A SOUTHERN CALIFORNIA
HISTORICAL ANTHOLOGY

A
SOUTHERN CALIFORNIA
HISTORICAL ANTHOLOGY

Selections from the Annual
and Quarterly Publications
of the Historical Society
of Southern California 1883-1983

Edited by Doyce B. Nunis, Jr.
Pictorial Editor, Abraham Hoffman

A Centennial Publication
Sponsored by the Historical
Society of Southern California
Los Angeles
1984

Library of Congress Catalog Card No. 83-81567
ISBN No. 0-914421-00-X
Copyright 1984 by the Historical Society of
Southern California. All rights reserved.

TO HONOR
THE FOUNDERS
OF THE
HISTORICAL SOCIETY OF
SOUTHERN CALIFORNIA

CONTENTS

LIST OF ILLUSTRATIONS

FOREWORD

When the Historical Society of Southern California was organized in November 1883, the members decided that the organization would be interested in "the collection and preservation of all material which can have any bearing upon the history of the Pacific Coast in general and of Southern California in particular." If this mandate now seems overly ambitious, is is useful to remember that there was at that time no other society in the state actively pursuing such a goal.

From the very first the members realized that collection and preservation alone were not enough. The Society also had to support scholarly research and publication. Before many months passed, the Society issued its first publication, and this activity has continued to the present day. For the first half century, a regular publication of the Society was issued annually. In 1935 the annual publication became a quarterly journal, and it has continued as such for nearly fifty years.

Various writers at various times have said the Historical Society of Southern California is "the oldest historical society west of St. Louis," or words to that effect. Perhaps this is so. Maybe not. It matters very little. The Society has certainly been issuing regular publications longer than any other historical society in the state, and that is no minor accomplishment. But more important than its age is the quality of its work. The Society has published studies of early exploration and settlement, original documents and maps, and monographs on the military, political, and social development of the region that still stand as major contributions to the understanding of American history.

In addition to this, the Society has worked actively to encourage the marking, preservation, and restoration of historic places. The Society has continued to sponsor a regular series of historical meetings, lectures, and pilgrimages to study the history of Southern California. And finally, the Society played the leading role in convincing Los Angeles County officials to build a Museum of History, Science and Art, as a place to display, study and interpret the history, the art, the flora, and the fauna of the region.

To celebrate a century of leadership, the Society has assembled this centennial volume, a sampler of the many fine publications issued by the organization during its first hundred years.

Altadena, California

Harry Kelsey
President

EDITOR'S PREFACE

This anthology was conceived as a testament to the Historical Society of Southern California's publication record, a record dating from 1884. With the exception of one year, the Society sponsored an *Annual Publication* from 1884 to 1934. The year following, the Society launched its *Quarterly*. Originally entitled the *Quarterly of the Historical Society of Southern California* or sometimes just *Quarterly Historical Society of Southern California*, the title was changed in 1962 to the *Southern California Quarterly*, the publication of the Historical Society of Southern California. A brief, but dated history of the Society's sponsored publications can be found in the March 1962 issue of the *SCQ*.

As the Society's Board of Directors moved to fashion a program of events to celebrate and honor the Society's centennial year, 1983-1984, one clear-cut objective which surfaced quickly was "a publication" to mark one-hundred years of service in the cause of California state, regional, and local history. As editor of the Society's quarterly publication since 1962, I was asked to chair a committee to consider the various alternatives. The newly formed group was styled the "Centennial Publication Committee." Committee members included Donald T. Balch, Pamela Ann Bleich, Robert W. Blew, Anna Marie Hager, Judson A. Grenier, Abraham Hoffman, Harry Kelsey, and Jacquelyn F. Wilson.

This hardworking committee quickly seized upon the essence of what should constitute a centennial publication: an historical tribute honoring the Society's distinguished record of annual and quarterly publication. Through a series of meetings, the contents were finally agreed upon by the committee. Thus the concept and the content of the Society's centennial publication is the handiwork of the Centennial Publication Committee.

With their task of selecting the essays to be included in the planned volume completed, it fell to my lot to serve as the editor of the manuscript text and prepare the draft for printing. A second responsibility was to see the manuscript through the various editorial phases required in book publication. Members of the committee also aided in the latter phase, while some had earlier made editorial suggestions on the selected materials. Thus this publication is a committee effort; it is a team endeavor. Each committee member played an important role in fashioning the finished product.

This centennial publication would not have been possible without grants from the Times Mirror Foundation, The John Randolph Haynes and Dora Haynes Foundation, J. B. and Emily Van Nuys Charities, The Ahmanson Foundation, Atlantic Richfield Company, Security Pacific Charitable Foundation, and more than one hundred Society members and business patrons. These benefactions underwrote publication costs. For this generous assistance, the Society is most deeply grateful.

Several special acknowledgments must also be noted. Abraham Hoffman served as pictorial editor; a demanding task which he ably discharged. The distinguished California printer/typographer, Ward Ritchie, the first printer to be associated with the Society's quarterly publication, gave of his time and talent in designing the book. The index was prepared by Everett and Anna Marie Hager who have given so much to the Society's publications by their published indices. Yeoman service was rendered in sharing the burden of proofreading by Anna Marie Hager, Joan Salz, and Mr. and Mrs. Robert D. Wayne. Lastly, Jacquelyn F. Wilson, the Society's executive director, handled the technical/business aspects of seeing the book through to final production.

It is with pride that the Historical Society of Southern California presents its centennial publication. The book's title sums up best what follows in the pages to come. Enjoy!

Doyce B. Nunis, Jr.
Editor

A SOUTHERN CALIFORNIA
HISTORICAL ANTHOLOGY

1

THE SENSE OF THE PAST

Lawrence Clark Powell

━━━━━━━━━━━━━━

I do not stand alone tonight, and though I shall speak personally, it will not be for myself alone. Our predecessors in this
unending work of recording regional history stand with me and
lend their voices to mine, as I shall do likewise in November
1983, when the Society celebrates its centennial.

Among these friendly shades whom I sense at my shoulder
are Colonel Warner, the founding president, whose inaugural
address in 1894 was wrought of mingled despair and hope; and
Robert Glass Cleland, who on the fiftieth anniversary in 1933
spoke eloquently of the power of historical knowledge to ani-
mate and people the landscape.

Now in November of 1958 has fallen to me the honor of
speaking on the seventy-fifth anniversary of the founding of
this Historical Society. I said I would speak personally, and
those of you who know me, know me in no other role. It is what
comes naturally, so bear with me, while I seek the sense of the
past, hoping at the same time to make sense in the present.

I have been trying to recall when it was that I first got the
sense of Southern California's past. Not while I was a boy. I
grew up in South Pasadena, on the sunny side of the Raymond
Hill, and my time was divided between reading books in the
library and raising hell in school. I was an imaginative boy, and
my reading led me to people the landscape with characters I
was reading about. There was a Kentucky Scout named Henry
Ware, and miscellaneous Texans, in the boys' books of Joseph

Altsheler. When I came to Zane Grey, my hero was of course Lassiter of the Purple Sage. All through grammar school and high school I was unaware that Southern California had a past. My immediate environment of the Adobe Flores, the Old Mill, and the Frémont Oak on the bank of the Arroyo Seco were taken for granted as part of the present. In back of our house on Marengo Avenue the concrete ditch in which we played Texan Scout or Mormon Villain was known as "The Sanky." It wasn't until years later I learned that the word was a Yankee corruption of Zanja.

As lovingly good as my father and mother were, they gave me no sense of Southern California's past. My father was a horticultural scientist whose collecting embraced the records of Caruso, the rugs of Armenia, and the chairs of Windsor. Although my mother and her people were Hudson River Valley Quakers from way back, she spent most of her life here in Southern California, until her death last year at 87, being homesick for England; and when she went there for the first time in her middle-age, she never wanted to leave. And so she was always filling her shelves and mine with books of English literature and lore. The only thing she liked about Southern California was the climate—and we all know what happened to that. She had not the least interest in local history back of 1900, the year she first came to Southern California. Nor was my education at Occidental College any help, even though I took history from Robert Glass Cleland—English history.

And so, paradoxically, it was not until I went to France to study in the University of Dijon that I began to get some sense about Southern California's past—and then it was by way of literature and landscape, not history. I lived a romantic student life for two and a half years in the old ducal capital of Burgundy, two hundred miles southeast of Paris, studying the poetry of Byron and Shelley, Whitman and Robinson Jeffers, and writing a book about our great Carmel poet.

And then I discovered Dana—a grubby copy of *Two Years Before the Mast* bought for sixpence in a London bookstall, which made me homesick, reading it in a boarding house in the lee of Primrose Hill, looking out on the rainy slope of London's only hilly park.

Dana was a lengthwise Californian, observing the harbors and the hills from San Diego and the point which bears his name to San Pedro, Santa Barbara, Monterey and Yerba Buena, and he described it miraculously in transparent prose of an enduring toughness. This is the gift all writers seek—to write language that incandesces, yet does not melt. There have been thousands of books about California, only a handful of which can stand with Dana. Why is this? Because the power to see, to sense, and to say is rarely united in a single writer in perfect proportions. It happened only once to Dana in this book of his springtime. He lived a long and useful life, but never again wrote anything to approach his California book. Let me read from it. But what to read in this altogether wonderful book whose every page is quotable? I have chosen the paragraph about Dana's first landing on the beach at Santa Barbara, perhaps because we now live above the beach on the Malibu, and nothing has changed in the century and a half since Dana saw and said:

> I shall never forget the impression which our first landing on the beach of California made upon me. The sun had just gone down; it was getting dusky; the damp night-wind was beginning to blow, and the heavy swell of the Pacific was setting in, and breaking in loud and high "combers" upon the beach. We lay on our oars in the swell, just outside of the surf, waiting for a good chance to run in, when a boat, which had put off from the *Ayacucho* just after us, came alongside of us, with a crew of dusky Sandwich Islanders, talking and hallooing in their outlandish tongue. They knew that we were novices in this kind of boating, and waitèd to see us go in. The second mate, however, who steered our boat, determined to have the advantage of their experience, and would not go in first. Finding at length how matters stood, they gave a shout, and taking advantage of a great comber which came swelling in, rearing its head, and lifting up the stern of our boat nearly perpendicular, and again dropping it in the trough, they gave three or four long and strong pulls, and went in on top of the great wave, throwing their oars overboard and as far from the boat as they could throw them, and jumping out the instant that the boat touched the beach, and then seizing hold of

[5]

her, and running her up high and dry upon the sand. We saw at once how it was to be done, and also the necessity of keeping the boat stern on to the sea; for the instant the sea should strike upon her broadside or quarter she would be driven up broadside on and capsized. We pulled strongly in, and as soon as we felt that the sea had got hold of us, and was carrying us in with the speed of a racehorse, we threw the oars as far from the boat as we could, and took hold of the gunwale, ready to spring out and seize her when she struck, the officer using his utmost strength to keep her stern on. We were shot upon the beach like an arrow from a bow, and seizing the boat, ran her up high and dry and soon picked up our oars, and stood by her, ready for the captain to come down.

When after three years of absence I returned to California in the Depression, poor in purse and rich in spirit, I saw the landscape with new vision, both clearer and sharper. There was only one difficulty: when I was little, the big houses had dwarfed the newly planted neighborhood trees. Now that I was grown to manhood, the trees too had grown, and now they made the houses seem small. Today Southern California has kept a few great immemorial trees—the Ellwood Queen in Goleta, the Moreton Bay fig at the Southern Pacific Station in Santa Barbara, the Santa Rosa deodars in Altadena, the cathedral camphor in Pomona—which are natural shrines. In general, however, trees are having a hard time these days—trees and pedestrians, those vestiges of a vanishing way of life.

In 1933 distance and reading had combined to lend enchantment to California's past, of which I had grown up in ignorance. As a boy I had worked two summers on the vast Di Giorgio Ranch southeast of Bakersfield, unaware that the shades of Garces and of Beale were at my side. Then in Europe I read *The Flock* by Mary Austin, and henceforth the mountains of Tehachapi and the southern plain of the San Joaquin merged in my imagination, with no time-barrier between the *entrada* of Francisco Garces, the camels at the Fort in the time of General Beale, and my own rabbit-hunting boyhood in the Weed Patch.

Now I came downstate through the passes of Newhall and Cahuenga with Frémont; and it was the same throughout Southern California. No more Kentuckians and Texans. I had found that my own land had pioneers and heroes. Drake and Cabrillo had sailed its shores. Portolá and Anza, Garces and Serra had been lost in its mustard fields and suffered its chaparral. And everywhere I went, from the dunes at Yuma, near the site of Garces' martyrdom, to the dunes at Oceano and landmarks named by Portolá, across the fertile landscape where the foliage of pepper and olive trees streamed like smoke in the wind, in the sunlit valleys and the shadow of the Sierra Madre, everywhere I sensed their presences at my side. Through a reading of history and literature, I had gained a sense of the past, and now this past made sense to me. This was the land of my childhood and youth, this was the land I loved, and my roots sought the nourishment in its soil.

The Depression was a bad time, and yet good came of it. Prepared to teach, I found no teaching jobs, and so I went to work in a bookshop on West Sixth Street in downtown Los Angeles. This move determined my future. The knowledge and experience I gained and the people I met led inevitably to the work I do now, as a librarian and writer.

This was the cultural heart of Los Angeles—public library, clubs, cafeterias, a park, the Philharmonic Auditorium, and the bookshops—what more could one ask? (Well, perhaps a river, which gives soul to a city). I came to know C. C. Parker and Ernest Dawson, Bishop Stevens, John I. Perkins, Elmer Belt and Donald Charnock, Bruce McCallister, Homer Crotty and W. W. Clary, Althea Warren, Phil Townsend Hanna, Ernest Carroll Moore, Henry R. Wagner, Robert Ernest Cowan, Frederick W. Hodge, Carl Wheat, J. Gregg Layne, W. W. Robinson, Paul Jordan-Smith, and my boss, Jake Zeitlin—all of whom, and many more, haunted the bookshops of the locale. The two years I spent on Sixth Street, and the earlier year on Colorado Street in Vroman's Bookstore of Pasadena, I count fully as important educationally as the years in college and university.

Chamber of Commerce literature measures the cultural level of a community by its churches, schools, libraries, and museums. Add bookshops. No city is civilized that does not support a variety of bookshops. The number and quality of bookshops in and around Los Angeles, as compared to those in the San Francisco Bay region, indicates to me that Los Angeles equals San Francisco as a center of civilization in California. One needs more strength to survive our centrifugal life here in Southern California, but from those strong survivors will come the children who will make the future. From our present dispersal of cultural centers—Santa Barbara and Ojai, Riverside, Claremont, Pasadena, San Diego, La Jolla, Laguna, Long Beach—will come eventual unification into one metropolis. Call it "urban sprawl," if you will. My imagination sees it as a kind of spiral nebula on earth, a vortex of actual power and potential beauty. Materially all we need will be abundant water and pure air. Spiritually we will need the inspired leadership of churches, schools, and civic groups.

And now I come at last to the Historical Society whose seventy-fifth anniversary we are celebrating tonight. What has the Society done in the region's growth to cultural maturity? What should it do in the years ahead? The first question can be answered by looking at the record; the second by looking at the radar screen of the future.

The "record" is a row of bound volumes which take up only a few feet on a library shelf. These in turn can be reduced to an inch of microfilm. The founders of the Society, who met together for the first time on November 1, 1883, have long since departed this life. Much of what they and others wrote about— the landmarks of Southern California—have disappeared, bulldozed into oblivion, and those that are left will soon be gone. The Prudential Building and the Park La Brea Towers are the look of the future. To survive at all, the remaining landmarks of wood and adobe need loving care.

For a month now I have lived with this short shelf of books, representing the Annuals and Quarterlies of this Society, published continuously since 1884, handling one or two before I went to work, and doing the same at night when I came home, sometimes just looking, skimming, sketching, other times reading an article clear through, and then leaning back and reflecting on what I read.

A strange, wonderful, rewarding experience it has been, as gradually my own life in Southern California since childhood was extended and enlarged to include all that the writers for our Society knew and were.

The history of these seventy-five years can be reduced to biography, to the biographies of a comparatively few thoughtful, persistent, dedicated men, who believed the work of the Society was worth doing.

No one of this great lineage is more heroic than the Society's first president, Colonel Jonathan Trumbull Warner, whose first two names gave the Spaniards trouble to pronounce, whereupon he changed them to Juan José. Colonel Warner stood six feet three, and his Spanish nickname was Juan Largo—Long John.

President Warner's inaugural address appears in the Society's first publication, which also includes the *Constitution, Standing Rules,* and *List of Officers and Members.* One of the primary purposes of the Society, seventy-five years ago, has pregnant meaning for us of this later age. Let me read President Warner's words,

> Just as we now eagerly prize the records of the early Colonial life and growth of our State and people, so will our successors prize the records which we shall preserve for them. . . . This is the underlying principle to which we owe our origin . . . Here is a new and unoccupied field. It has been the home of the white man for more than a century, and now, in the midst of the inrushing flood of immigrants, old landmarks are rapidly disappearing. Things which are now common, in a few years will be rare; and, after a few years more, will cease to be.

Colonel Warner wrote this in the Boom of the Eighties. How would he have expressed his emotion during the Boom of the Twenties, or of the post-war Forties and Fifties?

There is treasure locked in this file of our publications, and now at last it has been opened by the Bibliographical Abstracts and Index which Anna and Everett Hager have fashioned with love and skill. Throughout the first three decades it was James M. Guinn who nourished the Annuals with a hundred or more contributions, and also such stalwarts as H. D. Barrows, Laura Evertsen King, Rockwell D. Hunt, Edward A. Dickson, John C. Parish, Robert Glass Cleland, Owen Coy, Waldemar Wester-

[9]

gaard, Carl Wheat, Marshall Stimson, Ana Packman, Marco Newmark, W. W. Robinson, Justin Turner, and Gustave Arlt; and from 1937 until his death in 1952, J. Gregg Layne, editor of the Quarterly, the staunchest supporter of the Society since the passing of James M. Guinn. There was no need for a machine to retrieve information rapidly as long as there was Gregg Layne. The man was a walking-talking encyclopedia of knowledge about the West, California, Southern California, and Los Angeles in particular. He knew the answers to all the W's: *Who, What, When, Where,* and *Why,* and the answers were yours for the asking. Layne's *Annals of Los Angeles* should be brought up to date and reissued.

One of Gregg Layne's greatest contributions to the preservation of our past was his flair for collecting and reproducing in the Quarterly photographs of early Southern California. At the rate we are urbanizing the land, there will soon remain only these photographs to recall the way it once was. Layne's collection of them, and all his books and pamphlets on our region, were acquired after his death by the UCLA Library where they joined the library of Robert Ernest Cowan to form one of the best of all collections of Californiana.

Time can be stopped by a watch, can be measured by a gauge, say those who would have it so; and these include Shakespeare, for did he not say:

"And time, that takes survey of all the world, must have a stop."

This should make it easy for the historian in search of the past, if History were only the past. How much time separates the future from the present, and the present from the past? The rhythm of history is the beating heart, and Time is the interval between each heart beat. Our past history here in Southern California, in the few years since man has kept records, has been preserved largely by the efforts of this Society, by the foresighted hindsight of its founders and chroniclers. Up to 1900 much is known. Since 1900, and particularly during the booms of the Twenties and Forties, history has been happening too fast to be handled. It has been piling up data too numerous for any single agency to accumulate.

No library has all the telephone directories of all the towns in Southern California since the telephone was introduced. There is not even one complete file of the *Times*. Where can one find all the colored postcards of Southern California scenes since the beginning? Or the books and pamphlets, circulars, handbills, tickets, and other printing ephemera. The Huntington Library has the best collection before 1900. About ten years ago the UCLA Library began to collect anything and everything printed in Southern California since 1900, regardless of what form it is in or what subject it is on. We placed standing orders with book-scouts to "bring 'em in alive" and in bulk—and in these ten years we have amassed nearly ten thousand pieces of printed Southern Californiana which we keep in chronological order. This is the cultural humus that will fertilize studies in history and literature.

This is good, but it is not good enough. We need to divide the responsibility for local newspapers, directories, documents, and other printed records, not to speak of manuscripts and business papers, among the local institutions. It is too enormous a job for anyone.

We need to focus historical studies on this more recent past, for with every heart-beat of time it recedes from us, buried deeper and deeper beneath the records of the vanishing present. We need more studies such as the recent ones by Donald Duke of the Pacific Electric and the Angel's Flight. Of Green and Green Pasadena bungalow architecture. Sunkist packing houses. The little red Santa Fé stations, the burnt ochre buildings of the Southern Pacific. The resort hotels, of which only the beautiful Coronado.is left. Movie house stucco and studios. The Venice canals. Wooden oil derricks. Going, going, gone. We should employ a photographer to do nothing but photograph the local scene, day after day, up one street, down another, recording the present before it is lost to view. Southern California still has many beautiful backwaters, unknown to or disregarded by the Chamber of Commerce. Dare I speak of Bunker Hill?

Much *is* being done. Centers of study and publishing exist in the colleges and universities and museums. There are historical societies in the several counties. Magazines such as *West-ways*. Newspapers.

The teaching of history in the primary and secondary schools should begin with the bright interval called the present and work back, rather than the distant past, then come forward. By the first method, there is no break in the time-stream; one slips off the bank of the now and swims up stream against the gentle current. A very few swimmers, called mystics—and we are said to have more of them, at least self-styled, in Southern California than anywhere outside of India—a true mystic can swim either way on the time-stream, which is without beginning or end.

The sense of the past must be part of a culture's common sense if a culture is to call itself civilized; and not merely the distant past which the popular mind tends to make more romantic than real. The earliest heroes of Southern California— Portolá, Anza, Serra, and the first Yankees, have served us well. Let us come down the years and assemble a hall of later ones.

It is not enough to write and talk about history, or to make and show pictures of it. Needed to excite the imagination are symbols of beauty and truth. Monuments such as the one in limestone of Garces which is Bakersfield's noblest sight; or the ones in obsidian by Donal Hord in San Diego to Montezuma and to Water; or the Pioneer Memorial Wall and Waterfall at Fort Moore Hill.

Here in this semi-arid land, whose lifeblood is the water we have and have not, every town should rear a monumental fountain to the water-gods. One of them was William Mulholland, and we have honored him with a fountain on Riverside Drive. This is only a start. We should be inspired by St. Louis which commissioned Carl Milles to create the monumental fountain called The Meeting of the Waters, to symbolize the river union which takes place there, where the Missouri and the Mississippi flow together.

This Historical Society, allied with the County Art Institute, should take the lead in this. We have our own Millard Sheets who does not back away from monumental projects. And we have had public officials such as John Anson Ford who spoke the word *Beauty* without apology to the voters. Give us more of such!

I would hope that in the years to come this Society will increasingly assume the role of conscience of the community, of the region's self respect, of spokesman for survival. What other group is there without self interest? We have few or no material possessions. In the eternity of future-present-past we have the stability of mobility. As a group we are timeless, unhampered, unhindered, free. All the land we can claim as ours, all of nature's beauty, and man's ambivalent struggle to build and to destroy. I do not despair of the troubles that presently beset us because of industrialized over-expansion. We have the drive to catch up with ourselves, and when we find ways of curbing our aggressive vitality, then will we flower and fruit with great works.

In addition to preserving the Missions, we should not neglect the few remaining old California ranchos, taking as our model the Rancho Los Cerritos, so beautifully restored by the City of Long Beach and operated as a cultural center by the Public Library. The Casa de Adobe at the Southwest Museum is likewise an oasis in the urban wilderness. The Arboretum and the Casa Lucky Baldwin at Santa Anita are monuments to Supervisor Ford and his profound sense of the past. When form follows function, as it did in the Missions and the Ranchos, then a truly native architecture results. The Landmarks and the Pilgrimages conducted by our Society are works of piety to be maintained and increased.

From the farthest southeastern corner, where the Colorado drops the last load of silt into the Gulf, to that wavering boundary-line where wind and weather, landscape and flora, tell us that Southern California ends—all of this changed and changing region is our responsibility, to observe and report on man's transforming acts, to preserve the records, to fend off ruination and oblivion, and to imbue the people with *the sense of the past* in every meaning of the phrase. Only in this way will we keep faith with our founders. Colonel Warner had this long view—recall his nickname—and I end with his words, spoken seventy-five years ago:

[13]

THIS SOCIETY MAY, VERY WISELY, LOOK FORWARD TO THE TIME WHEN IT SHALL HAVE A BUILDING AND LIBRARY AND ARCHIVES OF ITS OWN; BUT, FOR THIS END WE NEED NOT MAKE HASTE. WE MAY BE AN ENERGETIC AND USEFUL SOCIETY AND HAVE NONE OF THESE, OR WE MAY HAVE THEM ALL AND NOTHING MORE, THE FORM BUT NOT THE LIFE OF A SOCIETY. IF WE CAN CATCH THE RIGHT SPIRIT, PERSUADE OURSELVES THAT WE HAVE BANDED TOGETHER FOR ACCOMPLISHING RESULTS BENEFICIAL IN THE FUTURE, WHEN WE SHALL BE AT REST, AND ARE NOT WORKING FOR THE POPULAR APPLAUSE; WE SHALL THEN, IN MY OPINION, HAVE MADE THE RIGHT START; AND MAY COUNT UPON A USEFUL CAREER, WHICH SHALL WIN THE LAUDABLE VERDICT, NOT OF THE DAILY NEWSPAPER, BUT OF THE FUTURE HISTORIAN, WHO WILL THANK US, WHEN WE ARE NOT HERE TO RECEIVE HIS THANKS, FOR PLANNING AND FOR EXECUTING SO WISELY.

2

LOS ANGELES, CALIFORNIA: THE QUESTION OF THE CITY'S ORIGINAL SPANISH NAME

Theodore E. Treutlein

━━━━◆◆◆◆◆◆◆◉◆◆◆◆◆◆◆━━━━

On a Tuesday, the fourth of September 1781, Lieutenant Josef Darío Argüello, on the orders of Felipe de Neve, governor of Californias [sic], led a party of settlers to a site on the banks of the Porciúncula River, and founded a *pueblo* with the title, *La Reyna de los Angeles* (The Queen of the Angels).

The background to the pueblo's founding had been Governor Neve's careful examination, a physical survey, from San Diego to San Francisco, early in the year 1777 to determine the water capability and soil conditions in upper California. In the Los Angeles region Neve wrote approvingly of the Santa Ana, San Gabriel, and Porciúncula rivers, and north, of the Guadalupe. His conclusion was to recommend the founding of two pueblos, one on the Guadalupe, which became San Joseph (San José), the other in the Porciúncula, which became Los Angeles.

When Neve's plans ultimately reached Don Teodoro de Croix, the governor and commandant general of the Interior Provinces, the latter gave his approval in a dispatch dated September 3, 1778. By that date San José had already been founded, and Croix gave specific permission for the establishment of the pueblo "en el Rio de la Porciúncula."

Although Governor Neve had initiated the idea of founding the pueblos (as well as other establishments), Commandant

Croix's position required him to write of the projects as his own. Croix now instructed Captain Fernando de Rivera y Moncada to recruit colonists for the Rio Porciúncula pueblo. In his order to Rivera, dated at Arispe, Sonora, December 27, 1779, we find the first use of the original Spanish name for Los Angeles.

Croix's words are of historic importance because they do define the city's title and also make clear his primary role in the higher echelon of Spanish administration. Croix wrote: "With the due aims of defense, conservation and development of the Province of Californias [*sic*], toward which the service of God and King is especially directed, I have resolved upon occupation of the Channel of Santa Barbara with a Presidio of this name, and three Missions; the erection of a Pueblo with the title of *la Reyna de los Angeles* on the River of *la Porciúncula*, and His Majesty has approved the [pueblo] named San Joseph which I ordered founded on the margins of the river of Guadalupe . . . ."

In almost the same language Commandant Croix then informed Viceroy Martín de Mayorga (the successor to Viceroy Antonio Bucareli who had died in April 1779) of his decision about the Channel establishments and of his order to found a pueblo with the title of *la Reyna de los Angeles* on the river Porciúncula.

On the 10th of February 1780 Commandant Croix also wrote to Governor Neve, stating in part, ". . . I have ordered the founding of a pueblo with the título de la Reyna de los Angeles sobre el Rio de la Porciúncula."

After the pueblo had been founded, Commandant Croix wrote to Minister of the Indies, Joseph de Gálvez, February 28, 1782: "The Governor of the Peninsula of California [*sic*] Don Phelipe de Neve informed me on November 19, of last year verifying that on the preceding September 4 there was founded 'el nuevo Pueblo de la Reyna de los Angeles al margen del Rio de la Porciúncula' with some of the settlers recruited by the deceased Captain Don Fernando de Rivera. . . ."

Minister Gálvez then wrote to Commandant Croix on October 29, 1782 telling him that the King had been informed of the establishment of the "nuevo Pueblo de la Reyna de los An-

*A statue of Felipe de Neve, who as Governor
of Alta California ordered the founding of the Los Angeles pueblo
in 1781, graces the downtown Plaza.*
Courtesy of California Historical Society.

geles al margen del Rio de la Porciúncula en la Peninsula de Californias."

The fact that The Queen of the Angels title was provided the King of Spain by the Minister of the Indies, Gálvez, would seem to confirm that this name for the pueblo was the accepted one. It should also be noted that when Croix referred to the Rio Porciúncula he was indicating the site of the pueblo; the river's name is not a part of the pueblo's title.

Later in the year 1782 Governor Neve was named inspector general of the Interior Provinces (September 4, 1782). In his instructions to his successor, Don Pedro Fages, in article 9, Neve expressed the view that very special attention be given to support the new pueblos, and he referred to "the pueblo of Nuestra Señora de los Angeles." This may be the only usage in the founding days of the form, *Nuestra Señora de los Angeles*, but the official form, as noted, had already been established.

However, generations of writers on California history have apparently disregarded the documentation and have compounded the name for the pueblo or have modified its name. The examples of misuse are very numerous and very easy to come by. Some special examples have been selected for this paper.

In the *Annual Publication* of Historical Society of Southern California, 1931, one finds a feature article by Thomas W. Temple II, "Se Fundaron un Pueblo de Españoles." In this article there is reference to the city's Spanish name, as follows: "Governor Neve's Reglamento of 1 June, 1779 approved the founding of two pueblos, one provisionally established [*i.e.*, San Joseph, or San José], the other to be known as Nuestra Señora de los Angeles, on the Porciúncula River."

Actually, the *Reglamento* states in the Fourteenth Title, "Political Government and Instructions for Settlement," Paragraph 1, ". . . the Pueblo of S. Joseph is already founded and settled, and the building of another is determined upon, for which settlers and their families must come from the Province of Sonora and Sinaloa . . . ."

In other words, unless the reader is very careful in interpreting Mr. Temple's wording he would form the impression that the famous Neve Reglamento provided the name of the new pueblo, which it definitely does not do. What makes the wording in the Temple article especially ironic and curious is that many of the documents reproduced in the extremely useful commemorative edition use the form, *La Reina de los Angeles.* Space will not permit citing all of these documents. However, it is worthy of special note that settlers were recruited in Sonora with the designation that they would be settled in the Pueblo de la Reina de los Angeles.

Also in the review of settlers to determine those "who enjoy wages and draw rations," made by Lieutenant Josef Francisco de Ortega (December 2, 1781), the title of the piece is Pueblo de la Reyna de los Angeles.

The census made in November 19, 1781, reads: "Padron del vecindario, el qe. tiene el pueblo de la Reyna de los Angeles fundado el 4 de Ste. del 1781, al margen del Rio de Porciúncula . . . ."

The confirmation of titles to pueblo lands ordered in August 1786 by Governor Pedro Fages refers to the Pueblo de la Reyna de los Angeles, as does the Act of Obedience, September 1786 by José Argüello.

There is also reference in the commemorative volume to a *Plano de el Pueblo de la Reyna de los Angeles, y tierras de Labor* [undated].

Considerably later, in another era, there is record of a litigation: "Transcript of the Proceedings in case No. 422. City of Los Angeles Claimants vs. The United States, Defendant, for the Place named 'Pueblo Lands'." In the first paragraph there is stated: "For the foundation of the Pueblo of la Reina de los Angeles in the neighborhood of the River of Porciúncula, and upon the land selected for this purpose; . . . Samuel D. King, Surveyor Genl. Cal. His seal affixed April 20, 1852. Filed in his Office, October 26, 1853. Geo. Fisher, Sec."

Returning to the theme of the apparent disregard of the documentary evidence by writers on the history of the beginnings of Los Angeles, one notes that Henry Raup Wagner in an early publication used the title: "The Earliest Documents of El Pueblo de Nuestra Señora La Reina de los Angeles" (1931).

[19]

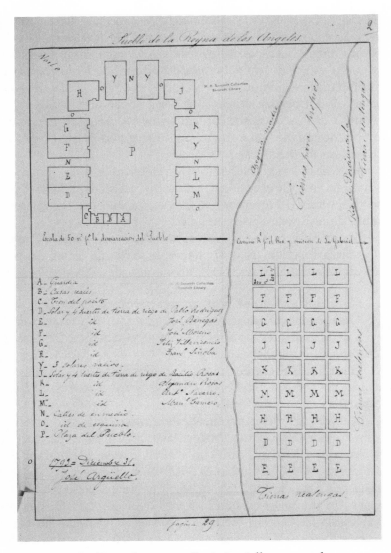

*In December 1793 José Argüello prepared
an outline map of the "Pueblo de la Reyna de los Angeles."
Unlike later generations of scholars, politicians, and
innocent newcomers, Argüello certainly knew
the correct name of the little settlement.*
Courtesy of Doyce B. Nunis, Jr.

Zoeth Skinner Eldredge, *The Beginnings of San Francisco* (2 vols.; San Francisco, 1912), I, 91, third footnote, goes a step farther than Wagner and asserts: "Portolá crossed the Los Angeles river on the 2d of August, 1769, the day of the Feast of Porciúncula and named it in honor of the day Rio de Nuestra Señora de los Angeles de Porciúncula. It is to this incident the city of Los Angeles owes its name which is in full Nuestra Señora La Reina de los Angeles de Porciúncula—Our Lady the Queen of the Angels of Porciúncula."

In writing this, Eldredge provided a clue to the cause for confusion which has surrounded the original Spanish name of the city; namely, he confused the official title (of which he was perhaps not aware), La Reina de los Angeles, with a religious festival which was celebrated by members of the Portolá expedition. It is very important to recognize that a pueblo was a civil, not a religious or a military community. No evidence exists that a priest was even present when the pueblo was founded.

The most recent example of this confusion, in this writer's knowledge and estimation, is found in the otherwise excellent article entitled "The Man Who Named Los Angeles," by Raymund F. Wood wherein is quoted from Father Juan Crespi's diary (1769): "This river [the Porciúncula] can be seen flowing down, its bed not deeply sunken below the surrounding ground, through a very green, lush, widespreading valley—an extent, north and south, of some leagues of level soil . . . so that it can truly be said to a most handsome garden [*sic*] . . . and in time to come there may be a very large and rich mission of Our Lady of the Angels of the Porciúncula, this being the day upon which we came to it, when this well-known Indulgence is gained [*i.e.*, noon of August 1 to midnight of August 2] in our Seraphic order; and so we have proclaimed it El Rio y Valle de Nuestra Señora de los Angeles de la Porciúncula."

In note 13 of the Wood article we find: "The addition of the words 'la Reina' into the title of the city, even though these words are not to be found in the original name given by Crespí to the river, has aroused considerable argument." Mr. Wood then goes on to cite the use of the words, La Reina, in the instructions to Rivera, December 27, 1779.

[21]

There truly should be no argument and the discrepancy noted by Mr. Wood has an obvious reason. The religious festival of August 2, 1769, provided the historical background for the name selected by Commandant Croix, *La Reina de los Angeles* (The Queen of the Angels) which is the original Spanish title for the pueblo, but the religious festival did not establish the title for the pueblo itself.

3

FIRST CENSUS OF LOS ANGELES

Translated by Thomas Workman Temple II

Census of the population of the City of the Queen of the Angels, founded September 4th, 1781, on the banks of the Porciúncula River, distant 45 leagues from the Presidio of San Diego, 27 leagues from the site selected for the establishment of the Presidio of Santa Barbara, and about a league and a half from the San Gabriel Mission; including the names and ages of the residents, their wives and children. Also an account of the number of animals and their kind, as distributed; with a note describing those to be held in common as sires of the different kinds, farming implements, forges, and tools for carpenter and cast work, and other things as received.

(1) Lara, Josef de, Spaniard,   50,
    Maria Antonia Campos,
        india sabina,   23,
    Josef Julian,   4,
    Juana de Jesus,   6,
    Maria Faustina,   2.
(2) Navarro, Josef Antonio,
        mestizo,   42,
    Maria Rufina Dorotea,
        mulata,   47,
    Josef Maria,   10,
    Josef Clemente,   9,
    Maria Josefa,   4.

(3) Rosas, Basillio, indian   67,
     Maria Manuela Calixtra,
        mulata,   43,
     Josef Maximo,   15,
     Carlos,   12,
     Antonio Rosalino,   7,
     Josef Marcelino,   4,
     Juan Esteban,   2,
     Maria Josefa,   8.
(4) Mesa, Antonio, negro   38,
     Ana Gertrudis Lopez,
        mulata,   27,
     Antonio Maria,   8,
     Maria Paula,   10.
(5) Villavicencio, Antonio,
        Spaniard,   30,
     Maria de los Santos Sef-
        erina, indian,   26,
     Maria Antonio Josefa,   8.
(6) Vanegas, Josef, indian,   28,
     Maria Maxima Aguilar,
        indian,   20,
     Cosme Damien,   1.
(7) Rosas, Alejandro, indian,   19,
     Juana Rodriguez, coyote
        indian,   20.
(8) Rodriguez, Pablo, in-
        dian,   25,
     Maria Rosalia Noriega,
        indian,   26,
     Maria Antonia,   1.
(9) Camero, Manuel, mulato,   30,
     Maria Tomasa, mulata,   24.
(10) Quintero, Luis, negro,   55,
     Maria Petra Rubio,
        mulata,   40,
     Josef Clemente,   3,
     Maria Gertudis,   16,

Maria Concepcion,	9,
Tomasa,	7,
Rafaela,	6.
(11) Moreno, Josef, mulato,	22,
Maria Guadalupe Gertrudis,	19.
(12) Rodriguez, Antonio Miranda, chino,	50,
Juana Maria,	11.

NOTE

That in addition to the cattle, horses, and mules, distributed to the first 11 settlers, as set forth, they were granted building lots on which they have constructed their houses, which for the present are built of palisades, roofed with earth; also 2 irrigated fields for the cultivation of 2 fanegas of corn to each settler; in addition, a plow share, a hoe and an axe: and for the community, the proper number of carts, wagons, and breeding animals as set forth above, for which the settlers must account to the Royal Exchequer at the prices fixed: with the corresponding charges made against their accounts, as found in the Book of Poblacion, wherein are also to be found the building lots, planting fields, farming utensils, and animals belonging to the settler, Antonio Miranda Rodriguez, which will be granted to him, as soon as he appears at said Pueblo.

San Gabriel, November 19, 1781.

PUEBLO DE LA REYNA DE LOS ANGELES

Extract of the review which I, Don Josef Francisco de Ortega, Lieutenant & Comandant of the Company which is to garrison the Presidio of Santa Barbara, made of the settlers, who enjoy wages and draw rations, in said Pueblo, on December 2, 1781.

Feliz Villavicencio,	Alejandro Rosas,
Antonio Mesa,	Antonio Rodriguez, absent in Loreto,
Josef de Lara,	Luis Quintero
Josef Vanegas,	Total—
Pablo Rodriguez,	With wages and rations . . 11

[25]

Manuel Camero,	1 absent at Loreto . . . . <u>1</u>
Antonio Navarro,	12
Josef Moreno,	
Basilio Rosas,	

NOTE: Having apprehended the deserter RAFAEL MESA, who recently arrived, and who claims to have enlisted as a soldier; [let it be known that] he enlisted as a settler, and is therefore excluded from the Company, having been a settler from the 12th of June 1780, until the 10th of October of said year when he deserted.

San Gabriel, December 2, 1781—Joseph Franco. de Ortega.

[NOTE: This manuscript is in the Provincial State Papers, Missions & Colonization, Vol. I: 101-102. In the original document accents, as in modern usage, were not used for personal names.]

4

CALIFORNIA PARTICIPATION IN THE SPIRIT OF 1776

Francis J. Weber

———————————————

The Declaration of Independence, certainly one of the most sublime assertions of human rights in recorded annals, triggered a series of social and political upheavals that eventually embroiled the whole of the civilized world. Though there was little more than a vast wilderness and a few French settlements between the Atlantic and Pacific Oceans in the late 1770s, the far away Spanish province of California was not totally immune from the aftershocks unleashed by the "Spirit of 1776." A careful gleaning of the historical sources indicates that Californians played at least a participatory role in the establishment of the nation to which their descendants would one day join forces as the thirty-first commonwealth.

It all began on March 22, 1778, with an order from King Charles III directing Spanish possessions in the New World to observe strict neutrality in the hostilities that had erupted between France and England. Shortly thereafter, the order was reversed and local officials were instructed to disallow British vessels landing privileges. The change of policy is important for it brought California within the revolutionary ambit, inasmuch as its soil ceased to be neutral territory.

The king was playing a close hand. In virtue of the so-called "Family Pact" between the Bourbon crowns, Spain and France were pledged to mutual military assistance. Yet Charles

Francis J. Weber

III initially procrastinated in honoring that commitment, for fear of the influence that a cluster of "free colonies" might exert on his own nation's immense and valuable possessions in the New World.

England foolishly failed to exploit Iberian hesitancy by continuing to antagonize her historic foe with stepped-up attacks on and seizures of Spanish merchant ships. Finally, on June 23, 1779, the two nations went to war.

During the years that followed, "Spain's attitude towards the American Revolution changed with the political situations of the times. Although she kept on friendly terms with the Colonies, her own interests were always at stake." The admittedly ambivalent Spanish policy served the crown well. For example, it was to King Charles' advantage to keep the Americans and their mother-country at sword's point, so as to divert English attention away from the attractive and vulnerable Spanish possessions on the continent. At the same time, officialdom at Madrid saw in the war a glorious opportunity for avenging past wrongs, acquiring fresh territories and crushing England's supremacy of the seaways.

News of the final rupture between Spain and England reached the Pacific Slope rather quickly. Fray Junípero Serra, the *Presidente* of the California Missions, learned about the ongoing hostilities during his second visit to San Francisco in the fall of 1779.

Confirmation came from Commandant General Teodoro de Croix who informed Serra on February 18, 1780, that on the previous June 24th, King Charles III, "inspired thereto by his sense of piety, and wishing above all things to implore the protection of the Almighty, on Whom depend the destinies of empires and the issues of wars, has given orders directing that, in all his possessions in Spain and America, public prayers be offered up for the prosperity of our Catholic armed forces." De Croix forwarded the full text of the royal directive "so that in conformity with His Majesty's command," the Presidente could "order public prayers to be offered" in the missions.

The commandant general's letter reached the Franciscan Presidente on June 13. Serra immediately drafted a circular to

[28]

the missionaries, outlining the king's wishes as spelled out by De Croix. He encouraged an unrestricted compliance because, as he pointed out, "we are in a special manner indebted here to the piety of our Catholic Monarch, who provides for us as his minister chaplains, and poor Franciscans, at his own expense, and, similarly, because we are interested in the success and victory of his Catholic armed forces, since by their means, especially are we to look for progress in our spiritual conquests here, which we have so much at heart."

Serra further asked each of the friars to be "most attentive in begging God to grant success to this public cause which is so favorable to our holy Catholic and Roman Church and is most pleasing in the sight of the same God Our Lord." Recalling the past two centuries of persecution against the Church in England, Serra reminded his confreres that "our Catholic Sovereign is at war with perfidious heretics. And when I have said that, I have said enough for all to join with His Majesty in the manner in which Heaven grants us to do so." The Presidente went on to say that "we should all be united in this purpose and display how we are one in spirit, an especial reason for offering to God our Lord our most pleasing if poor prayers."

The Mallorcan-born friar then outlined the form of prayers to be followed in the missionary foundations then serving the Indians of California. As for the public orations, which were to begin June 24th, he directed that at the principal Mass on Sundays, the litany of the Blessed Mother or the Saints along with the psalm, verses and prayers prescribed by the *Rituale Romanum* for "time of war," be said. At the conclusion of the services, all were instructed to recite the *Credo* or Profession of Faith three times in order "to help to soften the pride of our enemies." Provisions were also made for private prayers on behalf of the Catholic sovereign.

On the same day, the Presidente acknowledged De Croix's request for public prayers to hasten "the successful issue of His Catholic Majesty's undertakings in the present war" against England. Reporting that he had already circulated a letter to that effect, Serra assured De Croix that his orders would be carried out "to the last detail."

[29]

On August 12, 1781, De Croix notified Serra that all of the "free vassals in America" were expected to make a contribution to the war effort. Every Indian was to contribute one *peso* apiece, while Spaniards and other residents in the area were obliged to twice that amount. The commandant general expressed his hope that "Your Reverences will make them understand the importance of this small service which the king asks of all his faithful vassals in order to help him to meet the extraordinary expenses which the present war against the enemies of religion and of the state calls forth, realizing that no other means were found to this end. They are light and sensible and can be met by the Indians. This they can do from their community assets in that proportion and at the same time the instruction provides."

De Croix provided for those missions which might be poor and unable to comply with the royal directive, noting that it was not the mind of the king to "burden" the Indians, though he did anticipate a minimal or token compliance wherever possible. The insistence on conformance with the royal directive was not lost in the delicacy of De Croix's terminology, for, as one commentator put it, "nominally the contribution was to be voluntary, but in reality was so managed as to leave no convenient methods of escape."

Each of the friars was to draw up a *padron* of all the Indians eighteen years and older within his jurisdiction, along with an account of the produce turned over to the governor and sold by him for cash.

Obviously the royal mandate could not be literally fulfilled in California, where the peso had not yet been introduced. It was ultimately decided by Governor Felipe de Neve that the missions themselves would pay the tax on behalf of the Indians.

Fray Junípero Serra was unhappy about the whole idea of a tax, for, as he related to the Guardian at the Apostolic College of San Fernando, Francisco Pangua, the natives could not "understand why pesos are necessary to wage a war for they have had frequent wars among themselves and for them no pesos were necessary. Much less could they understand why the king of Spain, our master, must ask them to give him a peso apiece."

Though the resident friars at San Juan Capistrano and San Diego initially asked to be excluded from the tax, they ultimately joined the other missions in paying their assessment. This they did by pooling their Mass stipends and collecting debts owed by certain soldiers.

By the month of December 1782, California had contributed 4,216 pesos toward the expenses of Spain's war with England. The funds collected are thus recorded:

Mission San Carlos Borromeo	106	Presidio of San Diego	515
Mission San Antonio de Padua	122	Presidio of Monterey	833
Mission San Luis Obispo	107	Presidio of San Francisco (including Missions San Francisco and Santa Clara)	373
Mission San Gabriel	134	Presidio of Santa Barbara	249
Mission San Juan Capistrano and San Diego	229	Pueblo Los Angeles	15

for a total of 2,683 pesos

Teodoro De Croix attributed the overpayment to Governor de Neve. The Franciscan chronicler, Father Zephyrin Engelhardt, stated that the added money "may account for the honors" subsequently bestowed upon the governor.

The pittance of support for the crown's efforts came late, for the war between England and Spain was concluded by a treaty signed at Versailles in January 1783. Nonetheless, the record clearly shows that "if money constitutes the 'sinews of war,' the little towns of California make quite as good a showing as some of the older, richer cities of the Atlantic slope."

Though their prayers and material contributions were negligible to the overall war effort, the Franciscan missionaries and their neophytes in California can be credited with sharing, at least nominally, a common cause with their contemporaries in the American colonies.

[31]

Francis J. Weber

It may have been strictly fortuitous that Spain's conflicts with England reached fever-pitch at the precise moment as the War of American Independence. Yet the fact remains that during that struggle, "Spain and her colonies assisted the people of the United States in their gallant fight for freedom."

5

REMINISCENCES: MY FIRST PROCESSION IN LOS ANGELES, MARCH 16, 1847

Stephen C. Foster

The writer has witnessed forty celebrations of the 4th of July in this city, commencing with 1847, when he read the Declaration of Independence on Fort Hill, in Spanish, for the information of our newly-made fellow-citizens, who spoke only the Castilian tongue. As I marched in the procession the other day (July 4, 1887), I recalled the appearance of the city when I first knew it, so widely different from the present.

The outbreak of the Mexican War (May 1846) found the writer at Oposura, Sonora, which place he reached December 1845, on his way to California, by the way of Santa Fe and El Paso, from Missouri. The first news we had of the war was of the capture of Capt. Thornton's command of U.S. Dragoons by the Mexican cavalry, on the Rio Grande, and the people rang the bells for joy. But shortly after, we got the news of the battles of Palo Alto and Resaca de la Palma, and they did not ring the bells then.

In June 1846 a small party of Americans arrived at Oposura, headed by James Kennedy, a machinist from Lowell, Mass., who with his wife had come around Cape Horn, three years before, to the cotton manufactory at Horcasitas, Sonora: the husband to superintend the machinery, and the wife to teach the Mexican girls the management of the looms and spindles. As there was no chance to leave by sea, Kennedy had made up a party to see him safe through the Apache range to Santa Fe, where he expected to secure passage in the traders' wagons across the plains to Missouri, and I accompanied him; after a hard, hot trip, we reached Santa Fe safely in July.

August 18, 1846, I witnessed the entry of the American army, under Gen. Kearny, into Santa Fe.

In 1845, the Mormons were driven out of Nauvoo, Ill., and, under the leadership of Brigham Young, took up their march westwardly. Their first intention was to reach California, then occupied by a sparse Mexican population and few hundred American emigrants. They stopped one season at Council Bluffs, to raise a crop and procure means for their further progress. When the call was made for volunteers in Missouri, for service in New Mexico and California, none were willing to enlist as infantry, to make such long marches afoot, and Capt. James Allen, of the 1st U.S. Dragoons, was sent to Council Bluffs to try and raise a battalion of infantry, enlisted for twelve months, to be discharged in California. The order was given by Brigham, and within forty-eight hours five full companies (500 men) were raised and on their march to Fort Leavenworth. The conditions were, that they were to choose their company officers, but were to be commanded by an officer of the regular army, and were to receive army clothing at Fort Leavenworth. The Missouri troops furnished their own clothing, for which the Government paid each man $29.50 a year.

So, they started on their long march with their poorest clothing. When they reached the Fort they learned that the steamboat bringing their clothing and percussion muskets had been snagged in the Missouri, and everything was lost. Their commander, Capt. Allen, was taken sick and died. He had their confidence, and they objected to serving under another commander, and to start for California without the promised clothing; but the order was imperative to march, and the clothing could not be replaced in less than a month. So they sent to Brigham for advice, and he ordered them to push on, even if they had to reach California barefooted and in their shirt-tails. So, flintlock muskets, of the pattern of 1820, were furnished them, and they reached Santa Fe under the command of Lieut.

A.J. Smith, of the 1st Dragoons—the Maj. Gen. A.J. Smith of our Civil War. On their arrival at Santa Fe, Gen. Kearny ordered Capt. Cooke, of the 1st Dragoons, to command them, and Lieut. Smith went with them to California, to rejoin his company which had started a month before with Gen. Kearny. Lieut. (now Gov.) Stoneman, who had just graduated at West Point, also went with them.

Gen. Kearny had started with six companies of dragoons, but on the Rio Grande he met Kit Carson with dispatches for Washington, from Com. Stockton, announcing that California had been taken possession of, without resistance. So Kearny only took two companies, mounted on mules, with pack mules to convey their provisions, by way of the Gila River. At Santa Fe mules were scarce, and money scarcer with the quartermaster, who also had to provide transportation for the 1st Missouri Cavalry, under Col. Doniphan, then starting on their famous march through Northern Mexico to Camargo, where their period of enlistment expired. But seventeen 6-mule teams, hauling sixty days' rations, could be spared for Cooke's command, and no wagons had ever crossed from the Rio Grande to California; so, a road had to be found and made as they went, after leaving the Rio Grande.

Kit Carson had accompanied Kearny as guide, and Pauline Weaver, the pioneer of Arizona, who had come with Carson from California, awaited Cooke. Five New Mexican guides were hired, all under command of Joaquin Leroux, an old trapper, who had trapped on every stream from the Yellowstone to the Gila.

I was then clerking in a store, waiting for something to turn up, when I was informed that an interpreter was wanted to accompany Cooke to California, and I went to Capt. McCusick, the quartermaster, with my recommendations. Enoch Barnes, who was killed in a drunken brawl at the Ballona, in this county, some twenty years ago, who drove a wagon across the plains in 1845, in the same caravan as myself, was also an applicant. McCusick was a prompt, stern man, and the competitive examination of the Yale graduate and the Missouri mule-whacker was short, and turned on transportation and money. I

[35]

had a good mule, rifle and blanket, and as to money, I could wait until Uncle Sam was able to pay me, as long as my wages were running on and I got my rations. Barnes was just off a spree, in which he had drank and gambled off all his money, and pawned his rifle, and it would have cost $100 to fit him out. So I won the appointment, and the contract was quickly drawn, that for $75 a month and rations I was to serve as interpreter to California, furnishing my own animal, clothing and arms. The contract was made October 1846, and I served under it until May 17th, 1849, when the people of Los Angeles elected their *Ayuntamiento,* and the garrison evacuated the place, and the last seventeen months of my term I also acted as 1st Alcalde of the district of Los Angeles, without any extra compensation. On leaving the Rio Grande, I volunteered to join the guides, as there was nothing for me to do in camp, and we did not expect to pass through any Mexican settlements until we reached the Pima villages, on the Gila. Leroux's party, ten in number, started ahead, with six days' rations, on our riding animals, to find a practicable route for wagons, and wood, and water, at such intervals as infantry could march—fifteen to twenty miles a day, in one case forty miles, between camps; one man to be sent back from each watering place to guide the command until our rations were expended, and then all to return to the command. We thus found our way by the Guadalupe Canyon and San Pedro River to Tucson, from which place there was a trail to the Pima villages, and from there to California. Weaver had just come over the road, and there was no difficulty in finding our way. We ate our last flour, bacon, sugar and coffee by January 14th, 1847, on the desert, between the Colorado and Warner's Pass. A supply of beef cattle met us at Carrizo Creek, on the west side of the desert, and we lived on beef alone until April 1847, when supplies, brought from New York on the ships that brought Col. Stevenson's regiment, reached us at Los Angeles. At Gila Bend, we met two Mexicans, who told us of the outbreak that took place in Los Angeles, September 1846; and at Indian Wells, on the desert, we met Leroux, who, with most of the guides, had been sent ahead from Gila Bend, to get assistance from the San Luis Indians, who had declared for the

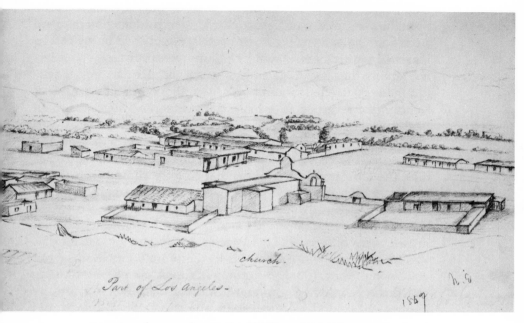

*Los Angeles, as drawn by William Rich Hutton
in 1847. The view is toward the northeast, with the Plaza Church
in the foreground.*
Courtesy of Huntington Library.

[37]

Americans, and held all the *ranchos* on the frontier; and he brought the news that Stockton and Kearny had marched up from San Diego to retake Los Angeles. We pushed on by forced marches towards Los Angeles, and at Temecula received a letter, stating that Los Angeles was taken, that Kearny and Stockton had quarrelled about who was to command, and that Kearny had returned with his dragoons to San Diego, to which place we were ordered to proceed. Arriving there, together with the dragoons, we were ordered to San Luis Rey, where, from the Rancho of Santa Margarita, we procured beef, soap and candles, the only articles of rations that country could furnish. In a few days, fifty of the men were attacked with dysentery, and the surgeon said breadstuff of any kind would be of more use to check the disease than all his medicine. So the commissary and myself were ordered to Los Angeles, to try and get some flour. We found the town garrisoned by Frémont's Battalion, about 400 strong. They, too, had nothing but beef served out to them, but as the people had corn and beans for their own use, and by happening around at the houses about mealtime, they could occasionally get a square meal of *tortillas y frijoles*. Here we met Louis Roubideau of the Jurupa Ranch, who said he could spare us some 2,000 or 3,000 lbs. of wheat, which he could grind at a little mill he had on the Santa Ana River. So, on our return, two wagons were sent to Jurupa, and they brought 1,700 lbs. of unbolted wheat flour and two sacks of beans—a small supply for 400 men. I then messed with one of the captains, and we all agreed that it was the sweetest bread we ever tasted.

March 12th, 1847, we received important news in six weeks from Washington overland. Stockton and Kearny had been relieved, and ordered East, and Com. Shubrick and Col. R.B. Mason were to take their places, and the military to command on land, and, what was of far more interest to us, that Stevenson's ships were daily expected at San Francisco, and that we should soon have bread, sugar and coffee again, and we were ordered to Los Angeles to relieve Frémont's Battalion. So, with beautiful weather, and in the best of spirits, we began our march to the city of the Angels. Our last day's march was only ten miles, and we camped on the San Gabriel at the Pico crossing, early, and all hands were soon busy preparing for the grand *entree* on the morrow. Those who had a shirt—and they were a minority—could be seen washing them, some bathing, some mending their ragged clothes, and as there was plenty of sand, all scouring their muskets till they shone again. We made an early start the next morning, and when we forded the Los Angeles River, at Old Aliso, now Macy Street, there was not a single straggler behind. The order of march was, the dragoons in front. They had left Missouri before receiving their annual supply of clothing, and they presented a most dilapidated appearance, but their tattered caps and jackets gave them a somewhat soldierly appearance. They had burned their saddles and bridles after the fight at San Pascual, but a full supply of horses to remount them had been purchased of the late Don Juan Forster, and all the Mexican saddlers and blacksmiths in the country had been kept busy making saddles, bridles and spurs for them. Their officers were Capt. A.J. Smith, 1st Lieut. J.B. Davidson, 2nd Lieut. George Stoneman; then came four companies of the Iowa Infantry, Company B having been left to garrison San Diego. In all we numbered 300 muskets and 80 sabres. The line of march was by Aliso and Arcadia streets, to Main, and down Main to the Government House, where the St. Charles now stands, where the dragoons dismounted and took up their quarters. The infantry turned out of Main street past the house of John Temple, now Downey Block, and pitched their tents in the rear, where they remained until they were mustered out, June 1847.

I have described the appearance of the dragoons, but cannot do justice to the infantry only by saying it was Falstaff's ragged company multiplied by ten. The officers had managed to have each a decent suit of clothes, but they brought out in stronger contrast the rags of the rank and file. On Los Angeles street were some 300 or 400 Indians, the laborers in the vineyard, who had taken a holiday to witness our entry, while a group of about 100 women, with their heads covered by their *rebosos*, who had met at the funeral of the mother of the late Don Tomás Sanchez, ex-sheriff of the county, stood looking at the ragged *Gringos* as they marched by. On Main street were some thirty or forty Californians, well dressed in their short jackets and

[39]

breeches with silver buttons, open at the sides, showing the snow-white linen beneath. I noticed they looked with most interest at the dragoons, so many of whose comrades had fallen before their lances at San Pascual that cold December morning, and lay buried in that long grave, or lay groaning in the hospital at San Diego. We had no waving flags, but waving rags, and many a one; nor brass bands, only a solitary snare drum and fife, played by a tall Vermont fifer and a stout, rosy-cheeked English drummer; and they struck up the "Star Spangled Banner" as we passed the Government House, and kept it up until orders were given to break ranks and stack arms. And then came a loud hurrah from all that ragged soldiery. Their long and weary march over mountain, plain and desert, of 2,200 miles, was over.

I will now describe two individuals who marched in that procession. One is the writer. 'Tis nearly forty years ago, and I was a younger and a better-looking man than I am now. I had left Santa Fe with only the clothes on my back, and a single change of under-clothing. I had been paid off at San Luis Rey, and had $200 in my pocket, and I tried to find some clothing in Los Angeles on my first visit, but could find none. So, I rode to San Diego, and through the kindness of a friendly man-of-war's man I got a sailor's blue blouse, a pair of marine's pants and brogans, for which I paid $20. My place in the column, as interpreter, was with the colonel, at the head, and I rode with my rifle slung across the saddle, powder-horn and bullet-pouch slung about my shoulders. My beard rivaled in length that of the old colonel by whose side I rode, but mine was as black as the raven's wing, and his was as grey as mine is now. But if I was not the best-looking, nor the best-dressed man, I was the best-mounted man on Main street that day. When the horses were delivered for the dragoons, a young man named Ortega, a nephew of Don Pío Pico, rode an iron grey horse, with flowing mane and tail, and splendid action. I tried to buy him for the colonel, but he would not sell him. The day we left San Luis, I had mounted my mule, and was chatting with Ortega, admiring his horse, when he offered to sell him, and I could fix the price. I gave him $25. The dragoon horses cost $20 each. A few days after my arrival in this city, Lieut. Stoneman was ordered to scout with a party of dragoons towards San Bernardino, to look out for Indian horse thieves, and I sold the horse to him; and well the Governor remembers the gallant grey that bore him on many a long and weary scout.

I have thus described my appearance at my first public entry into this city, from no spirit of egotism, but only to give my fellow citizens some idea of the appearance of the former Alcalde, Prefect, Mayor and Senator of Los Angeles.

But the most conspicuous man on Main street that day was of a different type. On our march, Dec. 1846, we were moving from the Black Water, just S. of the present Mexican line, towards the San Pedro River. The snow was falling steadily, but it was not very cold. Our order of march was, with an advance guard of twenty men, and twenty pioneers with pick-axe and shovel, commanded by Capt. A.J. Smith, to remove any obstruction to our wagons. I was riding that day, with the colonel and surgeon, when we overtook the advance guard. The pioneers had been cutting down some *mesquite* trees that obstructed our way, and had just finished as we overtook them. Their officer gave the order "fall in, shoulder arms," and they formed in ranks of four, so that for about fifty yards we could not turn out to pass them. The right-hand man in the rear rank was at least 6¼ feet tall. The crown of his hat was gone, and a shock of sandy hair, powdered by the falling snow, stuck out above the dilapidated rim, while a huge beard of the same color swept his breast. His upper garment had been a citizen's swallow-tailed coat, buttoned by a single button over his naked chest, but one of the tails had been cut off and stitched to his waistband, where it would do the most good, for decency's sake, and an old pair of No. 12 brogans, encased with rawhide, protected his feet. The right sleeve of the coat was gone, and his arm was bare from wrist to elbow, and, by way of uniform, the left leg of the pants was gone, leaving the leg bare from knee to ankle. His underclothing had long since disappeared. But the way he marched and shouldered his musket showed the drilled and veteran soldier. That ragged scarecrow had seen fifteen years' service in the British army, from the snows of Canada to the

[41]

jungles of Burma. The contrast between the soldierly bearing of the man and his dilapidated dress brought a smile to every face. After we had passed, the colonel pulled his long grey mustache, and said, "I never thought, when I left West Point, that I should ever command such a set of ragamuffins as these. But, poor fellows, it is not their fault; and better material for soldiers I never commanded." And that day, when I sat on my horse, where Ducommun's Block now rears its tall front, to see my old comrades march by, in the front rank of Company A, with cadenced step and martial mien, as he had marched in his younger days to the martial music of the regimental band, dressed in the scarlet uniform of a British grenadier, strode the old ragged veteran.

6

STORY OF ORD'S SURVEY
OF LOS ANGELES AND HIS MAP
OF SOUTHERN CALIFORNIA

W.W. Robinson

The following material has been drawn from the Los Angeles Archives.

(1) Superior Territorial Government Orders City Map To Be Made.
(From Minutes of the *Ayuntamiento* of June 9, 1849)

In view of a note received from the Superior Territorial Government ordering the making of a City Map to serve as a basis for granting vacant lots out of the unappropriated lands belonging to the Municipality, Council resolved—

1st That the said Sup. Gov't be assured of the Council's desire to give prompt and due compliance to its orders, and to inform the same that there is no City Map in existence to go by when concessions of land are made, and, furthermore, that there is no surveyor in this Town who could get up such a map.

2nd That this Honorable Body, desiring to have this done, requests the Terr. Gov't to send down a surveyor to do this work, for which he will receive pay out of the Municipal Funds, and should they not suffice by reason of other demands having to be met, then he can be paid with unappropriated lands, should the Gov't give its consent.

3rd That at the same time the Sup. Gov't be informed that the lands of the Municipality have not been defined, and that in making land grants within a perimeter of two leagues square, the City has acted in the belief that it is entitled to that much land as a pueblo. Upon this point Council begs to be advised by the Sup. Gov't so as to make sure that it is acting on proper lines.

> José del Carmen Lugo—Pres.
> Juan Sepúlveda—2nd Alcalde
> José Lopez
> Francisco Ruiz
> J. Temple—Syndic
> Jesús Guirado—Sec.

(2) *Appointment of Committee to Confer With Surveyor.*
(From Minutes of the Ayuntamiento of July 7, 1849)

The Syndic moved that a Com. be appointed to confer with the surveyor who is to make the Map of this City as to the means & details relating to the accomplishment of the undertaking, and it was resolved that the Syndic himself, together with Manuel Requena, to whom a notice shall be sent, act as such Com. and report back to Council as to the result of their labors.

> J. Temple—Syndic

(3) *Report of Committee Appointed to Confer With Surveyor.*
(From Minutes of the Ayuntamiento of July 18, 1849)

The Syndic submitted the report of the Com. appointed to confer with the surveyor who came to make a Map of this City and who made a proposition embodied in said report, which reads as follows:

"Your Com., encharged by your Hon. Body with the duty of conferring with Lieutenant Ord, the surveyor who is to get up a map of this City, has had a conference with that gentleman and he offers to make a Map of the City demarking thereon, in a clear and exact manner, the boundary lines and points of the Municipal lands, for which work he demands a compensation of fifteen hundred dollars in coin, ten lots selected from among

[44]

those demarked in the map, and vacant land to the extent of one thousand varas, in sections of two hundred varas each, and wheresoever he may choose to select the same, or, in case the proposition is refused, then he wants to be paid the sum of three thousand dollars in cash.

"Your Comm. finds the first proposition very disadvantageous to the City, because conceding to the surveyor the right to select not only the said ten lots, but also the thousand varas of vacant land, the City would deprive itself of the most desirable lands and lots which some future day may bring more than three thousand dollars, but as to the second proposition, it is the sense of the Comm. that it is preferable to the first.

"The City funds cannot now defray this expense, but should your Hon. Body deem it indispensable, a loan of that amount may be negotiated, pledging the credit of the City Council and paying an interest of one per centum per month. This loan could be repaid with the proceeds of the sale of the first lots disposed of, and until such sale is effected the payment could be secured by mortgaging in due form the lots which the Map will show as available."

The foregoing having been sufficiently discussed, it was resolved by Council that the same Com. should make the following proposition to the surveyor.

"That there should be embodied in the Map all the land actually under cultivation from the principal water-dam down to the last cultivated field below. As to the lots that should be shown on the Map, they should begin at the Cemetery and end with the house of Botiller. As to the commonalty lands of this City, the surveyor should determine the four points of the compass and taking the Parish Church for a center, measure two leagues in each cardinal direction. These lines will bisect the four sides of a square within which the lands of this Municipality will be contained, the area of the same being sixteen square leagues and each side of the square measuring four leagues. And the surveyor shall receive for his work the sum of 3000 dollars which is the amount he asked for, with the understanding, however, that he must pay his own help. Furthermore, that the same Com., accompanied by the Pres., be authorized to

[45]

submit a loan of 3000, bearing an interest of one per centum per month giving as security such lots as will be shown to be unappropriated when the City Map shall be finished, the City reserving itself the right to sell these lots in the meantime on three months time, which will .enable it to send notices to various points to the effect that these lots are being sold to pay the said 3000 and other incidental purposes.

"Furthermore, that parties intending to build on lots previously granted shall be governed by the Map which is about to be made, and that such lots must first be improved before their owner will be allowed to speculate on them."

Council adjourns.

Postscript: Resolved that the Pres. together with the Com. shall enter into a contract with the surveyor based upon the condition above mentioned, and he shall also execute the mortgage to be created in connection therewith. Any diff. as to the said conditions shall be adjusted by the Com. who are herewith empowered to do so in most convenient manner.

(4) Ord's Contract With the City
(Archives Book 13, Page 1 (in Spanish), Archives Book 22, Page 827 (in translation). Date: July 22, 1849.)

"The officer E.O.C. Ord binds himself to survey the City of Los Angeles, and to lay out streets and blocks, where there are no buildings, from the Church to the last house before the vineyard of Celis and from the vineyards to the hills; the streets to the southwest of 75 feet in width, and to each one (block) 112 yards, and the streets which run from the vineyards towards the hills of 60 feet width and to each one (block) 200 yards, from the Church northerly to the ravine beyond the house of Antonio Ygnacio Abila; placing stakes at each corner of the blocks embracing all the vineyards, lands, and roads which are within two miles to the river, in a direct line from the Church to the vineyard of Celis, and from where these two miles end at the river, he will follow all the bank to a point, where the Cemetery, and the uppermost point of the lands of Antonio Ygnacio Abila form a direct line.

"All the above has to be measured exactly and put on a map, as it actually exists, including streets, roads, zanjas outside of the fenced land, hills, plazas and crossings, between the vineyards and lands.

"Also he has to measure and fix four points, at two leagues from the Church to the four cardinal points, which four points will serve to form the square of the municipal lands, each one of them (the points) being the middle of the (side) of the square.

"And the said E.O.C. Ord on complying with all the aforesaid, the Ill. Ayuntamiento of this City binds (itself) solemnly to deliver three thousand dollars in current money, as compensation of said work. It is understood that the Ayuntamiento will furnish the lumber for the stakes.

"There shall be drawn two (copies) of the tenor of this contract, one for each party.

"Los Angeles, July 22nd, 1849.
"José del C. Lugo (rubric).
"J. Temple (rubric).

>"E.O.C. Ord,
>"Manl. Requena (rubric)."

(Book A, Page 671, Deeds, Original)

(5) Map Turned Over to Council
(From Minutes of the Ayuntamiento of Sept. 19, 1849)

In the City of Los Angeles on the nineteenth day of September, eighteen hundred and forty-nine, Council having convened in special session called at the instance of the 'Syndic' for the purpose of formally turning over to Council the new City Map which had just been finished, the minutes of the meeting held on the first of the present month were read and approved.

The 'Syndic' thereupon submitted the finished City map as well as a receipt showing that he himself had paid the surveyor

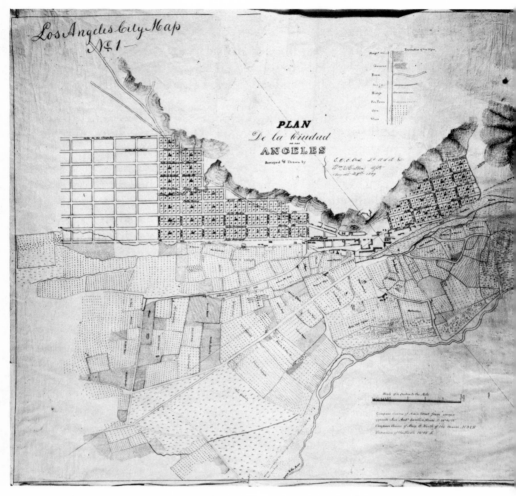

Edward O. C. Ord drew his map of Los Angeles in 1849.
Courtesy of Huntington Library.

the sum of three thousand dollars, this amount being a loan made by the 'Syndic' to the City to enable it to pay for the said map, the interest charge being one per centum per month.

The 'Syndic' also submitted a proposition offering to accept a piece of land lying in the rear of his house and having the same width as the latter, and extending as far as the high hill, in lieu of the three months' interest at the rate of one per centum per month on the three thousand dollars loaned the City for the new City map. Referred to a special Committee composed of Councilman Francisco Ocampo and the member representing the Committee on Vacant Lands, with instructions to report what may seem right and convenient in the premises.

(Signed)
José del C. Lugo—President
Juan Sepúlveda, 2nd Alcalde
José Lopez
Francisco Ruiz
Francisco Ocampo
J. Temple, "Syndic"
Jesús Guirado, Secretary

(The "Syndic's" proposition was approved at the next council meeting, on September 28, 1849. Book 4, Page 615.)

(6) The First Auction of City Lots
(From Minutes of the Ayuntamiento of Nov. 6, 1849)

Committee report they have selected lots to be sold on the 7th, has examined those demarked in the City Map & has selected 54 lots. In Block 4-5-7 & 8 in the lower & Nos. 32 & 34 in the upper district.

Syndic proposes:

1st—Lots sold at this auction must be paid for on spot in silver or current money. The respective title shall be made out in favor of the respective purchaser & signed by the President & Sec'y of the Council.

[49]

2nd—The buyer of a lot shall have privilege of securing at the same price, the lot adjoining in the rear & facing the parallel street on same Blk. If not taken at once, this privilege shall lapse.

3rd—On receipt of title each buyer shall put down stakes demarking his property, so that no question shall arise in future & when ready to build he shall abide by the line of the street as laid down in the City Map. Each lot is 40 varas wide by 56 deep.

(7) Results of First Auction
(From Minutes of the Ayuntamiento of Dec. 24, 1849)

Syndic reports that auction of lots produced $2490.00 & there still remains $510 due Temple for money advanced to pay for the City Map.

(Many subsequent auctions took place to raise needed City funds.)

(8) Fencing Land In Conformity With City Map.
(From Minutes of the Ayuntamiento of Mar. 23, 1850)

It was resolved that those intending to fence in their land should apply to the Syndic who will show them how to fence in conformity with the City Map. Also that every piece of property that since the new City Map was made resulted to be near a street can be extended up to the line of said street, the Council to make donation of the strip intervening———upon petition to Council and inspection.

(Thereafter there were many such petitions for alignment of lot lines with street lines.)

(9) Hansen's Comments on Ord's Survey—Nov. 19, 1869.
(Archives Book 13, Page 5)

"To the Hon. Mayor and Common Council of the City of Los Angeles: Gentlemen:

"In pursuance of your order I examined the survey of Frank Lecouvreur of Charity and Twelfth Streets, and the survey of Mr. Lothar Seebold of Block 21, fronting on Charity Street and Sixth Street, all within the limits of Ord's Survey.

"I find that both surveyors took for starting points of their respective surveys, stone monuments reputed to be "Ord's Rocks." I knew from numerous surveys and measurements, within the limits of Ord's Survey, that these same reputed "Ord's Rocks," are placed in an irregular manner, neither conforming to uniform directions and distances of the Blocks, nor marking in right lines Streets of the same width and directions.

"I learn from Col. J.J. Warner, that he is in possession of a letter from Genl. Ord, in which that gentleman states that he had not set any rocks to mark his survey, because the City failed to supply him with the necessary means. I learn also, that the said rocks were set by John Temple.

"The map of Ord's Survey states that the direction of Main Street South and North of the Church according to the magnetic needle and the variation of the same at the time of the survey; but does not state neither width of streets nor the dimensions of the Blocks. There are no field notes of Ord's Survey on record.

"The only evidence of the width of the streets and dimensions of the Blocks, I find in the contract between the Ayuntamiento and E.O.C. Ord for the survey of the City of date July 2, 1849, which is on record in the County Clerk's Office. In said contract it is stipulated, that the streets running South Westerly shall be 75 feet wide and 112 yards apart, and the streets running from the vineyards towards the hills shall be 60 feet wide and 200 yards apart.

"I find that the Surveyors Lecouvreur and Seebold made the streets running Southwesterly 80 feet instead of 75 feet wide, and the Blocks between them 110 yards in place of 112 yards as prescribed in the surveying contract above referred to.

"Whereas there remains at present nothing to guide the surveyor in laying out lots and streets except the old map in which the direction of Main Street, the mode of subdivision of Blocks and some objects on Main Street are laid down, and the above mentioned contract, in which the dimensions of Streets and Blocks are prescribed; I recommend that the City may employ a surveyor to lay out, and mark with posts or stones in a

[51]

permanent manner the corners of the Blocks of Ord's Survey in conformity to the old map and the dimensions fixed in the contract."

Most respectfully,

George Hansen.

Los Angeles
Nov. 19, 1869

(10) Lecouvreur's Comments on Ord's Survey—April 20, 1870.
(Archives Book 11, Page 154)

"This survey was made by Order of the City in the fall of 1849, if my recollection serves me right, and had for its purpose the subdivision of two tracts of city lands, into rectangular blocks and lots, one of them being south of First Street and West of Main, the other and smaller one, north of Short and likewise West of Main Street.

"It has generally been supposed that certain rocks, not marked but easily recognizable by shape and quality, were original corner monuments of that survey. This supposition has however been recently dispelled by a communication from General Ord to a private party, wherein in answer to inquiry, he states that the city not furnishing in time with the proper corner monuments, he was compelled to content himself with marking his survey by temporary stakes. Thus absolutely no indication at all exists where this survey (so often referred to in the records) or any part thereof, was actually located in the field. Further: no plan or other documentary evidence exists of this survey, except the "Official map" above referred to, from which no information can be derived, except the running numbers of Lots and Blocks, the amount of Lots contained in each Block and their relation to each other. As some of the deeds of record, described by the proper numbers of Ord's survey, state however the dimensions of the Lots be 120 by 165 feet deep, the size of the regular Blocks has been inferred to be 600 by 330 feet, and they have been so measured, or pretended to be measured, while the streets have been traditionally reported to be 80 feet wide for those running in a northerly and southerly, and 60 feet wide for those running in an easterly and westerly direction.

"My own experience as a surveyor warrants me however in the belief, that this assumption of width of street is incorrect, for I have come in more than one instance upon traces of old surveys, especially in the northern part of the city, made soon after the Original survey by Ord, when some of the original marks may be presumed to still have had existence, which do not tally at all with the figures given above, and raise the presumption that either the streets or the Blocks were not that wide. Probably the former was the case.

"Now in the absence of proper evidence from which to deduce distances and especially directions, and with the gradual disappearance of old landmarks, it is not surprising to find that often incompetent and careless surveyors, who had no interest in the work except the poor pittance which they were paid for their labor, and which latter in consequence they tried to get through with as rapidly as possible—in the course of time have done the rest.

"We now find ourselves in midst of a maze of lines conflicting, overlapping and intersecting each other, at all sorts of angles and curves in such a manner, that it has become utterly impossible for a surveyor even to approximate the location of any line, let alone to permanently fix it. On a previous occasion I have already stated to you, and I repeat it here as forcibly illustrating the present state of affairs, that I will undertake to shift any street or lot line in the "Ord's Survey" from where it may be now, 10 feet and even more, in any desired direction, if the choice of the so-called "Ord's Rock" from which to take my start, is left to me; for one of which rocks as good authority may be claimed as for the other."

"In the transfer of deeds of property which we find of record, reference is frequently made, either to the "Offical Map" of the city on file in the Mayor's office or the property is described by number of Lot and Block of a survey called "Ord's Survey," reference being likewise to the aforesaid Map. It is true that in the Mayor's Office a very dirty and ragged map may

[53]

be found, composed of several small sheets of paper cut into shapes to fit each other and pasted together, which pretends to be a representation of the City of Los Angeles as it was some twenty years ago. This map has traces of having once been drawn with great care and by a thoroughly competent drafts-man, but it is utterly valueless as a record, since it contains not a single word or figure which refers to dimensions, corners, distances, landmarks, starting points, or in fact anything that may be of service, or even give the smallest hint to a surveyor in attempting relocations. Moreover this map is drawn on such an exceedingly small scale, that even according to its positive cor-rectness and accuracy in all details, the rough expedient of de-ducing distances by the application of a scale could not be re-sorted to, since the finest dash of a straight line pen would represent some 3 or 4 feet in width, and an hardly perceptible dot cover an area in the field of from 9 to 10 square feet.

"I have been credibly informed that this map once con-tained all the required details in the form of marginal remarks, but that these were cut off—to reduce the map to a more handy size as is claimed—by some officious intermeddler. If so, and this act of vandalism was not prompted by a malicious design to create inextricable confusion, to further selfish ends, it would certainly crown the stupidity of a full grown baboon. Let the cause of this irreparable loss, however, be what it may, it is an incontrovertible fact, that this so called official map, is as utterly useless to the surveyor as so much waste paper."

* * *

THE ORD MAP OF SOUTHERN CALIFORNIA

Lieutenant E.O.C. Ord's map of the "Ciudad de Los Angeles" was not the only contribution of this officer to the cartography of this area. Somewhat later in the same year of 1849 he offered to his superiors a small, but highly interesting "sketch map" of the entire Southern California coastal region, under the title

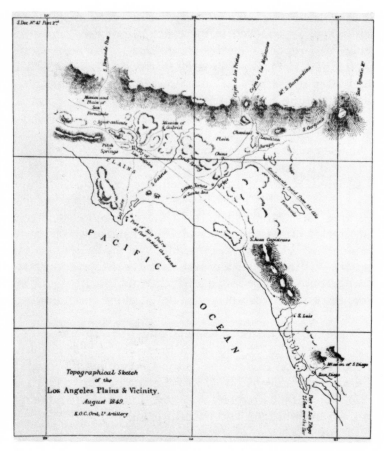

Ord's map of Southern California was done the same year as his map of Los Angeles.
Reprinted from the Quarterly.

"Los Angeles Plains and Vicinity." This delicate little map, which is here reproduced in the exact size of the original, was attached to a report made by Lieut. Ord to Brigadier General Bennett Riley, dated at Monterey, October 31, 1849. On December 30 of the same year he addressed a second report to the general, attaching a document dated November 6.

These several reports have to do with a tour of inspection made by Ord to San Diego by steamer and thence by land to Los Angeles, with a side excursion to Col. Isaac Williams' Chino Rancho and to Juan Bandini's Jurupa Rancho, where Riverside is now situated. He did not traverse either the Cajon or San Gorgonio passes, but his chief interest lay in possible means of preventing further depredations in the area called by him the "Los Angeles Plains" by Piutes and other Indians from beyond the mountains. He also recommended the dispatch of an expedition by way of the Cajon Pass and the Mojave country to explore a route to New Mexico which would make possible the avoidance of the hardships encountered along the more southerly Gila route.

These reports and Ord's sketch map of Southern California are contained in the "Report of the Secretary of War Communicating Information in Relation to the Geology and Topography of California," published in 1850 as Senate Executive Document No. 47, Thirty-first Congress, First Session. This document has long-since become rare and hard-to-come-by.

7

THE PLAN OF OLD LOS ANGELES AND THE STORY OF ITS HIGHWAYS AND BYWAYS

James M. Guinn

The history of the founding of our American cities shows that the location of a city, as well as its plan, is as often the result of accident as of design. Neither chance nor accident entered into the selection of the site, the plan, or the name of Los Angeles. All these had been determined upon years before a colonist had been enlisted to make the settlement. The Spanish colonist, unlike the American backwoodsman, was not free to locate on the public domain wherever his caprice or his convenience dictated.

The Spanish *poblador* (founder or colonist) went where he was sent. He built his pueblo after a plan designated by royal *reglamento* and decreed by the laws of the Indies. His planting and his sowing, the size of his fields and the shape of his house lot, were fixed by royal decree. He was a fief, a dependent of the crown. The land he lived on was not his own, except to use. If he failed to cultivate it, it was taken from him and he was deported from the colony.

The pueblo plan of colonization did not originate with the Spanish-American colonists. It was older even than Spain herself. In early European colonization, the pueblo plan—the common square in the center of the town, the house lots grouped around it, the arable fields and the common pasture lands beyond, appears in the Aryan village, in the ancient German mark, and in the old Roman praesidium. The Puritans adopted this form in their first settlements in New England. Around the public square or common, where stood the meeting house and the town house, they laid off their home lots, and beyond these were their cultivated fields and their common pasture lands. This form of colonization was a combination of communal interests and individual ownership. Primarily, no doubt, it was adopted for protection against the hostile natives, and secondly, for social advantage. It reversed the order of our own western colonization. The town came first, it was the initial point from which the settlement radiated; while with our own western pioneers the town was an afterthought—a center point for the convenience of trade.

The plaza is an essential feature in the plan of all Spanish-American towns. It is usually the geographical center of the pueblo lands. The old plaza of El Pueblo de Nuestra Señora, La Reina de Los Angeles (the town of our Lady, the Queen of the Angels) (*sic*) as decreed by Gov. Felipe de Neve in his "Instrucción para La Fundación de Los Angeles," was a parallelogram one hundred varas in length by seventy-five in breadth. It was laid out with its corners facing the four winds or cardinal points of the compass, and with its streets running at right angles to each of its four sides, so that no street would be swept by the wind. Two streets, each ten varas wide, opened out at the longer sides, and three on each of the shorter sides. Upon three sides of the plaza were the house lots 20 × 40 *varas* each, fronting on the square. One half of the remaining side was reserved for public buildings—a guard house, a town house, and a public granary; the other half was an open space. Around three sides of the old plaza clustered the mud-daubed huts of the pioneers of Los Angeles, and around the embryo town, a few years later, was built an adobe wall—not so much perhaps for protection from foreign invasion as from domestic intrusion. It was easier to wall in the town than to fence in the cattle and the goats that pastured on the *ejidos* or commons, outside the walls.

The area of a pueblo, under Spanish rule, was four square leagues of land, or about 17,770 acres, (a Spanish league contains 4444 acres.) The pueblo lands were divided into *solares* or house lots, *suertes* or planting fields, *dehesas* or outside pasture lands, *ejidos* or commons—lands nearest the town where the mustangs were tethered and the goats roamed at their pleasure; *propios*—lands rented or leased from which a revenue was raised to pay municipal expenses; *realengas*—royal lands, also used for raising revenue for the town government.

In 1786, five years after the founding of the Pueblo of our Lady of the Angels, Alferez José Argüello, aided by corporal Vicente and private Roque, put the nine settlers who had been faithful to their trust, in possession of their house lots and planting fields. Three of the pobladores originally recruited to found the pueblo had been deported for general worthlessness.

Lieut. Argüello spent but little time over surveys and probably set up no land-marks to define boundaries. The propios were said to extend southerly 2,200 varas from the dam (which was located near the point where the Buena Vista street bridge now crosses the river) to the limit of the distributed lands. The realengas were located on the eastern side of the river.

The boundaries of the Plaza *viejo* or old plaza, as nearly as it is possible to locate them now, are as follows: The southeast corner of the plaza would coincide with what is now the northeast corner of Marchessault and Upper Main streets. From the said northeast corner of these streets draw a line northwest one hundred varas (278 feet)—this line would constitute the easterly line of the old plaza. On this line construct a parallelogram with its opposite or westerly side one hundred varas in length, and its northerly and southerly sides seventy-five varas each. These boundaries will locate, approximately, as near as it is possible now to locate the *plaza real* or royal square of the old Pueblo of our Lady of the Angels.

. . . I have been unable to find any satisfactory reason assigned for the abandonment of the old plaza. The probable cause of the change was the location of the Church of our Lady of the Angels on its present site. The first church or chapel was a small building, 25 × 30 feet, begun in 1784, and completed in 1789. It fronted on the plaza. The new church was begun in 1814. By order of Governor Sola, in 1818, the site was changed to higher ground—its present location. The building was completed in 1822—forty-one years after the founding of the

[59]

pueblo. The open space in front of the church was part of the ejidos or commons, and was used for a place to picket mustangs while the owners were attending church. In course of time it became recognized as the plaza or public square.

Neve's streets that were to be free from the sweep of the winds, have disappeared. There are no land marks to show the location of the twelve house lots that clustered around the old plaza. Nor can we locate the boundaries of any one of the twenty-seven suertes or sowing fields that were laid off on the alluvial lands below the plaza. Time, flood, and the hated gringos have long since obliterated all ancient landmarks and boundary lines of the old pueblo as effectually as did Neve's pobladores all traces of the Indian town, Yangna, that once stood on the site chosen for the Pueblo of our Lady of the Angels.

As the town grew, it straggled off from its nucleus—the old plaza in an irregular sort of a way—without definite plot or plan. When a house was to be built the builder selected a site most convenient to his material—adobe. If his house did not conform to the lines of the street, the street must adjust itself to the house. Fifty years after the founding of the pueblo there was not a regular laid off street within its limits. Indeed there was but little necessity for streets. There were no wheeled vehicles, save a few old screaking carretas, used for hauling brea or asphaltum—the roofing material of the adobe houses. The *caballero* on his wiry and sure footed mustang, threaded its way among the scattered and irregularly built houses, and it mattered little to him whether the path zigzagged or ran in straight lines. Walking was a lost art to the native Californian. He was a centaur—half horse and half man—and only half a man, without his horse. As he never walked when he could ride, sidewalks he did not need.

With the growth of the town southward, the business center drifted from its first locality on Upper Main Street, and for a time became fixed at the head of Los Angeles Street where that street intersected with Aliso, Arcadia, Sanchez and Negro Alley. At that point Los Angeles was then a very broad street probably two hundred feet wide, it narrowed as it ran southward and widened again at its intersection with First Street. In the early part of the century it was known as Zanja (ditch) Street. In the early thirties it had been dignified into the Calle Principal or Main Street and with its continuation the Calle de Los Huertos—the street of orchards—(now San Pedro) formed the principal highway running southward from the center of the pueblo; later on it was known as Vineyard Street. (For information in regard to the old names of streets I am indebted to C. C. Grove of the West Coast Abstract company, Los Angeles.) First street at its intersection with Los Angeles and San Pedro was known as Broad Street or Broadway. A misnomer now but appropriate enough in the days of cheap lands.

Under Spanish rule the absolute title of all the lands in California was vested in the King. The individual occupant held only a usufructuary title. It was his to use so long as he used it for the purpose for which it was given him. Possession then was ten parts of the law. The occupant could hold on but he could not let go of it. To cease to use his land was to lose it. He could not sell it, he could not even indulge in that privilege so dear to the American land owner, he could not mortgage it. The land passed from father to son by the law of primogeniture.

When California became a part of the Mexican Republic the title to pueblo lands became vested in the *ayuntamiento* or town council. When the Pueblo of Los Angeles became a city in 1835, there was not a land owner in it who had a written title to his lands. Under Spanish rule the military *commisionados*, and under Mexican, the ayuntamiento made verbal grants. In 1836 owners were ordered to apply for written titles but little heed was given to the order. Efforts were made from time to time to induce the occupants of town lots to perfect their titles. But the easy-going methods of the pobladores had been transmitted to their descendants. Land was cheap and plentiful. There was no inducement to land grabbing, consequently disputes over titles and land boundaries were of rare occurrence and title deeds when given were loosely drawn. The more or less in a conveyance never worried the party of the second part. In the minutes

[61]

EL CIUDADANO RAMON RAYON,
General de brigada y Gobernador del Distrito federal.

El dia 6 del corriente he recibido por la Secretaría de Relaciones el decreto que sigue.

„El Exmo. Sr. Presidente interino de los Estados-Unidos Mexicanos se ha servido dirigirme el decreto que sigue.

„El Presidente interino de los Estados-Unidos Mexicanos, á los habitantes de la República, sabed: Que el Congreso general ha decretado lo siguiente.

„Se erige en ciudad el pueblo de los Angeles de la Alta California, y será para lo sucesivo la Capital de este Territorio.=Basilio Arrillaga, diputado presidente.=Antonio Pacheco Leal, presidente del Senado.=Demetrio del Castillo, diputado secretario.=Manuel Miranda, senador secretario."

Por tanto, mando se imprima, publique, circule, y se le dé el debido cumplimiento. Palacio del Gobierno federal en México á 23 de Mayo de 1835. =*Miguel Barragán.*=A D. José Maria Gutierrez de Estrada."

Y lo comunico á V. S. para su inteligencia y fines consiguientes.

Dios y libertad. México 23 de Mayo de 1835. =*Gutierrez Estrada.*=Sr. Gobernador del Distrito federal."

Y para que llegue á noticia de todos, mando se publique por bando en esta Capital y en la comprension del Distrito, fijándose en los parages acostumbrados, y circulándose á quienes toque cuidar de su observancia. Dado en México á 10 de Junio de 1835.

Ramon Rayon

Lic. José Francisco de Alcántara,
Secretario.

Certifico y doy feé que en el dra dela fecha que se espresa le fijó el Bando que antecede por las Calles acostumbradas y le fijó en los para

The printed proclamation declaring the pueblo of Los Angeles a *ciudad, a city, enacted by the Mexican Congress, May 23, 1835.*
Courtesy Henry H. Clifford.

of the ayuntamiento may be found the grant of a certain piece of land now known as the Requena tract which is described and deeded as that lot or tract on which the "Cows ate the apples."

On the 23rd of May 1835, Los Angeles ceased to be a pueblo. The following is a translation of the copy of the decree erecting it into a city:

> His excellency, the president ad interim of the United states of Mexico Miguel Barragan. The president ad interim of the United States of Mexico to the inhabitants of the Republic let it be known: that the general congress has decreed the following: That the town of Los Angeles, Upper California, is erected to a city, and shall be for the future the capital of that territory.

> Basilo Arrillaga,   Antonio Pacheco Leal,
>   President House of Deputies.   President of the Senate.
> Demetrio Del Castillo,   Manuel Miranda,
>   Secretary House of Deputies.   Secretary of the Senate.

> I, therefore, order it to be printed and circulated and duly complied, with. Palace of the Federal Government in Mexico, May 23, 1835.

> Miguel Barragan.

Although the Mexican Congress by decree had erected Los Angeles to a city yet to the Californians it was still the pueblo. Even now after sixty years of city life, to the old time native Californian it is still the "pueblo." The decree made it a city but it was ten years after, before it became the capital. The citizens failed to provide suitable buildings and the denizens of Monterey clung to the archives. The "Ciudad de Los Angeles" was a city of magnificent distances when it first took on metropolitan airs. The Departmental Assembly of 1834 designated the boundaries of the Pueblo of Los Angeles to be "two leagues to each wind from the center of the Plaza." This gave the Pueblo, when it was "erected into a city," an area of sixteen square leagues or over one hundred square miles. There was no survey of boundary lines, and the city fathers worried along ten years without knowing exactly where the city ended and country began. In 1846, an attempt was made to fix the boundaries but all that was done was to measure two leagues "in the direction of the four winds from the Plaza church" and set stakes as boundary lines. Then came the American invaders.

[63]

James M. Guinn

At the time of the American occupation (1846), the city had skirted along the foothills as far down as First (or Primero) Street with possibly a few scattered houses below that point.

The discovery of gold and the rush of immigration to the mines aroused the sleepy old "ciudad" of Los Angeles from its bucolic dreams. A stream of immigration, by the southern route, poured through its streets and gold flowed into its coffers from the sale of the cattle that covered the plains beyond. With increasing prosperity the city became ambitious to make a better appearance. The ayuntamiento decided to have a portion of the mesa lying to the south of Calle Primero and west of Calle Principal surveyed and subdivided into city lots and sold to procure a fund to make some needed improvements.

In the city clerk's office is a copy of a map of the first subdivision of Los Angeles city lands made after the American occupation. It is entitled, "Plan de la Ciudad de Los Angeles, by E. O. C. Ord, Lt. U. S. A., Wm. R. Hutton, Asst., August 29, 1849." Ord's survey embraces all that portion of the city bounded north by First Street and the base of the first line of hills, east by Main Street, south by Twelfth Street and west by Pearl Street. Also that portion of the city north of Short Street and west of Upper Main to the base of the hills. On the "plan" the lands between Main Street and the river are designated as "plough grounds, gardens, corn and vine lands." The streets in the older portion of the city are marked but not named. The blocks, except the first tier, are 600 feet in length, and are divided into ten lots each 120 feet front by 165 feet in depth.

Ord took his compass course for the line of Main Street S, 24° 45° W. from the corner opposite José Antonio Carrillo's house which stood where the Pico House now stands. This lot was granted Carrillo by the comissionado in 1821 and is one of the earliest transfers of which there is any record. On Ord's map, Main, Spring and Fort (Broadway) streets ran in parallel straight lines to Twelfth Street. How Main Street came to zigzag below Sixth Street, Spring to disappear at Ninth Street, and Fort to ignominiously end in Governor Downey's orange orchard (subdivided in 1884), are things that as Lord Dundreary says, "No fellow can find out." Ord probably made an accurate sur-

[64]

vey but many of the blocks now are irregular, some contain an excess and others are short and some of the streets have drifted away from their original locations. This, in part, is due to the easy going methods of those early days. The ayuntamiento was to have placed permanent monuments to mark the corners of blocks, but neglected to do so. The corner stakes were convenient for picketing mustangs and were rapidly disappearing. The council, a year or so after the survey was made, gave Juan Temple a contract to place stone monuments to mark the corners. He hired a gang of Mexicans to do the work. If they found a corner stake they placed a monument; if not, some one of the gang paced off the length of the block and set the corner stone. The excess in some blocks and the shortage in others might be accounted for if we could find out whether it was a long-legged or a short-legged paisano that did the stepping. The price of Ord survey lots on Spring Street in the fall of '49 and spring of '50 ranged from $25 to $50 each.

The names of the streets on Ord's plan are given in both Spanish and English; beginning with Main they are as follows: Calle Principal—Main Street; Calle Primavera—Spring Street, named for the season spring; Calle Fortin—Fort Street; Calle Loma—Hill Street; Calle Aceituna—Olive Street; Calle de La Caridad—The Street of Charity (now Grand Avenue); Calle de Las Esperanzas—the Street of Hopes; Calle de Las Flores—the Street of Flowers; Calle de Los Chapules—the Street of Grasshoppers (now Pearl Street). North of the plaza church the north and south streets were the Calle de Eternidad—Eternity Street, so named because it had neither beginning nor end, or, rather, each end terminated in the hills. Calle del Toro—Bull Street, significant of the national pastime of Spain and Mexico—the bullfight. Calle de Las Aspas—Hornet Street; an exceedingly lively street at times when the hornets had business engagements with the paisanos. Calle de Los Adobes—Adobe Street, well named. The east and west streets were Calle Corta—Short Street; Calle Alta—High Street; Calle de Las Virgines—Street of Virgins; Calle del Colegio—College Street, the only street that retains its primitive name.

[65]

The Calle de Las Chapules was for many years the extreme western street of the city. The name originated thus: On certain years, mostly during the dry or drought years, myriads of grasshoppers hatched on the low grassy plains of the Ballona and Cienegas. When they had devoured all vegetation where they originated, they took flight, and, flying with the wind, moved in great clouds towards the east—like the locusts of Egypt, devouring everything in their course. When the destroying hosts reached the Calle de Las Chapules, the *vinatero* knew his grape crop for that season was doomed. The voracious hopper would not leave a green leaf on his vines, and the vineyardist considered himself fortunate if the destroying host did not devour the bark as well as the leaves.

Calle Primavera—Spring Street, sixty or seventy years ago was known as the Calle de la Caridad—the Street of Charity. The aristocratic part of the city in those days was in the neighborhood of the plaza, and on Upper Main Street. Spring Street being well out in the suburbs, its inhabitants were mostly peons and Mexicans of the poorer class, who were dependent largely upon the charity of their wealthier neighbors. There is a tradition, which I have not been able to verify by written record, that back about the beginning of the century, Spring Street was known as Calle Cuidado—Lookout or Beware Street, so-called because of the numerous washes and gulches cutting across it from the low foothills. The name would be appropriate now, but it would be for other reasons.

Main Street below the junction, about that time was known as Calle de Las Allegria—Junction Street. The question is often asked why was Spring swung off on a diagonal to form a junction with Main? The historical facts of the case are that Main Street forms a junction with Spring. That portion of Spring Street between the junction and first, is the older street by many years. It is part of an old road made more than a century ago. It began at the old plaza and followed the present line of Main Street to the junction. In Ord's "plan," this old road is traced from the junction northwestward. It follows the present line of Spring Street to First Street, then crosses blocks 2 and 4, diagonally, to the corner of Third and Broadway. It intersects Hill at

Fourth Street and Olive at Fifth Street, skirting the hills it passes out of the city near Ninth Street to the brea springs from which the colonists obtained the roofing material for their adobe houses. This road or street was used for many years after the American occupation and was recognized as a street in conveyances. Within the past three years the city council gave a quit-claim deed to a portion of this street to a lot owner in Block 11½ O.S. It has been, by some poetical historiographers, claimed that this road was part of the Camino del Rey (the King's highway) of the olden times. "The King's horses and the King's men" may have galloped over it bearing royal mandates from pueblo to presidio, but creaking carretas, loaded with brea, were more common than the King's caballeros on this "royal road." On a map of the pueblo of Los Angeles, made in 1786, when Argüello surveyed the lands of the founders, there is a road marked as beginning at the southeast corner of the old plaza, from thence running southeasterly until it intersects what is now Aliso Street; thence following the present line of that street it crosses the river and passes out of the pueblo to the southeast. There are traces of this road in the old records. It leads southeastward through the Paso de Bartolo, thence to San Juan Capistrano and San Luis Rey, to San Diego; then down the coast of Lower California to Loreto, near Cape San Lucas. This, in the days of King Carlos III, was the Camino del Rey, or Camino Real. It was not like "the road from Winchester town, a good broad highway leading down," but rather a *camino de herradura*—a bridle path. Wheeled vehicles seldom traveled it. Although but the semblance of a road, yet time and again has this old highway echoed the tread of marching armies. In the troublous times of 1831-1833, when Echeandia of the south and Zamorano of the north waged a bloodless warfare against each other and fired off sesquipedalian *pronunciamientos* as ferocious in the rhetoric as they were harmless in effect, down this old camino from Paso de Bartolo rode Echeandía's faithful adherent, Captain Barroso, at the head of a thousand mounted Indians intent on the capture of the recalcitrant Pueblo of Angeles, but at the intercession of the beleagured inhabitants, this modern Coriolanus turned aside to regale his neophyte retainers on

[67]

the fat bullocks of the Mission San Gabriel. And via the Camino Real from Los Nietos rode Juan Gallardo, the cobbler, in command of his fifty Sonoran patriots, when, in imitation of the *hidalgos* of his native land, he essayed to play at the national game of Mexico—revolution. And by the same highway, he entered the pueblo in the small hours of the morning, and awoke its conscript fathers from their dreams of peace by the drum beat of war. And along the same Camino Real, from Paso de Bartolo, marched the Saxon conqueror, Stockton, with his invading army. On this roadway was fought the last battles of the conquest, when the boom of Stockton's cannon sounded the death knell of Mexican domination in California.

Going northward the Camino Real, or main highway, crossed the river near the base of the hills and followed up its valley to the Mission San Fernando; from there westerly to San Buenaventura, then on to Santa Barbara and the missions beyond, to Monterey. In the waning years of the last century out from the capital, Monterey, on the first day of each month, rode a courier southward, gathering from each mission, pueblo and presidio its little budget of mail as he made his monthly trip to Loreto on the Gulf—a perilous ride of a thousand miles over the old Camino del Rey.

There was one street in the older portion of Los Angeles that is not named in Ord's plan, but which, in the flush days of gold mining from 1850 to '55, had a more wide-spread notoriety than any other street in the city. It was the Calle de Los Negros in Spanish, but Americanized into Nigger Alley. It was a short and narrow street extending from the then termination of Los Angeles street to the plaza. In length it did not exceed 500 feet. Yet within its limited extent it enclosed more wickedness and crime than any similar area on the face of the earth. Gambling dens, saloons, dance houses, and disreputable dives lined either side. From morning to night, and from night to morning, a motley throng of Americans, Mexicans, Indians and foreigners of nearly every nation and tongue crowded and jostled one another in its dens and dives. They gambled, they drank, they quarreled, they fought, and some of them died—not for their country—although the country was benefitted by their death. In the early '50s there were more desperadoes, outlaws and cutthroats in Los Angeles than in any other city on the coast. In the year 1853 the violent deaths from fights and assassinations averaged over one a day. The Calle de Los Negros was the central point towards which the lawlessness of the city converged. It was, in its prime, the wickedest street on earth. With the decadence of gold mining the character of the street changed, but its morals were not improved by the change. It ceased to be the rendezvous of the gambler and the desperado and became the center of the Chinese quarter of the city. Even in its decadence its murderous character clung to it. That terrible tragedy known as the Chinese Massacre, took place on this street in 1871 when eighteen Chinamen and one white man were murdered. The extension of Los Angeles street obliterated it from the plan of the city.

When the United States Land Commission, in 1851, began its herculean task of adjudicating the Mexican land grants in California, the city of Los Angeles laid claim to sixteen square leagues of land. The Hancock survey of 1853, had divided the city lands south of Pico Street, to the Ranchos Los Cuervos (Crow Rancho) and the Paso de La Tijera, and on the west to the La Cienega, into 35-acre tracts known as city donation lots. The city limits on the south (west of the river) extended nearly three miles below the present boundary line of the city and on the west nearly two miles to the Cienega. All the territory sought to be annexed to the city at the recent election was once within the city limits. The streets, south of Pico, were named after the presidents. Beginning with Washington, in regular succession followed, Adams, Jefferson, Madison, Monroe, John Quincy Adams, and Jackson streets. All these streets, except parts of the first three, have long since disappeared in the orange groves of Vernon and the market gardens of University and Rosedale. The Mexican governors, after whom the north and south streets were named, have been more fortunate than the presidents. We still have Echeandia, Figueroa, Alvarado and Micheltorena streets, although considerably curtailed as to length south of Boyle Heights and east of the river, the Rancho San Antonio curbed the city's ambition to expand in that direction. On the north and northwest the Rancho Los Feliz and the Verdugos encroached on the city's area and the hostile owners refused to be surveyed into the city. On the east, from the center of the plaza it was two leagues to the city line. The area of the city according to the Hancock (or Hansen) survey of 1855 was a fraction less than 50 square miles—a magnificent city on paper. The land commission in 1856 confirmed to the city a grant of four square leagues (about 28 square miles) and rejected its claim to all outside of that. After many delays, in 1875 nearly twenty years later, a United States patent was issued to the mayor and council—and then the greater Los Angeles of the early '50s, shrank to the proportions of Felipe de Neve's pueblo of 1781,—"one league to each wind measured from the center of the plaza."

It was not to be expected that Neve's ease-loving pobladores would long preserve in its entirety the musical but long drawn out name of the new born town by the Rio Porciúncula, El Pueblo de Nuestra Señora *(sic)*, la Reina de Los Angeles, was inconveniently syllabic for every day use; in 1787 it had been abbreviated and changed to Santa María de Los Angeles, later on to Santa María. It was at one time proposed to change the name to Villa Victoria la Reina de Los Angeles so that it might not be confounded with Puebla in old Mexico. In the tumultuous days of '39 when the seditious and turbulent Angelenos vexed the righteous soul of good old prefect, Cosme Peña, he was wont to speak of it as the Pueblo de Los Diablos—the town of the devils. In official documents, under Mexican rule, it was simply Angeles. It is to be regretted that the Americans after the conquest did not continue the custom and thus save posterity the necessity of speaking and writing the prefix "Los."

In almost every "write up" of the early history of Los Angeles appears this venerable fiction "The founders of the town numbered twelve adult males, all heads of families." "There were forty-six persons in all." "The men were discharged soldiers from the Mission San Gabriel." This fiction has not that merit of the old time novels, "founded on facts." It is all fiction. There were not twelve founders—Rivera enlisted fourteen pobladores in Sonora and Sinaloa, two deserted, one was left behind at Loreto in Lower California (there is no evidence that he ever joined the colonists at Los Angeles) and then there were only eleven. There were not forty-six persons in all—only forty-four. Not a man of the eleven was a discharged soldier from San Gabriel. None of them had ever been at San Gabriel until they arrived with Zuñiga's expedition on the 18th August preceding the founding. Of the twenty-two adults, two were Spaniards, nine were Indians and one mestizo (one was classed as a coyote—wild indian) and ten were negroes and mulattoes. Early in 1782, three of the founders, one of the Spaniards and two of the negroes, were deported from the colony for general worthlessness and their property taken from them, and then there were but eight founders. In 1785, Sinova who had been a laborer in California for several years, joined the colony making nine heads of families, the number to whom Argüello distributed the house lots and the sowing fields in 1786. The founders left no lasting impress on the town. Not a street in the city bears the name of any one of them. Five of the Mexican governors have had streets named after them, but not one of the Spanish governors of California has been so honored. No street or landmark bears the name of good old Felipe de Neve, the real founder of Los Angeles. Nor have Portolá, Fages, or Borica, men of honor and high standing, been remembered in the nomenclature of its highways. Of the old Pueblo de Nuestra Señora (sic), La Reyna de Los Angeles, so carefully planned and so reverently named by Governor Felipe de Neve only an abbreviation of the name remains, and even the signification that that conveyed to the good old governor has been changed by the modern dwellers in the new city of The Angels.

8

LA ESTRELLA:
THE PIONEER NEWSPAPER
OF LOS ANGELES

James M. Guinn

In our American colonization of the Great West, the newspaper
has kept pace with immigration. In the building up a new town,
the want of a newspaper seldom becomes long felt before it is
supplied.

It was not so in Spanish colonization; in it the newspaper
came late, if it came at all. There were none published in California during the Spanish and Mexican eras. The first newspaper published in California was issued at Monterey, August 15,
1846—just thirty-eight days after Commodore Sloat took possession of the territory in the name of the United States. This
paper was called *The Californian* and was published by Semple
& Colton. The type and press used had been brought from
Mexico by Augustin V. Zamorano in 1834, and by him sold to
the territorial government; and it had been used for printing
bandos and *pronunciamientos*. The only paper the publishers of
The Californian could procure was that used in making ciga-
rettes which came in sheets a little larger than ordinary fools-
cap.

After the discovery of gold in 1848, newspapers in California multiplied rapidly. By 1850, all the leading mining towns
had their newspapers, but Southern California, being a cow

country and the population mostly native Californians speaking the Spanish language, no newspaper had been founded.

The first proposition to establish a newspaper in Los Angeles was made to the City Council October 16, 1850. The minutes of the meeting on that date contain this entry: Theodore Foster petitions for a lot situated at the northerly corner of the jail for the purpose of erecting thereon a house to be used as a printing establishment. The council—taking in consideration the advantages which a printing house offers to the advancement of public enlightenment, and there existing as yet no such establishment in this city: "Resolved, that for this once only a lot from amongst those that are marked on the city map be given to Mr. Theodore Foster for the purpose of establishing thereon a printing house; and the donation be made in his favor because he is the first to inaugurate this public benefit; subject, however, to the following conditions: First, that the house and printing office be completed within one year from today. Second, that the lot be selected from amongst those numbered on the city map and not otherwise disposed of."

At the meeting of the Council, October 30th, 1850, the records say: "Theodore Foster gave notice that he had selected a lot back of Johnson's and fronting the canal as the one where he intended establishing his printing house; and the council resolved that he be granted forty varas each way."

The location of the printing house was on what is now Los Angeles Street, then called Calle Zanja Madre (Mother Ditch Street), and sometimes Canal Street.

The site of Foster's printing office was opposite the Bell Block, which stood on the southeast corner of Aliso and Los Angeles streets. On the lot granted by the council Foster built a small two-story frame building; the lower story was occupied by the printing outfit, and the upper story was used as a living room by the printers and proprietors of the paper. Over the door was the sign "Imprenta" (Printing Office). The first number of the pioneer paper was issued May 17, 1851. It was named *La Estrella de Los Angeles, The Star of Los Angeles*. It was a four-page five column paper; size of page, 12×18 inches. Two pages were printed in English and two in Spanish. The subscription price was $10 a year, payable in advance. Advertisements were inserted at the rate of $2.00 per square for the first insertion and $1.00 for each subsequent insertion. The publishers were John A. Lewis and John McElroy. Foster had dropped out of the scheme, but when, I do not know. Nor do I know anything of his subsequent history.

In July, William H. Rand bought an interest in the paper and the firm became Lewis, McElroy and Rand. In November McElroy sold his interest to Lewis & Rand. John A. Lewis edited the English pages and Manuel Clemente Rojo was editor of the Spanish columns of the *Star* for sometime after its founding. The press was a Washington Hoe of an ancient pattern. It came around the Horn and was probably six or seven months on its journey. Even with this antiquated specimen of the lever that moves the world, it was no great task to work off the weekly edition of the *Star*. Its circulation did not exceed 250 copies.

The first job of city work done by *La Estrella* (as it is always called in the early records) was the printing of one hundred white ribbon badges for the city police. The inscription on the badge, which was printed both in English and Spanish, read "City Police, organized by the Common Council of Los Angeles, July 12, 1851." *La Estrella's* bill for the job was $25.00.

The burning political issue of the early '50s in Southern California was the division of the state. *The Star*, early in its career, took sides in favor of division, but later on, under a different management, opposed it. The scheme as promulgated fifty years ago was the division of the state into two parts—the northern to retain the state organization, the southern to be created into a territory. The professed purpose of division was to reduce taxation, and to "emancipate the south from its servile and abject dependence to the north." The real purpose was the creation of a slave state out of Southern California and thereby to increase the pro-slavery power in Congress. Bills for division were introduced in successive legislatures for eight or nine years; but all were promptly killed except one. In 1859, under the Pico law, the question came to a vote in the southern counties and was carried. The Civil War and the emancipation of the slaves virtually put an end to state division. In July 1853, William H. Rand transferred his interest in the *Star* to his partner John A. Lewis. August 1st, 1853, Lewis sold the paper to James M. McMeans. The obstacles to be overcome in the publication of a pioneer newspaper in Southern California are graphically set forth in John A. Lewis' valedictory in the *Star* of July 30, 1853:

"It is," writes Lewis, "now two years and three months since the Star was established in this city—and in taking leave of my readers, in saying my last say, I may very properly be permitted to look back through this period to see how accounts stand.

"The establishment of a newspaper in Los Angeles was considered something of an experiment, more particularly on account of the isolation of the city. The sources of public news are sometimes cut off for three or four weeks, and very frequently two weeks. San Francisco, the nearest place where a newspaper is printed, is more than five hundred miles distant, and the mail between that city and Los Angeles takes an uncertain course, sometimes by sea and sometimes by land occupying in its transmission from two to six weeks, and in one instance fifty-two days. Therefore, I have had to depend mainly upon local news to make the Star interesting. And yet the more important events of the country have been recorded as fully as the limits of the Star would permit. The printing of a paper one-half in Spanish language was certainly an experiment hitherto unattempted in the State. Having no exchanges with papers in that language the main reliance has been upon translations, and such contributions as several good friends have favored me with. I leave others to judge whether the 'Estrella' has been well or ill conducted."

Under Lewis's management the *Star* was non-partisan in politics. He says, "I professed all along to print an independent newspaper, and although my own preferences were with the Whig party, I never could see enough either in the Whig or Democratic party to make a newspaper of. I never could muster up fanaticism enough to print a party paper."

McMeans went to the States shortly after assuming the management of the paper. William A. Wallace conducted it during his absence. Early in 1854, it was sold to M. D. Brundige. Under Brundige's proprietorship, Wallace edited the paper. It was still published in the house built by Foster.

In the latter part of 1854, the *Star* was sold to J. S. Waite & Co. The site donated to Foster by the council in 1850, on which to establish a printing house for the advancement of public enlightenment, seems not to have been a part of the *Star* outfit. A prospectus on the Spanish page informs us that "Imprenta de la Estrella, Calle Principal, Casa de Temple,"—that is, the Printing office of the *Star* is on Main Street, in the House of Temple; where was added, the finest typographical work will be done in Spanish, French and English. Waite reduced the subscription price of the *Star* to $6.00 a year payable in advance, or $9.00 at the end of the year. Fifty per cent advance on a deferred payment looks like a high rate of interest, but it was very reasonable in those days. Money, then, commanded 5, 10 and even as high as 15 per cent a month, compounded monthly; and yet the mines of California were turning out $50,000,000 in gold every year. Here is a problem in the supply and demand of a circulating medium for some of our astute financial theorists to solve.

Perusal of the pages of the *Star* of forty-six years ago gives us occasional glimpses of the passing of the old life and the ringing in of the new. An editorial on "The Holidays" in the issue of January 4th, 1855, says: "The Christmas and New Year's festivities are passing away with the usual accompaniments; namely, bullfights, bell ringing, firing of crackers, fiestas and fandangos. In the city, cascarones commanded a premium and many were complimented with them as a finishing touch to their head dress." Bull fights, fandangos and cascarones are as obsolete in our city as the Olympic games, but bell ringing and firing of crackers still usher in the New Year. In June 1855, *El Clamor Publico—The Public Cry*—the first Spanish newspaper in Southern California was founded by Francisco P. Ramírez. The Spanish pages of the *Star* were discontinued and the advertising in that department was transferred to the *Clamor*. On the 17th

Los Angeles Star.

Saturday, October 16, 1858.

BY THE OVERLAND MAIL.
THROUGH IN 20 DAYS!!
TEN DAYS LATER!!

Dates from New York to the 15th and St. Louis to the 20th of September.

By the arrival here of the Overland Mail stage on Tuesday, we were put in possession of New York and St. Louis papers of the above dates.

The mail came through to this point, from St. Louis, in twenty days, including a stoppage of thirty-seven and a half hours at Fort Smith, waiting for the Memphis mail. This fact shows how thoroughly and completely the road has been stocked, and how well organized the whole system has been, from the very outset.

The passengers found everything ready at the stations, and no delay occurred, nor hurrying on to make up for lost time.

It is the opinion of all who have come over the road, that the journey will yet be made to San Francisco in twenty days.

From the New York *Herald* of the 15th ult. we obtain the following intelligence.—

The Incendiarism at the Quarantine Station.

The last mail brought us the intelligence of the total destruction of the Quarantine establishment at Staten Island, by the mob. This was brought

In Massachusetts, w
... seized for ...
their candidate for G
... Rip Van Wink
... by talking ...
... it cannot be
Buchanan's ... has
try. In the States w
votes he has made
stood opposed he h
... and prepar
... triumphs.

Under all these ci
of success, with the
heartened, the adm
day in convention a
tion stands better t
when the democ...
The grasping cup ...
misrule extravag...
the Albany lobby,
... if it is ...
... it is cer
... parti... Add
of Mr. Buchanan's
ularity of his ... mi
No party ever wen
auspices than that
to-day. The la t ...
... democracy w...
and squabbling for
... should be ch
visions, and shoul
will call out the str
ry section of the ...
the stump of the ...
supporting its pla
chanan's acts, an
State policy. Wit
... party will swe
Montauk, and giv
confidence as will
remainder of ...

The Los Angeles Star *was the first newspaper published in Los Angeles.*
Courtesy of California Historical Society.

of March 1855, the *Clamor* dropped from the proprietorship of the *Star* and J. S. Waite became sole owner.

In the early '50s a Pacific railroad was a standing topic for editorial comment by the press of California. The editor of the *Star*, "while we are waiting and wishing for a railroad," advocates as an experiment the introduction of camels and dromedaries for freighting across the arid plains of the southwest. After descanting on the merits of the "ship of the desert," he says: "We predict that in a few years these extraordinary and useful animals will be browsing upon our hills and valleys, and numerous caravans will be arriving and departing daily. Let us have the incomparable dromedary, with Adams & Co.'s expressmen arriving here triweekly, with letters and packages in five or six days from Salt Lake and fifteen or eighteen from the Missouri. Then the present grinding steamship monopoly might be made to realize the fact that the hard-working miner, the farmer and the mechanic were no longer completely in their grasping power as at present. We might have an overland dromedary express that would bring us the New York news in fifteen to eighteen days. We hope some of our enterprising capitalists or stock breeders will take this speculation in hand for we have not much faith that Congress will do anything in the matter."

Notwithstanding our editor's poor opinion of Congress, that recalcitrant body, a year or two later, possibly moved by the power of the press, did introduce camels into the United States, and caravans did arrive in Los Angeles. To the small boy of that day the arrival of a caravan was a free circus. The grotesque attempts of the western mule whacker to transform himself into an Oriental camel driver were mirth provoking to the spectators, but agony long drawn out to the camel puncher. Of all the impish, perverse and profanity-provoking beasts of burden that ever trod the soil of America, the meek, mild, soft-footed camel was the most exasperating. That prototype of perversity, the army mule, was almost angelic in disposition compared to the hump-backed burden bearer of the Orient.

In July 1855, the subscription price of the *Star* was reduced to $5 a year. The publisher informed his patrons that he would receive subscriptions "payable in most kinds of produce after harvest—corn, wheat, flour, wood, butter, eggs, etc., will be taken on old subscriptions." Imagine, if you can, one of our city newspapers today starting a department store of country produce in its editorial rooms. Times have changed and we have changed with them. In November 1855, James S. Waite, the sole proprietor, publisher and business manager of the *Star*, was appointed postmaster of Los Angeles. He found it difficult to keep the *Star* shining, the mails moving and his produce exchange running.

In the issue of February 2, 1856, he offers the "entire establishment of the *Star* for sale at $1,000 less than cost." In setting forth its merits, he says: "To a young man of energy and ability a rare chance is now offered to *spread himself* and peradventure to realize a fortune." The young man, with expansive qualities was found two months later in the person of William A. Wallace, who had been editor of the *Star* in 1854. He was the first principal of the Schoolhouse No. 1, which stood on the northwest corner of Spring and Second streets, where the Bryson block now stands. He laid down the pedagogical birch to mount the editorial tripod. In his salutory he says: "The Star is an old favorite of mine, and I have always wished to be its proprietor." The editorial tripod proved to be as uneasy a seat for Wallace as the back of a bucking bronco; in two months it landed him on his back, figuratively speaking.

It was hard times in the old pueblo. Money was scarce and cattle were starving; for 1856 was a dry year. Thus Wallace soliloquizes: "Dull time! says the trader, the mechanic, the farmer—indeed, everybody echoes the dull sentiment. The teeth of the cattle this year have been so dull that they have been scarcely able to save themselves from starvation; but buyers are nearly as plenty as cattle and sharp in proportion to the prospect of starvation. Business is dull—duller this week than it was last; duller today than it was yesterday. Expenses are scarcely realized and every hole where a dollar or two has heretofore leaked out must be stopped. The flush times are past— the days of large prices and full pockets are gone; picayunes, bad liquor, rags and universal dullness—sometimes too dull to complain of—have usurped the minds of men and a common obtuseness prevails. Neither pistol shots nor dying groans have any effect; earthquakes hardly turn men in their beds. It is no use of talking—business stepped out and the people are asleep. What is to be done? Why the first thing of course is to stop off such things as can be neither smoked nor drank; and then wait for the *carreta,* and if we don't get a ride, it will be because we have become too fastidious, or too poor and are unable to pay this expense."

Henry Hamilton, the successor of Wallace, was an experienced newspaper man. For five years previous to purchasing the *Star* he had been proprietor of the Calaveras *Chronicle.* He was an editor of the old school—the school that dealt out column editorials and gave scant space to locals. Hamilton's forte was political editorials. He was a bitter partisan. When he fulminated a thunderbolt and hurled it at a political opponent, it struck as if it came from the hand of Jove, the god of thunder and lightning. He was an able writer, yet with him there was but one side to a question, and that was his side of it. He was a Scotch-Irishman and had all the pugnacity and pertinacity of that strenuous race. His vigorous partisanship got him into trouble. During the Civil War he espoused the cause of the Southern Confederacy. For some severe criticisms on Lincoln and other officers of the government, and his outspoken sympathy for the Confederates, he was arrested. He took the oath of allegiance and was released, but the *Star* went into an eclipse. The last number, a single page, appeared October 1st, 1864. The press and type were sold to Phineas Banning, and were used in the publication of the Wilmington *Journal.* The City of the Sloo (Wilmington) was then the most prosperous seaport on the southern coast. After the war when the soldiers had departed and Wilmington had fallen into a state of "innocuous desuetude" the *Journal* died of insufficient circulation, and was buried in the journalistic graveyard of unfelt wants. The old pioneer press of the *Star,* after doing duty for fifteen years, took a needed rest.

On Saturday, the 16th of May, 1868, the *Star* emerged from obscurity. "Today," writes Hamilton, "we resume the

*Henry Hamilton, pictured at right, was a
controversial editor and publisher of the* Star. *His pro-Southern
editorials excited considerable opposition during the Civil War,
and at one point he was arrested and jailed, and his paper's
publication suspended.*
Courtesy of Huntington Library.

publication of the Los Angeles Star. Nearly four years have elapsed since our last issue. The little 'onpleasantness,' which at that time existed in the family, has been toned down considerably, and if perfect harmony does not yet pervade the circle, our hope is this brotherly feeling will soon be consummated."

The paper was no longer the bitter partisan sheet that it had been during the early '60s. Hamilton now seldom indulged in political leaders of a column length, and when he did they were of a mild type. The new *Star* was a seven column blanket sheet, and was devoted to promoting the welfare of the county. It was ably conducted, and was a model newspaper for a town of 5,000 inhabitants. June 1st, 1870, the first number of the *Daily Star* was published by Hamilton and Barter. Barter retired from the firm in September and founded the Anaheim *Gazette,* the pioneer newspaper of Orange County. He bought the old press and type of the Wilmington *Journal*—the first press of the *Star*—and again the old press became a pioneer. When the Anaheim *Gazette* office burned down in 1877, the old press perished in the flames. The last time I saw it it was lying in a junk pile, crooked and twisted and warped out of shape or semblance of a printing press. If the spirit of the inanimate ever visits its former mundane haunts, the ghost of that old press would search in vain for the half dozen or more office buildings wherein the body long ago ground out weekly stints of news.

After G. W. Barter sold out the Anaheim *Gazette* in 1872, he leased the *Daily Star* from Hamilton. He ran it less than a year, but that was long enough for him to take all the twinkle out of it. It had almost sunk below the horizon when Mr. Hamilton resumed its publication. In July 1873, he leased it to Ben C. Truman. The genial Ben put sparkle in it. He made it interesting to his friends, but more so to his enemies. Like Silas Wegg, he occasionally dropped into poetry, and satirized some of his quondam adversaries at "Sandy Ague" (San Diego), where he had recently published a paper. When they felt the pricking of Ben's pungent pen, they longed, no doubt, to annihilate time and space that they might be near to him to take revenge when their wrath was hot. Truman continued its publication until July 1877, when it was sold to Paynter & Co. Then it passed to

Brown & Co. The Rev. Mr. Campbell of the Methodist Church, South, conducted it for a time. In the last year of its existence it had several different publishers and editors. Its brilliancy steadily diminished until in the early part of 1879, it sunk below the horizon, or, to discard metaphor and state facts, the sheriff attached it for debt, and its publication was discontinued. Its remains were not buried in the graveyard of unfelt wants. A more tragic fate awaited them—they were cremated. The plant and the files were stored in an outbuilding of Mr. Hollenbeck's who was one of the principal creditors. His Chinese laborers roomed in the lower part of the building. In some of their heathen orgies they set fire to the house. For a few minutes *La Estrella* blazed up into a star of the first magnitude then disappeared forever.

Such in brief is the story of *La Estrella*, the pioneer newspaper of Los Angeles. Its files contain a quarter century's history of our city and its environs. It is to be regretted that its early editors deemed political essays of so much more importance than local happenings. If these editors could crawl out of their graves and read some of their political diatribes in the light of the twentieth century, they no doubt would be moved to exclaim, What blind leaders of the blind were we!

9

VIGILANTISM IN LOS ANGELES, 1835-1874

Robert W. Blew

Los Angeles is a city of violence. Murders, riots, slaughter on the highways, and crimes of passion seem to be daily occurrences in her history; furthermore, during the years 1835 to 1874, the first and last recorded lynchings in the city, the citizens resorted with distressing frequency to vigilante actions. During the 1850s, almost every issue of the local press noted several murders. Death by violence seemed so common that these crimes seldom received more than a few lines. Usually the announcement ran similarly to the following hypothetical example: Juan, an Indian, was found dead in the *Calle de los Negros* shot in the head and stabbed numerous times. Inquest found he died by violence from person or persons unknown. Even in the 1870s, when the local paper was a daily, most issues carried items about assaults, cuttings, and, less frequently, a murder.

In the first twenty-five years of Los Angeles journalism several patterns became obvious about reported murders. Near election time, there were few or no reports. One assumes this is because politics were more important than death. Not surprising, during times of economic crisis murders were more frequent. This is probably because the lower economic groups were reacting to the frustrations of poverty. During the last years of the Civil War, death reports were less common. The first years of the war coincided with a severe drought in southern California; the rise in violence may have been a reaction to financial conditions and not to the stresses created by the war.

The lessening of crime reports, in the last year of the war, may have been because it was during this period that the local newspaper was making its most vicious attacks upon the Lincoln administration and possibly slighted other news to have more space for its political editorials.

Not only does Los Angeles have a long record of individual (and mass) murders, but also her history includes the unenviable record of at least three major race riots. Obviously, an element of racial bias entered into vigilante actions, but since this factor would require an in-depth sociological study of personal attitudes, the press, and examples of overt and covert discrimination, this question will not be considered here. However, a cursory study of contemporary newspapers uncovers epithets of "drunken Indian," "cowardly Mexicans," "violent and brutal Mexican disregard for the law," "the heathen Chinese," and "John Coolie" which strongly indicates such feelings were rampant, especially against the Chinese. Just before the Chinese Massacre, there were several articles demanding the exclusion of Orientals. One in particular was designed to arouse public reaction with the remark: "We venture to the assertation that many a dark and terrible deed has been perpetrated by these heathens in their secret dens, which will never come to the knowledge of the Christians whose places they are usurping."

It is possible to formulate reasons for early violence in the "City of the Angels." Los Angeles was a frontier town. Because of the lack of police, of effective courts, and of a civic consciousness, settlements on the edges of civilization tended toward unrest. Apparently, though, Los Angeles outdid the rest. More than just a frontier town, it also served as a staging place for drifters. Fur trappers, the remnants of the mountain men, overland herders from Santa Fe, and soldiers from Forts Tejon and Yuma found the first taste of society and civilization here. In addition, it was the last stopping place for bands raiding into Sonora or fleeing to Sonora, after raids in the mining areas, as well as for various filibuster attempts.

Not only the drifters but the dwellers were also a source of potential trouble. Most were young, aggressive bachelors hoping to improve their fortunes. Many of the married men were without their wives and families. A portion of them did not plan to establish permanent ties here, but, rather, they planned to return to the eastern states. In addition, many of these men were Southerners, especially from Texas. Among this group, personal honor was not a trifle, and any slight or injury, real or imagined, required atonement. This touchy honor, combined with the "macho" of the native *Californio*, provided the spark to ignite many an explosive situation.

A survey of the northern California towns indicates that there the "Anglo" dominated, and usually the native or alien population was segregated to specific areas or even to separate settlements. In Los Angeles the economic and politically dominant "Anglo" group was outnumbered by the natives. Further, a large Chinese settlement existed near the center of town, and large numbers of Indians struggled to survive in the city. To this racial mixture, the possibility that *rico* Californio had joined forces with the more aggressive Americans to subjugate, or to continue to subjugate, the masses should be taken into consideration.

Like many restless towns, Los Angeles turned to popular tribunals to solve a rampant wave. One usually thinks of San Francisco when vigilantes are mentioned, but the first committee in California was organized in Los Angeles, and they continued to operate here for many years after they ceased to exist in the "City by the Bay." In San Francisco, the Vigilantes executed eight, but in "Los Angeles, Vigilante Committees hanged 32. . . . In addition, Los Angeles had 40 legal hangings and 38 lynchings. This does not include some 19 or 21 Chinese shot or lynched in the riot of 1871." In the year 1855 there were a total of forty-seven vigilante executions in the state and not one was in San Francisco.

It is difficult to determine the accuracy of the above figures since record keeping was very poor. As an example, one man was reported to have been executed in San Gabriel, Ventura, and Los Angeles on three consecutive days! There is also a confusion in names. One finds, on close scrutiny, that a "Juan," a "Juan Aliva," and an "El Gato," in actuality, were not three persons, but one. In the bargain it is difficult to make a geographic determination of what was meant by Los Angeles. The county consisted of the entire southern third of the state, and on occasion what is reported as a local event actually happened in San Bernardino or Yuma. Statistics would also differ if one were to use the present metropolitan boundaries rather than the boundaries of the smaller 1850 community.

Reporting even makes it difficult to determine if an execution were the result of a court ordered punishment, or if it were an extralegal action. For example:

> On Tuesday, a miserable imbecile looking creature, Thomas, an Indian, was executed in the jail yard, for the murder of his mother and wife. Some humane persons had an inquisition held before the Sheriff and a jury of twelve, as to his sanity, or moral accountability; the jury agreed that he was a proper subject for the operation of the law, and he was operated on accordingly.

Another problem that arises is what is a vigilante action and what constitutes a lynching. Webster defines a vigilance committee as a: "Volunteer committee of citizens for the oversight and protection of any interest, esp[ecially] one organized to suppress and punish crime summarily, as when the processes of law appear inadequate." Using this definition, it would appear that any extralegal action to punish a perpetrator of a crime could be considered as a vigilante action whether an organization existed or not. Even though organizations such as the Rangers or voluntary police were organized under the auspices of the law, they probably did not let legal procedures interfere with the accomplishment of their mission. With this in mind, every action not under the direction of the courts will be included as a vigilante movement, whether it was a Lugo sending his Indians after a band which had molested him and his home, or a formal committee, such as was formed during the Flores-Daniels excitement, or an informal lynching caused by the passion of the moment, as in the cases of the Cota boy and "El Gordo."

As noted before, the first vigilance committee was formed in Los Angeles. Generally, the shooting of María de Rosario Villa and her paramour, Gervasio Alipás, for the murder of her husband is accepted as the first, but Richard Henry Dana rec-

Los Angeles vigilantes tried extralegal methods of controlling crime in the city.
Courtesy of Security Pacific National Bank
Photograph Collection/
Los Angeles Public Library.

ords an earlier one. According to him, one of the early American settlers was stabbed in his home by a Californio. When it became apparent to the foreign settlers that nothing was to be done about this, the Americans and English in the pueblo joined forces with a band of thirty or forty fur-trappers, who were headquartered in town, tried, convicted, and shot the culprit. Since there is no other authority for this event, and because Dana did report gossip and anti-Californio rumor as truth, its veracity *must* be questioned.

The details leading up to the first authenticated vigilante committee were relatively simple. María had abandoned her husband, Dominigo Félix, and became the mistress of Gervasio. After attempting for two years to persuade his wayward wife to return home, Félix sought aid from the authorities, who ordered her arrest. An apparent reconciliation was made, and the couple, mounted on one horse, began the journey home. A few days later, Dominigo's body was discovered; María and her lover were arrested and brought to the village for trial. As there was no tribunal in California authorized to levy the death penalty, and because of the time required and the assumed futility of appealing to Mexico, some forty or fifty citizens, including fourteen foreigners, met at the home of John Temple and organized a *junta defensora de la segurida publica*. On that day, April 7, 1836, the committee, after an exchange of proclamations with the officials of the pueblo, removed the pair from the jail and shot them.

This was the only case of peoples' justice during the Mexican era. Soon after the American conquest, in 1848, a special tribunal consisting of Abel Stearns and Stephen C. Foster, was appointed to try some counterfeiters who had been apprehended.

In 1850 a committee of five was formed to drive a man from the city who had attempted to help some Negroes, who, knowing they were in free territory, had declared their freedom. He was given twenty-four hours to leave town, and, although the authorities tried to protect him, he was driven out. The correspondent, by his remark that mob law was triumphant in the district, suggests that this may not have been the only occurrence.

The murder of two teamsters, Patrick McSwiggen and Sam, a Creek Indian, resulted in charges against Francisco Lugo and two of his cousins. A Texan, John Irvine, who led a band of adventurers, offered, for a fee, to rescue the boys from jail, but, when the senior Lugo refused his offer, he decided to take his frustrations out on the three. Their lawyer, Joseph L. Brent, raised his own force of fifty mounted Californios to insure a fair trial. In addition to this force, a detachment of eighteen troopers was dispatched from Fort Tejon to help maintain peace and order. Outmaneuvered, the gang left the settlement. They attempted to rob Luis Rubidoux, who convinced them of his poverty and sent them to the Lugo ranch. The band attacked the Lugo home, broke in, rifled the place, and made off with some valuables. Señor Lugo, upon his return home, dispatched some of his Indians under his majordomo, Juan Antonio, to seek out the marauders. This group tracked Irvine and his men, trapped them in a canyon, and killed all but one. The next day, a posse under Stephen C. Foster appeared at the Lugo ranch and discovered what had happened. Whether this was a legal posse in search of Irvine, or a company of mounted volunteers is unclear.

Because of the exodus of criminals from San Francisco to avoid punishment by the First Vigilante Committee, a demand for protection and summary justice arose in many other towns. As the *Star* remarked: "In the absence of an efficient police, our citizens must take measures to protect their property." The populace had already taken measures. In the same issue, it was reported that a scouting party, which had been sent to San Francisco to ferret out undesirables, had returned to the Tejon Pass that day. On their tour, "They made one prisoner, and subsequently shot him."

As a result of the murder, in broad daylight, of the city marshal, Jack Wholy, on July 13, 1851, the city council authorized the organization of the first volunteer police force or committee of public safety. This one-hundred man organization, under the command of Doctor Alexander W. Hope, became the first of several officially ordained volunteer forces. Although no extreme action was reported at this time, the group had some psychological effect as one Wood, alias Otis, when arrested in August, supposedly remarked about his punishment, "I suppose that it will be just as the crowds say."

The committee found enough activity to justify its existence. Several army deserters, who had been apprehended after killing a Colonel Craig and a sergeant of the Bartlett surveying party were returned to Fort Yuma for court-martial, but "were it not that the military and not the civil officers were to try them they would have been disposed of by the people at once."

Three young men, Doroteo Zaveleta, Jesús Rivas, and the third unnamed, escaped from the inadequate Los Angeles jail. While apparently fleeing to Sonora, they met two American cattle buyers near San Juan Capistrano whom they robbed. Either Zaveleta or Rivas, depending on whose confession one reads, ordered the two men killed. The two killers fled to Santa Barbara, where with Francisco Carrillo, they were arrested for horse thieving. The trio were saved from lynching by a detachment sent from Los Angeles to return them to the southern city for justice. Upon returning to Los Angeles, the three were placed in the custody of a citizens' committee. Six men were appointed to examine the youths, and, after Carrillo turned state's evidence, Zaveleta and Rivas were brought to trial. A jury of seven Americans and five Californios was empaneled; the pair were found guilty and executed.

Major General Joshua H. Bean, a merchant of San Gabriel, sometime *alcalde* of San Diego, and the commander of the mounted rangers who scourged the southern areas of Indians, was set upon and assassinated in November 1852. Public indignation became quite vocal since General Bean, unlike his better known brother, Roy, "Law West of the Pecos," was very likable and an important figure in the community. The arrest of one of Solomon Pico's band and one of Joaquin Murrieta's men led to accusations against several for the crime. A committee was appointed to study the case, and it soon was indicated that:

*South side of the Los Angeles Plaza area
in the late 1850s. The white structure is the Carrillo Adobe and
Negro Alley is the street beyond.*
Courtesy of Huntington Library.

It is not improbable that these persons will be tried by a peoples' court, and the guilty ones punished as they deserve. There can certainly be no objection to this mode of procedure when we hear our very court officers acknowledge that the law is utterly incapable of bringing them to justice.

As the local paper predicted, the accused, "Eleulerio," Cipriano Sandoval, a cobbler of San Gabriel, Juan Rico, Reyes Feliz (or Felix), José Alivos, and Felipe Reid, the adopted Indian son of Hugo Reid, were brought to trial before a drumhead court. An eyewitness, years later, recalled the trial:

I believe it was about the fourth day after my arrival that the prisoners, who had been undergoing examination before the sub-committee, were brought to the Court House, where the final report of the committee was to be submitted to the great self-constituted court of justice-loving Americans.

Abbott's bath house was then used as a court house, and a high old court it was, too, I assure you. The place was packed to suffocation, with a dense crowd outside. *Old Horse-Face* presided over the court. The report of the committee was first read on the case of Reyes Feliz, and the President then in a solemn voice said: 'Gentlemen, the court is now ready to hear any motion.' Whereupon a ferocious looking gambler mounted a bench and said: 'I move that Reyes Felix be taken to the hill and hung by the neck until he be dead.'

'All in favor of the motion will signify the same by saying 'Aye!' said the president gravely.

'Aye! Aye! Aye!' yelled the mob, and Reyes Feliz was a doomed man. The same ceremony was gone through with in all the other cases, including Cipriano Sandoval, the poor innocent village cobbler of San Gabriel.

When they came to the case of the real murderer, a motion was made that 'Felipe Read [*sic*] be turned over to the legally constituted authorities,' and, strange to say, the motion was carried without a dissenting vote. Felipe, the red-handed murderer, was accordingly turned over to the sheriff, and immediately thereafter bailed and set at liberty. No effort was ever made to bring him to justice, and he died in his bed some years later in a natural way. So much for the wisdom of a mob.

All of this occurred on a Saturday, and the following day was set for carrying into execution the sentence of the court. By the time the town was astir next morning the ugly gallows could be seen on Fort Hill, with its horrid arms extended, as though defying the vengeance of man, or invoking the God of Justice. At 9 o'clock a herald paraded the streets, ringing a large dinner bell, and with a loud voice summoning the faithful to the feast; . . . When all was ready, the victims were given permission to speak. All maintained a dogged silence except the poor cobbler Sandoval, who made a brief speech. He hoped the great God would pardon his murderers as he pardoned them, and said that he died innocent, without a crime. They all kissed the crucifix, the rope was cut, the trap fell, and the five men were launched into eternity.

After dealing out punishment to the supposed killers of General Bean, the city settled back to its normal routine of murder and mayhem. In February a Smith and Williams stole some horses. Williams escaped, but Smith was captured. By public notice, a committee was formed, which removed him from the jail, tried him, and ordered that he be given seventy-eight lashes upon the bare back. He and a Mexican, who was apparently tried by the same jury, underwent flogging that afternoon.

This incident had further repercussions. Smith objected to being whipped by the Indian who had been hired for the chore. Thereupon a young American accepted the offer of ten dollars for the task. After he completed his commission, the crowd blanket-tossed him, which resulted in breaking his neck. This was felt only to be just for anyone who would carry out such a punishment on a fellow white.

Later in the month, a Colonel Watson killed a Doctor Overstreet and a Mister Cook whom he believed had participated in an earlier attack on his home. This caused the *Star* to editorialize:

> Such occurrences as these are too common. They bring reproach upon our city and leave a stigma upon the fair name of all our citizens. Is there no remedy? Is there no moral power in the community sufficient to check—nay to begin to check them. If the laws be powerless, as some assert, and as events seem to prove,—then we would recommend that in the 'peoples' courts,' which are sometimes held, such examples be made of violators of the peace as will show that there shall be no discrimination in men—only in crime.
>
> . . . there is no county where nature is more lavish . . . yet . . . there is no county where human life is of so little account. Men hack one another to pieces with pistols and other cutlery, as if

God's image were of no more worth than the life of one of the two or three thousand ownerless dogs that prowl about our streets and make night hideous.

When our neighborhood was infested by a band of robbers, our citizens rose and punished them until death and flight left only honest men and frightened knaves within our borders. Yet the cutting, and hacking, and shooting continue. It has become such a mania and its reoccurrence so common, that it has ceased to excite horror. It seems there are still some among us upon whom former example has lost their effect.

But we believe there is a remedy which if applied with the strong will of a people determined that the laws and decisions of the courts shall be respected will effect a huge reform among some of the social evils under which we groan.

Suddenly, the picture changed! No longer was the city plagued with normal domestic violence, but outside forces appeared. The infamous Murrieta and his band were raiding in the vicinity. Vigilante committees became the order of the day. A ranger company of one hundred was formed, for which the county provided one thousand dollars. And, the following year, the state legislature voted four thousand. Arms, equipment and horses were furnished by the local merchants and ranchers. Soon a city guard was formed to supplement the already existing rangers and police.

Once again, the *Star* furnished the battle cry. It charged the people, who in the times of Manuel Micheltorena had revolted and driven the governor and his *Cholos* from the province, that the time had arrived for another such revolution. A meeting was held at the El Dorado, and, after setting forth the conditions as they existed, it was further:

Resolved, That we organize a Mounted Police Force to range in the county, for the purpose of arresting all suspicious persons wherever we may find them and ridding the community of the same in such manner as may be advisable.

Resolved, That we warn all persons who have heretofore harbored robbers and assassins and furnished them means of escape, and in the event of their continuing so to do, that they be punished with the greatest severity.

Resolved, That we give three day warning to the whole vagrant class, taking down their names and description, and upon their failure to leave the county in the specified time, to remove them at all hazards.

Resolved, That we continue the system here adopted until the peace and security of the community are perfectly established.

A company was then formed, of which B. D. Wilson, Esq[uire], was chosen captain, and as we write this men are mustering preparatory to taking the field. Some have already started out. There are no officers subordinate to Mr. Wilson, but every man in the company pledged his honor and signed his name to an agreement to 'obey the command of our captain in carrying out the objects for which this company was organized; that we will faithfully stand by him and each other in the performance of the duties imposed by his command, and, as a consequence of responsibilities growing out of the same here or hereafter.'

The ranger company operated throughout southern California. Just how long it remained active is hard to determine. Horace Bell implies it was still active in 1857 and took part in the Flores-Daniels episode, but, after a few passing remarks about it, there is no mention of it in the newspapers more than a year later. At the time Bell states it was still in existence, the newspapers were clamoring that such a company be formed. Just what the company did is also difficult to ascertain. Bell never makes any positive statements and restricts himself mostly to humorous incidents or anecdotes about the members; the newspapers casually note from time to time that the Rangers had returned from a successful patrol, but seldom mentions any prisoners, nor gives any disposition of any captured desperado.

After Captain Harry Love and his California Rangers executed Joaquin, or somebody, a feeling of peace and security settled over the community even though murders were still reported to be almost daily occurrences. Jokingly, one was supposed to start breakfast conversation with, "How many were killed last night?" The Reverend Woods reported a murder, the second at the same spot within a month. Five days later, he noted a shooting in which one died and another was wounded; at the end of the month, he recorded that three men were being tried for murder, all of which had occurred within a month. By mid-summer, the newspapers complained: "Shooting in our streets is a daily occurrence, to the danger of the lives of our citizens." By October the paper was demanding more action be taken against the criminal element, especially the formation of a volunteer night police to patrol the streets.

At this time, a young gambler, David Brown, knifed Pinckney Clifford, a friend of his, the result of which was the most famous vigilante action in the city's history. The mayor resigned his post to head the mob. A committee met the next day to mete out summary punishment to Brown, but the mayor, Stephen C. Foster, by promising to help hang him if justice were not done, convinced the body to turn the culprit over to the courts. On November 20, 1854, District Judge Benjamin Hayes, faced with an unruly crowd which was threatening to take immediate action, duly sentenced Brown to suffer capital punishment the following January. Unfortunately, due process of the law now intervened. About the same time that Brown had murdered Clifford, Felipe Alvitre had been sentenced to death for the murder of James Ellington. The lawyers of both defendants appealed for stays of execution; one was received for the American, but none for Alvitre. Public opinion was that neither was entitled to a stay, but, if one were given a delay, they both should have one; therefore, certain persons decided that if Alvitre were executed, then Brown would be also. Disregarding the great excitement in town, Sheriff Barton ordered the execution of Alvitre to be carried out. The hanging was bungled which contributed to the surly mood of the crowd. As soon as Felipe was dead, a force of men commanded by Foster, Colonel McClanahan, J. D. Hunter, Juan Sepulveda, and Frank Bell overpowered the jailer and dragged Brown from his cell. He was quickly prepared and the execution about to proceed when the young gambler objected to being hanged by a "bunch of greasers" and a substitute hangman had to be found.

There are two other versions. An unnamed "old resident" swore, years later, that the lynch mob was agitated by two fellow conspirators of Brown, who wished to prevent him from naming them as participants in an earlier plot to rob John Temple. Horace Bell, writing about the same time, stated:

Dave was hung at Los Angeles in 1854, by an irate mob of Californian Mexicans, most of whom were his personal friends, and hung him only in vindication of principle. That is to say, the Americans of the Angel City were in the habit of amusing themselves by hanging some luckless Mexican, and the Mexicans wished to show that they could play the same game, and so seized on poor Dave as a fit subject for demonstration, apologized for the liberty they were taking with him, which Dave laughingly accepted, and was then swung up. Dave had always lived the life of an unprincipled fellow, he died in vindication of a principle, that is, to show that the native Californians knew how to hang a man in the most approved *gringo* fashion.

The town began to achieve an appearance of stability when suddenly in July 1855, another unfortunate incident occurred. William Jenkins, a deputy constable, shot Antonio Ruiz while attempting to repossess a guitar on which Ruiz owed a small debt. After Ruiz' death, the native community rose up in revolt. During the next week committees of vigilance were formed to patrol the streets, the sheriff was fired upon while patrolling the outskirts of the town, and the populace armed expecting an immediate outbreak of revolution. One of the citizen groups was a "Committee of Twenty," who were "to inquire into and hear of any and all persons making complaint or accusation into the character, conduct, and occupation of all disorderly or suspicious persons, and that upon the order of such Committee the said persons may be released, or sent out of the county. . . ."

"The City and vicinity during the past week has been rejoicing in its usual quietude," was the optimistic report of the newspaper, but the worst was to come. Several bands of native discontents, estimated to number one hundred, were raiding throughout the county. The most daring and successful of these bandits were led by Juan Flores and Pancho Daniels. Sheriff James Barton, informed that the two leaders were hiding in San Juan Capistrano, formed a small posse to capture them. At the Rancho Laguna, the sheriff was warned that the outlaws were aware of his plans and had prepared an ambush. Nevertheless, the posse continued to press down the main road and were attacked; Barton and three deputies were killed, but two es-

caped and hastened back to Los Angeles with news of the tragedy. The people panicked; quasi-military law under Doctor
John S. Griffin was imposed. For further protection, several
armed bodies were organized. These included: a committee of
safety to protect the town itself and to round up any suspected
person within its limits, a Ranger company of Americans under
W. W. Trist, a company of Germans under Joseph Weibel, a
Chives formed a company of French, and Andrés Pico and Tomás Sanchez organized the Californios. A volunteer company
from El Monte and troops from Fort Tejon provided additional
force. The Rangers scoured the countryside and, during the next
few days, captured many suspected outlaws. Because Flores had
escaped, after the El Monte company captured him, Pico, to
prevent the same thing from occurring again, hanged the two
prisoners he had, or as he reputedly said, "he confessed them."
A summary court presided over by Judge Jonathan R. Scott decreed the death penalty for eleven of the prisoners. In town the
Committee of Public Safety apprehended some forty or fifty
persons, who were interrogated, and some thirty released. The
remaining were apparently turned over to the civil authorities.
On February 14, the crowd mandated that Flores, who had been
recaptured and lodged in the city jail, should also pay the extreme penalty. The new sheriff, Trist, was lured out of town by
a fraudulent alarm, the crowd took Flores from the aged jailer,
marched him to an improvised gallows, and executed him. At
the same time, Miguel Blanco, who was in jail for assault upon
the sheriff, was hanged. In addition to these fifteen, other alleged members of the band were dispatched in San Gabriel,
Buenaventura, and Santa Barbara. It is difficult to determine
exactly how many were lynched, since Diego Navarro was reportedly put to death in three different places, and several were
recorded simply as name unknown, which may have been mis-
reporting or rumored deaths.

The alleged leader of the desperados, Pancho Daniels, was
still at large. He was finally captured under a haystack in San
Jose and returned south for trial. After his lawyers managed to
procure two delays, Pancho was granted a change of venue to
Santa Barbara. The people decided that the courts had abdi-

cated authority over the bandit, and they must insure that he was properly punished. "On Tuesday morning, the good people of our city were somewhat astonished on waking up from their peaceful slumbers, by the rumor that Pancho Daniels was then hanging by the neck from the cross beam of the gate of the county jail yard. On proceeding to the place, we found the rumor was well founded," reported the local press.

Another result of all the commotion was that Jack Powers, who had roamed the state robbing and murdering for some time, was, along with one follower, ordered into exile in Baja California.

After this affair, peace and quiet returned to the pueblo, until Francisco Cota senselessly and brutally murdered the wife of Lawrence Leck, a local grocer. The boy was quickly captured by the aroused neighbors and with great difficulty was taken into custody by the police. Judge Peterson examined him immediately and granted him until the next morning to secure counsel. As the officers attempted to escort him to jail, a mob seized the boy, marched him down the street, and in spite of several attempts to rescue the youngster, lynched him. An eyewitness remembered the crowd captured the boy and that he was never in the hands of the civil authorities. Moreover, they lynched the youth even though he had been repeatedly stabbed while being marched down Aliso Street and was nearly dead at the time.

Shortly before the Cota boy was executed, the *Star* reported that Claudio Alvitre was lynched in San Gabriel for murdering his wife, and, some months afterward, it mentioned that five persons were rumored to have been hanged near Lake Elizabeth, presumably for cattle rustling.

During the summer and fall of 1863, lawlessness in a more virulent form once again broke out in Los Angeles. A former police officer, Boston Daimwood [or Damewood] and his cronies returned from the Colorado mines with a large amount of money. The rumor was that in Colorado, or on the desert, or in Los Angeles, they had killed and robbed a miner, R. A. Hester. Because Daimwood was making loud threats against the lives of various local citizens, the sheriff Tomás Sanchez, arrested him and his three cohorts. During the arrest, the law officers were fired upon by other local toughs, but the quartet was, nevertheless, lodged in jail. On the morning of November 21, a crowd of approximately two hundred broke down the doors of the jail and removed the culprits. A young man, named Wood, who was in jail for stealing chickens, was also taken. These five were lynched, and the crowd dispersed. Sheriff Sanchez attempted to form a *posse comitatus* to arrest the ring leaders, but the public refused to support him. He did issue a proclamation demanding that the committee disband. In this he was supported by the press which remarked if the citizens wished for law and order, instead of hindering the sheriff in the process of his duty, just as the lawless had assaulted him the day previous, they should serve on juries and carry out their other civic duties.

Even though there had been no previous mention or hint of the formation of this committee, apparently it was well organized. In the same paper, an advertisement appeared answering the Sheriff. It stated that the committee stood only for law and order and waited to support the peace officers when called upon. It was signed "21, Secretary." Structure, notwithstanding, there is no further indication that the committee remained in existence; although, when the Chinese Massacre occurred in 1871, someone referred to an organized vigilante group, to which the editor admitted having no knowledge.

Earlier, John Rains, a local rancher, was murdered near Azusa. Suspicion fell upon Manuel Cerredel, who, shortly after his arrest, was stricken with smallpox. Fearing death, he confessed a conspiracy against Rains and implicated five or six others. He recovered, was tried, and sentenced to ten years at hard labor. The night the sheriff boarded the *Cricket* to take the prisoner north to San Quentin, an unusually large number of passengers also enshipped. The guard was overcome, Cerredel was hanged from a yardarm, and the body was dropped overboard.

Within days of Cerredel's departure, Charles Wilkins murdered John Sanford, a local merchant. Wilkins evaded the troops who were searching for him, but he was apprehended in Santa Barbara and returned to Los Angeles. He was quickly indicted by a special grand jury, and, while being taken to Judge Hayes' court for trial, one of Sanford's brothers attempted to kill him, but failed. The accused was adjudged guilty and re-manded to jail until the next morning when sentence would be pronounced. A crowd, suddenly, charged into the court room, dragged the prisoner away, and hanged him at a nearby corral. An eyewitness maintained that Phineas Banning, whose wife Rebecca was the sister of the murdered man, was the one who had attempted to assassinate Wilkins, and that Banning "led the Vigilance Committee which strung up Wilkins on Tomlinson & Griffith's corral gateway where nearly a dozen culprits had al-ready forfeited their lives."

For many years there were no vigilante actions in Los An-geles. Murder became less frequent, but other crimes were con-stantly reported in the press. Toward the end of the 1860s, stage coach robbery became very common in Los Angeles County, and the *Star* once again reported the formation of a vigilance committee. As usual, the editor opposed but admitted that when "the law be found powerless to interpose in defense of society and to punish the aggressor, then, in that case the people must protect themselves." There is no further mention of this group or indication they took any active measures, unless they were the group referred to at the time of the Daimwood epi-sode.

For several years Los Angeles seemed to be losing her fron-tier character. Murders became less frequent, assaults were still common, the citizens still carried pistols, but the violence of the earlier period seemed to have passed. But in late 1869 and early 1870, crime and violence became more noticeable once again.

In November 1870 another vigilance committee of five hundred of the best and most influential citizens was formed. They issued a proclamation that the association was "not to inaugurate mob law . . . we do, however, . . . intend to protect the life and property of innocent persons to the best of our ability. . . . Our actions are based upon humanity and jus-tice. . . ."

Michael Lachenais set the wheels in motion again by mur-dering Jacob Bell over the use of water from the *zanja*. Lache-nais had been forced to leave the area a few years earlier for the murder of a countryman and was suspected of at least two other

[103]

homicides, one his wife. After he was arrested, the sheriff started to take him to court for examination; however, a crowd formed which threatened to seize him. The sheriff returned his prisoner to jail and called for a *posse comitatus* to stand guard; only two men appeared for duty. An armed body of about two hundred marched into the jail yard and demanded the keys. While this was happening another group of approximately the same number stormed the jail from the other side and removed the prisoner. The condemned was taken to the near-by corral, given confession, and hanged.

In October 1871 some trouble over a lady in the Chinese quarter led to a shooting there. When the city marshal attempted to arrest several Chinese to preserve the peace, he and his party were fired upon. He then called for a citizens' posse to help capture the culprits, who had barracked themselves in the old Coronel adobe. By the next day, when sanity was restored, eighteen Chinese had been shot or lynched. Reaction turned public opinion against the persons who had perpetrated this fulsome crime, and a full inquest was ordered. Unfortunately, no one was able to recognize anyone else, but the grand jury did indict over one hundred. This assault is considered here only because it started out as a duly authorized citizens' posse, and because there were rumors that peace had been partly secured by the assistance of an existing vigilante committee which is the last recorded event of any such organization functioning in the city.

One more lynching took place, not in Los Angeles, but in El Monte. A Californio named Romo, alias "El Gordo," attempted to rob the store of William Turner. Mrs. Turner, worried because her husband was late, arrived at the store at that time and attempted to drive "El Gordo" away with a pistol she was carrying. In the fracas that followed, both Turners were seriously wounded, and Romo escaped. He was quickly captured and lynched by the aroused neighborhood. It is possible this mob reaction, after several years without any lynchings, could partly be due to a residue of fear from the depredations of the Vasquez gang, which had just recently been captured or killed. Some may have feared that Romo was aping the ways of

One of the last vigilante actions in Los Angeles
occurred in December 1870 when Michel Lachenais was hanged for
the murder of Jacob Bell. The view looks south across
Temple Street to Pound Cake Hill, later the site
of the county courthouse.
Courtesy of California Historical Society.

the more feared bandit. With this event, the history of extralegal punishments drew to a close.

Not all was horror and death; even this grim recital had a moment of grisly humor. The law firm of Edward J. C. Kewen and James G. Howard had developed a very lucrative and successful criminal practice. So successful, in fact, that one of the vigilante committees decided to hang both of them. When Howard was seized by the group, he said: "We are all friends; be generous, let's compromise. Hang Kewen, he's the head of the firm."

Conclusions may be drawn about vigilantism in Los Angeles. First, there were no formal organizations as in San Francisco. The *Angelinos* took a very pragmatic approach. Crime existed, an organization was formed, summary executions were inflicted, and then the group dissolved. Each crisis resulted in the formation of a new committee, frequently with the same personnel. The implication that a continuous committee existed in the late 1860s and the early 1870s does not seem to be borne out in fact.

Second, the persons involved did not seem to be historically conscious of their actions. In the collection of letters available, there are very few references to the events. In the Abel Stearns papers, for example, only one letter mentions vigilantes, and that referred to the second San Francisco committee. A comparison of newspaper accounts shows that except for the early years and for very popular movements, such as the reaction to the Flores-Daniels raids, a careful avoidance was made of names, which were provided by memoirs written after 1880. An element of protection as well as a lack of historical perspective is present here. The actions of the vigilantes were illegal and criminal charges could have been pressed against the participants. As some of the leaders were the most substantial men of the community, business leaders, large ranchers, lawyers, and judges, it would not have been economically feasible for the editors to have been indiscreet.

Third, the more literate members of the community did not approve of summary law, but believed that existing conditions forced its application. As Harris Newmark expressed his feelings:

> While upon the subject of lynching, I wish to observe that I have witnessed many such distressing affairs in Los Angeles; and that though the penalty of hanging was sometimes too severe for the crime (and I have always deplored, as much as many of us did, the administration of mob-justice) yet the safety of the better classes in those troublous times often demanded quick and determined action, and stern necessity knew no law. And what is more, others besides myself who have always repeatedly faced dangers no longer common, agree with me in declaring, after a half a century of observation and reflection, that milder courses than those of the vigilance committees of our young community could hardly have been followed with wisdom and safety.

Abel Stearns expressed similar feelings at the time the events were occurring. In regard to the San Francisco committee, he stated: "Although we may all regret the necessity that the people have to, so frequently take the law into their own hands, to make the necessary examples that crime must be punished. . . ."

Fourth, even though the editors protested innocence, the motivation to create the committees often came from the press. Almost in every instance before any violence there were a spate of editorials which deplored summary justice, but indicated that sometimes it was a harsh necessity. Horace Bell clearly indicated the belief that the Chinese Massacre was caused by the *Star*.

Finally, like most popular tribunals, the lack of effective law enforcement, inefficient courts, and lax punishments were set forth as justification for the lynchings. As late as 1870, the newspapers were crusading against "the failure of the courts to inflict proper punishment upon the murderers who infest the county." This was similar to an editorial that had appeared fifteen years earlier. Some, however, realized that the laxity in the administration of justice was in part due to the failure of the respectable class to perform their civic duties, such as serving on juries.

One may conclude that the committees in Los Angeles were spontaneous happenings, brought about by specific events, and, as soon as the danger disappeared, they dissolved. Many of the participants lamented the occurrences as a grim but necessary duty, an unimportant unpleasantness that was part of developing a new society.

10

THE STRUGGLE FOR NEGRO TESTIMONY IN CALIFORNIA, 1851-1863

James A. Fisher

For twelve years, 1851 to 1863, Negroes in California, along with white allies, fought against laws which forbade them from testifying for or against white persons in state courts. As emphasized in petitions, speeches, conventions, public meetings, and editorials, California Negroes lived in a constant state of anxiety and insecurity under the state's testimony prohibitions. They knew that such prohibitions on their testimony could be, and often were, interpreted by some whites as license to abuse Negroes without fear of penalty. With the courts—traditionally the channel for redressing grievances—closed, Sacramento Negro James Carter described the situation confronting the state's black citizens in 1855: "The Statute books and the common law, the great bulwark of society, which should be to us as the rivers of water in a dry place, like the shadow of a great rock in a weary land, where (the) wretched should find sympathy and the weak protection, spurn us with contempt and rule us from their very threshold and deny us a common humanity." Similar apprehension was stressed in a statement issued by the Colored Convention of 1857: "We, the colored people of California, believe that the laws which invalidate our testimony in the Courts of Justice, compel us to labor and toil without any security." Little did Carter and the convention delegates realize that the testimony situation would become much worse before it improved.

James A. Fisher

In 1850 the California legislature had passed a law which denied the right of testimony to Negroes, mulattoes, and Indians in criminal cases involving white persons. The following year that denial was extended to civil cases as well. The latter legislative action was strongly influenced by Governor Peter Burnett's annual message of January 1, 1851. Considering equality a mere theoretical assumption, Burnett emphasized that "the colored races are inferior by nature to the white, and . . . it may be safely affirmed that no race of men, under the precise circumstances (of colored races) . . . in our State, could ever hope to advance a single step in knowledge or virtue."

In that same year, 1851, a group of San Francisco Negroes, led by Mifflin Wistar Gibbs, Jonas H. Townsend, William Yates, J. J. Moore, and William H. Newby, drew up and published resolutions protesting the legislature's action. Gibbs wrote in his memoirs a half century later that those resolutions protesting the restrictions placed upon Negro testimony represented the beginning of Negro Californians' determination to use "all moral means to secure legal claim to all the rights and privileges of American citizens."

This early act of protest by Negroes accomplished little. One effort, however, seemed potentially fruitful. On March 22, 1852, Assemblyman Patrick Cannay of Placer County, induced by the Gibbs group, presented to the legislature a petition signed by San Francisco Negroes. The petition asked for a change in the state's testimony laws in order to allow Negro citizens the right to protect their property. Such an assertion may have seemed too bold for the tastes of some legislators, and a resolution which declined to accept "any petition from such source" was unanimously passed.

By 1853 a growing petition movement was afoot in California. In that year a petition from Negro citizens was again unanimously rejected. Sentiments in the Assembly were perhaps best expressed by Assemblyman George Carhart's suggestion that any petition "from such source" be thrown out the window. His colleague A. G. McCandless would have liked the petition burned.

Throughout the 1850s Negro petitions to the state legislature, as the San Francisco *Pacific Appeal,* a Negro weekly, later recalled, "met with adverse fate; they were either indignantly thrown out the window, or laid on the table, no (legislative) member being bold enough to advocate a consideration." A. Odell Thurman is perhaps a bit overly oratorical when he describes the rebuffs of petitions to the legislature as having left Negro citizens "weary of the struggle, apprehensive for the future, but still stout in heart, with an abundance of purpose." However, it was becoming apparent to some Negroes that different tactics and approaches, as well as other "moral means," were necessary if the right of testimony were to be attained. This would have called for organizing and soliciting the material and moral support of the entire Negro community of California.

Between 1851 and 1855 Negroes had held small local meetings in the cities of San Francisco, Sacramento and Stockton to denounce the testimony restrictions. Such meetings were more or less spontaneous and unorganized. Meeting in September 1855 at the Athenaeum Library of San Francisco, Negro leaders James Carter of Sacramento, Jonas H. Townsend, Peter Anderson, David W. Ruggles, and Jeremiah B. Sanderson, all of San Francisco, discussed and laid the plans for a statewide convention of Negro citizens. The general purpose of the convention, traditionally a collective endeavor to refute charges of Negro inferiority and a vehicle of protest, was to make "careful inquiries into our social, moral, religious, intellectual, and financial condition." According to its secretary, the specific purpose of the convention was "to get the right of testimony in the courts." Thus, California's first Negro convention, formally called the State Convention of the Colored Citizens, assembled in the city of Sacramento on November 20, 1855.

The Colored Convention of 1855 was neither abolitionist in temperament nor radical in leadership. A proposal, for instance, to send a transcript of the proceedings to *The Liberator* and to Frederick Douglass' *North Star* was rejected by the convention delegates in order to not identify their cause with abolitionism. The apparent moderation of the convention, however, was somewhat contrary to the backgrounds of at least two of its foremost leaders. William H. Yates, president of the convention, was an ex-slave who, after having been hired out as a janitor, served throughout the 1830s as a pamphleteer in Philadelphia. In the early 1840s he engaged in conveying fugitive slaves along routes taken by the Underground Railroad, often using his own hayloft as a rest station. Arriving in San Francisco in 1851, he quickly established himself as an activist and spokesman for the city's Negro community, donating practically all of his time to the cause of equal rights. Yates had the dubious distinction of being considered by one California Assemblyman to be more intelligent than a third of that Assemblyman's colleagues.

Likewise, the secretary of the convention, Reverend Jeremiah B. Sanderson, was no stranger to protest movements. In 1842 after hearing Sanderson speak at an antislavery rally in New Bedford, Massachusetts, Frederick Douglass was moved to write that Sanderson had put on "a brilliant demonstration" of his talents. Sanderson, since his arrival in California in 1854, had constantly been called on by the states' Negroes to work in a variety of capacities. It was in the field of Negro public education, however, that he was most successful and best known.

Even resolutions passed by the 1855 convention emphasized a certain restraint and sobriety often absent in those of abolitionist persuasion. Such resolutions stressed the favorable comparison Negroes made with other segments of the general community, and the belief that the state legislature should formulate a sound and positive policy toward its colored citizens. A positive policy, the convention suggested, would certainly be one which considered bona fide petitions of redress, particularly those advocating the abrogation of the hated testimony laws. Also stressed in the resolutions were the need for the "statistical and other evidences of our advancement and prosperity"; the need to encourage education among Negro children; the means to alleviate Negro apathy "in refusing to take part in any public demonstration"; and the desirability of creating a "twenty thousand dollar fund" to further the general "amelioration of our condition."

The strategy of moderation on the convention's part was obviously deliberate. To present an appealing image and to persuade—rather than pressure—public opinion were the ever present guidelines followed. Indeed, one resolution encouraged "all classes" interested in removing barriers to Negro testimony to make themselves known. This, as such, was an indirect call for liberal white support. Later, in a letter to his abolitionist friend, the writer William C. Nell of Boston, Sanderson revealed: "We have got among our young men here the right material for devising and carrying out plans for our general good." Speaking specifically of the 1855 convention, he continued: "We anticipated opposition from the press, and this is apt to stir up the baser sort to indulge in some excess. Those papers, however, which spoke, did so calmly, and encouragingly in regard to the objects of the convention (which was mainly to get the right of testimony in the courts), and though we heard distant grumbling and dark threats, it passed off." Apparently Sanderson was trying to make it clear to the easterner that another road besides that of abolitionism would be taken by Negroes in California.

The 1855 Colored Convention had no effect on the state legislature. But one side effect was the founding of the first Negro owned and operated newspaper in California, the San Francisco *Mirror of the Times*. Actually, the short-lived weekly was not published until late in 1856, but it was the convention planners (Townsend, Ruggles, and Moore) and then the convention itself which set the newspaper's moderate tone and attracted the initial interest in the venture.

Another result stemming from that first Negro convention was the organizing of the permanent Colored Executive Committee. Politically oriented, the body's original function was to adopt methods which would be effective, if not expedient, in the struggle against the testimony laws. Growing more and more autonomous and, seemingly, breaking with the moderation of the Convention of 1855, the Executive Committee proved itself more than capable in the field of agitation. It held public meetings, set up and delivered speeches to other Negro groups; it organized smaller committees in the various colored communi-

[113]

ties; it initiated petitions and sponsored resolutions. Where and under what circumstances future Colored Conventions were to be called were decisions made by the Executive Committee alone. Its traveling agent and director, as well as being a minister and editor of the *Mirror,* Jonas H. Townsend, was definitely the most influential and respected man in the Negro community during the 1850s.

The Colored Convention of 1856, again held in the city of Sacramento, signaled increased Negro concern and participation in the testimony question. Seventeen counties were represented—the Mother Lode counties especially—by sixty-one delegates. Clearly, the Convention had much appeal as an organ or form of protest. And, possibly, the ruling handed down the previous year by United States Circuit Judge McAllister in San Francisco served to increase support as well as to widen interest in the 1856 convention. In his ruling Judge McAllister stated that the testimony of a Negro sailor who had witnessed the murder of a fellow white sailor was inadmissible. McAllister based his decision on the fact that the laws of the state in which the federal court was held had predetermined that Negroes were not competent to testify in cases involving white persons.

In 1857 Negroes from seven different counties sent seven petitions to the state legislature; all seven were summarily rejected. The recently founded *Mirror* reacted to the legislature's actions in uncharacteristic indignation:

> But, you cannot expect a class of intelligent people in your midst . . . (owing to) their industry and enterprise . . . to tamely sit down and quietly submit to a law that denies them any protection, and on the other hand give license and security to thieves and robbers to plunder us with impunity; burn our houses; destroy our property, ravish our wives and daughters before our eyes and then turn around and laugh at us—and the lawmakers and politicians have the audacity to ask us, as intelligent men, to submit tamely and quietly to such outrages.

Supporting the *Mirror's* position was the 1857 Colored Convention's resolution to continue petitioning the legislature to repeal the state's onerous testimony laws.

Support for the Negro citizens' efforts—sometimes coming from the highest quarters—surprisingly increased (or became more vocal) among sympathetic whites after 1857. But even prior to that year Sanderson had written to William C. Nell that some of the best and most influential white persons in California were in favor of Negro testimony. Prominent voices like those of Colonel Edward D. Baker, Republican party lawyer and strategist; David Broderick, Democratic party leader, and Governor John Neely Johnson were heard up and down the state. In January 1858, Governor Johnson, making one of the addresses of his administration, asked the legislature to amend the law which excluded the testimony of Indians and Negroes. "This indiscriminate prohibition," he argued, "(is) at variance with the spirit of our Constitution and a wise and judicious governmental policy." Nevertheless, Johnson's words fell on deaf ears in the legislature. As the *Mirror* pointed out later: "A new governor (John B. Weller, who succeeded Johnson), hostile to all our interests is soon to be inaugurated, and a Legislature of the same stripe is about to assemble."

Between 1858 and 1861 the testimony question seemed to have gone into abeyance. During these years, the issue of Negro immigration to California occupied public attention (to say nothing of sectional bitterness and strife). Indeed, it was only later made clear just how closely related the two controversies really were, even merging along certain lines. If Negroes were given the right to testify in California, so some legislators argued, a massive influx of Negroes to the state would begin. Statistical data for the closing decades of the century belied this presumption.

The Sacramento *Daily Union*, almost alone (the *Mirror* went out of existence in 1858), attempted to keep the question of Negro testimony before the public. Incidences of criminality committed against Negroes were constantly printed. For example, a case of arson committed against a Negro in the city of Auburn was reported in the summer of 1858. After stating that the damage caused by the fire ran to a thousand dollars, the newspaper added: "Other acts of wrong are alleged to have been committed, and yet no redress could be had. If these things be so, the offense is doubly atrocious, having been perpetrated against those who are placed by the law in a position of civil disability."

The question of testimony for Negroes was regenerated in the early 1860s—and from unsuspected sources. Andrew Wilson, a contemporary journalist for the *China Mail,* wrote that respectable San Francisco merchants supported the Bishop of Victoria's call for Californians to allow the Chinese to testify against white persons in court. The California Supreme Court, in 1854, had decided that the "Chinese and all other people not white are included in the prohibition from being witnesses." Indeed, Wilson saw the question of Chinese testimony as being "too much mixed up with that relating to Negroes to be settled on its (own) merits." Wilson continued: "It would scarcely do to allow the Chinese coolie to testify against a white man and refuse the same privilege to an intelligent Negro. Many of the Californians consider the Chinaman to be 'a little lower,' and some of them 'a damned sight lower' than the Negro." Congressman Aaron A. Sargent from California seemed to have validated Wilson's observation when he stated on the floor of the House: "I tell the gentleman from Tennessee I never saw a Negro population anywhere which was not infinitely superior to these Chinese in character, morality, and intelligence. It would be an infinite work to elevate them."

So great, even at this early date, was animosity felt for Chinese in California that the suggestion that they be given the right to testify, or any other right for that matter, only served to have them compared to Negroes. In fact, as Wilson noted, the arguments used against allowing Chinese the right to testify stripped the quasi-logic from the arguments used against Negroes being granted that right. Negroes themselves, concerned for their own interests, were prone to use those same arguments. The *Pacific Appeal,* for instance, reminded its readers that "a more plausible excuse might be offered for depriving the Indian and Chinese of their oaths than the colored American: they being heathens and not comprehending the nature and obligation of our oath or obligation which would be binding on their consciences." On the other hand, the newspaper reasoned, "the Negro is a Christian: there is a strong religious sentiment in his nature, a feeling of awe and reverence for the sanctity of an oath which renders his judicial testimony sacred to him."

It was clearly revealed that the attitude of self-interest on the part of Negroes ruled out the possibility of a meaningful coalition with Chinese in order to combat the equally restrictive testimony laws. The fact that some Negroes employed Chinese as servants quite possibly reinforced general Negro reluctance to identify with Chinese. Indeed, statements in the legislature suggested that testimony for Negroes might mean testimony for Chinese also. Since Chinese testimony was so strongly resented, Negroes, perhaps more than many white legislators, ignored the idea that justice for all should be equal for all—for Chinese as well as Negroes.

Economics and leadership provided another explanation for the testimony question's prominence in the early 1860s. By 1860 the economic position of Negroes in California had substantially improved, and their leadership had reached a new level of distinction and articulation. The historian Rudolph Lapp notes that Negroes had accumulated more wealth in a shorter period of time in California than anywhere else in the nation. The *Union* estimated that in 1862 Negroes constituted a population of five thousand and a total wealth of 1.5 million dollars on which they paid $50,000 in annual taxes. It became increasingly more difficult to ignore the demands of a portion of the state's population which was proving itself to be not only economically efficient but rather economically sophisticated as well. This point was well illustrated in the lives of Basil Campbell and Mary Ellen Pleasant.

Born a slave in Cooper, Missouri, in 1823, Basil Campbell was sold by his master in 1853 to J. D. Stephens, a banker in California. According to the terms of an agreement between himself and his liberal-minded owner, Campbell would receive one hundred dollars a year for a total of ten years, after which he would be freed. If, however, he could buy his freedom in less than ten years, a reasonable price would be determined by Stephens. In 1861, after seven years of servitude, Campbell paid

Stephens $700 for his remaining three years and, as a conse-
quence, was freed. It seemed that all the time Campbell had
worked for Stephens, he had also been successfully investing
his annual 100 dollars in various San Francisco stocks. Thus, at
the time he bought his freedom it was estimated that he was
worth $10,000. By 1870, Campbell had become the richest Ne-
gro in California.

Mary Ellen Pleasant, affectionately called "Mammy" Pleasant, was born a slave in Georgia. Arriving in San Francisco after
several misadventures in the East, Mammy quickly established
herself as an operator of a chain of laundries. Her margin of
profit resulted from a cheap labor source: hired immigrant Negroes from the South. At one point in her laundry enterprise as
many as fifty Negroes were her employees. With capital from
her laundries, Mammy expanded into the boardinghouse business, catering only to well-to-do San Franciscans "on the
make." Defiant when racial slurs were spoken within her hearing, yet gracious when gain was at stake, she was able to make
valuable contacts and gather pertinent financial information at
her establishments. Mammy built up an indeterminable amount
of wealth, having invested in stocks, real estate, and other lucrative ventures—even blackmail whenever she overheard com-
promising conversations among her boarders. By 1858, as a
well-known story goes, she was in a position to guarantee John
Brown, whom she had known for some time, $30,000 for arms.
Brown's haste, however, prevented his ever receiving the money
before Harper's Ferry. While "feathering her own nest," Mammy's generosity to poor Negro families in San Francisco was not
unknown. Indeed, the "angel," as she was known to some,
started many Negroes in small businesses of their own.

An articulate leadership also provided California Negroes
with a much-needed unity and personal voice in the awakened
emphasis on his right to testify. Such leadership extended beyond the question of testimony. Jonas H. Townsend, as editor
of the *Mirror*, held a pervasive influence in the Negro community throughout the 1850s. It was he who authored the 1855
Colored Convention's resolutions and a most informative article
on the efforts of California Negroes to achieve equal educa-

tional facilities. This article first appeared in the New York journal *The Anglo-African* in March 1859. His editorial, "What We Want," should be a classic in the bibliography of California social history; it is a definitive statement of the plight of the Negro in the 1850s.

Along with Townsend, other Negroes—for example, William Yates, John J. Moore, and Jeremiah B. Sanderson—were also in the vanguard of leadership in California by 1860. After 1861, Negroes in California found new and more aggressive voices to articulate their grievances. Peter Anderson, Philip A. Bell, James Madison Bell, and Ezra R. Johnson, to list a few, were names which composed this new Negro leadership.

By March 1862, a long-awaited bill to repeal the anti-Negro testimony laws of 1850 and 1851 was introduced in the state legislature and, after heated debate, was enacted a year later, March 1863. Indeed, in conclusion, it is difficult to know precisely how great an impact the Civil War had upon the issue of testimony for Negroes in California. The humanitarian impulse emanating from the struggle was undoubtedly a significant force. The California historian and moralist Theodore Hittell viewed the testimony issue as "merely a special and exclusive movement in favor of the Negro brought about by the war." Admittedly, the war did create an adverse reaction to pro-Southern members of the state legislature. Yet, in the final analysis, without initial action and persistent agitation for twelve years on the Negro's part, one wonders what the fate of Negro testimony in California would have been.

11

EARLY SOUTHERN CALIFORNIA VINICULTURE
1830-1865

Iris Engstrand

The wine industry in California is as old as the state's earliest settlements. After the Franciscans established their first mission at San Diego in 1769, they began cultivating vines brought in from Baja California to produce their necessary sacramental wine. With the subsequent founding of new missions, wine making spread northward, although the area of major concentration remained in Southern California until the late 1850s. Padres particularly noted for their success in viniculture were those at San Fernando, San Gabriel and San Antonio. Today visitors to Mission San Antonio may still see the remains of the great *bodegas,* or vats, in which wines pressed from mission grapes were kept for future use.

The padres, however, concentrated all their attention on a single variety of wine, somewhat mediocre in quality, which is now called by the appropriate, if not very original, name of Mission. Probably the reason the mission fathers failed to develop a superior type grape is that even though they considered wine an article of commerce, they produced it mainly for their purposes.

Prior to 1830 very few vines were cultivated by private individuals, although in 1824 Joseph Chapman, an early Los Angeles settler, planted 4,000 vines in a rather unsuccessful attempt to break into the wine industry. The greatest stimulation to the industry on a private commercial basis was provided by the secularization of the missions after 1830. This act on the part of the Mexican government caused the padres generally to abandon their vineyards and orchards, and consequently to relinquish their chief source of income—the production of wine. Since grape growing and wine making had become a major factor in the economy of the missions of Southern California, immigrants to the territory were quick to realize the potentialities of commercial viniculture.

The suitability of California and particularly Los Angeles County as a grape producing area resulted from a combination of several factors. The virgin soil and temperate climate were ideal and California vineyards generally yielded a much larger crop than those in other parts of the world. A lack of severe storms and frost insured the success of the grape crop; the grapes required no irrigation; it was possible to make wine by fermentation without artificial heat during the winter; a greater variety of grapes could thrive on California soil than on soils elsewhere; and in the latter half of the 19th century land was relatively inexpensive in Los Angeles. In addition to wine making, the production of raisins and table grapes also proved to be a lucrative business.

Of the early pioneer settlers who capitalized upon this industry after 1830, two men were noted as becoming particularly successful viniculturists in the Los Angeles area. The first of these, a Frenchman bearing the somewhat appropriate name of Jean Louis Vignes, arrived in Los Angeles in 1831 from Monterey and immediately purchased 104 acres of land for the purpose of setting up a vineyard. The second, William Wolfskill, a native of Kentucky, also arrived in 1831 but did not purchase his first vineyard until 1838.

Apparently Louis Vignes was not satisfied with the variety of grape cultivated by the mission fathers as he began to import cuttings of prized French wine varieties which were shipped first to Boston and then around the Horn to California. Several varieties were in large enough quantities to be used in wine making in the early thirties. By 1839 Vignes had more than

Artist Edward Vischer made this drawing of the "El Aliso"
winery of Louis Vignes.
Courtesy of California Historical Society.

forty thousand vines thriving on his acreage which was located on part of the site of the present Los Angeles Union Station. By 1840 Don Luis was chartering ships, which he loaded at San Pedro, for regular shipments of wines and brandies to the ports of Santa Barbara, Monterey and San Francisco. Vignes continued his wine-making enterprises until 1855 when he sold his vineyard, called El Aliso, to his two nephews, Jean Louis and Pierre Sansevain, for $42,000. The Sansevain brothers later became famous not only as producers of quality wine but as pioneer wine merchants.

Following his arrival in Los Angeles, William Wolfskill, who had led a party of trappers from New Mexico to California and opened the Old Spanish Trail, engaged in an unsuccessful venture to hunt sea otter on the California coast. This proving to be an unprofitable business he soon directed his activities

[123]

*The Los Angeles Vintage Company in 1852 typified the efforts
of early winemakers.*
Courtesy of Huntington Library.

toward viniculture. In 1838 William and his brother John, who
had arrived in Los Angeles in 1837, acquired a vineyard located
on land formerly occupied by the Southern Pacific's Arcade Station. The Wolfskills received 4,000 vines with the purchase of
this vineyard and by 1846 they had planted 32,000 vines.
Through the acquisition of adjacent lands, William—called
"Don Guillermo" by his Spanish neighbors—had increased his
holdings to 145 acres and 60,000 vines in 1858. John S. Hittell
lists the Wolfskill vineyards as containing 85,000 vines in his
statistics for the year 1862.

The quality of wine produced by Wolfskill is expressed by
Edwin Bryant, who visited the ranch in 1847, and commented
that the wine "compared favorably with the best French and
Madeira wines." An article appearing in the Wilmington *Journal* in 1857 stated that "H. D. Barrows of Los Angeles . . . sailing
for the east tomorrow is taking on a barrel of Los Angeles wine
to President Buchanan from the celebrated Wolfskill Vineyard." The paper later reported that Mr. Barrows "had called on
President Buchanan and for himself and Mr. Wm. Wolfskill . . .

presented Mr. Buchanan with various specimens of California wines and fruits, which he brought from the Pacific side for that purpose. They consisted of a barrel of fine old California port, made by Mr. Wolfskill from his own vineyard, probably the largest in California. . . ."

Before the fruit was raised to any great extent in the central and northern part of the state, and even some time into the 60s, Wolfskill and other Los Angeles vineyardists, which included John Rowland, the Sansevain Brothers and others, shipped large quantities of grapes to San Francisco. These grapes in 1851 and 1852 brought twenty cents per pound in the city and as high as seventy-five cents in the interior. Arpad Haraszthy states that in 1852 and 1853 grapes selling in and around Los Angeles on the vines for two to six cents per pound brought from fifty cents to one dollar in San Francisco as there was no one there to supply the demand.

During the grape season of 1857, according to the records kept by the port of San Pedro, 21,000 boxes were shipped to San Francisco; and at times Mr. Wolfskill shipped as many as 500 boxes of grapes on a single steamer. However, this does not mean he had ceased his wine-making activities. In 1859, which was reported as an unfavorable season, the total vintage for the state was 340,000 gallons of wine of which William Wolfskill produced 50,000 gallons or a little over one-seventh of the total.

An idea of the value of the vineyards in Southern California can be gained from the Los Angeles County Assessor's returns for 1858 as corrected by the Board of Equalization. Those taxpayers whose property was assessed at $10,000 or more included William Wolfskill, $80,000, third highest in the county; Sansevain Brothers, $40,000; John Rowland, $35,712; and Matthew Keller, $35,325.

The man whom Bancroft calls "the first wine manufacturer of the state" was one of the leaders of an expedition which arrived in California in 1841 from New Mexico. John Rowland, a native of Pennsylvania, engaged in beaver trapping west of Santa Fe until his marriage to a Spanish woman in Taos. Having built a flour mill and distillery and established himself in the mercantile business, it took some resolution and considerable

*Matthew Keller's calling card advertised his California-grown
wines and brandies.*
Courtesy of Huntington Library.

planning for Rowland to dispose of his holdings and make necessary arrangements for the journey and for starting anew in a
strange country. He and his partner, William Workman, led a
party of about twenty-five men and several families over the
Old Spanish Trail to California.

Rowland and Workman worked fast and successfully in
the territory and within three months after their arrival they had
obtained the excellent La Puente Rancho of some 48,000 acres
near the San Gabriel Mission. Planting extensive vineyards on
his portion of the ranch, Rowland cultivated a tremendous
grape crop. He constructed a still on his property and began
producing large quantities of wine which he sold commercially
throughout the 1850s and 1860s.

A large part of the grape yield was bought by the firm of
Kohler and Frohling who established a wine house in San Francisco in 1855. These two men had fled Germany after the up-
heaval in 1848 and came to America as musicians. Kohler, who

organized the German Concert Society in San Francisco, intended to dispose of the wines in the city while Frohling, his flutist, was to manufacture them in Los Angeles. When they lost in wine ventures they played in theaters until they had saved up enough to get back into the business. By 1857 the firm of Kohler and Frohling was established on a sound basis and the volume was sufficient to warrant the full-time hiring of a wagon and team of horses.

From a total production in 1856 of 15,000 gallons, their vintage increased to more than 100,000 gallons in 1858. By 1860 the firm had shipped over $70,000 worth of wine outside of California and had established a branch office in New York. Besides the produce from their 22,000 bearing vines in Los Angeles, they annually purchased the grape crop of more than 350 acres of Los Angeles vineyards, which they stored in the cellars of the City Hall as well as at nearby wineries. During the vintage they employed an average of 150 men to pick, crush and prepare the wine for fermentation.

Kohler and Frohling bought the grapes from the vineyards of William Wolfskill, John Rowland, Antonio Coronel, Matthew Keller and others for about three cents a pound, and the firm was entitled to use the wine cellars and presses located on the property of the various grape producers. In a column entitled "Letter from Los Angeles" which appeared weekly in the San Francisco *Daily Bulletin,* Henry D. Barrows describes the process of wine-making at Wolfskill's vineyard as it was carried on by Kohler and Frohling in 1859. He uses this vineyard as a representative sample of the general mode of operation in Los Angeles at the time and states as follows:

> They employ about 40 hands, two-thirds of whom are engaged in picking and hauling in the grapes; the balance are at work about the presses or in the cellars. The grapes are cut off by the stem from the vine and carried in baskets to the crossroads running through the vineyard and turned into tubs holding from 150 to 200 pounds (or as large as two men can easily handle) which are hauled in one horse cart to the press where they are weighed, and then turned into a large "hopper" which has an apron or strong wire sieve, through which they are "stemmed."

[127]

*This California wine press had already
seen many years of service when this photograph
was taken around 1895.*
Courtesy of California Historical Society.

It was generally the practice of European wine makers to use a stemmer with a wooden grating because most of the baser metals were corroded by the acid of the grape. Californians, however, seemed to favor the wire grating. After the stems were thrown out, the next step was to mash the grape. This was done

> . . . when the latter is run through a mill consisting of two grooved iron cylanders (sic) so gauged as to run as closely as possible together without mashing the seeds. The grooves of one cylinder are longitudinal and of the other spiral. This method is quicker, less laborious and far more decent than the old way of "treading out" the grapes, which in a measure has passed away, as it should.

> Although this method (treading with bare feet) is as old as the hills and is still followed in many extensive wine-growing countries, allow me to suggest through your columns, as a good field for Yankee ingenuity to spread itself, the invention of the best machine for washing grapes for making wine. The machine described above in most respects, however, works admirably—better than any other I ever saw. By it the mere crushing of the grape is done by two men more easily than probably ten men could do the same work by any of the old methods of tramping, malls, or what not.

In regard to the crushing of the grapes, E. H. Rixford comments that "many of the best writers of today (1883) are of the opinion that the wine is better when the grapes have been well trodden with the bare feet . . ." but continues to say that Californians, in contrast to many Europeans, regard treading as an antiquated practice and a relic of the past. He further surmises that "those who are fastidious in this matter may rest assured, that if they will drink California wine, they run but very small risk of imbibing a liquid which a man has had his feet in." By 1865 various machines and processes had been invented for the purpose of crushing and extracting the juice from the grape, a popular one consisting of Indian rubber covered cylinders which crushed the berry without breaking the seed.

Mr. Barrows continues to describe what happens to the grape as it is being made into wine:

> After being ground, the pommace runs down into a vat, on the bottom of which is a grating through which the juice of the grape runs, whence it is conveyed into tubs for white wines. The pom-

[129]

mace is taken directly into spiral screw presses and subjected to moderate pressure, the runnings from which make pale or yellow wine, like sherry. The grape skins are then put into large tubs to ferment six or eight days for red wine, or longer, when the residue of their vinous property is extracted in *aguardientes* by distillation.

The process of fermentation followed in these early days generally consisted of pouring the juice into large casks, usually holding about 140 gallons each, until they contained about 115 gallons of must. A considerable surface of the wine was left exposed to the air in order to favor fermentation. The process began in three or four days and the period of greatest activity was completed in another three or four. The maintenance of the temperature at the proper degree of 65°F. was of great importance in preventing spoilage. The winemaker poured in six or eight gallons of fresh juice every day until the cask was full, and then the long process of aging began. The casks were generally stored in cellars although at times they were sent on long sea voyages to complete the aging of the wine.

Meanwhile, back at the ranch, Mr. Frohling is directing the activities of his workers.

> . . . He has in his employ four men who are cleaning off the stems; this they do by pushing the grapes through the sifter with their hands; two men turn the mill by cranks; two feed the hopper; one weighs the grapes; three or four attend to the wine as it comes from the mill and the presses; five or six do the pressing and carry off the pommace to the fermenting vats; one, two or three attend to washing, cleansing and sulphuring of grapes; and three teams are constantly employed in hauling in the grapes. Every night all the presses and appliances used about them are all washed thoroughly to prevent acidity. Everything that comes in contact with the grape juice from the time the grape is bruised till it reaches the cask is kept as pure as an abundance of water and hard scrubbing can make it.
>
> During five days of last week, commencing on Tuesday, 160,000 pounds or 80 tons of grapes were turned into wine at Mr. Wolfskill's place, yielding about 10,000 gallons of wine, exclusive of a balance left in pommace for brandy, which is considerable.

Apparently E. H. Rixford knew even faster workers as he writes that on an average five men—one to handle the boxes of grapes,

*The Pomona Valley in 1886 featured a number of
well-established vineyards.*
Courtesy of Historical Society of Southern California.

two to stem, standing on opposite sides of the stemmer; one to
operate the crusher; and one to take the stems and remove the
remaining grapes—could stem and crush with hand machines
twenty tons of grapes per day, enough to make three thousand
gallons of wine.

Further in his article Barrows cites the progress of work at
other vineyards in the area.

> Mr. Frohling finished making wine out at "Puente" last week
> both at Mr. Workman's and Mr. Rowland's vineyards. This week
> he commences on his own and Mr. Coronel's vineyards besides
> continuing operations at Mr. Wolfskill's place where he is nearly
> half done. During the present vinification he employs something
> over 60 men.

During the period from the late 1830s to the early 1860s
William Wolfskill, John Rowland and the others previously
mentioned were certainly not the only vine growers in the Los
Angeles area, but they were among the most successful. Others
who entered the industry during the 1860s were later to become
leading producers. Leonard J. Rose, whose first vintage from his

ranch at Sunny Slope near the San Gabriel Mission was in 1864, had shipped wine around the Horn to New York by 1869. Also during the sixties the extent of the grape acreage and the productivity of the vine and soil made Anaheim, a German settlement east of Los Angeles, one of the leading viticultural areas of California.

Among the problems faced by the wine industry at this time were the falsification of labels, giving rise to a bad reputation for California wines, and the lack of suitable containers for both domestic sale and out-of-state shipment. For some time much of the better California wine was bottled under a foreign label while the poorer wines both from within the state and elsewhere were marked with California labels. As California became better known as a wine-producing area and the demand for its wines grew, this type of activity was eventually reduced. To solve the container problem, the Pacific Glass Works was incorporated in October of 1862 with the support of Charles Kohler, and the first wine bottle was blown in June 1863. Financially unprofitable in the beginning, the consistently large demands of the wine growers insured its success in a short time.

From its earliest beginnings the wine industry in Southern California especially Los Angeles was big business. Although it suffered a few major setbacks, the most important ones resulting from the ravages of the insect phylloxera in 1870 and the ruination of the market by Prohibition in the 1920s, commercial viniculture has remained an important factor in the economy of Southern California, as well as the entire state, until the present time.

12

A LITTLE GIRL OF OLD CALIFORNIA: A REMINISCENCE

Sarah Bixby Smith

A long time ago when the first railroad into California had found its winding way over the high mountains and down to the sea there were not many people outside San Francisco, and the country was wide and empty. Father and two of his cousins had come with the Argonauts, but had chosen to raise sheep rather than to follow the uncertainties of mining, and that meant the control of much land for grazing. On one of these large sheep ranches, the San Justo, near the little old town of San Juan Bautista, I was born.

Home was in the foothills whose velvety slopes, sometimes brown, sometimes green, were dotted with live oaks; and over all was the wide blue sky, a little patch of it seeming to have fallen into the pond in the nearby hollow. This was a wonderful pond, for it attracted water which appeared to run up hill through a roadside ditch, and it contained fish which never consented to be caught on the bent pin with which I fished for many an hour.

The large house, built about 1860 to accommodate the three cousins and their families, was white, with green blinds; Maine memories bodied forth in a far land. It contained conveniences of modern plumbing that I fear the eastern prototypes had to await for still many a year. Under the long front veranda there could be found sweet potatoes very good for nib-

A view of Los Angeles north of the plaza area in the late 1880s which was called Sonora Town.
Courtesy David Workman.

bling, and sacks of beet seed, reminders of an early interest in the manufacture of beet sugar. Beside the house there were horse barn and fine sheep barn, men's house and shed, all as white as the house itself.

There was an old-fashioned flower garden with Johnnie-jump-ups, honeysuckle, mourning-bride, and an orange tree that gave blossoms but no oranges, important enough for me to remember; there was a vegetable garden where little onions and horseradish grew, and an orchard whose chief glory was several cherry trees. On top of a nearby hill was the family burying ground where a few lay under the wildflowers, some babies, and Uncle Solomon, father's young brother, who, while reading poetry in a lonely sheep camp, had been shot to death by some unknown hand.

No other houses were in sight, but not many miles away, down a winding road, and over the bridge, lay the town with its postoffice, store, a few houses and friends, and its old mission, which had a long corridor, arched and tile-paved, and an enclosed garden where peacocks used to walk and drop long, shining feathers for little girls to pick up. Inside was dim silence, with strange dark pictures on the walls, some old music books with large notes, and a precious Bible, chained to its desk. There was another church in the place, one that was light and bare and small, where I learned from a tiny flowered Sunday school card, "Blessed are the peacemakers," which, being interpreted for my benefit, meant, "Sally must not quarrel with little sister." And I ate up a rosebud and wriggled in my seat during the long sermon, and wondered about the lady who brushed her hair smooth and low on one side and high on the other: had she only one ear? And that is all I remember of the little church where I went almost every Sunday.

My earliest memory is of sitting in my mother's lap in a stage full of men, and of being unbearably hot. But once when I asked my father if I had ever been taken on such a trip he maintained that I could not remember that terrible trip up through the San Joaquin Valley during the hottest weather he ever knew there, for I was not quite a year old. But I know I do remember.

[135]

There were many long rides with father in those very little girl days, when he was going the rounds of the sheep camps or over to Salinas or Gilroy. For a time I would sit up very straight, but soon would retire to the bottom of the buggy for a nap, with father's foot for a pillow, and I remember when I grew so long that I could no longer lie straight, but must put my feet back under the seat.

There was one time when father and I cleared land for many days together, burning oak stumps and grubbing out brush, and on the hillside above this I walked with mother, and she made me chaplets of oak leaves, fastening each leaf to the next in a most ingenious way.

There is a memory also of a trip to a circus at Hollister, where I saw Mr. and Mrs. Tom Thumb, Minnie Warren and Commodore Nutt, whose pictures, with Mr. Barnum, I still have. Minnie Warren was supposed to be the height of a six-year-old girl, and children of that age in the audience were invited to measure with her. But it must have been eastern six-year-olds that she was supposed to match, for I was quite a little taller. My first heroine was a lady of this same circus who rode bareback in tarleton skirts and jumped through tissue-papered hoops, but, alas! I have lost her name!

All day there was play, except for an occasional stint of patchwork, every day but Sunday, and then there were stories, oh, such stories! Mother would say, "When I was a little girl away down in Maine" until Maine seemed Paradise. We had no brooks nor river, no snow nor sleds; we had no Susan and Ella. Why were there only boys for me to play with, and why did not something interesting happen to me? It was nothing to me that there was the big ranch with horses and cows, pigs, dogs, and sheep, hens and ducks, turkeys and geese—they were commonplace; it was nothing to me that Dick and I could make figure-four traps and catch live quail, or that once we found our trap disturbed and bear tracks all about! It was not exciting to hunt tarantulas and to pry open the door that the mother spider was holding closed with all her strength, nor to see the baby tarantulas running in every direction when the nest was finally raided. No, life in California was very tame, compared to that in

Maine—only the same things to do that I had done all my long life!

Once mother took me "way down to Maine" to see grandfather and grandmother. There I learned many strange things. Leaves were not green, but red and purple and yellow and brown, and they were so loose on the trees that of a sudden they all fell off; but they were very nice for scuffing in, and when the wind blew them after one they looked like all the rats following the Pied Piper of Hamelin. Mother gathered some of the prettiest leaves and pressed them, and polished them with wax and a hot iron, and we took them back to California and pinned them on our lace curtains.

Soon after we reached Maine the air filled with goose feathers, only it wasn't feathers, but wet snow! And then came sleds and sleigh rides, and Christmas with a piggy-back ride on grandfather to the tree at the church.

In those days I learned smells as well as sights, and now know for always the smell of snow in the air, the weeds in winter, the woodshed and the winter-bound barn, and of the old, old house so long lived in.

But we were not going to stay always in Maine, so father came all the way from San Juan to get us. He took us to Boston, where Miss Three-Year-Old was dressed up in her bottle green dress and bottle green coat, with stockings and velvet bonnet to match, and white kid gloves, and taken to call upon the cousins in Beacon Street, opposite the Gardens. At the side of the entrance steps was a low coping, just right for a handrail for the little girl, and she eternally disgraced herself, proving that she was no child of prim Boston, by dragging her little Western hand in its white kid glove up that rail. Poor black gloves! I am afraid she took more naturally to comfort and mud-pies than to elegance and formal calls.

Soon we reached Chicago, where Uncle Jo lived, and the big cinnamon bear in Union Park. That night there was a fire in the business section, and it was not so long after Chicago's great fire that people had forgotten the horror. There was fear and panic, and we must leave the hotel and fly to safety. We made our way slowly in the night, when children should be asleep, through streets packed with frightened, pushing, shouting people, to a house beyond the reach of danger. And from the seat in Uncle Jo's buggy we could look back over the heads of the people to the red fire dancing at the end of the street. The house where we went, so far as I remember, had nothing in it but mosquitoes and a red balloon, and a talking doll that the dear uncle bought.

In those days it took a week to reach San Francisco from Chicago. What fun it was to have the table for lunch, and the basket opened and the good things laid out—fried chicken and a long, green bottle of olives, and a can of patent lemonade—a tiny bottle of extract in a can of the queerest, greenish sugar, and wanting only train water to make it into ambrosia. Then hands were washed in water made soft and white by Florida Water, something that never happened at home. There were Indians to be seen at the stations, with little Hiawathas on their backs, and cunning beaded moccasins to sell; and once at night, with my nose pressed against the window, I saw by the light of a flaring torch a big buffalo head upon a pole.

San Francisco came next, with a ride on the octagonal street car, and a visit to Woodward's Gardens, and then home by train and stage. It was good, after all, to get back to California. Here was our own sitting room, with its marble mantle, its pretty flowered carpet, its pictures of L'Allegro and Il Penseroso, hanging by their crimson cords with tassels; and here were old toys and the boy cousins who lived at the other end of the house. And here soon came little sister, who was the cunningest baby that ever was, but what a long time it did take for her to grow up enough to play with anyone who was born so much as three years ahead of her!

We lived at San Justo forever, and then when I was seven, we moved to Los Angeles. And if I wanted I could tell many things of the little town of less than ten thousand people, a town with orange orchards and *zanjas,* of vineyards and cottage homes where now are paved streets and skyscrapers; of the dentist who traveled in a golden chariot, and did a Painless Parker business in the open at the Plaza; of the tight-rope walker who flipped flapjacks on the rope across Main Street at

*The Plaza Church, the heart of early Los Angeles, presented an
everyday sight to Sarah Bixby Smith.*
Courtesy of Doyce B. Nunis, Jr.

the Baker Block; of the visit of President Hayes and his party, and the reception given him in the fashionable St. Elmo Hotel, alas! no longer fashionable, tho' still standing. But why talk of Los Angeles? It was the place of business, going to school or buying shoes at the Queen or cloth for a doll's dress at Coulter's or Christmas presents at the Crystal Palace, or some other commonplace living. The fun of life was at the sheep ranches, the Alamitos or the Cerritos, at each of which lived an uncle and aunt and some double cousins, and at which I made long and frequent visits.

It was at the Cerritos that I had my particular crony, Harry, and it was there that the most interesting things happened to me. The old house now lies on the brow of the hill like a tired dog that has thrown itself down to rest with its paws stretched out before it. Little do the gay people that motor past it on their way to the beach dream of the past glory of the old adobe, of its charm, its comfort, its active life. It was one of the largest and finest of old homes, a two-storied adobe, and it is a pity that it has been deserted.

The main portion of the house, with its lower windows protected by iron bars, was one hundred feet long. On the north were two wings even longer, and the court was closed by an adobe wall with large wooden gates. On the south side of the house there was a long porch extending the full length, which was floored with brick that had come "around the Horn," while above it was the wide covered balcony on whose floor might possibly still be found little round patches of brea which we children dug with sticks from the roof and wings when the covering was softened in the summer sun. In front of these verandas there was a garden laid out in many beds with more of the travelled bricks, and a well-built hexagonal summer house covered with Madeira vine in the center, the whole being surrounded by a ten-foot fence to keep out the winds that swept in from the neighboring ocean.

The house was built about 1840 by Don Juan Temple (probably plain John Temple when he was baptized in faraway Massachusetts), and it must have known all the hospitalities and festivities common to the life of those early haciendas. In 1866

[140]

Don Temple, growing old and wishing to close up his business affairs, sold to my people for twenty thousand dollars in gold the rancho of twenty-seven thousand acres and the house upon which he had lavished so much care and money. The bulk of this ranch was sold many years ago, and the towns of Clearwater and Hines and the city of Long Beach west of Alamitos Avenue, are upon it, the eastern part being upon the Alamitos Ranch. A short time after Don Temple made this sale he died and his wife and daughter, who was the wife of a French gentleman, went to Paris to live. People familiar with Los Angeles will remember the street starting from the old center of town which bears the name of Temple in honor of this old don.

When my uncle and his beautiful young wife first began to live at the ranch they found some primitive conditions. The cooking in the kitchen was done before an open fireplace, supplemented by a brick oven in the yard. Clustering about the house were many little huts or jakals made of tule or willow brush, in which lived many old retainers of mixed Spanish and Indian blood, but as the business of the ranch was changed they gradually drifted away. There were few neighbors, except the Dominguez family, and Los Angeles, the sleepy little town, was too far away to offer much social life, but there were occasional visitors from San Francisco or far east, and trips to these places were taken. My aunt was a passenger, I have been told, on the first through train from San Francisco to the East.

Once Admiral Thatcher, an old friend of the family, and at that time in command of the Pacific fleet, came in his flagship, "Pensacola," to San Pedro, and he and his officers were guests at the ranch for several days. I have seen a letter of his written soon after this in which he makes recommendations for the construction of a suitable harbor at San Pedro, which are interesting in the light of the developments of half a century later.

It is around this old house that happy memories of my later childhood gather. We children ranged about freely from morning to night during our vacation days. On rare rainy days I read, lying crosswise on one of the stuffed chairs covered with dark red leather, or curled up in one of the deep windowsills—the walls of the lower floor were four feet thick, so that the win-

*Los Angeles in 1870 showed little promise of the great expansion
the city would experience in a few short years.*
Courtesy of Security Pacific National Bank
Photograph Collection/Los Angeles Public Library.

dows, perhaps, functioned better as cubby holes than as sources of light.

But it was out of doors that we usually played. We could go down to the orchard, where all summer long there were ripe apples and pears, or we could shed our usual shoes and wade in the San Gabriel, reduced to its safe summer level. I remember once sitting down, clothes and all, in a deeper pool, and grinning over the surface at Harry, similarly seated. We could watch the hundreds of pigeons flying in and out of the deserted old adobe, known to us, because of its condition, as "The Flea House," or we could go to our retreat in an enlarged coyote hole in the pasture on the other side of the hill. We could play in the old stage that stood in the weeds just outside the high garden fence, a stage that remained from the earlier day before the railroads when father and his cousin partners ran the stage lines, carrying mails, express and passengers between San Diego, Los Angeles, and San Francisco.

In the right wing of the house was a store room of unfailing interest, but locked and barred. Here were barrels of brown sugar, so good by the handful, and sweet chocolate that tempted to petty larceny; big boxes of Chinese tea with gay pictures on the outside and a heavy lead foil that carried the smell of tea for many days in our pockets.

One day I discovered heavy white smoke pouring out the iron-barred window, and my hurried search for father brought him and several men to fight a most difficult fire caused by the drying out and self-ignition of some sticks of phosphorus kept for preparing poisoned wheat for the army of squirrels that wanted our grain. Next to this room was the dark blacksmith shop, with the wide, black chimney, the old forge and bellows, the anvils where we pounded lead pipe into the semblance of little books, and ornamented them with designs of nail pricks; and high up in the wall the mysterious funnel-shaped holes that were meant for guns in the early days when defense might be needed. The next room was a carriage room, beyond that a dark room whose entire floor I have seen covered with apples, and the last room was a man's room where lived one of our good friends, who later deserted the ranch to open a saloon on Commercial Street in Los Angeles.

Across the court in the other wing of the house was the kitchen where Ying reigned supreme, and Fan was his prime minister. Next came the men's dining room, with oilcloth-covered table, and always the smell of mutton stew and onions, good to the hungry noses; then the woodroom, a very necessary adjunct to a kitchen where cooking for as many as thirty people had to be done with willow wood for fuel. Then came the wash room, where every week we could watch the inimitable skill of the Chinese method of sprinkling clothes with a spray blown from the mouth—those were the days before the propaganda against germs. The last room on that side was the dairy room, with its rows of pans of milk and its fascinating barrel churn. From that room used to come unlimited supplies of milk, butter, and cream that could be spread with a knife, a variety of cream that seems to have vanished from the earth.

Back of this wing was a second court with barns, granary (where we sometimes raced over the deep, loose grain catching mice in our hands), pig-pens, chicken house, and private accommodations for Silverheel, father of all the colts, the wise stallion who, when once caught in a burning stable, dashed out and smothered the fire in his burning mane by rolling in the dust, an example that was remembered and followed successfully later by my little cousin Fanny when her dress caught fire. In this rear court stood also the brick oven where, every Saturday, Ying baked pies and rolls and bread, and, at Christmas time, the whole little pig.

But the sheltered, spacious garden, lying in the sunshine, was the best of all. Old cedars, whose cones we were told by an older boy, were bats' eggs; locust, orange and lemon blossoms, lilac and lemon-verbena, roses and oleander, heliotrope and honeysuckle, and the odor of honey stored for years by the bees, made a heaven of fragrance. The linnets, friendly and twittering, built about the porch and the swallows nested under the eaves; the ruby-throated and iridescent humming birds darted from flower to flower and built their tiny felt-like nests in the trees, and great, lazy yellow butterflies floated by. There were oranges and lemons, olives, pomegranates and figs; and grapes, green, blue-black and rose-colored, hanging under the low canopies of leaves and inviting us to lie in the pale green light and feast without stint. Over by the windmill was a boggy bed of mint, and many a brewing of afternoon tea it furnished us—mint tea in the summer-house, with Ying's cookies, scalloped and sparkling with sugar crystals.

Cookies were not the only things in which Ying excelled. There were cakes fearfully and wonderfully decorated with frosting curlycues and custard pie so good that grandfather always included it with the doughnuts and cheese that little David carried in his lunch-basket when he went up to visit his brothers on the famous occasion when he slew Goliath with his slingshot.

Grandfather had left his old Maine home and now sat on the wide brick veranda and charmed his child audience with versions of the Hebrew stories that I judge he did not use in the pulpit of the dignified village church where he had ministered for so many years. We learned how Samson's strength returned to him, when, in the temple of the Philistines, the hooting mob threw rotten eggs at him (grandfather knew how mobs act, for he had met them in the days when he was an early speaker for the Abolitionists), and we learned more about David, how, when the lion attacked his sheep, he ran so fast to the rescue that his little coattails stuck out straight behind him; how, when the lion opened his mouth to roar, David reached down his throat and caught him by the roots of his tongue and held him, while with his other hand he pulled his jackknife out of his trouser pocket, opened it with his teeth, and promptly killed the beast; how he then sat down upon a great white stone, played on his jewsharp and sang "Twinkle, twinkle, little star."

Grandfather not only told us stories, but to me he opened Sunday for secular reading, telling me one day when the question of my reading Grimm's Fairy Tales on Sunday had been raised, and I had been sent to him as the highest authority—I see him looking over the tops of his spectacles at the wishful child—that a book that was fit to read any day was fit to read on Sunday. I bless the memory of grandfather.

I treasure a little lacquer box that he bought for me once from a Chinese peddler who had walked the dusty miles from Los Angeles, balancing on a pole over his shoulder the two large, round bamboo baskets, so familiar in those earlier California days. We all gathered while on the floor of the shady porch were spread the wonders of China; nests of lacquer boxes, with graceful sprays or curious designs in dull gold; bread boats, black outside and Chinese vermilion inside; Canton china, with its fascinating ladies and flowers and butterflies in pink and green; teapots in basket cosies, covered cups, chopsticks and ivory back-scratchers; carved ivories; crepe or embroidered handkerchiefs, cerise, white, apple green; gorgeous hanging baskets of flowers fashioned from bright colored silk, feathers and tinsel; sandalwood boxes and fans, puzzles, tiny tortoise-shell turtles with quivering legs and head, safely fastened in little glass-covered green boxes, and lichee nuts and cocoanut candy. How could so many things come out of those two baskets?

If the Chinaman was an essential part of the housekeeping, the Mexican was no less important in the ranch work. There were many of them, several Josés, Miguel (who, by the way, is spending his last days with various of his descendants in the old house), Allesandro, and others, but the one who stands out was Juan Cañedo, a dignified figure who had come with the ranch, insisting that he belonged with the land and had been sold with it by Don Temple. He was the best vaquero in the country, being equally skillful with either hand in the use of the lariat. When not otherwise occupied I remember him setting out on horseback, surrounded with the hounds, Duke, Queen, Timeroso, and a dozen others, to hunt coyotes, the constant menace to the sheep. Old Juan never condescended to speak English, although he understood it, and as I did not speak Spanish I never talked with him. The boys learned Spanish, and so were able to enjoy the tales he told. They also, being boys, had the privilege of riding with him to the rodeos at the Palos Verdes, but I, being only a girl, must stay at home and be a lady, whether I was one or not.

Sheep, however, were the main interest. We ate sheep, smelled sheep, saw sheep, heard sheep, talked sheep; we lived, moved and had our being in, for and by sheep. There were sometimes as many as thirty thousand on this ranch alone. We had got into the business in the early days of our being in California, long before I was dreamed of.

My father, Llewellyn Bixby, and two cousins, Benjamin and Thomas Flint, all young men in their twenties, came from Maine by way of the Isthmus of Panama to California, reaching San Francisco on the S. S. Northerner on July 7, 1851. They landed in a small boat at Clay and Montgomery streets, and left the same evening for Sacramento. From there they went by freight wagon to Volcano, Amador County. Sooner or later my father's seven brothers and two sisters found their way to this land of promise, and now all lie sleeping under its sunny sky.

A week of mining satisfied the three cousins and they looked for other work, my father finding a job with a butcher who paid him $150.00 a month, with board, no small item in those days when the cost of living was higher even than now. After a year and a half the young men had accumulated five thousand dollars, which they decided to combine, and therewith make a business venture as partners. So on Christmas Day, 1852, they left Volcano, sailing from San Francisco on the same S. S. Northerner on the following New Year's Day. I have been told that one of them sat on the precious box of gold dust all the way.

While the gold was being minted at Philadelphia they visited the home in Maine, then took the train for the west, going to Indianapolis, the western limit of rail travel at that time. There they formed the partnership of Flint, Bixby & Co., a well-known firm of early California. From here they started on horseback. At Quincy, Illinois, they purchased their outfit for the trip across the plains and bought 2400 sheep. They crossed the Mississippi on June first, went on to Council Bluffs, thence by the Mormon Trail to Salt Lake City. Here they bought 110 head of cattle, and, it being too late to cross the Sierras, took the

Fremont Trail into Southern California, arriving at San Bernardino on January first, 1854, just a year to a day from their sailing from San Francisco. They arrived at San Gabriel a week later and went into camp on the present site of Pasadena, where they stayed until March, when they started up the coast. They camped at Santa Teresa Ranch, near San Jose, for a year, then moved to Monterey County, and in October purchased the San Justo Ranch from Francisco Perez Pacheco, one-half of which was later sold to Colonel William Hollister.

How I wish I knew more of the details of the venturesome trip, but I remember only a few of the incidents that my father told me as a child. I recall his boast that he had walked across the plains, explaining that the sheep moved so slowly that it was pleasanter to walk than to use his horse. Just before reaching Salt Lake City their caravan came upon a stranded party of Mormons, whom they rescued and took in safety to their goal, the oasis of the City of the Saints. Brigham Young was so pleased at their kindness to his followers that he entertained the young Yankees, their cattle and sheep for two weeks, in order that they might be in good condition to meet the hardships of the coming trip across the desert. Our party escaped any general attack of Indians, but one young man who was standing guard for father one night was shot and killed. On one occasion some Indians brought in venison, which was bought and greatly enjoyed until it was discovered that the number of supposed deer corresponded exactly to the number of their colts that had disappeared mysteriously. They lost other of the stock, especially during the last stretch of desert, where there were one hundred miles without water, but on the whole the venture was a great success, and we were launched in the sheep business, almost the first of any Americans to do so in California.

It had grown to large proportions long before I knew it, with many bands of sheep on many ranches in different parts of the state. At one time these men imported some valuable Merino sheep, materially improving the quality of California wool. I remember a wonderful ram with wool that hung to the ground, and great curling horns, an honored gentleman who lived in state in the "Fine Stock Barn" with a few favored wives.

It was impressed upon the little girl that it was not wise to get familiar with him, for he was neither polite nor gentle.

Most of the sheep, however, lived out on the ranges in bands of about two thousand under the care of a sheepherder and several dogs. These men lived lonely lives, usually seeing no one between the weekly visits of the man with supplies from the ranch. Often there was some mystery about the men who took this work—a life with the sheep was far away from curious observation, and served very well for a living grave. Once I overheard talk of a herder who had been found dead in his little cabin. He had hanged himself. And no one knew what tragedy in his life lay behind the fatal despondency!

Once every week a man from the ranch made the rounds of the sheep camps, carrying mail and tobacco and food, brown sugar, coffee, flour, bacon, beans, potatoes, dried apples. On the mornings when this was to happen I have watched the flickering light of the lantern travel back and forth over the ceiling of the room where I was supposed to be asleep, as the finishing touches were put on the wagon-load, and the horses were brought and hitched to the wagon before daylight, so that the long rounds could be made before night.

Twice a year, spring and fall, the sheep came up to be sheared, dipped and counted. Father usually attended to the count himself, as he could keep tally without confusion. He would stand by a narrow passage between two corrals, and as the sheep went crowding through he would count and keep tally by cutting notches on a willow stick.

During shearing time we heard new noises out in the dark at night, after we were tucked in our beds, the candle blown out and the door to the upper porch opened. Always there were crickets and owls and howling coyotes, and overhead the scurrying footsteps of some mouse on its mysterious errands, or the soft dab of an errant bat on the window, but now were added the unceasing bleatings of thousands of sheep in a strange place; and separated, ewe from lamb, lamb from ewe.

Shearing began on Monday morning, and the day before the shearers would come in a gay band of Mexicans on their prancing horses, decked with wonderful bridles made of rawhide or braided horsehair, and trimmed with silver, and saddles with high horns, sweeping stirrups and wide expanse of beautiful tooled leather. The men themselves were dressed in black broadcloth, with ruffled shirts and high-heeled boots and high-crowned, wide sombreros, trimmed with silver-braided hatbands, and held securely in place by a cord under the nose. The men would come in, fifty or sixty at a time, and stake out their *caballos*, put away their finery, and appear in brown overalls, red bandanas upon their heads, and live and work at the ranch for a month, so many were the sheep to be sheared.

Once at the Alamitos a number of men had chosen places in the hay in the barn to sleep, each man holding his chosen place most jealously from invasion. Half a dozen of us children, starting out after breakfast on the day's adventure, after each taking a slice from the raw ham stolen from the smokehouse and secreted in the hay, spied some clothes carefully hung on the wall above the haymow, and the idea of stuffing the clothes into the semblance of a man was no sooner born that it was adopted. Our whole joy was in doing a life-like piece of work and perhaps of fooling somebody. Little we knew how seriously a hot-tempered Mexican might object to being fooled. In the evening when the men came to go to bed the owner of the particular hole in which our dummy was sleeping was furious at finding his place occupied. He ordered the stranger out. No move. He swore violently. Still no move. He kicked. And as he saw the man come apart and spill out hay instead of blood, his rage knew no bounds, his knife came out, and it was only by good luck that we children were not the cause of a murder that night.

There were similiar wool barns at all three of the ranches that I knew, but I officiated at shearing more often at the Cerritos. Here the barn was out beyond the garden, facing away from the house, and towards a series of corrals of varying sizes. The front of the barn was like a wide veranda, with big cracks in the floor. Before this were two small enclosures into which a hundred sheep might be turned. The shearer would go out among these sheep, feel critically the wool on the back, choose his victim and drag it backward, holding it by one leg, while it hopped on the remaining three, to his regular position on the shearing floor. Throwing the sheep down, he would hold it with his knees, tip its head up, and begin to clip, clip, clip, until soon its fleece would be lying on the floor, the sheep would be dismissed with a slap and the wool gathered up and placed on the counter that ran the length of the barn back of the shearing floor. Here the big boys of the family tied each fleece into a ball and tossed it into the long sack suspended in a frame a few feet back, another responsible boy or man tramping the fleeces down tight into the long bag. When the shearer brought his fleece to the counter he was given a little copper check, about the size of a nickel, and marked J. B., which he was to present Saturday afternoon when father and uncle exchanged checks for money. It was a fact that frequently the most rapid shearers did not get the most pay on payday, simply because they were less skillful as gamblers than as shearers. I remember going one night out into the garden and peeking through the knothole to watch the dark-skinned men squatting around a single candle intensely interested in a game of cards. The pile of copper checks were very evident, and the cards were curious, foreign-looking, quite different from the ones in the house.

I had several parts in these busy days. Sometimes I was allowed to walk back and forth on the counter and give out the checks to the men when they brought a fleece, and much time I spent up on this same counter braiding the long, hanging bunches of twine that was used for tying up the fleeces in balls. I worked until I became expert in braiding any number of strands, either flat or round. A few times I was allowed to climb up the frame and down into the suffocatingly hot depths of the hanging sacks, to help tramp the wool, but that was not a coveted privilege, it was too hot. I loved to hold the brass stencils while the name of firm and number of sack was painted on the prone roll before it was put aside to wait for the next load going to Wilmington. Never was there a better place for running and tumbling than the row of long, tight wool sacks in the dark corner of the barn.

And many a check was slipped into our hands, that would promptly change into a watermelon, fat and green or long and striped, for during the September shearing there was always just outside the barn a big "Studebaker," not an auto in those days, full of melons sold always, no matter what the size, for a nickel apiece. It has ruined me permanently as a shopper for watermelons; nothing makes me feel more abused by the H. C. L. than to try to separate a grocer and his melon.

I seem to have gotten far way from my subject, but, really, I am only standing in the brown mallows outside the open end of the wool barn, watching the six-horse team start for Wilmington with its load of precious wool that is to be shipped by steamer to "The City," San Francisco, the one and only of those days.

As soon as the shearing was well under way the dipping began. This was managed by the members of the family and the regular men on the ranch. In the corral east of the barn was the brick fireplace with the big tank on top where the "dip" was brewed, scalding tobacco soup, seasoned with sulphur, and I do not know what else. This mess was served hot in a long, narrow, sunken tub, with a vertical end near the cauldron, and a sloping, cleated floor at the other. Into this steaming bath each sheep was thrown, it must swim fifteen or twenty feet to safety, and during the passage its head must be pushed beneath the surface. How glad it must have been when its feet struck bottom at the far end, and it could scramble out to safety. How it shook itself, and what a taste it must have had in its mouth. I am afraid Madam Sheep cherished hard feelings against her universe. She did not know that her overruling providence was saving her from the miseries of a bad skin disease.

Now the sheep are all gone, and the shearers and dippers are gone too. The pastoral life gave way to the agricultural, and that in turn to the town and city. There is Long Beach. Once it was cattle range, then sheep pasture, then, when I first knew it, a barley field with one shed standing about where Pine and First streets cross. And the beach was our own private, wonderful beach; and we children felt that our world was reeling when the beach was sold and called Wilmore City. Nobody now knows what a wide, smooth, long beach it was. It was covered with shells and piles of kelp and a broad band of tiny clams; there were gulls and many little shore birds, and never a footprint except the few we made, only to be washed away by the next tide. Two or three times a summer we would go over from the ranch for a day, and beautiful days we had, racing on the sand or going into the breakers with father or uncle, who are now thought of only as old men, venerable fathers of the city. Ying would put us up a most generous lunch, but the thing that was most characteristic and which is remembered best is the meat cooked over the little driftwood fire. Father always was cook of the mutton chops that were strung on a sharpened willow stick, and I shall never forget the most delicious meat ever given me, smoky chops, gritty with the sand blown over them by the constant sea breeze. I wonder if the chef of the fashionable Hotel Virginia, which occupies the site of our outdoor kitchen, ever serves the guests so good a meal as we had on the sand of the beautiful, empty beach.

All these things happened once upon a time in the long ago, and now we children are all grown up, and grandfather, father and mother and uncles and boon companion Harry live only in the changeless land of memory.

13

LANTERN IN THE WESTERN SKY:
THE CHINESE MASSACRE IN
LOS ANGELES, 1871

Paul M. De Falla

On the evening of October 18, 1871, a date squarely in the middle of the era when the "Chinese Question" was a burning issue in California politics, a Los Angeles *Daily News* reporter whose name has not come down to us in history, gazed reflectively at the heavens over the Angel City and wrote the following day:

> The young moon, in setting, has presented a most peculiar appearance for the last few evenings, strongly resembling a semicircular Chinese lantern of bloodshot hue, suspended in the air over the Western horizon.

Aside from revealing his strong awareness of things Chinese in those days by seeing the moon over Los Angeles as a Chinese lantern, this *Daily News* reporter was also being unconsciously prophetic when he juxtaposed in his story about the moon the word "Chinese" and the words "of bloodshot hue," because, a few nights later, on October 24, 1871, some very authentic Chinese objects of a genuine bloodshot hue could actually be seen in Los Angeles suspended in the air—the bodies of seventeen Chinese men dangling from ropes where they had been hanged by the Angelenos during a massacre of Orientals that evening, an occurrence which constituted the first major explosion in California against the spirit of the three-year-old

Burlingame Treaty between the United States and the Chinese Empire—an occurrence which tended to place America in the spotlight of international scrutiny, as the savagery in Los Angeles had been reported to the world *via* San Francisco almost while it was taking place.

The dead Chinese in Los Angeles were hanging at three places near the heart of the downtown business section of the city; from the wooden awning over the sidewalk in front of a carriage shop; from the sides of two "prairie schooners" parked on the street around the corner from the carriage shop; and from the cross-beam of a wide gate leading into a lumberyard a few blocks away from the other two locations.

One of the victims hung without his trousers and minus a finger on his left hand. The trousers had been hastily pulled off the Chinese by the men who had hanged him because it was suspected that he had some money in them which could not be readily obtained—and the finger had been severed from his hand because it had a diamond ring on it which would not readily slip off.

The seventeen Chinese had been hanged by members of a crowd of Angelenos which was estimated to number five hundred men, as reported by an Associated Press dispatch over the telegraph from Los Angeles to the San Francisco *Daily Examiner* at 9 p.m. the evening of the massacre, an on-the-spot report made precisely at the time the riot started which resulted in the Chinese hangings.

If the Associated Press estimate of the number of men involved in the riot is correct, it means that approximately eight percent of the total population of the city of Los Angeles took part in the program, as there were less than six thousand persons living in Los Angeles at that time—counting men, women, and children. Actually, so large was the crowd of men which hanged the Chinese on October 24, 1871, that one observer present estimated it as numbering three thousand persons, a number which is obviously much more out of reason than the Associated Press estimate.

The crowd which committed the depredations against the Chinese was composed on the whole of members of the large hoodlum class which resided in Los Angeles, and, as the coroner later put it, "of people of all nationalities." Nine years later, in 1880, poet-historian A. J. Wilson said of this Los Angeles crowd and its work at the Chinese massacre that "American 'hoodlum' and Mexican 'greaser,' Irish 'tramp' and French 'communist'—all joined to murder and dispatch the foe. He who did not shoot, could shout; he who feared to stab, could steal; there was work for all."

At the time of the Chinese massacre, the city of Los Angeles was almost completely surrounded by vast vineyards and orchards, except on its western and northern side, where steep hills had blocked the advance of agriculture, presenting a semibucolic appearance which belied its big-city toughness.

Leaving out its ingrained civic hardness, about which he apparently knew nothing, a very good description of Los Angeles as it existed just after the Chinese massacre was given by a Reverend J. W. Hough of Santa Barbara, when, after climbing the hill on which Fort Moore once stood, he gazed at the Angel City spreading out below him to the east and south and said, as reported by the Los Angeles *Star* on May 28, 1873:

> The general view of Los Angeles from the old fort more nearly resembles that of Damascus, the 'Pearl of the Orient' than any city I have elsewhere seen. The hills skirt it on the north and west as the range of anti-Lebanon does the Eastern city, while from them your eye sweeps over the same broad, brown plain, in the midst of which lies an island of verdure (El Mej, or the meadows, as the Arabs call it), with the city embowered in its midst. True, there are no minarets rising in the modern town, and the Los Angeles River is a poor substitute for the ancient Abana—nor are the desert schooners which take their departure for the Colorado river much like the caravans which leave Damascus for the Euphrates. But the vineyards have the same luxuriance, the pomegranates the same regal blossom, and the orange groves the same ravishing beauty—while an occasional palm, the stateliest of trees, gives an Oriental air to the scene. One misses the ocean view, and the mountains lie away upon the horizon, and the city itself is rather irregular and has but a few fine buildings. The beauty is in the environs, where lovely cottages and lofty mansions peep out from amid bowers in which lemons and limes and apricots are mingled with oranges and walnuts and grapes.

[157]

Paul M. De Falla

Reverend Hough also had an eye for those geographic and economic factors which are necessary to sustain a city. He goes on to remark:

> Los Angeles owes its future promise, as Damascus does its past greatness, to the water, which flows freely in its zanjas, and to its situation in reference to the interior country. It lies on the lap of a wide farming country, and in the midst of thrifty settlements such as El Monte, Los Nietos, Anaheim, and Compton—while one who stands at the depot and sees now and then a carload of bullion passing down to the sea, or a great wagon loading for Arizona, discerns therein a promise of a mighty inland traffic, which, unless diverted when the railroad systems of the region shall be determined, must make Los Angeles an important center. A gentleman, whose business has compelled him to traverse all parts of this state for years, remarked to me that in his view, Los Angeles was destined to be the second city in California.

So far, Reverend Hough's observations about the new Damascus and its environs had been very sound, as history will attest, but when it came to the issue of the society of men who lived in the city of Los Angeles, the good reverend's horn let out a note which was distinctly off key. Reverend Hough said:

> Society in Los Angeles is a curious mosaic, in which Jew and Gentile, Protestant and Catholic, Spaniard and American, Northern and Southern elements, are intermingled—yet, all seem to be possessed of the generosity and open-heartedness that is a characteristic of California.

It was true, that all of these elements were intermingled in Los Angeles—but nothing could have been further from the truth than that these same elements were possessed of generosity and open-heartedness. Less than two years before, a few days after the great Chicago fire, the newspapers of the city, on October 14, 1871, called upon this very same mosaic of citizens to gather at the county courthouse for the purpose of taking up a collection for the victims of the fearful conflagration—and only three persons put in an appearance.

After gazing at this puny gathering, the Los Angeles *Daily News* said in bitterness: "Anything more disgraceful than this on the part of the inhabitants, Los Angeles could not have been guilty of!"

[158]

But precisely ten days later, this same curious mosaic mustered up approximately five hundred persons at one place for the purpose of committing a massacre.

* * *

The road to the sensational eruption in Los Angeles against the Chinese residents of the city had been paved for the Angelenos eight years before, when, during the height of the Civil War, the California Legislature, in 1863, placed in the statute books a law which clearly and categorically placed the Chinese in the state outside the protection of the courts by establishing that henceforth, no Mongolian, Indian, Indian half-caste, or Chinese, could testify in a court of law in any criminal case (as well as any civil case) wherein a "white" man was involved, either in favor of, or against, said white man.

This extraordinary law meant that any white man who was so inclined could rob, maim, rape, injure, or swindle any Mongolian, Indian, Indian half-caste, or Chinese, and the victim could not testify against his aggressor; and that any "white" man could murder any person belonging to the Mongolian, Indian, or Chinese race living in California in the presence of any number of witnesses belonging to the same race as the victim, and no testimony from such witnesses could be allowed in court or official hearing. And since the law of 1863 was plainly aimed at the multitude of Chinese immigrants in California, it would appear that the legislature was inviting attempts on the part of the non-Oriental population of the state to solve the vexing "Chinese Question" in California by making it easy to drive out the Chinese by injury, and to decimate their numbers by murder—an invitation which hundreds of Angelenos took up with a glint and a glee on the evening of October 24, 1871 . . .

* * *

[159]

The chain of events which led to the massacre of Chinese in Los Angeles can of course be traced back to the law of 1863 placing the Orientals in California outside the protection of the courts, but the closest link in time to the debacle was forged in Los Angeles itself just four days before the hangings; on Friday evening, October 20, 1871.

On that evening, a marriage between two Chinese was solemnized in Los Angeles by Justice of the Peace Trafford, and the following day, the Los Angeles *Daily News* reported the event as follows:

> MELICAN MARRIAGE CEREMONY—The White's marriage ceremony is becoming quite fashionable among the followers of Confucius in this city. Such a contract was consummated between a "John" and a "Maly" last evening by Justice Trafford.

Then, the *News,* out of intimate knowledge of such matters, went on to observe:

> It is supposed that these marriages are contracted to evade paying the purchase money to the Company whom the woman may have been previously bought by.

The *News'* supposition implying that the marriage of the two Chinese by Justice Trafford had been contracted solely for the purpose of having the groom attempt to evade paying for the girl was most heartily concurred with by a Chinese association called the Nin Yung Company, one of the many such Oriental groups in the city popularly known as "Tongs." First, the Nin Yung Company claimed that the girl involved in the marriage belonged to that association body and soul—and second, that the bride had actually been "abducted, held, and secreted" by its rival, the Hong Chow Company of Los Angeles before being taken to Justice Trafford to be married to a member of the aforementioned Hong Chow group. The girl's name was Ya Hit, and it is quite probable that she was very handsome.

Thus a bitter quarrel between the Nin Yung and Hong Chow companies quickly developed over the nuptials of the girl claimed by the Nin Yung Company, as the introduction of an American-type marriage into Chinese male-female affairs threw

CHINESE MASSACRE

out of gear the system of female ownership then in practice among the Oriental companies which dealt in Chinese women; women who were relatively scarce in America.

If there had been no "Melican Marriage Ceremony," as the *News* had put it, and the girl Ya Hit had been simply spirited away and hidden from her previous owners (as was the custom in such disputes) the situation would have presented no real problem for the Nin Yung Company. All this association would have had to do was to go before a magistrate and swear out a bogus complaint to the effect that the girl had run away after having stolen something, and a warrant would have been issued for her arrest. Simultaneously, the Nin Yung Company would have offered a generous reward to the officers of the law for her "capture," since, once the warrant was issued, she was technically a fugitive from justice.

The officers of the law, now empowered by an order from the court to arrest the girl, and spurred on by the offer of a reward for her capture, would have then searched high and low for Ya Hit and seized her wherever she might be, even if a hundred miles away in Santa Barbara or San Diego, and brought her back to Los Angeles. Then, after having been privately notified by the arresting officers that the girl was back in town, the Nin Yung Company would have put up Ya Hit's bail, and taken her home—and when her case came up in court, there would have been no victim of a theft or witnesses to testify against her, so the case would have been dismissed. It was that simple.

The workings of this system, by which Chinese companies in California kept their prostitutes in absolute bondage until they sickened and died was open knowledge to everyone in the state, including the helpful magistrates who issued the warrants for the arrest of these women, and the peace officers who served these warrants. Thus, on December 24, 1870, less than a year before the quarrel between the Nin Yung Company and the Hong Chow Company took place over the girl Ya Hit, the Los Angeles *Daily News*, in reporting an arrest of a Chinese woman by some Santa Barbara officers who had come to Los Angeles with a warrant for her, openly charged:

> The woman arrested in this City on Thursday has been several
> times arrested in a similar manner, and her possession as often
> changed hands from one Company to that of another—through
> the instrumentality of law.

But in the case involving Ya Hit, the Hong Chow Company, through the machinations of its leader Yo Hing, had gummed up the system—by introducing into the situation the instrumentality of an American marriage. Therefore, certain Chinese tempers in Los Angeles flared, and those members of the Nin Yung and Hong Chow companies who already had revolvers, began to check them to see that they were in good working order—and those who did not have them, went to Caswell & Wright's store at the southeast corner of Aliso and Los Angeles streets and bought some.

These warlike preparations did not take long to complete, and on October 23, just three days after the marriage of Ya Hit had taken place, the first skirmish between the Nin Yung and Hong Chow companies took place, when two of their warriors exchanged pistol shots in Negro Alley, a narrow thoroughfare lined on both sides with Chinese residences and business houses near downtown Los Angeles.

In this fight, neither of the participants was injured, and both of these bravos managed to flee the scene before the Los Angeles police arrived. The following day, however, Tuesday, October 24, 1871, they were ferreted out by the officers of the law and taken to Justice Wilson H. Gray's court for a preliminary examination. The result of this examination was that both of the Chinese fighters were held to answer to the grand jury on charges of having attempted to murder each other.

After the examination, the question of bail for the litigants arose, and Sam Yuen, a merchant in Negro Alley and the leader of the Nin Yung Company, stepped forward to offer the court sureties for his fighting man, Ah Choy. At this time the Chinese merchant stated to Judge Gray that he had six thousand dollars in gold in a trunk in his store in Negro Alley to back up his position.

Judge Gray was disinclined to believe that Sam Yuen actually had that much money to offer as surety for Ah Choy—and instructed Los Angeles police officer Emil Harris to proceed to the Yuen establishment in Negro Alley to check the merchant's story.

At this point, attorney Andrew Jackson King, a former city attorney, county judge, and state assemblyman, who was representing the Hong Chow man, stepped forward—to voice his own disbelief that the leader of the opposing Nin Yung Company had that much money to offer as surety for Ah Choy. Judge Gray then permitted attorney King to accompany officer Emil Harris to Negro Alley to check Sam Yuen's statement. Negro Alley was only four short blocks from the court, running north and south for one block along what is now the west side of the four hundred block of North Los Angeles Street.

In a short time, policeman Harris and attorney King returned to the court to tell Judge Gray that Sam Yuen did in fact have six thousand dollars in gold in his store as he claimed. Thus Ah Choy of the Nin Yung Company was allowed to go out on bail.

Ah Choy, upon being released in court, was then personally escorted from the courtroom to where he lived in the Beaudry Block, on the east side of Negro Alley, by police officer Emil Harris, a courtesy and a vital service which could hardly have gone unnoticed by members of the Hong Chow Company and their leader, Yo Hing.

Yo Hing, who had been responsible for the marriage of Ya Hit, was a man who had at one time been attorney Andrew Jackson King's cook, and who was now manufacturing cigars. He was generally popular with many influential Angelenos— although he was once described by a non-Oriental contemporary of his as a "guttersnipe Talleyrand."

* * *

Approximately a half an hour after officer Harris had taken his friend Ah Choy home, one of the city of Los Angeles' other six policemen, a mounted officer named Jesús Bilderrain, a former city assessor, made a leisurely tour around the Chinese quarters in Negro Alley, apparently checking for trouble, as it was open knowledge in town that the Hong Chow and the Nin Yung companies were not through fighting over the marriage of Ya Hit.

Officer Bilderrain first rode east along Arcadia Street for two blocks, starting at Main Street. He rode past Sanchez Street to Caswell & Wright store which was located diagonally across the street from the south entrance to Negro Alley. While near the store, he had a leisurely chat with one of its owners. Then officer Bilderrain entered Negro Alley itself, proceeding north along its entire length of one block until he came to Plaza Street, turning west at that point to Main Street two blocks away. There, where the Pico House hotel still stands, he turned south and back to his starting point at Arcadia and Main Streets, where he stopped at Higby's Saloon to refresh himself after his tour. He had found everything quiet at Negro Alley; and at Higby's he found his brother officer Estevan Sanchez, another mounted policeman, refreshing himself at the bar.

While officers Bilderrain and Sanchez were drinking at Higby's, shots were suddenly heard, coming from the direction of Negro Alley, and it was not difficult for anyone to surmise that the Hong Chow and Nin Yung companies were at it again—which in fact was the case. And once again, Ah Choy was involved. This time, the Nin Yung man was shot in the neck by an unknown Hong Chow man, receiving an injury from which he died three days later in a wash house in Negro Alley.

Upon hearing shooting going on in the direction of the Chinese quarters, police officer Jesús Bilderrain immediately left Higby's and rode hastily to Negro Alley, where he came upon what he later described as a big battle taking place between several Chinese, who were fighting in the middle of the narrow thoroughfare. There was already one man down in the dirt, with blood spurting from a hole in his neck: it was Ah Choy, of the Nin Yung Company. The events which were to take place immediately thereafter probably hinged upon whether or not the policeman recognized him as Sam Yuen's man.

Upon dismounting, officer Bilderrain dropped his gun, which was quickly retrieved for him by a man named D. W. Moody, a hanger-on who had been watching the Chinese fighting in the alley prior to the arrival of the policeman—and the fighting Chinese, upon sensing the presence of the officer, promptly scattered and ran, all of them dashing into the adobe houses which comprised the Coronel Block on the west side of Negro Alley, across from the Beaudry Block, where Ah Choy lived.

At this point, as the only victim of the shooting who was visible was Ah Choy, a Nin Yung man, the officer should have naturally been looking for Hong Chow men. Officer Bilderrain, however, apparently without differentiating between members of the Nin Yung and Hong Chow companies, instructed a certain Adolph Celis, another hanger-on present at the alley, to help him catch any of the fleeing Chinese fighters.

Upon being asked for assistance by the officer, Adolph Celis instantly moved to obey—but his eagerness to help was just as quickly checked by the fact that two Chinese had suddenly emerged from one of the houses in the Coronel Block and begun to fire their pistols at him and Bilderrain. One of the shooters was Sam Yuen himself, the leader of the Nin Yung Company—and according to Celis later on, Sam Yuen, before beginning to fire at him and policeman Bilderrain, called out to the officer saying "Over here!" Bilderrain, however, apparently assigned no particular significance to the fact that Sam Yuen was actually calling out to him, and charged straight at the Nin Yung leader, pistol in hand, calling out to Adolph Celis to help him. It was at this point that Sam Yuen and his friend then opened fire upon officer Bilderrain and Celis—immediately afterward fleeing back into the house from which they had emerged. Their bullets had missed Bilderrain and Celis, however, striking some hangers-on standing near the Beaudry Block on the east side of Negro Alley, wounding them superficially.

Now with a leap and a bound, policeman Bilderrain charged into the house where he had seen Sam Yuen and his brother gunman disappear—but he did not remain out of sight of those watching him in the alley for long. In a few moments he reappeared on the long porch of the Coronel Block houses minus his hat, his pistol, and with a gunshot in his shoulder. He stood panting on the porch and blew a long blast on his police whistle.

Almost at the same time that policeman Bilderrain was blowing his whistle, an ex-saloon keeper lately turned rancher named Robert Thompson appeared on the scene, accompanied by none other than officer Estevan Sanchez, whom Bilderrain had left at Higby's. After a brief conference with the wounded Bilderrain, who was preparing to leave the scene to get medical attention, citizen Thompson and policeman Sanchez began to pour pistol shots into the houses in the Coronel Block. Officer Sanchez, however, who was apparently off duty at the time, soon ran out of ammunition, and hurried away to get more, leaving Robert Thompson to pepper away at the Chinese houses.

As the Chinese in the Coronel Block were not returning the fire, Thompson climbed on the porch of the house into which he had been pouring shots, and walked toward the front door, the upper portion of which was partially made of glass. Adolph Celis, who had just a few moments before sneaked a glance into the very house Thompson was now approaching and had seen it was full of armed Chinese, instantly warned Thompson that the occupants there would kill him, but Thompson disregarded the warning, stating to Celis: "I'll look out after that!" and pistol in hand, boldly stepped up to the door. He was met there by a barrage of shots fired from the inside of the house, and staggered backward with a bullet in his chest, muttering, "I am killed." Citizen Robert Thompson died approximately an hour later at Doctor Theodore Wollweber's drugstore a couple of blocks away on Main Street.

At precisely the moment Robert Thompson was staggering away from the door of the Chinese house, the city marshal and titular chief of police of the city of Los Angeles, Francis Baker, arrived at Negro Alley, having heard the shooting going on and Bilderrain's whistle. He did not waste any time in ordering the entire Coronel Block surrounded, obtaining his guards from among the crowd that had gathered in the vicinity of the Chinese quarters. The city marshal ordered his guards to shoot any Chinese that might try to escape their houses on the west side of the alley.

At this time, policeman Estevan Sanchez returned to Negro Alley, accompanied by Cyrus Lyons, an old-time "Judge of the Plains" for Rancho Cahuenga—and together with Lyons, ran north along Negro Alley to the end of the Coronel Block and tried to enter the corral at the back of the building for the purpose of intercepting any fleeing Orientals who might be attempting to leave the compound to gain the freedom of Plaza Street to the north of the block. But he and Lyons were met by a rear-guard action on the part of some of the fleeing Chinese fighters, and were driven back into Negro Alley proper by their shooting.

Policeman Sanchez then joined forces with a special police officer named Robert Hester, an ex-deputy constable, and Sanchez and Hester then tried the same maneuver that Sanchez had tried with citizen Lyons—but with the same result. They were driven back into the alley by the gunfire from the corral. No more attempts were made after that to intercept any Chinese fleeing the Coronel Block.

When Marshal Baker had worked his way completely around the Coronel Block placing his sentries, and was back at the south end of Negro Alley on Arcadia Street, he saw that a group of men had seized a Chinese, who, as it turned out, had bolted out of one of the houses in the Beaudry Block on the east side of the alley. Marshal Baker quickly went to where the Chinese was being held, and questioned him. The man's name was Wong Tuck, and he had a pistol—a four-barrelled affair, with one shot spent.

After briefly examining Wong Tuck on the spot and taking away his pistol, Marshal Baker released the Oriental—and himself walked away from the excited crowd which had seized the fleeing Chinese and did not return to Negro Alley for several hours. He had decamped from the vicinity.

In the meantime, after having been so unexpectedly and suddenly released by the marshal, Wong Tuck quickly made a run for his house in the Beaudry Block, managing to get inside his quarters just ahead of several shots fired at him by members of the crowd who had just seized him. If Marshal Baker heard the shots as he walked away, he did not show any signs of it.

Not long after Marshal Baker had taken leave of the vicinity of Negro Alley, the sheriff (and ex officio tax collector) of the county arrived at the scene of all the shootings and commotion. He was James F. Burns, former county school superintendent and city treasurer, who the month before had been defeated for reelection to the sheriff's office by William "Billy" Rowland—and who consequently, was to relinquish his lucrative office to Sheriff-elect Rowland in March of the following year, 1872. James F. Burns, in short, was at that time a lame-duck sheriff of the county—and while at Negro Alley, all he did was to supplement the city marshal's original guard around the Coronel Block with some impromptu deputizations of his own, and then, like Marshal Baker, he too left the vicinity of Negro Alley, not to be seen around those parts for several hours.

Sheriff Burns, however, while at Negro Alley, had apparently seen that the situation around the Chinese quarters had some serious possibilities, and after leaving the area, sent a man named Madigan, a printer by trade, around to the home of the mayor of Los Angeles, to tell his honor to either come to his office for a report or to go to Negro Alley and see for himself, as there was one hell of a row developing there over the shooting of some whites by the Chinese.

Subsequently, Mayor Cristobal Aguilar, one of the most durable politicians in the history of the city, appeared at Negro Alley, mounted on his horse. Mayor Aguilar, who since 1850 had been a city councilman seven times, a county supervisor eight times, and who was now serving his third term as mayor of Los Angeles, surveyed the turbulent scene around Negro Alley quietly—then just as quietly departed, not to be seen near there again all that day or night. And at about this time, policeman Estevan Sanchez also decamped from the area, not to be seen around there any more that day.

Meanwhile, other officers of the law began to make their casual appearance near the south end of Negro Alley, where Los

The locale of the 1871 Chinese massacre.
Courtesy of Doyce B. Nunis, Jr.

Angeles Street came to a dead-end at Arcadia Street. They were police officers Emil Harris and George Gard—as well as the constable of the county, Richard Kerren.

These officers, however, also made no effort to enter the Coronel Block to investigate if the shooters who had wounded Bilderrain and Thompson were still in the building, nor did they attempt to disperse the excited crowd gathering in the vicinity of the Chinese quarters—a mob that was becoming larger and more bellicose by the minute. Instead, the officers merely loitered across the street from the south end of Negro Alley, near the hay scales at the southwest corner of Los Angeles Street and Arcadia Street.

Then, at approximately six o'clock, an hour or so after he had been shot, the news that the daring Robert Thompson had died at Wollweber's drugstore reached Negro Alley, and a passion seized the crowd guarding the Coronel Block.

One of the first persons to learn that citizen Thompson had been killed by the Chinese was city councilman George E. Fall, and he, along with many other prominent Angelenos, hurried to the vicinity of Negro Alley. Indeed, news had by then traveled throughout the city to the effect that the Chinese in Negro Alley were "killing whites wholesale."

On his way to the scene of the shootings, Councilman Fall encountered a Chinese stealthily scurrying south on Main Street; a "Celestial" obviously meaning to put as much distance between himself and Negro Alley as he could. Councilman Fall then picked up a loose plank from the board sidewalk and hit the Chinese over the head with it, chasing the Oriental into the Blue Wing Saloon, where he lost him.

Soon after he arrived at Negro Alley, Councilman Fall, who was also president of the one and only volunteer fire company in the city, and who had in fact just returned from San Francisco by boat where he had gone to contract for the purchase of some new fire-fighting equipment for Los Angeles, was prevailed upon by some ingenious members of the crowd surging around the Coronel Block to let the city fire hose be used in an attempt to drown out the Chinese from their quarters in the Coronel Block.

Coronel Adobe, c. 1875, where hapless Chinese were massacred that fateful night in October 1871.
Courtesy of Huntington Library.

Councilman Fall agreed to let the fire hose be used by the mob for the purpose explained to him, subsequently justifying his actions by stating that he had wanted the firefighting equipment to be on hand around Negro Alley in case some one in the mob decided to fire the building in which the Chinese were penned. This, of course, was an excellent excuse, as the monstrous Chicago fire was then less than two weeks old and its memory was fresh in everyone's mind. Also, the Coronel Block was adjacent to some buildings facing Sanchez Street on the north, and thus just across that narrow thoroughfare from the buildings on Main Street, which came all the way back to Sanchez Street, such as the new Masonic Lodge, the Merced Theatre, and the Pico House Hotel.

But as it turned out, the crowd soon tired of playing with the fire hose, and the attempt to drown out the Chinese in the Coronel Block was abandoned.

Not long after the news of Robert Thompson's death had reached Negro Alley, firing up the crowd gathered there to a fever pitch, the once-captured and once-released Wong Tuck made another try to get away from his house in the Beaudry Block across Negro Alley from the Coronel Block. This time Wong Tuck had a hatchet with him, but was quickly overpowered by a man named Ramon Sortorel.

While Sortorel and Wong Tuck were struggling, another member of the mob ran up to Tuck and attempted to plunge a two-foot-long piece of broken sword into him, crying; "Oh you Chinaman, you had a gun!"

Peace officers Emil Harris and Richard Kerren immediately took charge of Wong Tuck, and with the assistance of a man named Charles Avery, started to walk the Oriental to the jail four blocks away. The eager crowd churned around them, shouting for Tuck's life.

The officers and citizen Avery continued west on Arcadia Street, and finally managed to get around the corner at Main Street with their prisoner, but once there, someone planted a blow on the back of citizen Avery's ear, and someone else pinned policeman Emil Harris' arms behind him, and Wong

Tuck belonged to the crowd. There is no record to the effect that any one attacked Constable Kerren at this time.

A rope was quickly furnished the crowd by the owners of Broderick & Reilly's book store near the corner of Main and Temple Streets, and a few minutes later, Wong Tuck could be seen dangling from a corral gate a block away, at the northwest corner of Temple and New High Streets, just across from the St. Athanasius Episcopal Church, the first and only Protestant church in Los Angeles in those days.

For a while, a few members of the crowd amused themselves by banging the dead Wong Tuck's head back and forth against one of the gate's uprights, while Constable Kerren stood quietly by. In the meantime, policeman Harris had returned to the mouth of Negro Alley, where he joined his brother officer George Gard. The mob around these officers grew larger and larger as time passed.

This crowd, which was allowed to develop from a mere gathering of loiterers who happened to be present when the Chinese companies had first begun to fight, until it became a mob of formidable proportions, was, by past and contemporary standards, a most extraordinary gathering not only in size but also in character; a mob which in all probabilities could not have been mustered up in the year 1871 in any California town excepting Los Angeles.

It was a San Francisco crowd of twenty years earlier recreated in Los Angeles, composed in the majority of scores of hoodlums, thieves, gamblers, thugs, and shady idlers of all nationalities; a San Francisco crowd of a type to have been found in the Bay City only before the famous "Businessman's Revolution" in the form of the Vigilance Committee of 1856 took over the reins of San Francisco's government and brought some semblance of order to the town.

But these characters now gathered around Negro Alley in 1871 were Los Angeles' very own; a mob attracted to the bosom of Damascus of the West and nurtured there by the remarkable amount and scope of civic corruption in the town. For Los Angeles was, in 1871, and had been ever since Company E of

[173]

Stevenson's Regiment (the Bowery Company) mustered out there in 1848, a wide-open town in the fullest sense of the word.

Even the casual student of criminology will come to the conclusion that a town such as Los Angeles was in 1871, where fortunes were being made in real estate, mining, transportation, and agriculture, and which at the same time did not even have a simple gambling, prostitution, or drunk ordinance, was bound to attract to itself hordes of rough-and-ready individuals looking for a chance to make some easy cash. Such was the City of the Angels in the early seventies; the richest, the largest, the most influential, and at the same time the most wide-open community in Southern California; a town in which a man could buy a drink in a full one hundred and ten out of its approximately two hundred and eighty-five business enterprises; where he could gamble and carouse in girlie houses to his heart's content. It was a haven for thugs.

It follows, therefore, that being wide-open, the incidence of criminality in the city of Los Angeles in those days, and the incidence of criminality around the area it dominated, was extraordinary. In 1872, when the city of Los Angeles comprised over forty percent of the total population of Los Angeles County, the number of felons in the state's prison at San Quentin who had been committed to custody from the Los Angeles area was double that of any other county in California, and fully one half of the total number committed from San Francisco City and County, which at that time had a population eight times greater than Los Angeles County. The Los Angeles *Daily News* printed these statistics on May 30, 1872.

Actually, so generally disproportionate were the criminal statistics coming out of the Los Angeles area, that on May 18, 1872, the Superintendent of the Census Office in Washington, D.C. wrote to the clerk of Los Angeles County asking if there hadn't been some mistake made in the felony figures the clerk had sent in for the year ending June 1, 1870, cautioning the clerk that misdemeanor figures should not be included in the yearly tabulation of criminal statistics, only felonies. The superintendent of the census office advised in his letter to the clerk of Los Angeles County that "An impression very unfavorable to your section might be created by the publication of these statistics, unaccompanied by some explanation."

The clerk of Los Angeles County could have also pointed out an explanation to Washington regarding the criminal activities in his area. He might have pointed out that the principal city in his county was governed on the basis of a city charter which specifically granted to the City Council the power to license such lively and crime-breeding places as bawdy-houses, one-night-stand "dance halls," and gambling joints—and that the city council of Los Angeles had always been very much inclined to use this extraordinary civic prerogative on the theory that the license fees which these activities brought into the city coffers were indispensable.

The clerk of Los Angeles County could have also pointed out to Washington that not only was Los Angeles a wide-open town without even a drunk ordinance, but that its police department was completely ineffectual for the following reasons: One—the police officers of the city were political appointees, being put on their jobs by interested members of the City Council formed into a "Board of Police." Thus, it would hardly be wise for an officer to put too much pressure on a crime-breeding place when a member of the City Council might have vested interest in it. Two—the titular head of the police department, the City Marshal, was, throughout 1870-71-72, utterly without power to discipline his officers as he could not suspend them from their positions for any cause whatsoever. This power was tightly held by the "Board of Police" of the city council. (It was not until ordinance 322 and 323 were passed on January 10, 1873, that the chief of police of the city of Los Angeles could suspend an officer in his department.) Three—the titular head of the police department, the City Marshal, was not only a dog catcher, but also the city tax collector, a job which netted him two and a half percent of all the tax monies he collected for the city, a job which directed his efforts away from the task of running the police department, leaving the police force of the city without a head, and further demoralizing its officers.

In fact, in asserting that the ineffectuality of the police force of the city of Los Angeles was a contributing issue to the crimi-

[175]

nality of the Los Angeles area, the clerk of the county could have sent to the Census Office, as an "accompanying explanation" to any future statistics he might forward to Washington, an editorial published in the Los Angeles *Star* on May 9, 1872, entitled "An Ineffectual Police Force"—and the Superintendent of the Census would have gotten the hint. The editorial reads:

> The incompetency of our police force has so often been demonstrated that it no longer remains questionable to anyone. It has become a byword, that whenever and wherever officers are required to preserve the public peace, or to protect the private property of citizens, they are least likely to be on hand at the opportune moment. The law itself recognizes neither person nor position, and its officers are expected to deal it out with like impartiality, but in this respect, even the faithfulness of the members of our police force is impeached. It is alleged, however, that when a Chinawoman escapes from a brothel, there is wonderful activity manifested in certain quarters to recapture the runaway and return her to her vile den wherein she has shown a disinclination to reside, a special pecuniary benefit accruing from such services being represented as the inducement. Presiding over a low gambling hall and participating in the business therein, instead of exerting themselves in putting down such illegal institutions, are openly avowed to be the regular nightly avocations of more than one of its members. It is insinuated that the Marshal has greater regard for those secondary duties from which he obtains fat prerequisites in the way of fees than he has for the proficiency of his subordinates. There are probably men employed on the force who desire to do their duty as public officers, in all occasions, but as a whole, the organization is rotten from head to foot and wants to undergo a thorough cleansing. It has become an absolute necessity.

The clerk of Los Angeles County could have also pointed out to Washington another feature of the city of Los Angeles which attracted "hard cases" to its environs by the scores, and consequently, also increased the criminality of the community; that is, that Los Angeles was also politically wide-open; a place where a man could sell his vote at election times as easily as he could buy a drink at all other times.

A few weeks before the Chinese massacre, on September 6, 1871, during a state-wide primary, when the city had only approximately twenty four hundred registered voters, the Los

Angeles *Express* estimated that approximately twenty thousand dollars had changed hands that day for the purpose of vote-buying and selling—a process which was made easier to manipulate by the fact that a good portion of the electorate was under the influence of alcohol, as (according to the Los Angeles *Star* of the next day) there had been served and consumed in the city of Los Angeles during the election seven thousand lagers, three thousand whiskeys, and two thousand glasses of wine, for a grand total of twelve thousand drinks. This in a city of less than six thousand population, counting women and children.

The following year, on March 8, 1872, since matters had not improved, the Los Angeles *Star*, in an agonizing reappraisal of its community, asked of its readers: "What is the matter with Los Angeles?" then went on to remark: "To our mind, the chief cause is obvious, and lies in the fact of the unfavorable and unsettled condition of our society, the apprehended insecurity of capital and prosperity, the manifest disregard of the sanctity of human life, and those moral obligations so essential to peace and safety of all communities and which to the orderly and law-abiding are prerequisites of happiness and prosperity."

The *Star* then added: "That both our city and county have been loosely governed cannot successfully be denied, and so long as our statutory laws are rendered inoperative by the want of proper local enforcement, and their almost daily violations acquiesced and winked at by the people, we need not expect any change for the better."

Thus, with all its built-in attractions for the reckless and the dissolute, it is not difficult to understand how on October 24, 1871, the city of Los Angeles was able to produce a relatively enormous crowd of hoodlums of all types and nationalities to surround the Chinese penned up in the Coronel Block at Negro Alley. The city council was the host to this dangerous legion; the city charter was the Magna Carta of this mob; and the disorganized police its corrupt chaperone. Now this large crowd, much of which was armed, milled around the vicinity of Negro Alley, waiting for a chance to pounce upon the officially-hated Chinese and their property. For was it not open talk around town that one of them had six thousand dollars in gold in his store in the Coronel Block?

* * *

Sometime after the death of Robert Thompson had been avenged by the mob and Wong Tuck had been strung up by the neck until he was dead, two more of Los Angeles' six police officers appeared in the vicinity of Negro Alley. They were officers Sands and Bryant, bringing the total number of peace officers present there to six: Harris, Gard, Sands, Bryant, Constable Kerren, and special policeman Robert Hester—with mounted officers Bilderrain and Sanchez not present, along with their chief, Marshal Francis Baker.

As these officers congregated in the vicinity of Negro Alley, so did many other residents of the city, who came there either to watch the fun or to join in the target shooting going on, with the Coronel Block being the object upon which all gunsights were trained. At one time, when two Chinese women appeared at the doorway of one of the houses, the crowd fired at them, and one of the marksmen was Constable Kerren. One of the women was obviously hit, and staggered back into the house. The crowd continued to pepper away at the Chinese quarters until long after darkness had fallen upon the town.

At one time, according to officer Bryant, someone firing at the Chinese houses discharged a pistol so close to his ear as to deafen him—at which time policeman Bryant remonstrated with the careless shooter but did not arrest him.

A fiery-tongued orator also appeared in front of the Coronel Block between six and nine p.m. He was a man named King, an employee of Los Angeles' only railroad at the time, which ran from the city to the harbor at Wilmington, twenty miles away. Mr. King worked at the depot on Commercial and Alameda Streets, and was known as "King of the Depot." This orator made inflamatory speeches against the Chinese in general, an easy subject to talk upon in those days, and the patriotic crowd of yeggs cheered him heartily.

Officer Gard attempted at one time to put an end to Mr. King's silver-tongued orations, but finding that Mr. King was not easily dissuaded, and that the crowd listening to him was not in a temper which would allow any heavy-handed tactics to be used against him, gave up his attempt, and Mr. King continued his speeches.

Then, as night descended upon Los Angeles, the gas lights in the dozen-or-so saloons in the vicinity of Negro Alley were turned on, while inside these lively establishments, many hoodlums planned further strategy to be used against the Chinese being held prisoner in the Coronel Block.

At approximately nine in the evening, or a full four hours after Robert Thompson had been shot, a maneuver against the Chinese was put into effect. This scheme was generally credited to have been the brain-child of a man named Refugio Botello— and was ingenuity itself. Some men climbed up on the flat roof of the Coronel Block, and using pickaxes, chopped holes in it over every apartment below, then poured gunfire through the holes.

The result was immediate. Two Chinese ran out of their houses and into the street, where they were instantly cut down by gunfire from the marksmen stationed around the Coronel Block.

One of the holes chopped in the roof was apparently cut over a lantern hanging from the ceiling in one of the apartments below, and flames could be seen coming out through it into the night air. This brought a quick reaction from officer Gard, who quickly climbed onto the roof to see that the fire did not spread, and once satisfied that the flames were out, climbed back down to the street.

While on the roof, and while helping douse out the flames in the hole, officer Gard let a young man named A. F. Crenshaw "hold" his shotgun, and subsequently, Crenshaw was accused of having fired with this weapon upon some Chinese huddled in the corral among some horses at the back of the Coronel Block, a charge which officer Gard helped Crenshaw disprove by testifying that the shotgun he had let Crenshaw hold was as fully loaded when he got it back from the young man as when he had first let Crenshaw hold it.

A. F. Crenshaw, who was known as "Curly Crenshaw" to his friends, was a typical member of the Los Angeles underworld fraternity. At the time of the Chinese massacre, Crenshaw gave his age as twenty-two, but according to the newspapers, he appeared to be no more than seventeen or eighteen. The Los Angeles *Daily News* said of him on February 20, 1872: "Since being here, his associations have been of the lowest character. His favorite resort was a rendezvous of low women, pickpockets, and cut-throats."

After the two Chinese had run out of their houses and had been cut down by gunfire, no more Orientals came out of the Coronel Block, no matter how many shots were poured into the apartments through the holes in the roof. Time began to hang heavy on the hands of the mobsters prowling around the Chinese quarters.

Then two daring hoodlums found a large rock on Requena Street which had fallen off a wagon earlier in the day, and using it as a battering ram, broke down one of the doors in the Coronel building.

The mobsters quickly ran off the porch after breaking the door down, remembering what had happened to the lion-hearted Robert Thompson, who even now was developing rigor mortis in his house on New High Street, not far from where Wong Tuck dangled at the end of a rope. But the Chinese inside the apartments made not a move or a sound, and this emboldened a carpenter named Charles Cox, who fashioned some kind of fireball and threw it inside the apartment through the opening made with the rock.

This maneuver on the part of the carpenter brought an immediate response from police officer Emil Harris, who was also a prominent member of the brand new volunteer fire department organized just the month before. The officer ordered Mr. Cox to enter the building and retrieve his fireball, and when the carpenter refused to go inside the building alone, officer

Harris went in with him. A few moments later, the fireball could be seen sailing through the air and out into the middle of Negro Alley, where it burned for a long time, throwing a flickering light on part of the startling events which were about to take place.

Since nothing happened to Cox and officer Harris when they entered the building, the crowd instantly realized that it was safe to enter the Coronel Block, and began to pour into the Chinese quarters in an ever-surging, eager throng.

The Coronel Block was an L-shaped affair, like two dominoes set at right angles to each other, with half of it running east from Sanchez Street to Negro Alley on the north side of Arcadia Street, and half of it running north from Arcadia Street to Plaza Street, forming the west side of Negro Alley. A long porch, raised about three feet off the ground, ran around the entire building, both on its Arcadia Street and Negro Alley side. The apartments in the building were almost all connected by doors, and once inside the houses, the mob found dozens of Chinese men and women cowering in their quarters.

The Chinese who were found already dead inside the apartments, probably killed by the gunfire through the roof, were thrown out into the streets, where their bodies were kicked and pummelled by drunken and infuriated mobsters and then dragged off to be hanged. At this time some of the mobsters cut off the queues from some of the Chinese victims for souvenirs. Of those Chinese who were found alive in the Coronel apartments, some of them were dragged along the street, conscious or unconscious, to various hanging places. Pandemonium reigned.

As soon as the now unmanageable crowd had gained access to the Chinese quarters in the Coronel Block, three of the peace officers present at the riot immediately cast their lot with the Chinese. Policeman Bryant and special officer Hester wrested the Chinese women from the crowd and took them to the safety of the jail. Police officer Sands took it upon himself to rescue as many Chinese males as he could, and in a fury, gun in hand, managed to save four of them.

[181]

Policemen Harris and Gard, however, instantly became concerned with one thing alone: the safety of Sam Yuen's store, where a few hours before, officer Harris had seen with his own eyes six thousand dollars in gold.

During their struggle to get to Sam Yuen's business establishment, officers Gard and Harris became separated, and while Gard was wandering through the apartments in the Coronel Block, he heard an aged Chinese calling out to him from under a bed. Gard went over to the Oriental and tried to help him out from under his hiding place, as the old man was wounded. While policeman Gard was holding the Chinese's hand, a group of men rushed into the apartment and poured a fusillade of pistol shots into the Oriental, leaving Gard holding the hand of a dead man. Officer Gard then dropped the man's hand and continued his search for his brother officer Emil Harris.

Soon afterward, policeman Gard ran across a young Chinese woman in one of the apartments, one that Bryant and Hester had apparently missed. This woman Gard personally turned over to "Curly" Crenshaw, with instructions to the young man to take her to jail. The ultimate fate of this girl is not known, as later, Crenshaw could not remember what he did with her that night.

Meanwhile, somewhere else in the Coronel Block, officer Emil Harris was busy personally turning Chinese males over to the mob, instructing the eager hoodlums to take the Orientals to jail—whereupon all the Chinese handed over to the crowd by officer Harris were summarily hanged within sight of the south entrance to Negro Alley. One of these victims was a young Chinese doctor named Chien Lee Tong, known around town as "Gene" Tong, who, before being hanged, was shot through the mouth and robbed. Among the hoodlums to whom doctor "Gene" Tong was entrusted by policeman Harris was the ubiquitous "Curly" Crenshaw.

The busiest gallows for a time was the porch roof of John Goller's wagon shop, at the southwest corner of Commercial and Los Angeles streets, just one block down the street from the south entrance to Negro Alley. Goller, an ex-city councilman who lived over his shop, objected bitterly to the actions of the mob, but his objections were silenced very effectively when a tall teamster with a rifle told him to shut up or he would get it too. The ropes used to hang the Chinese from Goller's shop porch were cut from a clothesline furnished to the crowd by a woman who ran a boarding house across the street from the wagon shop. During the hangings, a mobster who had climbed on the roof of the porch to help haul the Chinese up on ropes, danced a jig on his perch and sang out, "Come on, boys, patronize home trade!" obviously trying to compete with the men who were hanging Chinese to the sides of some prairie schooners parked in the street around the corner on Commercial Street, wagons that were from out of town and therefore not "home" establishments as Goller's shop was. Meanwhile, other mobsters were hanging Chinese from the corral gate where Wong Tuck had met his fate three hours earlier.

Eventually, officers Harris and Gard found their way to the Sam Yuen store, after battling their way through the eager and violent mob. And once there, they did not budge from the premises the rest of the night, while bedlam reigned around them.

While the hangings were going on, none other than Marshal Baker returned to Negro Alley, where he at once set about the task of trying to make the looters at work there disgorge their booty. But as there were scores of men milling about in the Chinese quarters, with dozens of them busy seizing anything of value available in the apartments, the marshal found his task an impossible one.

Here was a man scurrying out of the Coronel Block with a roast goose and several bottles of wine under his coat. And there was another one carting off some sacks of rice—while another man was making off with some bolts of silk. Marshal Baker did not know where to begin in his efforts to stop the looting of the Chinese houses.

But as to hangings, the marshal saw nothing—subsequently stating that while at Negro Alley during the riot, he had seen "no ropes or hangings." And as to Wong Tuck the marshal said that he had "heard" that some one had hanged him after he had set him free earlier in the afternoon.

[183]

Paul M. De Falla

At approximately the same time that Marshal Baker returned to Negro Alley, so did Sheriff James F. Burns, who immediately attempted to intercede on behalf of the Chinese—at one time making a speech to the rioters asking them to stop their depredations. He made his plea while standing on top of a barrel, and his speech suddenly came to an end when the top of the barrel gave way, plunging the sheriff to the ground amidst the delighted hoots of the mob. Then, when the infuriated sheriff attempted to physically rescue some of the Chinese victims from the crowd, he was confronted by pistols and a threat to lynch him too. At this time Sheriff Burns decided that the situation was completely beyond remedy, and that discretion was the better part of valor; probably also reflecting that it would have been too ironical to be murdered by some of the very men who had probably already helped to deal him a political death-blow at the polls a month before during the gay election of twelve thousand drinks.

Adding to the success of the mob in its lynchings and looting was the speed with which the crowd worked; speed born partly out of the fear that the federal troops stationed at Drum Barracks in Wilmington, only twenty miles away by railroad, would show up any minute during the riot. Two of the mobsters subsequently testified that they thought that the "dough" boys from Wilmington would surely arrive—but as the soldiers had not been notified of the *émeute* in the Angel City, they did not come.

Of course, among the citizenry of Los Angeles present at the riot, there were some persons who were not hoodlums or professional politicians, and who consequently tended to view the Chinese in California with a somewhat dispassionate turn of mind; persons who did not want to see the Orientals in Los Angeles hanged without some kind of legal show being afforded them first if the Chinese had committed some kind of crime. And at least two such citizens took an active part in trying to rescue Orientals from the mob. This they did at a great personal risk, as the mob was well armed and was not to be denied its victims.

[184]

One of these citizens was Robert Maclay Widney, an ex-schoolteacher turned real estate entrepreneur who was subsequently to become judge of the Seventeenth Judicial District of California and one of the founders of the University of Southern California.

Robert M. Widney, upon being notified by a friend that a crowd was murdering Chinese wholesale around Negro Alley, obtained a pistol from his brother and went to the scene of the killings, where he waded into a group of mobsters and rescued four Chinese from its clutches. At this time, Widney, like Sheriff Burns, was also threatened with instant "liquidation" by the mobsters confronting him, but being more hot-headed than Burns, openly challenged the crowd to go ahead and try to liquidate him. The mobsters then let Mr. Widney go ahead to the safety of the jail with his rescued Orientals.

A twenty-seven-year-old attorney named Henry Hazard, who had just three years before gotten his law degree at the University of Michigan, and who was later to become the mayor of the city of Los Angeles, was another man who attempted to dissuade the maddened crowd from murdering Chinese. Young Hazard had witnessed the Chinese quarters being broken into with the rock, and saw carpenter Cox throw his fire-ball into the open apartment—and subsequently, overtook three mobsters who were dragging an Oriental to his doom at Goller's wagon shop and prevailed upon them to let the Chinese go. There is a slight hint in the records to the effect that one of these mobsters was Constable Kerren, who, upon realizing that he had been recognized by attorney Hazard, was probably only too glad to set his Oriental victim free.

Immediately after having caused the Chinese to be released by his tormentors, Hazard went to where the crowd was hanging Orientals from the prairie schooners on Commercial Street, and mounting one of the wagons, began to harangue the mob, urging the hoodlums, in the "name of Christianity," to stop murdering the hapless Chinese. While Hazard was standing on the wagon, some one in the crowd fired a pistol at him but missed. At this time some of Hazard's more discreet friends

[185]

Los Angeles Street looking north, a decade after the Chinese massacre took place.
Courtesy of California Historical Society.

hauled him down from his perch and took him away before he got killed.

A man named J. M. Baldwin, upon encountering a group of mobsters hanging Chinese from the corral gate at Temple and New High streets, took it upon himself to attempt to persuade the crowd not to commit any more murders. Like Henry Hazard, Mr. Baldwin was unarmed, while the crowd hanging the Chinese was guarded from any interference by a teamster with a rifle. Mr. Baldwin began to make a speech to the mob in Spanish, as this particular portion of the general mob was composed mostly of Hispanic-Americans—whereupon a merchant named John Hicks began to interpret Baldwin's speech into English for the benefit of the English-speaking members of the mob, using ironical terms, and causing merriment among the mobsters.

The crowd went on hanging Orientals while their comic interpreter displayed his prowess—but later on merchant Hicks denied that he could understand Spanish at all let alone speak it, saying that all the Spanish he knew were the few words necessary to wait upon any Spanish-speaking customer who might come into his store.

Meanwhile, as a great many persons in Los Angeles employed Chinese in their homes, every one who had a Chinese cook or servant hid his Oriental from the fury of the mob. The census of 1870, a year before the massacre, reveals that attorneys Chapman and Glassell each had two Chinese employed at their homes, and that doctors John Griffin, J. P. Widney (brother of Robert Widney), and Clement Rheims each had a Chinese cook. Also, ex-mayor Manuel Requena and ex-governor John G. Downey had Oriental cooks—and even Frank Carpenter, the jailkeeper, had a Heathen Chinese working in his kitchen.

All of these Chinamen had to be concealed from the mob, and in fact, Judge W. H. Gray is reputed to have hidden a score of Orientals in the basement of his house, and it was subsequently reported that Judge Trafford had hidden Sam Yuen himself, in, of all places, his courtroom.

But all of the Chinese males whom the crowd had managed to ferret out in the Coronel Block in Negro Alley were hanged, including a fourteen-year-old boy and doctor Chien Lee Tong. In speaking of this massacre, Major Horace Bell, author of *Reminiscences of a Ranger* and *On the Old West Coast*, two works about old Los Angeles which are of such a revealing nature as to make Major Bell the Boris Pasternak of Los Angeles historians, paraphrased the Prophet Hosea and said that the Angel City had "sown the wind and reaped the whirlwind." By eleven o'clock of the evening of October 24, 1871, the grim harvest lay in the jail yard at Franklin and Spring streets, where the cadavers of seventeen Chinese lay in a neat row upon the dirt. The eighteenth victim, Wong Tuck, who had been hanged first as early as six p.m., had been dragged to the cemetery back of the old fort on Moore Hill.

14

DAILY LIFE IN EARLY LOS ANGELES
Maymie R. Krythe

The native Californians loved amusements of all kinds. They delighted in races, bull or cockfights, picnics, *fiestas, fandangos,* the celebration of national and religious holidays all of which gave them the opportunity of enjoying themselves with their friends. When the gringos arrived, and the American regime began, they, in turn, introduced their own pastimes; therefore, there was an abundance of varied entertainment in the sleepy pueblo during its transition period.

Sunday, was naturally, the day when many came into town to see their friends and take part in various sports. Of course some of the Angelenos attended Mass at Our Lady Queen of the Angels, at the west side of the Plaza. But according to Judge Benjamin R. Hayes, who arrived here in 1851, few men went to church; the congregation consisted mostly of women, "many of them richly dressed, graceful, and handsome."

An interesting description of Sunday around the Plaza is given in a diary kept by the Reverend James Woods, who arrived in the pueblo, via the Horn, in October 1854. There was much revelry around his small shack near the Plaza—men racing past on horseback, dogfights, crying children, and much loud cursing on the part of drunks. The noisy, jabbering crowd stayed close to the minister's home to see the horse racing and the almost unbearable bedlam continued for hours.

The Reverend Mr. Woods started church services at the Court House, with a few women and children in attendance, but became quite discouraged and, as he was in ill health, had to give up his attempt. However, he stayed until he had secured a successor.

Some years later, the *Star*, January 15, 1871, spoke of the way Sunday was kept in the pueblo.

> Today is Sunday, and those of our people who do not prefer horse-racing, chicken-fighting, hunting and shooting, will probably celebrate the day by going to church, or by remaining peacefully in their several places of abode.

During the 1850s there was much gambling in notorious Nigger Alley, that began at the southeast corner of the Plaza. The gambling dens in this narrow street were frequented by the varied population of the period—Mexicans from Sonora, Americans and foreigners. The proprietors of the gaming tables were well supplied with weapons and never hesitated to settle gambling quarrels with pistols. If anyone lost his money and started to argue about it, he was beaten or shot, and his body thrown out into Nigger Alley.

Inside the hot, dusty, low-ceilinged adobes, gold slugs, guarded by armed men, were piled up on the tables, where faro or monte games were going on. The most infamous of the gambling dens was the Golden Eagle, where criminals, prostitutes, and murderers mingled in their mad efforts "to beat the game."

North of the Plaza was a collection of adobes, known as Sonora Town—a section untouched by American influence. Here the lowest class of native Californians lived. The district was as truly Mexican as if it had been brought from Old Mexico itself. This kind of life continued until into the 1870s. There were numerous saloons and many "fair, frail ladies" lived here. There was continual drinking, smoking, dancing, fighting, and quarreling. On Sunday there was always much excitement; sometimes drunken Indians got into fights with Mexicans. Women, too, took part in such combats as described in the *News*, March 26, 1872:

> Last Sunday a couple of squaws, mad with the poison they had imbibed, were tearing away at each other's hair, until they had to desist from sheer exhaustion.

[190]

Cockfighting was a popular sport in Sonora and owners walked around with fighting cocks under each arm. Some Mexicans made their living dealing on these birds. When a cockfight was going on there was "a mystic circle" around the contestants. Once, according to the *Star* (January 25, 1871), four birds of almost equal size were pitted against each other. First, the preliminaries and bets were arranged. In this fight, "the red was the quickest bird and like an arrow from a Piute bow, sprang at his antagonist, who dodged, escaping with the loss of a few feathers, and in his turn, made a pass at the head of his enemy." Then the cock buried his weapon in the shoulder of his enemy and cut a gash "large enough to let out the light of his soul. He expired in the arms of his friends, who mourned for their loss, and would not be comforted—for had they not bet on the losing fowl?"

In 1872 a reporter wandered through Sonora and wrote a detailed picture of what the section was like in the early seventies:

The Keno Game

Main Street, the principal avenue, passing through it, is lined on each side by a series of brothels, gambling dens, and miserable billiard and dancing halls. As passing by an open doorway, the voice of one calling out at regular intervals, and a deeply interested crowd standing or sitting in the interior, pronounce it to be a gambling house. We step inside. The game is called "Keno." The caller stands at a small table, facing the open doorway, and has in his hand a tin cylinder containing the dice. These dice bear figures representing various animals and vegetables, counterparts of which are supposed to be on the cards in the hands of the players. A few vigorous shakes of the cylinder, and the game and the singsong call commence. So intent are the players in listening to the words falling from the caller's lips, and to the cards lying before them, that the entrance of a stranger into the room is unnoticed, and consequently attracts no attention. A girl of 15 or 16 years of age utters an exclamation in Spanish, and after comparing the dice with her card, is pronounced the winner of the "pot."

After the reporter left the gambling den, he saw a group of drunken Indian women, singing a native song. In front of the crumbling adobes were game cocks soon to be pitted against each other; and the *News* man prophesied that a hand-to-hand "fight with knives will close the day's orgies."

The Spanish sport—bullfighting—was popular for many years in Los Angeles and was enjoyed both by the gringos and the natives. It was not so cruel here as in Spain, for a bull was seldom killed. The main part of the sport consisted of shaking *serapes* before the bull to anger him. Then men tried to seize the animal by his tail, and throw him to the ground. There was much rough riding; and when the horsemen collided, sometimes both the riders and horses were hurt.

These bullfights took place on Sundays or holidays, and were often held in conjunction with rodeos. Sometimes the contests lasted three days and were sponsored by prominent citizens. Each fight was advertised by placards which lauded the skill of the *toreador* and magnified the bull's ferocity:

GRAN FUNCION DE TOROS
El Domingo Proxima Lastres a la Trade

At first, these bullfights were held at the Plaza near the church, Our Lady Queen of the Angels. But, since they caused much noise and commotion, church officials asked that they be removed to a distance. Then such contests took place in the *Calle de Toros,* which ended in a natural canyon, where the animals could be kept safely.

The area was surrounded by a fence of green willow posts, lashed together by rawhide thongs and fastened to stout poles, forming a forty-foot circle. Some Angelenos paid admission to the elevated seats, arranged on one side, but the rest of the populace peeped through the fence. On a platform a Mexican string band played "brave, solemn airs." Although the toreador was advertised as directly from Mexico City, he was usually a cowhand from a nearby rancho.

A herald announced the entry of the *lazadores, picadores, banderilleros,* and lastly, the *matador,* all dressed in bright costumes. With a great flourish and gay music, the brave toreador

[192]

Los Angeles around 1860.
Courtesy of El Pueblo de Los Angeles State Historic Park.

entered the ring; the ladies then threw flowers in his direction. He immediately made a speech, declaring he was the bravest man in the world, and the bull, the fiercest one in all California. However, the bull usually proved to be so tame that the spectators would hiss at him, run into the arena, twist his tail, and drive him ignominiously from the scene.

If a horse was killed, there was much excitement. One paper reports that at a bullfight in 1860, a child lost its life. The *Star*, July 5, 1851, told of one such contest:

> This afforded amusement to many. The fight was simply a race with some capital feats of horsemanship. The bull was driven into a large corral where a dozen or more Californians provoked the animal by shaking their blankets in his face. The sport consisted of seeing the daring riding.

Twenty years after this fight, the *News* gave the following account of a bullfight in the Mexican section of town:

A Real Bullfight in Sonora

> At the hour of commencement, three individuals dressed as clowns stepped into the pit, each bearing in his hand a red flag attached to a small stick; these were the *picadores*. One of them was well advanced in years and shortly after the first animal had been turned into the arena and had became sufficiently enraged to make it somewhat warm for his tormentors, the old fellow, not having the elasticity of youth, was impaled; by the infuriated brute against the fence and finally tossed over it. Besides being badly gored, it transpired afterwards that some of his ribs were broken . . . the other two continued to worry the poor bull and succeeded for some time to avoid all his plunges. Finally one of them taking the wrong direction, was slightly elevated on the horns of the bull, the points of which had been sawed off. Nothing daunted, he continued to torment the beast with increased ardor. Several brads to which were affixed various appendages in the way of ribbons, leaves of colored paper, etc. were then passed to the *matadores*. With a brad in one hand, and a banner in the other, they awaited the onset of the bull, and as he came within reach, prodded him in the neck, and at the same time, darted aside. The poor bull tore the ground with rage, the brad meanwhile sticking in his neck, and a dozen various colored ribbons streaming in the wind, as he rushed blindly, foaming at the mouth, at the agile *picadores*, who would then stand aside to receive the plaudits of the fair senoritas that were in attendance.

The bull was then taken out, and the band struck up a lively air. The clown who had hitherto kept at a safe and respectful distance from the bull, being perched on the fence, then danced a polka and sang, a song full of Mexico and *"Liberto."* Another bull was then driven into the ring and the same performance passed through.

As before, the bull in the present case . . . tossing the *picadores* several times. What was considered the best sport of all was the "Grand Ride," performed by the second bull. The animal being lassoed and thrown to the ground, a *riata* was tied around his body. To this the *picador,* who was to ride the bull, was to hold. A novel crown, ornamented with firecrackers and immense back gear made of wires covered with firecrackers was then placed on the bull, being joined together by means of a fuse. The *picadores* then asked the crowd to contribute their mites as it would probably be their last ride. Mounting and grasping the *riata,* the animal was relieved of its bonds and the fireworks attached to its tail ignited. Plunging round the ring at breakneck speed, both bull and rider seemed enveloped in flame and smoke, which continued until the poor creature fell from sheer exhaustion. The enthusiastic delight of the spectators beggars description. Cries were then raised for a third animal, which being fresh and more furious than the others, soon compelled the weary *picadores* to abandon the field. The clown then extended an invitation to anyone from among the crowd to take their places, but no one felt disposed to do so. And the performance was declared at an end.

—*News,* October 27, 1872

There was a fight between a bull and a bear in the pueblo in 1854, the young bear weighing about 600 pounds. This fight took place within a strong wooden fence and a short distance away, a platform was built for the women and children. Men on horseback held their loaded guns ready in case the bear should jump over the enclosure.

In the contest, sometimes the bull and bear were joined together; the crowd taunted and goaded the animals on to fight, even if they didn't want to do so. Sometimes, in such fights, the bear won, and sometimes, the bull. These spectacles are said to have been very popular with the "ladies." At such contests, shrill feminine screams could be heard. However, this was not considered a very desirable type of entertainment. Bullfights were continued through the first quarter of a century under

[195]

American rule in Los Angeles. The *Herald,* September 18, 1879, reported the details of a bullfight held on the Mexican Independence Day.

Before the coming of the Americans, the native Californians were passionately fond of the turf. All the important *rancheros* had their own racing horses, and bet large sums of money, hundreds of cattle, sheep, and horses on this pastime. On Sundays, on Upper Main Street, north of the Plaza, there would be arranged impromptu races, with people coming from long distances to take part, or to see the contests. In the 1850s, (before the droughts had caused the death of so many thousands of cattle), many Angelenos still had plenty of money and didn't hesitate to spend it on the "sport of kings."

On August 16, 1851, Don Pío Pico and Teodosio Yorba sent a printed challenge to the North, saying, "The glove is thrown down; let him who will, take it up." They wanted to run a nine-mile race, or a four-and-a-half one, and return. The stakes consisted of one thousand head of cattle, worth $20 apiece, and two thousand dollars in cash. The backers asked for two additional races, one of two leagues and back, the other of 500 *varas.* The sum of two thousand dollars and two hundred head of cattle made up the prizes of each of these contests.

From earliest times there had been a decided rivalry between Don José Sepulveda and ex-Governor Pío Pico. Although the former had many fine horses, both blacks and palominos, his horses were usually beaten by Pico's *Sarco.* Sepulveda became frantic over these defeats; so at great expense, he imported *Black Swan* from Australia. He himself went up to San Francisco to meet the horse on its arrival. His trainer, Bill Brady, brought the imported animal down to Los Angeles.

The race between *Black Swan* and *Sarco,* March 21, 1852, was so well advertised that many people came down from San Francisco, others from San Diego, and from intervening points. It was the largest crowd that had ever gathered in the pueblo. The course began on San Pedro Street, near the edge of town, ran south for a league and a half, then back, so that the excited spectators could see the finish of the nine-mile race.

[196]

On the day set for the race, Señora Sepulveda rode out to the starting point. She carried a box full of fifty-dollar gold slugs, in case her husband wanted to add to his bets. She also gave some of these gold pieces to friends and servants to place on *Black Swan*.

Finally everything was ready. The race was started with the usual signal, "Santiago"—the battle cry of Old Spain. The Negro who rode *Black Swan*, and the young Mexican on *Sarco*, had been told to hold their horses in, but were unable to do this. At the turning post, the two horses were neck and neck. But *Black Swan* didn't want to make the turn; so *Sarco* ran far ahead of her. However, on the return, *Black Swan* caught up; and to the chagrin of the *Sarco* backers and the delight of the Sepulvedas, *Black Swan* finished as the winner. She made the nine miles in 19 minutes and 20 seconds, winning by 75 yards. Blood was streaming from her nostrils when Don José Sepulveda threw a gold cloth over her and told his *vaqueros* to take her to his *rancho* at Ventura. There she could live happily the rest of her life, for he would never race her again after this victory.

Betting was vigorous at the time of this outstanding race; it is said that not less than $50,000, 500 sheep, 500 horses, and 500 calves were won and lost. This race was a hard blow for Pío Pico to take, and showed "another example of the way his enormous wealth was thrown to the winds."

After this epoch-making contest, horse-racing continued to enthrall both the Californians and the gringos. That same year—1852—Don Andrés Pico and Don José Sepulveda put on two other races, one with stakes of $1,000, the other for $1,600 and 300 head of cattle. On October 20, 1852, the last named race took place, with *Canelo*, backed by Pico, and *Alison* (a horse from Santa Barbara), the favorite of Sepulveda. *Canelo* was declared the winner by half a length; but this contest finally ended up in the courts. Don Manuel Rojo, holder of the stakes, refused to turn over the $50 slugs to either of the rivals, as he was not satisfied that *Canelo* had won the race.

In March 1853, Moore and Brady's horse, *John Smith*, beat Powell's *Sarah Jane*, by one length, with the stakes valued at $2,100. Later a Sepulveda horse, named *Muchado*, was pitted

[197]

against a mule belonging to Moore for $550, and the horse won the race. There was another meeting in February 1857, between the Picos and Sepulvedas, when the latter's *Pinto* easily won the purse of $3,000 from Pico's *Don Johnson.*

There was also much rivalry between the Picos and Avilas, which came to a climax in February 1860. Then all the race-loving Angelenos rode down to San Juan Capistrano to see the contest between Juan Avila's *Coyote,* and Pío Pico's *Azueljo.* The latter won $3,000 for his owner in the 300-yard race; and one backer is said to have carried winnings of $8,000 away with him that day.

The formation in March 1871, of the Southern California Agricultural Society, by such leaders as L. J. Rose, Colonel J. J. Warner, Judge Henry O'Melveny, John G. Downey, Harris Newmark, and others, promised the breeding of fine horses in this region. Each year the society sponsored a week of trotting races at Agricultural Park—now the site of Exposition Park—and so promoted the sport so loved by the early Californians.

Another favorite pastime of the twenty-five year period (1850-1875) was dancing; and before the coming of the Americans, balls were attended by old and young, many coming long distances to enjoy such affairs. The musicians were harp, violin, or guitar players, assisted by singers. A master of ceremonies was in charge of dancing, which usually continued all night; at wedding fiestas the gaiety often was kept for several days and nights.

At first they danced folk dances, but later the waltz, mazurka, polka, and other European "round dances" came into fashion. The waltz was frowned upon by the clergy, but Juan Bandini introduced it into California in 1830. Richard Henry Dana describes a fandango, which he saw in 1836 at Santa Barbara, and spoke of the grace and agility of the dancers, especially the skill of Juan Bandini, who was highly applauded by the spectators.

In 1838, the *Ayuntamiento* apparently found it necessary to curb the Angelenos in their dancing, for they passed this ordinance:

> Every individual giving a dance at his house, without first hav-
> ing obtained permission from the *Alcalde,* will be fined $5 for the
> first offense, and the second and third punished according to law.

After dances it was the custom for young men to go around
to serenade the ladies; this must have caused some disturbance
as the Council also passed this rule:

> All individuals serenading promiscuously around the streets of
> the city at night, without having first obtained permission from
> the *Alcalde,* will be fined $1.50 for the first offense, $3 for the
> second, and the third punished according to law.

Bailes, or formal dances, were given in the large halls, or
salas, of the better homes, and were attended by both sexes.
However, at public fandangos, usually only the men of the aris-
tocracy attended, and danced with ladies not quite so high in
the social scale. The room was usually crowded to suffocation.
There was an abundance of food and drink at such large parties,
and *cascarones*—egg shells filled with bits of colored paper, or
perfume—were broken over the heads of favored guests.

One of the first balls, in which many Californians and
Americans took part together, occurred on July 4, 1847. That
morning a celebration was held at Fort Moore; and in the evening an elaborate dance was given at Lieutenant Davidson's
headquarters for the officers and aristocratic Spanish Californians and their wives. Meantime, the enlisted men were also
enjoying a dance at their quarters. Another "brilliant" Fourth of
July ball took place in 1851 at *El Palacio,* the home of Abel
Stearns. A military dance, enjoyed by many, occurred on Independence Day, 1857, when soldiers from Fort Tejon arrived
with their band to help the Angelenos in their celebration.

During the 1850s the young men about town, headed by
Dr. J. B. Winston (who had married a daughter of Juan Bandini)
used to organize dances for their friends. These were usually
held at Widow Blair's home, on Main, across from the Bella
Union Hotel. It contained one of the largest rooms in town, 18
by 30 feet, and was popular for private dances. The young men
would collect money for candles, refreshments (usually cake
and lemonade), and the musicians, each of whom received a

dollar or more for his services. The ladies were escorted, on foot, to the dance, through the muddy or dusty streets, of course properly chaperoned by "female relatives."

By 1860 public dances were largely attended at *Tivoli Gardens*, on Wolfskill road, conducted by Charles Kaiser. Each Sunday from 2 p.m. on, dancing was enjoyed. *Sycamore Grove*, too, furnished facilities for this pastime; every two hours on Sundays and holidays an omnibus carried Angelenos to this resort. In addition, other dancers congregated at Lehman's *Garden of Paradise*, and later, at *Washington Gardens*.

In 1861 the City Council declared that the sum of $10 must be paid for a permit, per evening, for any dance held within the city limits. Music for these affairs was usually furnished by a German barber, Fred Dohs, who also directed a string band.

When the first railroad in Southern California—from Wilmington to Los Angeles—was opened in 1869, the celebration closed that night with a ball at the new depot, gaily decorated for the occasion.

Balls also were given at the *Bella Union Hotel*, the *Temple Theatre*, the *Merced*, or the *Turnverein*. Frequently they were sponsored by such fraternal groups as the Masons, Ancient Order of Hibernians (who of course always had a "Grand Ball" on St. Patrick's Day), the Order of Red Men, and the Odd Fellows. Some were put on to raise funds for charitable organizations.

Several private social clubs were formed, the most important being the Los Angeles Social Club, organized by leading business and professional men as charter members. This group frequently gave balls attended by the "socially elite."

Dancing became more popular than ever with the opening, in 1871, of a dancing academy in *Stearns Hall*, by the "pioneer dancing master of California," S. J. Millington. He conducted morning classes for children and evening sessions for adults. Costume dances were popular with his students; "elaborate toilettes and variety of dress marked an advance in these harmless diversions."

During the first quarter of a century of California's statehood, dancing was always a popular diversion in Los Angeles. One of the finest balls ever given in the pueblo occurred on

*Women and children take a peaceful stroll along Main Street near
the Plaza Church in the 1880s.*
Courtesy of El Pueblo de Los Angeles State Historic Park.

September 6, 1876, when the Angelenos entertained their distinguished guests from San Francisco on the day the Southern
Pacific Railroad completed its tracks to Los Angeles. This elaborate banquet and ball at Union Hall (on Spring Street, opposite
the old Court House) ended the period in a genuine "blaze of
glory."

Angelenos patronized all types of entertainment that came
to the pueblo. From the 1850s on, a circus would arrive, from
time to time, and perform to appreciative audiences. At first
these companies came from Mexico; but later Californians
formed their own circuses. The *Star*, October 1859, told of the
arrival, for several performances of the *Washington Circus*, under the direction of T. W. Tanner. The most popular troupe was
the *Lee Circus and Hippodrome*, which first appeared here in
1859. They advertised that they would have a "grand change of
program, Saturday and Sunday nights, with brilliant equestrian
scenes and gymnastics extraordinary." They included, too, "a
grand cotillion," and "Mascaroni, the Italian banditti." Patrons
paid $1 for cushioned seats in the Circle, while those in the Pit

[201]

Maymie R. Krythe

cost only 50 cents. This circus showed originally in a small tent, at the present site of the Los Angeles *Times* building.

By 1867, when the show again was seen in Los Angeles, Lee had joined with a partner in the *Lee and Ryland Circus*. They had "a splendid band," which took part in a long parade on Main Street, while they displayed American, French, and Spanish flags in the procession.

The performers "elicited general applause"; but Lee's two daughters, Polly and Ellen, seemed to be special favorites. With her father as Dick Turpin, and mounted on *Black Bess*, Polly "electrified the town" as she was carried away by him to the freebooters' den. New feats in "classical positions and gymnastics" were offered; but one of the best was the riding and dancing act of William Franklin, as an American sailor. There had been heavy rains during this January; but in spite of muddy streets, "elegantly dressed ladies" went with their families to be thrilled by the performers of the incomparable *Lee and Ryland Circus*.

15

SOME EARLY CALIFORNIA INDUSTRIES THAT FAILED

James M. Guinn

Historians generally speaking are not partial to failures. The enterprise, be what it may, that fails fills but a small space in history and the actors in it are usually relegated to oblivion; or if it is commemorated at all it is by the briefest of notices. Scattered at intervals along the highway of California's march to wealth and progress are the ruins of enterprises that failed, the remains of industries that died in their infancy and the unmarked resting places of Napoleons of finance who met their Waterloos in the collapse of some undertaking that almost succeeded—that by all signs and omens ought to have succeeded. Success would have brought them fame and fortune—failure doomed them to poverty and oblivion. It is the story of some of the industries that failed, of some of the enterprises that brought neither fame nor fortune to their promoters yet should have brought both, that I shall attempt to tell.

For three-quarters of a century California's sole commercial industry was cattle raising. Its only product that would bear eighteen thousand miles shipment was the dried hides of its tens of thousands of slaughtered cattle.

The famine years of 1863 and 1864, when for two years in succession the rain fall amounted to little more than a trace and cattle died of starvation by the hundreds of thousands, virtually put an end to the cattle industry in Southern California. It had been declining for a decade. The high price of beef in the mines from the discovery of gold up to about 1855 had not only stimulated the industry in the cow counties of the south, but had expanded it over Northern California, which in the days of the padres was a *terra incognita*.

Overproduction forced it into a decline and drought was the death of it. The cattle kings were ruined. They had no means to restock their desolated ranges, and without cattle their myriads of acres were worthless for production. Besides the *rancheros* were encumbered with debt. Cancerous mortgages bearing interest at 5 and 6 per cent a month were eating away their possessions. With nothing to sell to pay interest or principal, the end soon came. The Shylocks foreclosed the mortgages—took their pounds of flesh—and the ancestral acres of many a proud Don passed into the possession of the money lenders. The cattle kings were uncrowned. Their kingdoms despoiled, and the olden time industry that once had made them rich and powerful was their undoing.

After the change of owners came the era of subdivision. The new owners cut the great *ranchos* into fractions and sold pieces large or small as the buyers wished at prices ranging from $2 to $10 per acre on time. Thrifty farmers from Central California and the "states" drifted down into the cow counties and bought themselves farms and started a new industry for the south,—"grain raising." Where a few years before lowing herds covered the plains, now fields of barley and wheat billowed in the breeze. The soil was rich and the yield of grain enormous, but machinery was expensive and labor costly and of poor quality. After the harvest came the problem of transportation. The only market on the coast then was San Francisco, five hundred miles away, and there were no railroads. Los Angeles then was a city of vast area but limited population and no commerce. A ton of barley would have demoralized its market for a month. The people pastured their horses on Spring Street lots and kept dairy ranches out on Grasshopper Street, now Figueroa. In the olden time cattle transported themselves to market, but grain sacks had to be carried. The farmers found the lighterage charges, freight charges, commissions, storage and all the other

*Wheat was one of the successful crops in the San Fernando Valley.
Here is a threshing scene in the 1880s.*
Courtesy of Spectrum, L.A. 200.

*Olive groves in the San Gabriel Valley proved another successful
agricultural venture toward the end of the nineteenth century.*
Courtesy of Spectrum, L.A. 200.

charges that commission merchants and middlemen could trump up as cancerous as the old time mortgages. The farmer was fortunate indeed if after marketing his crop he did not have to mortgage his farm to pay the deficit; actually pay a penalty for cultivating his land. It was clearly evident that grain growing for a market five hundred miles away would not pay. The query of the agriculturists was what can we produce that transportation charges and commissions will not eat up. Then began an era of agricultural experiments.

One of the first of these was the seri-culture venture. Louis Prevost, an educated Frenchman, who was familiar with silk culture in France, in a series of letters in the newspapers, proved beyond a doubt that California was superior to France in the conditions required for the success of the silk industry—that the Golden State would eventually out-rival France in silk production and put China out of the business.

To encourage silk culture in California, the legislature in 1867 passed an act giving a bounty of $250 for every plantation of 5,000 mulberry trees two years old, and one of $300 for every 100,000 merchantable cocoons produced. This greatly encouraged the planting of trees and the production of cocoons, if it did not add to the number of yards of silk in California. In 1869 it was estimated that in Central and Southern California there were ten million mulberry trees in various stages of growth. One nursery in San Gabriel—"The Home of the Silkworm," as its proprietor called it—advertised 700,000 trees and cuttings for sale. Two million trees were planted in and around Los Angeles City. Prevost had a plantation of 50 acres on South Main Street.

The Los Angeles *News* of April 11, 1869, says: "We risk nothing when we express the belief that in two years from this time the silk products of this county will amount to several million dollars."

The California Silk Center Association was formed with a large capital on paper. The Association bought four thousand acres which now forms part of the site of the city of Riverside. It was the intention of the Association to found a colony there of silk growers and silk weavers. Sixty families were reported ready to locate on the colony grounds as soon as negotiations were completed. Prevost, the great head center of the scheme, died shortly after the purchase was made, and the colony project died later. At first the profits from the seri-culture fad were large, not, however, from the manufacture of silk, but from the sale of silkworm eggs. When the industry was launched, eggs sold at $10 an ounce and the worms were good layers. One seri-culturist reported a net profit of a $1,000 an acre made in sixty days from the sale of eggs. Another realized $1,260 an acre in a single season. The net profit from his three acres of trees and cocoons exceeded the net profits on his neighbor's 30,000 acres of grain. With such immense returns from such small investments it is not strange that the seri-culture craze became epidemic. Mulberry plantations multiplied until the bounties paid threatened the state treasury with bankruptcy. A sanguine writer in the *Overland Monthly* of 1869 says: "It is almost startling to think that from a calling so apparently insignificant we may be able to realize in a short time a larger sum and infinitely greater gains than from one-half of all our other agricultural productions in the state." With the increased supply the price of eggs declined until it was all supply and no demand. Then the seri-culture epidemic came to as sudden a stop as a yellow-jack does when a killing frost nips the fever breeding mosquito. The worms died of starvation and the bounty-bought mulberry plantations perished from neglect. Of the millions of trees that rustled their broad leaves in the breeze not even the fittest survived. They all died.

Out of the hundreds of thousands of bounty-bought cocoons only one piece of silk to my knowledge was manufactured and that was a flag for the state capital. Proudly that homemade "Old Glory" floated above the dome of the state house, and proud indeed it might be, for indirectly it cost the state a quarter million dollars.

The experiment failed, but not because California was unsuited to silk culture. The defects were in the seri-culturists, not in the soil or climate of the state. There was no concert of action among the producers. They were scattered from Dan to Beer-sheba, or what was a much greater distance, from Siskiyou to San Diego. There were not enough producers in any one place to build a factory, and not enough weavers in the country to manufacture the raw silk produced; nor could capital be induced to invest in silk factories.

After the failure of the seri-culture industry a number of minor experiments were made on various products that it was hoped after paying transportation charges, storage, commissions and other charges, would leave a small margin of profit to the producer.

Col. Hollister of Santa Barbara County planted a small forest of tea trees and imported Japanese tea growers to cultivate them. The trees flourished and seemed to enjoy the soil and climate of California, but somehow the home grown tea did not reduce the prices of the imported article.

A coffee planter from Central America planted an extensive grove of coffee trees near San Bernardino, and there were great expectations that Southern California would rival Central America in coffee production. The climate was all right, the soil was adapted to the tree, but home-grown coffee, like home-grown tea and homemade silk, never affected the price of the imported articles, nor brought fortune or fame to the promoters of these industries.

Another agricultural experiment that we tried in the later 1860s and early 1870s was cotton growing. Experiments on a small scale had proved that cotton could be grown in California equal in quality to the finest Sea Island and Tennessee Upland of the Southern States. These induced planting on a more extensive scale.

Col. J. L. Strong, a cotton planter from Tennessee, in 1870 secured from the Los Angeles and San Bernardino Land Company a lease of 600 acres located on the Santa Ana River in the Gospel Swamp country, a region famous in early times for mammoth pumpkins and monster camp meetings. On this he planted a large field of cotton. It grew like the fabled green bay tree, and produced fabulous returns, but not in money. On the Merced River bottoms near Snellings was a plantation of a thousand acres and in Fresno County were a number of smaller ones, aggregating about 500 acres. The California Cotton Growers' and Manufacturers' Association purchased ten thousand

Cotton bales await shipment.
Courtesy of Los Angeles County Museum of Natural History.

acres of land adjoining to, and covering part of the present site of Bakersfield, the oil metropolis of Kern County. On account of the difficulty of obtaining seed only 300 acres were planted the first year. A portion of this made a fine crop of excellent quality. The Association announced that it would plant two thousand acres next year (1873); and to encourage planting would furnish growers with seed and gin their cotton free. To secure laborers, the members of the Association imported a colony of Negro cotton-field laborers from the south, built cabins for them and hired them to plant, cultivate, pick and gin the prospective crop. The colored persons discovered that they could get much better wages at other employments and deserted their employers. The cotton crop went to grass and the cotton growers went into bankruptcy.

Along about 1869 or 1870 a large portion of Los Angeles City was a cotton field. The late Don Mateo Keller tried the experiment of cotton growing on irrigated lands. West of Figueroa Street and extending from near Ninth Street down to Ad-

[209]

ams there was an extensive field of cotton. The plants grew luxuriantly and produced abundantly. The bursting bolls of cotton whitened the expanse like the snows of winter an arctic landscape. The experiment was a success as far as producing went, but Don Mateo did not turn cotton planter.

The experiments tried in various parts of the state demonstrated beyond a doubt that cotton of the finest quality could be grown in California, but when it came to figuring profits in the business—"that was another story." The Negro cotton picker was not much in evidence here and those that were, were too "toney" to stoop to cotton picking in California. The Mexican peon and the Mission neophyte could pick grapes, but when it came to cotton picking they simply bucked and that was the limit with them. White labor was too scarce and too expensive. So the coast winds did most of the picking. For that which was gathered and baled there was no market nearer than Lowell or Liverpool—eighteen thousand miles away via Cape Horn. There were no railroads then in Southern California, and no cotton factories on the Pacific Coast; so the cotton boll, like the silk cocoon, disappeared from the land of the afternoon.

The next industry that came to the front guaranteed to lift the agriculturist out of the slough of financial despond was the cultivation of the castor bean. California from away back in the days of the padres has always been as famous for raising beans as Boston has been for eating them. But the castor bean is not that kind of a *frijole*. It is the bean or nut from which castor oil is manufactured. Its cultivation in Southern California was introduced by the late George H. Peck and for a time the industry paid fairly well. Somewhere along about 1870 a castor oil factory had been started in San Francisco. The proprietors, to secure a supply of beans, furnished the farmers with seed and contracted to buy their crop at a stipulated price. The beans were planted in rows like corn and cultivated in a similar manner. The bean stalk or bush grew to be from six to eight feet high the first season. On the branches the beans were produced in spike-covered pods that were uncomfortable things to handle. The bean grower prepared to harvest his crop by first clearing off an earthen threshing floor and tamping the soil until it was smooth and solid. This floor he surrounded by a circular board corral. With a large box fastened on a sled drawn by a horse he drove between the rows, cutting off the clusters of bean pods and throwing them into the box. The loads were dumped in the corral and spread out over the threshing floor. As the sun dried the pods the beans came out with a pop like the report of a toy pistol. This was kept up until the pods were emptied. The popping of the beans in the corrals resembled a Chinese New Year celebration. It was a source of joy to the small boy, who had Fourth of Julys galore as long as there was any pop in the beans.

The industry held its own for several years, then the castor bean pod joined the silk cocoon and the cotton boll in the haven of "has beens." The elements that were its undoing were similar to those that wrought the ruin of the others: scarcity and high price of labor, excessive freight rates and long distance to market.

The castor bean plant had some faults of its own that did not commend it as an agricultural standby. It had a trick of volunteering its services when they were not needed. Once planted it was as difficult to get rid of as the Canada thistle. Its staying quality was one of the causes that finally banished it.

A series of experiments had convinced us that it was not so much a new product that we needed as it was more population and a home market. We were all producers; we needed consumers.

Forty years before, Dana, he of *Two Years Before the Mast,* had decried against the want of enterprise in the native Californians. With all the ingredients to tan leather they sold the hides of their cattle to the Boston hide droghers at a dollar a piece to be carried around the world to tanneries, and returned two or three years later in leather boots and shoes for which the Californians paid a thousand per cent above the cost of the raw material. California had been a quarter of a century under the domination of the most energetic people on earth, and yet we were doing the same thing that the cattle kings had done generations before.

Sheep take a midday rest on Lucky Baldwin's ranch.
Courtesy of Los Angeles Museum of Natural History.

We were producing millions of pounds of wool every year and sending it around the world to hunt a market. Tufts of the finest raw cotton were wafted hither and yon by the gentle sea breezes and there was no one to gather them and manufacture them into cloth. We were paying an aggregate of a thousand per cent to middlemen, shippers, manufacturers and dealers for returning to us the finished product from our own raw material.

A few would-be political economists of the southland, myself among the number, wrote stirring articles for the local press advocating the building of woolen mills and cotton factories. Bring together producer and consumer, save cost of transportation, cut out the profits of the middlemen and we would all get rich. To obtain power for our factories conserve the waste waters of our rivers in great reservoirs, set these to propelling hundreds of mill wheels, these in turn would set tens of thousands of spindles in motion to twist our wool and cotton into

[212]

thread, and would start thousands of shuttles flying to weave these threads into cloth. The building of factories would make a Lowell of Los Angeles and boom all the cities of the south.

A few years before, the City Fathers of Los Angeles had given to a syndicate as a consideration for constructing a reservoir and digging a ditch, all of the northwest corner of the city from Diamond Street, now West First, north to the city's northern boundary and from North Figueroa west to the city limits, except Elysian Park, and that would have gone, too, but the syndicate scorned such refuse real estate. All that the city has today for the donation of thousands of acres of canal and reservoir lands is that hole in the ground called Echo Lake.

The ditch, which was intended to irrigate the desolate regions down by West Adams Street, meandered along what is now Lake Shore Avenue to old Pearl Street, now Figueroa. There was considerable fall to it and it afforded water power. On this ditch along about 1872 the Bernard brothers of Illinois built a woolen mill of ten-loom capacity. The political economists rejoiced greatly. We were on the king's highway to prosperity. The mill's long suit was blankets, but the proprietors did manufacture some blue serges and mixed cheviots. Some of us economists had suits made of these and pointed with pride to our clothes made from home-grown wool, spun and woven in a homemade mill and fashioned by a homemade tailor. When the glorious sunshine of California got in its work on the alleged fast colors of the cloth they faded away into nondescript shades; Joseph's dress suit—his "coat of many colors"—would have gone out of business at sight of our garments. Nevertheless, we were proud of our homemade clothes, but when one of us went to San Francisco we borrowed an imported suit, not but what our own homemade was good enough, but then the San Franciscans were envious of our growing manufactures and might make invidious comparisons.

Our great expectations of becoming a manufacturing center were blighted by that financial frost that chilled the nation to its heart's core—"Black Friday on Wall Street." No more capitalists from the east could be induced to come west to build up the country. They had need of their capitalists at home. Our lone woolen mill did its best to furnish us with a very good quality of blankets, but one day a frost struck it and it was changed to an ice factory. The only reminder of the first and last woolen mill of Los Angeles left us is the name of the subdivision where it was located, "The Woolen Mill Tract." Many a newcomer, no doubt, has puzzled over the appearance of such a name on the city map.

Such are some of the trials and tribulations through which the pioneers of Southern California passed in their attempts to develop the land of sunshine. The pioneer, like the prophet, is without honor in his own country. He blazes the trail for the army of occupation that follows his lead into new lands, but he seldom profits from his adventures. The new arrivals regard him as a silurian—a relic of a remote age—and shove him aside. The newcomer who buys a piece of real estate on a rising market and sells it a few months later at an advance of a hundred per cent, regards with contempt the old resident who years ago sold leagues of land for less than he, the newcomer, has sold feet. Let this Napoleon of finance try selling land or lots on a falling market when all are sellers and there are no buyers; and to add to his misery a cancerous mortgage eating away at his possessions day and night. His plaint of woe would be painful to the ear. He would not submit to the decrees of Fate with the fortitude, the manhood and the courage with which the cattle kings of long ago met misfortune and were overwhelmed by conditions beyond their control.

16

ADVERTISING SOUTHERN CALIFORNIA
BEFORE THE BOOM OF 1887
Glenn S. Dumke

Advertising is described by Daniel Starch, author of a classic text on the subject, as "the presentation of a proposition to the people, usually through print, in such a manner as to attempt to induce them to act upon that proposition." Of all classic campaigns, that of selling California and its products to the rest of the world is surely a *chef d'oeuvre* of the advertiser's art. It is, of course, recent examples that come most readily to mind—Sunkist oranges, Sunmaid raisins, the movies. But even in the years which advertising historians have dubbed the "period of expansion", Southern California was being hailed by enterprising publicists for its natural advantages, its successes, and its potentialities.

California advertising first became standardized in the period between the gold rush and the real estate boom of 1887. The southland was, naturally, more or less of a silent partner in the gold frenzy; there is no doubt, however, that it reaped its share of benefit from the attention, however cursory, bestowed upon it by the influx of people thus drawn to the West. And in later and more leisurely years the Anglo-Saxon *Californios* of the south were joined by an ever-increasing number of enthusiasts who perceived that gold was not the state's only asset.

The new population had heard about California from many sources: accounts of returning gold-seekers, descriptions written by eager travellers and residents, railroad propaganda, material from western newspapers and other agencies, and, finally, letters from friends and relatives who had found the southland to their liking and who had become permanent citizens. Of the items listed only one, the first, will not be considered a proper part of this article; for the returning miners were for the most part either disappointed and thus not good advertisers, or else primarily interested in the northern part of the State. The others, however, each merit a brief discussion.

Probably the first tenuous hint of Southern California advertising which filtered into the eastern mind was that provided by travellers' and other descriptive accounts. There were an immense number of these written after the gold rush and before the boom; and they range from the encyclopedic *Resources* of John Hittell to the jocund and slightly mocking "Golden Hesperides" of Charles Dudley Warner. Although the spirit varies, the content is similar in all—high praise of miscellaneous benefits and the following seven attributes of the region: the climate, rapid disappearance of the frontier, agricultural potentialities, cheap living costs, healthfulness, picturesqueness, and money-making opportunities.

The climate was (and is) a perennial favorite. Warner was enthusiastic:

> This is Paradise. And the climate? Perpetual summer (but daily rising in price). . . . The night temperature throughout California is invariably in great contrast to that in the daytime; nearly everywhere fire is necessary at night the year round, and agreeable nearly all the year, even in Southern California.

"The architecture of this region," another adds, "will remind you that you are in a land where it is never very cold. The dwelling is a secondary matter here, and it results that many people are satisfied to live in very small and slight houses." William Henry Bishop was even more outspoken: "The temperature, this late November day—on which there are telegrams in the paper of snowstorms at the North and East—is perfection. It is neither hot nor cold. A sybarite would not alter it."

It was necessary to abolish the idea prevalent in eastern minds that California was still frontier territory. Much space

Los Angeles with its dirt streets in the 1880s.
Courtesy of Spectrum, L.A. 200.

Los Angeles as it would have appeared to a visitor in the late 1880s.
Courtesy of Spectrum, L.A. 200.

was devoted to assuring timid newcomers of the safety of life in the West.

> The whole number of persons in the whole southern half of the State (where thousands sleep all summer on the open ground) injured by snakes and poisonous reptiles, animals, etc., in the last ten years is not equal to the number killed by lightning alone in one year in one county in many Eastern States.

Charles Nordhoff, a traveller-publicist whose volume, *California for Health, Pleasure, and Residence,* was given "more credit for sending people to California than anything else ever written about the section," went so far as to say that

> There are no dangers to travellers on the beaten track in California; there are no inconveniences which a child or a tenderly reared woman would not laugh at . . . when you have spent half a dozen weeks in the State, you will perhaps return with a notion that New York is the true frontier land, and that you have nowhere in the United States seen so complete a civilization.

As Southern California did not have precious metals to exploit, and as the cattle business suffered a sharp decline in the sixties, more and more of the advertisers turned to agriculture as the real basis of the southland's prosperity. "Possibly Southern California should be described as a garden rather than an agricultural region," says Warner. "There is . . . no doubt that nearly every kind of wine known to the market is made from the same field." Nordhoff seconds with: "After a thorough examination, I believe Southern California to be the finest part of the State, and the best region in the whole United States for farmers." Van Dyke, the historian of the boom, noted the variety of products which could be grown: "Southern California seems to produce with proper care nearly every kind of tree, shrub, grass, grain, herb, or tuber that is at all common or useful in the temperate zone, together with a large number of those of the tropics."

There were, of course, extravagances. Bishop, for instance, states that ten or even five acres were "a comfortable property. On Lake Guarda half an acre in lemons is sufficient for the support of a family. It is in evidence here that returns of from $500 to $1000 an acre are had from orange, lemon, and lime, after the trees have arrived at full bearing." And Warner recounts the oft-quoted tale of a vigorous booster, who claimed that vine-growth was so rapid that melons were bumped along and bruised on the ground. "If you want to pick a melon in this country, you have to get on horseback." These tall stories were somewhat neutralized by the criticism of more level-headed promoters, such as Van Dyke, who states:

> It is just as true that beets here reach the size of one hundred pounds and over, that sixty bushels of wheat are raised to the acre . . . as that in the Mississippi catfish have been caught weighing fifty pounds. . . . So, too, those who call it the land of 'perpetual' or 'eternal' sunshine do not mean that literally, but suppose the reader capable of making the proper exceptions.

Another advantage of the region was the cheapness of living costs. Nordhoff claims that living expenses (before the boom) were less by a third than in any eastern state. California was, at this time, he says, "the cheapest country in the United States to live in."

One of the most important talking points for Southern California was its healthfulness. Bishop remarks:

> Invalidism is heard of with considerable frequency as an excuse for the migration hither. Certainly many advantages offer to the invalid. The climate permits him to be almost constantly out-of-doors. The sky is blue, the sun unclouded, nearly every day in the year, and he can go into his orchard and concern himself about his Navel or Brazilian oranges, his paper-rind St. Michaels, and his Tahiti seedlings, with little let or hindrance.

Much attention was given to the value of the climate in curing tuberculosis, or, as it was then called, "consumption." One writer says:

> The purity of the air of Los Angeles is remarkable. Vegetation dries up before it dies, and hardly ever seems to decay. Meat suspended in the sun dries up, but never rots. The air, when inhaled, gives to the individual a stimulus and vital force which only an atmosphere so pure can ever communicate.

There was, it must be admitted, some mild criticism, but never enough to detract in any measure from the praise bestowed.

The Spanish and Mexican periods had given California a picturesque aura which was capitalized by the advertisers. Los

Angeles was described as "cosmopolitan," and said to be "the product of one era of barbarism, two or three kinds of civilizations, and an interregnum." Warner praises Camulos Rancho and Santa Barbara for their preservation of the older Latin atmosphere.

The possibilities of profit in California investment were not neglected by any means. Warner says:

> It has been a subject of regret ever since that I did not buy Southern California when I was there last March, and sell it out the same month. I should have made enough to pay my railway fare back, and purchase provisions to last through the deserts of sand and feeding-places, and had money left to negotiate for one of the little States on the Atlantic coast.

Another writer boasts that Los Angeles "takes the first place by all odds for booms in lands and building."

Finally, there were plenty of general statements which attempted to sum up the glories of California for the prospective settler. A typical example follows:

> In this newer and nobler life which is growing up here upon the shores of the Pacific . . . it seems to him that [the writer] he can discern the fair promise of a civilization which had its only analogue in that Graeco-Latin race-flowering which came to the eastern shores of the Mediterranean centuries ago.

But travellers' accounts, whether in books or magazines, were not the only means of advertising California. Much of the publicity was financed by the railroads, primarily the Southern Pacific, for two main purposes: one, to sell their own granted land; and two, to induce a large population, whose future business and travel would be profitable, to settle along their lines.

One of the most effective methods used by the railroads was the employment of agents, who wrote, lectured, and planned exhibits in various parts of the world, expounding the glories of the West. A noted example was Jerome Madden, the Southern Pacific's land agent at San Francisco. His books, *California: Its Attractions for the Invalid, Tourist, Capitalist, and Homeseeker,* and *Lands of the Southern Pacific,* attained a wide circulation. Other agents were maintained by the same road in

GRAND FREE EXCURSION AND FREE LUNCH

—TO—

GARVANZO!

FRIDAY, MAY 6, 1887.

Train leaves L. A. & S. G. V. R. R. Depot at 9:30 A. M.

Auction Sale at 10 o'clock A. M.

Don't fail to examine the Business and Residence Lots in the healthful town of Garvanzo. Only four and one half miles from Los Angeles, on the line of the L. A. & S. G. V. R. R.—has five trains daily each way.

The A. T. & S. F. R. R. will have completed their Connection at Garvanzo by June 1st.

Water is piped to this property from the Mountain Water Company, and charged for at the Los Angeles City water rates.

This Sale is Peremptory, and it is to the interest of all persons desiring good investments to be in attendance at this sale.

For Further information apply to

ROGERS, BOOTH & CO.

134 North Main Street, Los Angeles,

OR ON THE GROUNDS AT GARVANZO.

NEWHALL'S SONS & CO., Auctioneers,

225 & 227 BUSH STREET, SAN FRANCISCO.

A newspaper advertisement proclaims the virtues of Garvanza (now Highland Park) in the Boom of the 1880s.
Courtesy of Security Pacific National Bank
Photograph Collection/Los Angeles Public Library.

many parts of the United States and Europe. The railroads also cooperated with the immigration agencies, which were promotional organizations formed to encourage westward migration. The California Immigrant Union and the Pacific Coast Land Bureau, both founded in San Francisco, maintained agents in many countries. The latter published the *California Guide Book.*

The railroad companies also subsidized editors and writers. The outstanding example of the former was the Southern Pacific's financing of Marcus D. Boruck's *Spirit of the Times,* a San Francisco weekly. Land advertisements were often written up in the form of pseudo news articles and inserted in ordinary news columns. Among the writers paid by the railroads were Charles Nordhoff and Benjamin Truman, whose pointed allusions to the lines in their various volumes leave little doubt as to their chief interest. In addition, the railroad companies published pamphlets and folders which were distributed by means of station-agents throughout the country. One of the more ambitious efforts of the "Big Four" was the *Southern Pacific Sketch Book,* which at one time attained a circulation of ten thousand copies.

Western newspapers did their share in advertising the southland. Their circulation was, of course, more limited than that attained by descriptive accounts and railroad propaganda, but it was much more direct and served to guide the enthusiasm of the newcomer into the proper paths of investment. Newspaper advertising reached its zenith in 1886 and 1887, with the real estate boom, and many were the tricks which promoters employed to urge their wares.

There were several types of newspaper advertisements, and some exhibited a strangely modern approach to the advertising problem. First, there was an abundance of realtors' announcements which were little more than expanded business cards:

Office of
E. H. Lockwood
Cor. Colorado St. and Fairoaks Ave.
Dealer in
GILT EDGE REAL ESTATE

Newspaper copy-writers also delighted in long descriptions of various tract offerings. An ad in the *Pasadena Daily Union* grew quite confidential:

> This is an era of town building in Southern California, and it is proper that it should be so, for the people are coming to us from the East and from the North and from beyond the sea, and for the great multitude whose faces are turned with longing eyes toward this summer land and who will want homes among us, we must provide places. And while there is much room in Pasadena and in Monrovia and in other pleasant towns, yet Pasadena prices, and even Monrovia prices are rather high for the purses of many who will come, and these places are rapidly filling, and the prices are getting higher. . . .

This long-winded discussion was followed by an even lengthier description of the location of a proposed town, its benefits for the sick, a pledge as to the prohibition of saloons, and a presentation of the stock issues offered. The town thus treated was La Verne, which is still not a metropolis.

Some of these descriptions included glib statements which today seem rather humorous: "Elsinore is the center of a coal mining and manufacturing district, which makes it a natural business center." Still others resorted to poetry, of which the following is perhaps the most popular effusion:

> When the Angel of Peace to earth first descended,
> To bless with his presence the children of men,
> 'Mid the fairest of scenes his pathway e'er tended,
> And unto his smile the glad earth smiled again.

> He joyed in the fragrance of orange and roses,
> And loved 'mid their glances to linger or roam,
> And he said: 'Here in Tustin, where Beauty reposes,
> I also will linger or build me a home!"

A favorite trick of the newspaper advertisers was to make a flamboyant announcement to arouse the curiosity of the reader, then to follow it up with a more detailed explanation. As early as October 1887, the following ad was printed:

Linda Rosa!   Linda Rosa!
—WHERE IS—
Linda Rosa!   Linda Rosa!

During November the explanation appeared, as a half page of copy:

Linda Rosa! Linda Rosa!
WHERE IS LINDA ROSA?
WE GIVE YOU THE PARTICULARS NOW

It is nestled in the far-famed Temecula Valley, the home of Alle-sandro and Ramona. It is situated in San Diego County on the line of the California Southern Railroad, which being connected with the Atlantic and Pacific, and Atchison, Topeka, and Santa Fe lines, gives us not only a direct Eastern outlet, but also one with the port of San Diego. . . .

Another example will suffice to illustrate these real estate no-tices:

HO! FOR THE CORSON TRACT
For the accommodation of all desiring to examine these
Lots, whose attractions and good quality it is
not desired to hide under a bushel
A FREE CARRIAGE DAILY
(except Sunday) will leave the Santa Fe Station
at 1:36 p.m.

The use of pseudo news articles to advertise realty offices, railway land, or tract offerings was widespread. The Los Ange-les *Times* printed the following on its front page:

Bargains in Real Estate

Do not fail to read the advertisement of J. C. Byram and Co., in the 'wants' column of today's *Times*. This firm is having great success in handling city, suburban, and ranch property. You will make no mistake in placing any kind of real estate in their hands for sale or exchange.

Special supplements, like that of twelve pages issued by the *Times* on New Year's Day, 1886, contributed to the publicity about Southern California. In this particular issue, the types of people who would benefit by life in the region were listed in detail, with an eye to eastern readers. The *Herald* also had a supplement of eight pages on the same day.

An examination of local newspapers shows a great increase in real estate advertising during 1886 and 1887, reaching a peak during the latter year. There was a sharp decline in 1888, how-

A view of Los Angeles spans the basin from
the mountains southwest to the Pacific Ocean, as envisioned by
real estate promoters in 1887.
Courtesy of Huntington Library.

ever, when the boom broke, and by July of that year the only land advertisements printed resembled the following, in which the realtor begged for business:

WANTED! WANTED!
Resident Lots and Acre
Property Listed With
Us For Sale
Good Property Will Sell
Arnold & Mills Co.

Among the local agencies which aided the newspapers in their dissemination of propaganda was the first Los Angeles Chamber of Commerce, whose brief existence embraced the years 1873 to 1877. The second Los Angeles Chamber of Commerce was formed partly as a result of the boom in 1888, and thus did not contribute to the earlier advertising. Another institution interested in increasing migration westward was the realty syndicate, a group of promoters interested in booming a certain district; many of these flourished during boom years. Like the newspapers, however, the syndicate's influence was largely local. One of the earliest was the New York Committee on California, a group of Eastern businessmen who collected information on California agriculture and advertised the state's resources.

Perhaps the most important local publicist, at least immediately before and during boom years, was the individual real estate promoter. His methods were variegated and colorful. He made lurid promises to construct hotels, colleges, and banks in unimproved townsites, and in some cases began construction on a shoestring. He utilized brass bands, processions, menageries, and freaks (in one case, at least, remnants of a stranded circus) to attract attention to land auctions and real estate excursions. He held mass meetings, ostensibly for some worthy cause, but which usually ended in real estate auctions. Free lunches and excursions, posters and broadsides, auctions and lotteries, all played their part in selling California land.

Threats of periodic rises in price caused investors to desire to be first in line when new subdivisions were opened. Lotteries became popular; after subdivision, certain lots would be offered as prizes in a raffle. In one case, chances were sold for $350 each; drawings were often held at the Turnverein Hall in Los Angeles.

Sometimes the schemes devised were outstandingly original. George E. Gard urged the contribution of lots by each town in Southern California for the purpose of raising money to advertise the region in the national G.A.R. convention of 1887. The lots were sold, and $10,000 was collected, which provided for an exhibit. William Monroe, the founder of Monrovia, when invited to send a delegation to the Pasadena Republican rally in the fall of 1886, mustered one hundred and fifty-three representatives of his town, who proceeded to parade with a large banner, stating: "As Goes Monrovia, So Goes the Nation." This illustrates the general modesty of promoters' methods.

Two harbor projects are worthy of mention. Ballona Creek was hailed, in 1887, as the "future harbor of Southern California." In August of that year a huge celebration was held to inaugurate it; and General Nelson A. Miles and ex-Governor Stoneman were featured as speakers. Another harbor was plotted by J. R. Tuffree, who bought the Palos Verdes Rancho and announced his intention of building "Catalina Harbor" at Portuguese Bend. A large hotel was to be erected, and a railroad to Point Fermin was planned. These are typical of the lures used by promoters to attract land buyers.

A fourth type of publicity manifested itself in the activities of enthusiastic newcomers. Such people exerted their influence chiefly by personal correspondence. It is often impossible to learn, of course, just what arguments they used to persuade their friends to come to California; but a survey of postal activity, particularly during boom years, shows that many letters travelled eastward. And as the population of California continued to increase magnificently, it is perhaps safe to assume that some migration, at least, was due to the urging of personal friends and relatives. Letters mailed in Los Angeles alone increased from some 2,083 per month before the boom to 21,333 at its height.

Pioneer settlers like B. D. Wilson praised California in their letters. "No country could be more healthy than this," he wrote

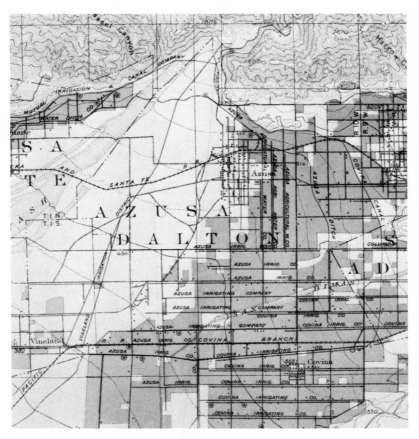

Plat of the Azusa-Dalton area of the San Gabriel Valley, a prime location for real estate promotion.
Courtesy of Historical Society of South California.

his brother in 1854. "Here besides the finest climate in the world we produce every species of grains and fruits in the greatest abundance." Prospective immigrants often wrote Wilson asking for information about agriculture and living conditions, and his replies were consistently enthusiastic. His son-in-law, J. De Barth Shorb, answered many of these requests for information. "Los Angeles County," said Shorb in a typical reply, "is the third county in the State in point of productiveness and it is only in its infancy of development." Also: "I think Los Angeles City the best place to start a bank in this vicinity, or at any place in California." But he added: "A more economical disposition of a larger banking capital could be easier made by simply renting an office and loaning on real estate securities which in this county affords [sic] such first class security." Harrison Gray Otis was another example of the California resident whose eastern contacts made his influence as an advertiser important. He arrived in California in 1882 from Ohio, a typical Civil War veteran in his forties, looking for a place to make a new start. His editorship of the *Grand Army Journal,* while in the east, gave him an influence among army men which he utilized effectly to persuade them to move to California.

These four types of publicity—descriptive accounts, railroad propaganda, newspaper and local agency material, and, finally, the work of enthusiastic residents—combined to make Southern California perhaps the best-advertised portion of the country during the third quarter of the last century. Quaint as this advertising was, it illustrates perhaps better than anything else the economic tendencies of the period, and it forecasts the astounding success of modern publicity methods in the same region.

That it seems primitive is no sign that it was ineffective, however. Besides statistics, the best evidence of its value was the critical attitude of the North. " 'Our brethren of the city and would-be state of the Angels understand how to advertise,' " said the San Jose *Times-Mercury* in 1885. " 'The average Eastern mind conceives of California as a small tract of country situated in and about Los Angeles. . . . The result shows the pecuniary value of cheek.' "

17

THE EUCALYPTUS CRUSADE

Viola Lockhart Warren

———◦◦◦◦◦◦◦◦❨3❩◦◦◦◦◦◦———

The mere outline of a eucalyptus tree against the horizon serves
to identify California to the rest of America, because our state
alone has the tree, and we have it in fantastic abundance. It is
easy to forget that Southern California, now so well clothed
with eucalyptus, was once almost barren of any kind of a tree.
No forests grew here; only tangles of willows along the stream
beds, sycamores in the deepest canyons, and live oaks on the
moist side of a few coastal hills. A single isolated stand of Tor-
rey pine throve in the dampness of the southern coastline, and a
ragged clump of native palms struggled in a hidden canyon near
Palm Springs. The rest of the arid land accommodated only
chaparral, cactus, and wild mustard.

The Franciscan missionaries were the first to rebel against
the absence of trees. They brought pepper trees from Spain to
shade the mission courtyards, imported fruit trees, and encouraged the olive to grow on their irrigated lands. The natives of
Los Angeles were slower to plant trees, because the only water
available to the pueblo ran from the Los Angeles River in narrow, weed-grown ditches, or was carried to the householder in a
barrel on a donkey cart. As late as 1840, the pueblo could boast
only two large trees, a lofty and wide-branching pepper tree in
front of a Mexican adobe north of the Plaza, and a giant sycamore in front of the winery of Don Luis Vignes on Aliso Street.
When a flagpole was needed in 1850 to furl the first United
States flag over Los Angeles, it was necessary to send a crew of

Indians to the pine forests of the San Bernardino Mountains to drag back two pine trunks.

In 1855, the School Trustees of Los Angeles bought a dozen or more black locust trees at "eight bits each" and had them planted on the school grounds. The schoolmaster watered them so faithfully from the school barrel that the water carrier protested to the Trustees about the waste of water. In the ensuing controversy, only a few of the locust trees were saved, the only trees growing on city land. The old Plaza and the vacant area then known as Central Park, now as Pershing Square, were bare of trees until 1870. Meanwhile, the drastic need for firewood was reducing the scant supply of willows, sycamores, and oaks, and was even destroying the peppers and olives in the abandoned mission gardens.

Eventually, the ranchers introduced walnut trees by importing seeds, brought almonds from the Mediterranean, and chestnut seeds from Bordeaux, France. It became a delightful custom in the pueblo to share a small packet of imported seeds with friends and neighbors, and then to compete for the best stand of the foreign trees. Large fruit orchards were finally cultivated successfully on the river bank, or in nearby areas where the water of small streams could be impounded for irrigation. Home gardens began to display exotic trees brought by sailing vessels from faraway lands. The welcome shade of trees was deepening in the settled communities, but the vast empty plains and the rounded hills were still sunburnt and sterile, waiting for the eucalyptus crusade.

The crusade started in a small way, in San Francisco immediately after the gold rush, when Dr. H. H. Behr, a native of Germany and a pupil of Alexander Humboldt, began to talk about the importation of eucalyptus and acacia from Australia. He may have sent away for the seeds. At any rate, by 1853, there were fourteen species of eucalyptus growing in the garden of a Mr. Walker of San Francisco. Hayward had a large planting in 1856, and in 1860, Stephen Nolan, a nurseryman of Oakland, had seedlings ready to sell to the public. In Southern California, William Wolfskill planted eucalyptus on his Santa Anita rancho sometime after 1859. A cluster of five trees was still standing there when Harris Newmark bought the ranch in 1873.

The very name "eucalyptus" was a curiosity to the people of California. The combination of two Greek words, suggested by the formation of the seed pods, might be translated, "I conceal well," or "well hidden." The tree itself, an evergreen, with smooth bark, long graceful branches, and blue-green foliage, was an even greater curiosity. Single seedlings were planted experimentally in home gardens all over the state, with high hopes for ornamentation and shade.

For a dozen years, the planting of eucalypts continued to be sporadic and experimental, until a modest educator, president and principal of the small, private Santa Barbara College, started a crusade with his plea that a barren state be converted into a continuous forest of eucalyptus trees. Ellwood Cooper had seen eucalyptus trees in San Francisco when he first arrived from the East, and he determined to plant some on his Dos Pueblos ranch, twelve miles west of Santa Barbara. Taking advantage of previous acquaintance with Thomas Adamson, Jr., United States Consul-general at Melbourne, Australia, Cooper wrote to ask how to obtain some eucalyptus seed. He also asked about books on the cultivation of the tree, because he could find none in America. Mr. Adamson sent the seeds and reported that Baron Ferd von Mueller, a botanist stationed in Melbourne by the British government, had delivered some lectures on the subject. The lectures had been printed, but the copies had all been sent to the government in London. However, Baron von Mueller would send his one precious original to Mr. Cooper, provided Mr. Cooper would have it published in America and give the Baron fifty copies.

By this devious and thoroughly academic process, Ellwood Cooper got his seeds, read all about their culture, and began to plant. His first trees were three years old, and the little college which his three children attended, and where he had accepted leadership responsibility, was five years old in 1875. When the officers of the college asked their president to be the speaker at a benefit to raise money for the college library, Ellwood Cooper fused his two absorbing interests into a lecture entitled, "Forest Culture and Australian Gum Trees."

Although Cooper had read all of Baron von Mueller's hyperbole about the eucalypts as a money-making proposition, and although he did stimulate his audience gently with visions of income from trees, yet his heart was obviously in the more aesthetic and patriotic aspects of eucalyptus culture. He decried the wanton destruction of the forests in the eastern part of America and in Europe, and pleaded for their replacement by the planting of new forests of eucalyptus trees in California.

> The preservation of forests is one of the first interests of society, and consequently one of the first duties of government. All the wants of life are closely related to their preservation; agriculture, architecture, and almost all the industries seek therein their aliment and resources, which nothing could replace. . . . Their existence is of itself of incalculable benefit to the countries that possess them, as well in the protection and feeding of the springs and rivers, as in their prevention against the washing away of the soil upon mountains, and in the healthful influence which they exert upon the atmosphere.

He promised his listeners joy in the planting. "It may be questioned whether, in the whole range of rural occupations, one more interesting presents itself than the superintendence of a growing wood, presenting to the eye at every season new objects of interest and solicitude. Where is the planter who would wish the workmanship of his hands undone, and who does not look with honest pride on the beautiful creation which, in a generous spirit, he has raised up around him?"

Ellwood Cooper could speak with authority on the gratifications of the planter, because he now had 50,000 eucalypts growing at Ellwood, his home ranch. Some were on steep hillsides, some on level ground. Some had irrigation, some had none. Some were cultivated, some not. Every species was identified, and the rate of growth of each recorded. He could tell his audience that a tree grows to forty-five feet in three years from seed, with a diameter of nine and a half inches; that young trees reach six feet in five months. He could explain exactly how to propagate the seeds and how to transplant into the open

A grove of various species of eucalyptus trees
at the County Arboreta and Botanic Gardens in Arcadia.
Photo by William Aplin.
Courtesy of the Los Angeles County Arboreta and Botanic Gardens.

ground, "as easily as setting out cabbage plants." Most persua-
sive of all, he could describe an acre of land planted with trees
six feet by seven feet apart, one thousand trees on the acre. At
the end of five years the planter takes out three fourths of the
trees and sells them for 700 fence posts and fifty cords of firewood. The remaining trees become so valuable at the end of
fifty years as to return 100% on the investment. "What we have
therefore to do, as individuals, is to begin at once to plant. It is
an obligation we owe to the possessory title to land; and financially we will be amply rewarded for our labors."

President Cooper's address to the little group in Santa Barbara stirred up so much interest that he was persuaded to pub-
lish his material. In his little book of 1876, he fulfilled his promise to Baron von Mueller by including a large section of the
Baron's writings: his definition of species; his discussion of industrial uses; his description of the Australian eucalyptus. The
book devoted a chapter to a listing of twenty varieties of eucalyptus available from the plant catalogue of Anderson Hall &
Co., of Sidney, Australia, and at the very end of the book, as if
by accident, there was inserted the Fifth Annual Catalogue of
the Santa Barbara College.

With the naive mixture of patriotism and acquisitiveness
which Ellwood Cooper had inspired, Southern California began
to plant. At least, as good citizens, the planters would be serving
their community, even if they never made money on fence
posts or cord wood, and even if their eucalyptus trees were
never used, as were those in Australia, for ships, bridges, piers,
railroad ties, telegraph poles, wagons, furniture or any of the
other hardwood objects that Cooper had enumerated. The nurserymen took advantage of the crusade spirit, collected seeds
locally, and supplied seedlings in abundance. Cooper had recommended windbreaks planted at right angles with the prevailing direction of the wind, and windbreaks were planted. Cooper
wanted the highways lined with trees, closely planted and two
or three rows deep, and the inspired land holders edged their
property with belts of little seedlings and watered them carefully for the first year. As they watched the trees grow, they

[236]

came to agree with Cooper, "In its juvenile period, it is a finished type of elegance. In its adult period, it is a magnificent representation of strength."

When the State Legislature created the Board of Horticulture in 1883, Ellwood Cooper was made a member, without salary. He was still on the board twenty years later when it was converted into a commission. For four years more he served on the commission. Of course, he carefully tended his eucalyptus grove at home while he carried his crusade into the state arena. In December 1885, his good friend in Santa Barbara, Judge Charles Fernald, also an officer of the Santa Barbara College, joined the eucalyptus campaign by supplying seeds of a new species to horticultural societies and other agencies interested in forestry. The letter that went out with his little packets of seeds indicates the amateur character that still marked the eucalyptus crusade:

> I have received very recently from Mrs. Charles Hutton of Bath, England, a small package of the seed of the "Jarvah," the giant eucalyptus of West Australia, forwarded by the Manager of one of the estates of that lady in the last mentioned place. I desire to distribute this seed as widely as possible throughout California, especially to the members of the various Horicultural Societies and to those who take an interest in "American Forestry," trusting that the noble and valuable tree may, in time, become acclimated and thrive here.
>
> I therefore take pleasure in sending herewith a small portion of the seed to you, which I beg you will accept, and distribute in such a manner as you may deem wise and proper for the accomplishment of the purpose above named.
>
> It has occurred to me to recommend the setting of young trees, if the seed should grow, in as many different soils, localities, and exposures as possible, until the habit of the tree shall be better known.

With good luck, Judge Fernald's seeds could probably have planted the entire state, because there are over 10,000 eucalyptus seeds in a single ounce. But the hazards in planting are many. A large proportion of the early seeds from Australia were sterile, this despite the fact that a fertile seed remains fertile for as long as six years, until it is moistened in a seed bed. More serious for Judge Fernald's dream of spreading the new species, correctly known as "Jarrah," was the fact that seeds from Australia were seldom true to name. Gathered by the natives in the Australian bush, the seeds might represent any one of the 150 species of the genus, or might be a mixture of many species.

Moreover, conditions of planting differed widely with the different species. Some required moist soil with the water table near the surface. Others could thrive on dry soil if they were exposed to ocean fog. No variety could tolerate frost in its early years, although some mature trees could withstand temperatures slightly below freezing. Excessive heat was fatal to some species, of little danger to others. Some grew easily in solitude, whereas they did not survive if planted closely in a grove. Some could be harvested early and would sprout again, others would not. Each species reacted so violently to its soil and temperature environment as to produce quite a different tree in each environment, some resembling neither their brothers in California nor their ancestors in Australia.

The resultant confusion in identifying species and in determining the special conditions for planting each, resulted in many failures with the seedlings and in growing discouragement with the idea of trying new varieties. The most generally successful species was the *Eucalyptus globulus* or "blue gum." Although it was not the tallest, nor the best for timber, it was the fastest growing; it would thrive easily under average conditions; it produced effective windbreaks and spectacular corridors along the streets and highways. It could be "cropped" every five years for firewood and would sprout again for a new cropping. It would even seed itself, if the wind should blow its seeds into a hospitable spot. With the blue gum, then, in possession of the field, the crusade gathered momentum.

Patriotic school children planted blue gum on Arbor Day, especially in the north. The Presidio, Sutro Forest, Mount Davidson, and other public areas were planted almost wholly by school children. On a hot November day in 1886, 3,000 public-spirited citizens went by boat to Yerba Buena Island to plant blue gum while the First Infantry Band played background music, and such distinguished men as Mayor Sutro, Joaquin Miller, and General Mariano Vallejo gave them encouragement. The University of California campus in Berkeley was planted by a group of enthusiastic neighbors.

The Forest Grove Association was formed in Los Angeles in 1875, seeking "to convert the barren horizons into both beauty and profit by planting eucalyptus trees on a large scale." This group was interested in the experimental planting at "Santa Monica Heights," now Riviera Heights, and in converting Sullivan Canyon into a eucalyptus forest. The State Forestry Bureau built an experiment station in Santa Monica and, under the management of W.S. Lyon, Forester of the Bureau, tried many different species.

Closely associated with the Forestry Bureau, and its chairman from 1886–1888, was a new apostle in the crusade, Mr. Abbot Kinney, better known as the founder of Venice and Ocean Park. While road master of Santa Monica in 1876, he had planted the streets of Santa Monica, the highways leading to the city, and his own home gardens in Santa Monica and in the San Gabriel Valley, with many different varieties of eucalypts. As State Forester, he distributed seeds and seedlings throughout the state without charge, asking only that records be kept of their adaptation. He lectured widely, pleading for more intelligent utilization of the many diverse species of eucalypts. Finally, in 1895, he published a monograph on the subject, describing again the different species and the special growing conditions and uses of each, wishing to "make the knowledge of the eucalyptus accessible to the largest possible number of inquirers."

To prove that variety in species is possible in California, Kinney gave the location of sample trees of fifty-one species, urging that these successful plantings be visited and reproduced in other areas. In addition to the value of certain species for timber, he stressed the use of other species for medicinal oil; tannin; kino or red rosin for insecticides and astringents; nectar for honey bees; paper pulp; bark for mats; moth balls; nest linings to control the lice; scouring material for encrusted boilers. Above all, he emphasized the ability of the eucalyptus tree

Abbot Kinney, prominent real estate developer, advocate of Indian reform policies, and promoter of eucalyptus trees.
Courtesy of Security Pacific National Bank
Photograph Collection/Los Angeles Public Library.

to "draw water" and thus drain swampy land and reduce the incidence of malaria.

Mr. Kinney's enthusiastic but disorganized book is of value today chiefly for its precise location of the large plantations of 1895, and of the occasional trees of note in private gardens and on public streets. Almost invariably he found a good specimen of every species in the twenty-three-year-old planting of Ellwood Cooper at Santa Barbara.

But a more urgent incentive than Mr. Kinney's enthusiasm was necessary to keep the crusade rolling, and this incentive was provided in 1904 when the Forest Service of the U.S. Department of Agriculture announced that the supply of eastern hardwood would be exhausted in about sixteen years. As a result of the increasing scarcity and the rising price of oak, hickory, ash, walnut, maple, and mahogany, manufacturers of hardwood goods began to look for a substitute. Tests with Australian eucalyptus showed this hard wood to be the equal, if not the superior, of the accustomed eastern woods.

Here was a new and urgent reason for planting groves of Australian eucalyptus in California. A plantation set out immediately would be ready for cutting just as the eastern hardwood went off the market. The Panama Canal would be completed then, and lumber from California could be shipped at low cost all over the world. The eager planters studied again the list of species, decided which would produce the best hardwood for commercial use, and planted feverishly.

At least fifty nurserymen swung into action with seedlings; newspapers and periodicals carried encouraging and instructive articles; new industries were organized to process the timber and to make use of its by-products. A one-time Assistant State Forester, Mr. C. H. Sellers, published a book of "authentic data" for the guidance of the commercial planters. Its title was *Eucalyptus, Its History, Growth and Utilization*. Utilization was the key word in the treatise. The book was studded with testimonial letters from furniture makers, flooring firms, agricultural implement houses, dry dock builders, and other users of hardwood, all describing eucalyptus wood as excellent for their purposes. By-products were listed, with conjectures as to profit:

[241]

some dozen medicinal and cosmetic products made from the distillation of the oil and resin (one Santa Monica firm distilled nine tons of eucalyptol a year); souvenirs such as pipe bowls and canes made from the highly polished wood; tannin, in vigorous use for tanning leather; a superior grade of charcoal; paper veneer; paper pulp; bee nectar; paving blocks.

For several years, tree planting became a commercial obsession. The Santa Fe Railroad planted a giant grove at what is now Rancho Santa Fe, and put in thousands of trees along their right-of-ways so that railroad ties could be cut at the spot needed. Furniture manufacturers bought land in California and planted it heavily. The Pullman Company planned to finish the interiors of their cars with the beautiful grain of the eucalyptus, and planted accordingly. Jack London planted 100,000 trees on the slope of Sonoma Mountain. Forty square miles of trees were set out south of Pismo Beach, between Highway 101 and the beach. Good agricultural land was ripped up for the planting of trees, which promised to be a more profitable crop than grain or beans. A coal mining company planted a grove on good land in Compton, expecting to produce strong timbers for shoring up the mine shafts.

Meanwhile, owners of some of the mature groves started to take their timber to market. The first difficulties they encountered seemed trivial and easy to overcome. The trees had to be sawed immediately after cutting, or the wood became too hard to work. Perhaps the wood was cut at the wrong time of year—would it be easier to work if it was cut while the sap was flowing, or while the sap was not flowing? And should the lumber be cured in the sun, or in a kiln? Should the kiln use dry heat or steam heat? Everyone worked valiantly to solve these "trivial" problems, but little by little it became painfully obvious that the problems were not trivial. Whenever cut, or however cured, the lumber was not satisfactory. It warped, twisted, checked, and even opened into huge cracks. A Nevada railroad reported that its railroad ties were perfect in every particular but one—not enough solid wood could be found between cracks for the insertion of bolts.

What was the difference between the Australian eucalyptus

that had long been successful in the hardwood market, and the California eucalyptus of the same species? Remembering the wide limits of variation of a given species under different growing conditions, there could be a dozen answers. Possibly the superiority of the Australian trees was just a matter of age, but the California planters could not wait until their trees were a hundred years old to see if their timber had improved.

Sadly, the lumber mills shut down and the furniture factories moved back East. The planters counted their losses and figured how much they could salvage by cutting down entire groves for firewood. The pharmacologists withdrew their endorsement of eucalyptol as a valuable drug, and the cold cream, cough drop, and liniment factories closed. Only a few products retained the eucalyptol ingredient. Orchardists removed the eucalypts from their lines of fruit trees, because the surface roots of the shade tree stole water from the fruit. City maintenance crews cut down eucalyptus trees because their roots would go as far as a hundred feet in search of water, breaking water pipes and cisterns. As they grew tall, the shallow-rooted trees were apt to blow over on the city streets and their brittle branches sometimes dropped on pedestrians. The blue gum became anathema to subdividers, who began to specify in their deeds that no blue gum could ever be planted on any lot in the subdivision. Nurserymen still had eucalyptus seedlings for sale, but, rather than blue gum, they were now smaller varieties, designed for ornamentation and for shelter from wind and sun. In preference even to these, the nurserymen recommended the new favorites, jacaranda and magnolia, which would take up less room in a land where there was no longer room to spare.

The crusade had come full cycle, back to its modest beginning in the home garden where one tree was enough. But in the forty years since Ellwood Cooper sounded the clarion call, the crusade had clothed a major portion of California with forest, relieving the monotony of the bare hillsides and uncultivated wastes. The great trees rose tall and stately on every hand. What matter if individual dreams of profit were disappointed? The State has been beautified, and that was the beginning dream of the crusade.

[243]

18

DON BENITO'S PATHWAY:
THE STORY OF THE MT. WILSON TRAIL

John W. Robinson

One of the premier attractions of the San Gabriel Mountains, particularly if one is a hiker, is the old Mt. Wilson Trail from Sierra Madre. Beginning near the junction of Mira Monte Avenue and Mount Wilson Trail Drive in Sierra Madre, the trail ascends the chaparral-coated west slope of Little Santa Anita Canyon to Orchard Camp, located in a sylvan glen near the head of the canyon, then switchbacks steeply up to the southeast face of Mt. Harvard to a junction with the old Mt. Wilson Toll Road. The hiker then ascends the latter to the summit of Mt. Wilson, a total distance of eight miles from Sierra Madre. Nowadays, on clear winter and spring weekends when fire closure is not in effect, the famous old footpath feels the tread of hundreds of walkers. In fact the trail is so popular today that the city of Sierra Madre has erected numerous signs directing would-be hikers to the trailhead.

The trail dates back to the days before the white man entered California. Indian peoples of Shoshonean linguistic stock, called Gabrielinos by recent anthropologists because of their later association with Mission San Gabriel, blazed the first known footpath up Little Santa Anita Canyon, over Mt. Wilson, and down into the West Fork of the San Gabriel River. Although their homes were generally below the mountains, these peoples depended heavily on the San Gabriel Mountains for food, water, materials, and to trade with other peoples across the range.

With the coming of the Spaniards and the Mexican Californios, the Gabrielinos were incorporated into the mission community and the trail evidently fell into decay. At least that was its condition when Benjamin Wilson decided to utilize the old footpath to reach the mountain peak later named in his honor.

Benjamin Davis Wilson, proprietor of the Lake Vineyard Ranch, needed lumber for his fences and wine barrels. The peak on the northern skyline, above the green-carpeted ridges in the foreground, possessed plentiful stands of sugar pine and incense cedar, so he had been told. To get this timber Wilson, in the spring of 1864, set his Mexican and Indian help to revamping the old Indian trail up Little Santa Anita Canyon.

Wilson, born 1811 in Tennessee, was a wide-ranging fur trapper and trader when he arrived in California in 1841, intent upon continuing to China. He never went on. Instead he bought some land near Riverside and tried his hand at cattle ranching. In 1844 he married Ramona Yorba, member of a prominent Californio family. Two years later, during the Mexican War, he joined up with the "gringos," was captured, and spent the remainder of the conflict as a prisoner. After the war he entered business in Los Angeles, became involved in local politics, and was elected mayor of the little pueblo in 1851. In 1854 he bought the 128-acre Rancho La Huerta del Cuati, where present-day San Marino stands, and renamed it Lake Vineyard. Here Don Benito, as he was known to his many Spanish-speaking friends, lived out the rest of his years until his death in 1878.

By April 1864 Don Benito's trail had reached a wooded glen in upper Little Santa Anita Canyon, about half way up the peak. Here Wilson built his "Halfway House"—a small three-room cabin, stable, blacksmith shop and chicken house—a well-supplied construction camp for the steep work ahead.

One clear April day Don Benito and William McKee, the Wilson children's tutor, decided to go on to the summit without benefit of trail. With horses, food and camping gear, they scrambled all afternoon up unstable slopes and through thorny chaparral. Just before sunset they reached the stands of big cone spruce near the top. They looked down over an inspiring panorama. Far below sprawled the green ranchos of the San Gabriel Valley; beyond, the small towns of the Los Angeles basin; on the horizon, floating in a crimson and gold carpet of the sinking sun, the glimmering Pacific. They followed bear tracks over to a bubbling spring just west of the summit. McKee reminisced years later, "I thought then, and do still, that that water was the best I ever tasted in my life. We camped there that night. Oh, how beautiful . . . I shall always remember it as one of the most pleasant trips I ever had with Mr. Wilson; and we had many."

Next morning they discovered the crumbling remains of two log cabins, evidence that someone had preceded them to the mountaintop. McKee described the relics: "They were two parallelograms, well marked by a pile of what appeared to be ashes. Removing the ashes, we found the lower logs of the cabins not decayed. Americans must have built them. Mr. Wilson said so. Michael White, who came to San Gabriel in 1825, knew nothing of them." The identity of these original Mt. Wilson pioneers remains a mystery. Pasadena historian Hiram Reed speculated that they were horsethieves. During the middle decades of the nineteenth century, horse stealing was of epidemic proportions in southern California.

Work continued on the trail, tougher now as it switchbacked up the precipitous upper slopes of the mountain. By late summer the crude but passable pathway was completed. Wilson then built a small log cabin near the summit and commenced logging the rich stands of pine and cedar. Several weeks later his stepson, Edward S. Hereford, brought down the first pack train toting lumber.

The timber on Wilson's Peak, as the mountain became known, evidently didn't suit Benjamin Wilson, for within a few weeks he abandoned the venture. But Wilson's trail remained for many years the only pathway to the mountaintop from the south.

A few years later after Wilson gave up his mountain timber enterprise, his halfway house in Little Santa Anita Canyon was occupied by George Islip. Islip planted a small grove of cherry,

*Benjamin D. Wilson's old halfway house was being used as
a store and refreshment stand, along with tourist accommodations,
under the name Orchard Camp in 1907.*
Courtesy of Huntington Library.

apple, pear and plum trees just above the house. With the maturity of these trees, the place became known as Orchard Camp, and by this name it has been known ever since. Islip also kept bees and made wood shingles for a meagre living. Several years later Islip was joined by George Aiken, and the two of them made Orchard Camp a busy place. Fruit from their orchard was sold to travelers enroute to the mountaintop. The honey and shingles they produced were transported by burro down to the valley to sell. Sometime before 1880 the two colorful mountaineers left Orchard Camp, and for a number of years the place was unoccupied, a favorite overnight camping spot for Mt. Wilson travelers.

As the valley and foothill towns grew, Wilson's Peak became a favorite target of energetic hikers and horsemen. Some holiday weekends in the 1880s saw as many as seventy persons camping on the summit or at the small spring just below the top.

Jennie Hollingsworth Giddings, pioneer Pasadena settler,

described a trip up the trail she made with some neighbors in 1880:

> Our trail was not a tourist trail. . . . It was strictly a commercial trail as far as construction was concerned. At the beginning it was very steep and dusty.
>
> The sun was warm and we were not too comfortable. But when the shadows lengthened and we gained altitude our spirits rose correspondingly.
>
> We reached Half Way House about six o'clock. This was a free-for-all establishment consisting of one room. Two bunks furnished one end and a cook stove filled a corner at the other end. Nearby was a blacksmith shop which had been useful, no doubt, to the packers of the Wilson pack-mule trains. An apple orchard was still holding forth against time and the elements. . . .
>
> The sound of Eugene's good axe cutting firewood broke the stillness of the early morning . . . Someone had the bright idea of baked apples for breakfast and stoked the old stove for their baking. I remember that we ate by candlelight. All of us were young and eager to gain the mountain top.
>
> The trail which we took for this early morning start was a path through slopes and vales of bosky beauty. In those days the mountains were not scarred with fire-breaks nor spotted with resorts. Along the way our trail narrowed as it led into a slide of loose decomposed granite. Here the trail zigzagged several times in mule-ladder fashion and the horses set their feet down with caution. . . .
>
> Beyond this shaly portion the trail curved around huge mountain shoulders crossing steep escarpments where we gazed down thousands of feet into the depths of Eaton Canyon . . . About noon we reached the top.

The Giddings party spent the night in Wilson's crude log cabin, described as having "a roof of shakes, a dirt floor, no windows, no bunks, no stove." Women making the mountain trip usually slept inside the cabin while men camped outside. Occasionally the mountaintop campers were visited by bears and awoke in the morning to find their food gone.

In those days it was customary for those making the trip to build a huge bonfire after sunset on Signal Point, a south-facing prominence overlooking the valley, to let friends below know they had arrived without mishap. Miss Giddings described such an event on her 1880 trip.

[249]

At evening we retraced our footsteps and went up on the point to build our signal fire, as this was the custom used by people who made the trip in those days. I knew that my mother and father and others would be watching for the all-safe signal. Not knowing how many nights we would stay on the mountain we had agreed to light one signal fire on the first night in camp and two fires on the night before our return to the foot of the trail. After the signal fire died down we returned to our cabin and built a good log fire out in front where we relaxed and told stories.

In 1886 a Los Angeles *Times* correspondent made the trip up Wilson's trail and after describing his experience, made the prophetic observation: "Perhaps some shrewd Yankee may come along who will put money in his purse by improving the trail, establishing a house of entertainment at the summit, and providing trains of burros and other facilities for tourists." How true this would become in a few years!

In August and September 1886 hordes of prospectors rushed up the trail during a brief flurry of gold excitement on the mountaintop. Two prospectors named Frank Dunham and Ed Pettibone discovered a promising quartz ledge near the summit and the rush was on! The Los Angeles *Times*, August 31, 1886, reported, "A large number of people from various parts of the state are flocking up to Wilson's peak, and if the discoveries continue, Pasadena will be converted into a mining camp." Three weeks later, the *Times*, on September 18, exclaimed," . . . the entire summit is already staked . . . the mountains are full of men from Switzer's trail to the headwaters of the San Gabriel, . . . all anxiously looking for the gold that glitters."

Then, just a suddenly, it was all over. Gold was not on Wilson's Peak in paying quantities. The miners drifted to more profitable diggings elsewhere, and the Mt. Wilson Trail returned to its usual fare of weekend hikers and horsemen.

But not for long was the trail neglected. In January 1889 Dr. William H. Pickering, director of the Harvard University Observatory in Cambridge, Massachusetts, arrived in Pasadena intent upon testing atmospheric conditions on Mt. Wilson. Harvard was considering the placement of a telescope on the summit. Along with telescope-maker Alvan Clark, Benjamin Eaton and other Pasadena civic leaders, Pickering journeyed up the trail on horseback, observed the heavens at night, and upon his descent pronounced that "the climate here is far superior to the East and for that matter to any other portion of the world. . . . I consider this the point of all others to place the finest and largest telescope in the world."

Upon returning to Harvard University, Pickering announced that a thirteen-inch photographic telescope would be shipped west to be installed on Wilson's Peak. Judge Benjamin Eaton, pledged financial aid by the Pasadena Board of Trade, agreed to improve the Wilson Trail in order to transport the instrument to the summit.

On February 20, 1889, the thirteen-inch telescope arrived at the railway station on Baldwin's ranch and was transported to the foot of the trail. It was readily evident that an error had been made as to the weight of the instrument. Instead of a supposed 1,600 pounds, it scaled in at 3,700 pounds—in Eaton's words, an embarrassing thing to take up a mountain trail."

Eaton set to work without delay. The first step was to improve the trail, smoothing the rough stretches and widening narrow spots. Then the telescope was started on its tedious, eight-mile journey up the mountain. The instrument was packed in a dozen packages, the heaviest one being the base and the longest the sixteen-foot telescope tube. To move the heavier part, a small "dolly" was specially constructed, consisting of a platform with a wheel twenty-four inches wide secured under the center, and a six-inch pivoted bandwheel in the rear.

Six men and two horses constituted the working crew. It was slow, painstaking work. The trail was narrow and steep, with many switchbacks. When the path was wide enough, both horses were used to pull the dolly. More often, the work was done by one horse or by manpower using block and tackle. Hiram Reed explained how the telescope was hauled up some of the more precipitous places on the trail: "At some points where there was a sharp angle in the trail, they had to pick and drill and blast out rock to widen it before they could make the turn safely; and at some places where there were a series of sharp angles constituting a zig-zag traverse, they had to drill into the mountain side for a secure anchorage at the upper lap of the traverse, and then with heavy ropes and pulleys hoist the car and its load bodily up the steep declivity."

The trip went slowly but without incident until the instrument was within two miles of the summit. Then a sudden storm left a foot of snow on the mountain. The crew abandoned the packages and beat a hasty retreat to Halfway House. Here they waited a week for the snow to melt sufficiently to continue the work.

Success crowned the difficult effort. The Pasadena *Star* of April 3, 1889, reported: "A big blaze on the summit of Mt. Wilson last night announced that Judge Eaton had succeeded in placing all the boxes containing the Harvard telescope on the spot where the observatory is to be built." It had taken slightly more than a month. In May Harvard astronomers commenced their heavenly work.

Even before the astronomers started their star-gazing, two enterprising entrepreneurs moved quickly to capitalize on the publicity surrounding the scientific venture. Peter Steil, a young Pasadena restaurateur, started a tent camp along the trail in the saddle between Mt. Wilson and Mt. Harvard, within easy walking distance of the observatory. He initially called it. "The Eyrie," but it soon came to be known simply as Steil's Camp. For three dollars a tourist was provided with round-trip transportation by burro, overnight lodging and meals.

Almost at once Steil's Camp became a popular trail resort. During the summer of 1890, an estimated 1,000 persons enjoyed the hospitality of the camp.

Steil's success encouraged A. G. Strain, who had previously homesteaded several acres on the north side of the mountain, to open his own camp. But not before the farcical, bloodless "Mt. Wilson War" was settled. Strain became convinced that others were infringing on his rights. As a result he erected a fence across the trail, blocking access to the mountain-top. Steil ripped down the fence, and "an altercation ensued that augured a great deal of bad blood." The Pasadena *Star*, June 18, 1890, under a headline "War on the Peak," reported the results of the battle: "No blood was shed, but tents were torn down and other hostile demonstrations indulged in that bordered close upon open warfare." A few days later, Strain brought suit against Steil.

The *Star*, March 11, 1891, announced the court decision, a victory for Steil:

> In the case of A. G. Strain against Peter Steil, judgment was yesterday rendered denying the application of plaintiff for an injunction and awarding him damages in the sum of $1. This is the case that grew out of the attempt of Strain to bar Steil from crossing his land on Mt. Wilson. Peter broke down Strain's gate in order to take a party over the trail leading past the observatory, and the irate owner of the gate claimed he was trespassing on his land and then brought this suit for $100 damages and asked for an injunction restraining the defendant from further trespass. The $1 damages awarded pays for the gate probably, but in denying Mr. Strain's application for an injunction the court holds that the trail is a public highway, and cannot be closed against travel.

This settled the issue, although huffy feelings continued between the mountain landowners for some time.

Strain then erected his own tourist camp in a grove of sugar pines near Benjamin Wilson's old spring, several hundred yards northwest of the summit. He did a flourishing business right from the first. It seemed that mountaintop camping was a popular pastime among valley residents.

Early in 1891 Steil sold out to Clarence S. Martin, who built a frame dining room and added sufficient tents to accommodate forty persons. Strain then expanded his facilities to handle upwards of sixty visitors. Almost every summer weekend during the 1890s, tourists on foot, burro-back and horseback ascended the Mt. Wilson Trail to the two popular camps.

Down at the head of Little Santa Anita Canyon, Don Benito's old Halfway House, now known as Orchard Camp, was turned into a trail resort by James McNally. Small guest cabins were erected alongside the stream, and tents were added to handle the overflow. By the late 1890s Orchard Camp was a flourishing weekend hostelry, often crowded with relaxing hikers and campers. For those who cared not to make the four-mile uphill trudge from Sierra Madre, burros were offered, $1.00 one way, $1.50 round trip. The camp rate for two was

$5.00 per week, which included "one tent, double bed and bedding, towels, furniture, stove, dishes and cooking outfit for two people."

In July 1891 the Mt. Wilson Trail from Sierra Madre lost its status as the sole thoroughfare to the summit. In that month the newly-formed Mt. Wilson Toll Road Company opened its toll trail from the mouth of Eaton Canyon (above Altadena) to the top, 25¢ round-trip for hikers and 50¢ for riders. Since the new trail was more gently graded and wider, it rapidly gained popularity at the expense of the "old" Mt. Wilson Trail. For about a decade and a half, the old Mt. Wilson Trail went through a period of decline, as many hikers and riders utilized the new trail from Eaton Canyon to reach the summit.

In 1905 William M. Sturtevant, who operated the Mt. Wilson Stables at the foot of the trail in Sierra Madre, packed all the material and equipment for the first Mt. Wilson Hotel up the old Mt. Wilson Trail. Sturtevant's horses, mules and burros were long a familiar sight along the trail, lugging equipment and supplies not only for the new hotel, but also for the new Carnegie Observatory that was established on Mt. Wilson in 1904.

Mention needs to be made of these many pack and saddle animals who played such a key role in supplying the observatory and hotel during the years before the completion of the Mt. Wilson Toll Road in 1907. These sure-footed beasts of burden carried almost everything imaginable up the mountain—lumber, cement, structural steel, and even bathtubs—and they usually arrived with their cargo intact. The limits set by such methods of transportation necessarily affected every feature of the design of the early buildings on the mountaintop. It is of interest to note that no single structural part of the Snow Telescope (first of the Carnegie Institution telescopes on Mt. Wilson, completed in 1906) building exceeded eight feet in length. The speed of transportation by pack animal was limited too. Trailwise burros knew exactly how fast they wished to move, and no amount of mule-skinners' prodding could hasten their pace. Books could be written about the personal characteristics of these sagacious animals and the infinite variety of their individual behavior. One wise old mule would deliberately expand his

*A mule train wends its way up the Mt. Wilson Trail. The
photograph was taken by B.D. Jackson around 1905.*
Courtesy of Huntington Library.

chest when the load was strapped on his back; then, at some
awkward point on the trail, the package would slip off, allowing
the unburdened animal to complete the journey in comfort. It
took several such episodes to enlighten the frustrated packer as
to what was happening. Another pack animal possessed an almost irresistible desire to roll over, frequently selecting a stream
bed for this purpose. A third beast, used primarily for carrying
passengers up the mountain, would groan painfully when the
grade became steep, but once the rider dismounted, he would
be fortunate to overtake his mule within several miles.

There were a few misfortunes. In 1907, after a particularly
heavy snowstorm that completely obliterated the upper section
of the trail, a loaded mule stumbled and rolled over and over far
down the mountainside, finally coming to rest in the bed of a
canyon. The deep snow prevented injury to the animal, but

[255]

there was no possible way to retrieve him until the snow had melted considerably. So for some weeks the positions of the mule and the driver were reversed, the driver packing hay on his back to feed the mule, who apparently enjoyed the vacation. The language of the driver in describing the situation was notable even among the remarks of his highly profane fellows.

In 1906 the Pacific Electric Railway extended its trolley service to Sierra Madre, reaching to within a mile of the trailhead. Once again the old Mt. Wilson Trail vibrated under the tramp of many boots and the pounding of hoofs every fair-weather weekend. This was in the midst of the great hiking era. Every Saturday morning, hundreds would disembark from the Big Red Cars at line's end, knapsacks slung over their shoulders, and ramble up the trail—some to travel only as far as Orchard Camp, some to continue on to Martin's Camp in the Harvard-Wilson saddle, and the hardiest to scramble all the way to Mt. Wilson's summit. Sunday afternoon, weary and footsore, the hikers would emerge from the mountains to find the big PE cars waiting, ready for the homeward journey. The peak year was 1911, when an estimated 40,000 persons passed through Orchard Camp.

Charles W. Jones, first mayor of Sierra Madre, related his memory of that period.

> After the coming of the electric line the popularity of the Mt. Wilson Trail grew by leaps and bounds, which continued until the automobile became too common for using shanks' mare. It was estimated, about the years 1908-15, there was an average of 200 hikers per day who began the long climb to Mt. Wilson. In 1909 after an exceptional fall of snow on Mt. Wilson, one Sunday 2,500 people were on the trail at one time. Saturday night trains of two to six cars filled with riotous youth would unload at Mt. Trail Avenue and begin their shouting, shooting off pistols and in every way creating a disturbance of Sierra Madre's peace and quiet. Finally the city marshall and his deputies had to meet these crowds and escort them through the streets to the trails, where their noises no longer could be heard.

Orchard Camp was a thriving trail resort during this period. James McNally was the congenial host until 1912, when he sold out to Foster W. Huston. Huston enlarged the camp, adding more tent houses, a spacious pavilion for Saturday night dances, and even a croquet court.

Orchard Camp was not the only resort along the Mt. Wilson Trail. In another streamside nook, about halfway between Sierra Madre and Orchard Camp, was the Quarterway House, also known as The Old Trading Post. The spot was homesteaded by Emile Deutsch, Belgium-born cigar maker, in 1888. Around 1912 Deutsch's small cabin was converted into a trailside refreshment stand, catering to tired and perspiring hikers.

For those who wished to savor the delights of Little Santa Anita Canyon without traveling by foot or burro-back, there was Carter's Camp, right at the canyon mouth. Established by the Carter brothers of Sierra Madre in 1906, the resort grew into a tree-shaded village of five cottages and thirty-seven tent houses; for several years the Carters did a flourishing business. In 1913 the property was sold, subdivided and renamed Sierra Madre Canyon Park.

Perhaps the most interesting chapter in the long saga of the Mt. Wilson Trail was the annual Sierra Madre-to-Mt. Wilson footrace, held during the years 1908 through 1913, and intermittently after that. The strenuous contest was the idea of Richard K. Fox, publisher of the *Police Gazette,* and was managed the first three years by his son Charles Fox of Sierra Madre. In 1911 it came under the sponsorship of the Sierra Madre Board of Trade. The race drew contestants from throughout the Southwest. Spectators lined the eight-mile course all the way from Sierra Madre to the summit, cheering on the participants in this gruelling, lung-bursting competition. First prize was a gold medal, valued at $150, and a gold watch. All who finished received a gold button. The winner in 1908 was Joseph King of San Francisco's Irish-American Club, who ran the uphill course in 1 hour, 25 minutes and 30 seconds. In 1912 Paul Westerlund of San Francisco broke King's record in a phenomenal 1 hour, 21 minutes and 56 seconds, a time that many thought would never be bettered. But the following year two men bettered Westerlund's time. The winner was Albert Ray, an Indian from the Sherman Institute of Riverside, in 1 hour, 19 minutes and 54 seconds, followed closely by W.G. Brewster of Pomona College in 1 hour, 21 minutes and 30 seconds. The Pasadena *Star*, April 30, 1913, in a front-page story, reported the race:

> The race was a close one between Brewster and Ray over almost the entire course. The fact that the white man was not familiar with the trail handicapped him, for he did not save himself where he should have done so, and was not prepared to take the fullest advantage of difficult conditions. He hung closely to the Indian, however, up to the last mile, when he began to lag behind. . . . The runners were well taken care of at the top by manager Ross of the Mt. Wilson Hotel.

The race was revived briefly in 1930, 1939, 1940 and in recent years.

Orchard Camp and the Mt. Wilson Trail reached their zenith of popularity about 1924. After that a series of happenings caused the resort and the famous footpath to lose their mass appeal. The first misfortune was the outbreak of hoof and mouth disease in the San Gabriels during the early months of 1924. To prevent the spread of the disease, the Los Angeles County Health Department prohibited all people and animals from entering the mountains. Orchard Camp and other mountain resorts had just stocked up with supplies, many of them perishable, in anticipation of Easter week; thus the travel ban was a serious financial blow. Unfortunately this was only the beginning. No sooner was the quarantine lifted, in August 1924, than one of the most disastrous fires in the history of the San Gabriels broke out near San Gabriel Canyon and burned all the way across the range. Orchard Camp was spared, but the hillsides above were charred.

In the early 1930s came the depression, and most people had neither the time nor the money to engage in such peripheral activities as mountain hiking. The great destructive flood of March 1938 wiped out large sections of trail and damaged trail resorts. New high-gear highways provided rapid access to mountain regions formerly reached only by hours of hiking. Perhaps most important was the distraction of World War II. Trails that once vibrated with the busy tramp of boots and the merry singing of hikers became almost deserted. One by one, the trail resorts succumbed. As one old-timer sadly reflected,

"Only people who hike for the love of hiking use these trails now.

Orchard Camp continued to operate as a trail resort throughout the 1930s, managed by M.A. DeTemple. But these were trying years, and the camp was a marginal success at best. The camp reached its end as a resort in February 1940, when the city of Sierra Madre purchased 760 acres in Little Santa Anita Canyon including half interest in Orchard Camp, for the purpose of utilizing the canyon's water resources. Herbert and Harriet Martin, last managers of the camp, abandoned it, and for several years the buildings lay empty. In 1945 the Forest Service and the city of Sierra Madre, which now owned the property, removed the buildings because they were considered a fire hazard.

The Mt. Wilson Trail, although little used, remained in passable condition until 1953. In that year heavy winter rains, following a particularly destructive forest fire, washed away large sections of the trail. "Unsafe to Travel" signs were posted at the top and bottom of the historic pathway. Because of the beauty of the area, many persons still ventured into the canyon and some had to be rescued. The Forest Service considered removing the trail from their maps.

If it were not for the concern and efforts of a handful of Sierra Madre residents who did not want this original Mt. Wilson trail to become just a bygone memory, there would be no passable trail through Little Santa Anita Canyon today. Leader of the trail restoration project was Bill Wark. With his wife and son and fellow Sierra Madre residents Barney Decker and Ambrose Zaro, Wark spent many weekends with shovel and pick making the old footpath passable again. Some weekends they were assisted by the Sierra Madre Search and Rescue Team and church youth groups. With the completion of the restoration project in 1960, the Angeles National Forest district ranger handed Wark the "Unsafe to Travel" signs, and the Little Santa Anita Canyon trail to Mt. Wilson regained its place among the major pathways of the San Gabriels.

Even before the restoration was completed, the Sierra Madre Historical Society, in collaboration with the Sierra

Madre Search and Rescue Team, designed a bronze plaque to commemorate the trail. This Mount Wilson Trail Monument, placed in a granite boulder from Little Santa Anita Canyon, was dedicated in an impressive ceremony presided over by Charles W. Jones, Sierra Madre's first mayor, on June 28, 1959. Today the monument stands for all to see at the corner of Mira Monte Avenue and Mount Wilson Trail Drive.

Today, most of the Mt. Wilson Trail lies within the Sierra Madre Historical Wilderness Area, established by the Sierra Madre City Council on land owned by the city on January 24, 1967. The trail is maintained in good condition by volunteer citizen efforts. Orchard Camp, only the stone foundations of the old resort remaining, is now a shady picnic area alongside the singing creek. Every weekend during seasons of low fire danger, hundreds of hikers stroll the footpath, pausing often to enjoy the sylvan delights of the canyon. Little Santa Anita Canyon and its famous trail should stay this way as long as the citizens of Sierra Madre and other nearby communities care about their mountains.

19

INFLUENCE OF THE RAILROADS IN THE DEVELOPMENT OF LOS ANGELES HARBOR

Franklyn Hoyt

For more than a century the main seaport for Los Angeles had been the miserable harbor at San Pedro. When Dana visited San Pedro Bay in 1835 he complained that it was the worst harbor he had seen, "exposed to every wind that could blow, except the northerly." But it was the only port for eighty miles and for this reason handled a large amount of shipping and was the leading hide port on the coast.

During the Spanish and Mexican period transportation from Los Angeles to the harbor was by mule and ox-cart. After the American conquest some large freight wagons began to be used, but even in the 1860s a large amount of freight was still carried by the creaking carts. Agitation for a railroad between Los Angeles and San Pedro was begun by the newspapers in 1861, and eight years later the Los Angeles and San Pedro Railroad was completed.

In 1873 the Southern Pacific Railroad acquired this pioneer Southern California railway as a reward for extending its line south to Los Angeles and building a branch to Anaheim. Not only did the Southern Pacific own the railroad to the harbor, it also owned the pier and the lighters which carried cargo to the waiting ships. Freight rates were cheaper than before the advent of the railroad, but it still cost a farmer $3.00 per ton to ship his wine from the Los Angeles depot to the waiting ship. Grocers were charged $5.00 per ton to get their merchandise from Wilmington to Los Angeles; lumber dealers added $7.00 to the price of every thousand feet of Oregon lumber to pay the freight from Wilmington.

This monopoly was threatened briefly in December 1875, when the Los Angeles and Independence Railroad completed a line from Los Angeles to a deep-water pier at Santa Monica. But the Southern Pacific was quick to meet the challenge, and freight rates between Los Angeles and San Pedro were cut as much as eighty percent. This competition, coupled with the depression which had just reached Southern California, proved too much for the Los Angeles and Independence Railroad.

In 1877 Senator John P. Jones gave up the fight and sold his railroad to the Southern Pacific for an estimated $195,000. The Southern Pacific had purchased what Colton called "a bad egg at best," but the Big Four once more controlled the port facilities of Los Angeles.

The fine wharf at Santa Monica, which reached deep water without the use of lighters, was declared unsafe by Southern Pacific engineers and was demolished. Once more it was necessary for all shipments to be made through Wilmington, although it is to the credit of the Southern Pacific that it did not take advantage of its monopoly to restore the high freight rates which had existed before 1875.

For nearly a decade control of Los Angeles' port facilities by the Southern Pacific went unchallenged. Then in 1883 the Atlantic and Pacific Railroad reached Needles and began making plans to build a line to some deep-water port in Southern California. This forced the Southern Pacific to compromise with its enemy; an agreement was reached which allowed the Southern Pacific to build a line from Mojave to Needles. The Atlantic and Pacific was permitted to use Southern Pacific tracks into Southern California.

The Atlantic and Pacific had little choice in the matter, since the powerful Southern Pacific lobby had been able to get a provision inserted in the Atlantic and Pacific charter allowing the Southern Pacific Railroad to connect with the Atlantic and

Pacific "at such point, near the boundary line of the State of California, as they shall deem most suitable for a railroad line to San Francisco."

An uneasy truce continued until August 1884, when the Southern Pacific agreed to sell the line between Mojave and Needles to the Santa Fe Railroad, successor of the Atlantic and Pacific. President Strong of the Santa Fe was able to persuade the Southern Pacific to sell by threatening to parallel the Southern Pacific line to San Francisco. At this time the Santa Fe was in no financial condition to engage the Big Four in a struggle to the death, but the Southern Pacific was not certain of this and decided not to call the Santa Fe's bluff.

The California Southern Railroad, a subsidiary of the Santa Fe which had been built between San Diego and San Bernardino in 1883, was quickly pushed through Cajon Pass to Barstow on the Mojave-Needles line. At last the Santa Fe could run trains over its own rails to salt water, and the first passenger train from the East reached San Diego the middle of November 1885.

San Diego had a wonderful harbor, but it was more than a hundred miles south of the center of population and never gave Wilmington any real competition. The Santa Fe was quick to realize this, and soon after the line was opened to San Diego, plans were made to build a railway through Los Angeles to some nearby seaport.

Toward the end of May 1887, an extension was completed from San Bernardino to Duarte, and at the same time purchase of the San Gabriel Valley Railroad was announced. The first Santa Fe train steamed into Los Angeles over its own tracks one month later, but the Santa Fe Railroad still did not have a seaport capable of competing with the Southern Pacific monopoly at Wilmington.

In the fall of 1886, the Santa Fe had started work on a railway from Los Angeles to Port Ballona, now called Playa del Rey, and this line was opened September 23, 1887. The Santa Fe tried hard to make a port at Ballona by dredging a canal eighty-eight yards long from the ocean to a saltwater lagoon called Lake Ballona, but it was a dismal failure.

[263]

The following April the Santa Fe tried again by building a branch from Inglewood to Redondo Beach, where a $100,000 iron pier was being constructed by a real estate promotion company. Redondo Beach was hardly more than an open roadstead which offered little protection from winter storms. Its chief advantage was a submarine canyon which brought deep water close to shore.

In the summer of 1890, a second railroad began operating between Los Angeles and Redondo. This was the narrow gauge Redondo Railroad, built by the Redondo Beach Company which was promoting real estate developments at Inglewood and Redondo Beach. By 1891 the Port of Redondo was becoming a threat to Wilmington, and it was not uncommon for over a million board feet of lumber to be unloaded at the Redondo pier during a single week.

Some writers have overestimated the importance of Redondo as a seaport. Charles D. Willard says that "over sixty per cent of all the water traffic in and out of Los Angeles, if coal and lumber were excluded, was passing by way of Redondo." Certainly Redondo managed to lure considerable shipping away from its rival, but Wilmington continued to handle twice as much freight as Port Redondo. During 1891, for example, 54 million feet of lumber was unloaded at Wilmington and 21 million at Redondo. Ships loading or unloading were in about the same ratio: in 1889 Redondo was visited by 101 ships, while 588 called at Wilmington; in 1890, 211 unloaded at Redondo and 492 at Wilmington; in 1891 there were 255 at Redondo, and 585 at Wilmington.

Competition from San Diego and the new port of Redondo Beach caused the Southern Pacific some concern, but its monopoly was not broken until the completion of the Los Angeles Terminal Railroad in 1891. The Terminal Railroad, which was the result of a merger of several bankrupt railways, ran from Altadena, through Pasadena and Los Angeles to Long Beach, where it turned west along the bay to Rattlesnake Island. Warehouses and a wharf were built on Rattlesnake Island, as Terminal Island was then called, and the new railroad was ready to challenge the supremacy held by the Southern Pacific.

[264]

*A busy day at San Pedro Harbor in the 1880s. Dead Man's
Island and a breakwater are in the background.*
Courtesy of Los Angeles County Museum of Natural History.

Since 1888 Los Angeles had been fighting to get Congress to vote money for improvement of the harbor at San Pedro. The Los Angeles Chamber of Commerce, which was founded in that year, was one of the leaders in this struggle for a deep-water harbor. One of the Chamber's favorite methods was to fasten upon some unsuspecting senator or representative who happened to be visiting Los Angeles and escort him to San Pedro, accompanied by a group of enthusiastic Angelenos. The Southern Pacific was a strong supporter of harbor improvement, and Senator Leland Stanford usually accompanied these parties to San Pedro.

In the fall of 1889, the Senate Committee on Commerce was touring the country, inspecting harbor projects which the committee had under consideration. The committee reached Los Angeles on October 24, and was taken to the harbor in a special train which had been chartered by the Los Angeles Chamber of Commerce. As the party climbed a bluff behind Timm's Point, the chairman of the Committee on Commerce, Senator Frye of Maine, asked "what do you want with a harbor here anyhow? I don't see any ships."

One of the Chamber of Commerce officials explained that at this season of the year conditions were not very favorable for shipping at San Pedro. Senator Frye then grumbled that it would cost $5,000,000 to improve the harbor, and "you can buy all of California for that." Senator Stanford, president of Southern Pacific Railroad said, "Don't say that to these Los Angeles fellows," and whisked him off for a quick tour of Pasadena and Los Angeles.

During the summer of 1890, largely through the efforts of Senator Stanford, $5,000 was appropriated for the purpose of surveying possible harbor sites near Los Angeles. The Secretary of War was authorized to appoint three army officers "to examine the Pacific Coast between Points Dume and Capistrano, with a view to determining the best location for a deep-water harbor."

In December 1891, the Mendell Board submitted its report. All of the possible harbors near Los Angeles were quickly dismissed except for Santa Monica and San Pedro, which were examined in detail. There would not be a great deal of difference between the cost of the two harbors—$5,700,000 for Santa Monica and $4,600,000 for San Pedro. The report recommended that the harbor be constructed at San Pedro because it would afford "better protection both from prevailing winds and from dangerous storms," and this protection would be "secured at less cost for equal development of a breakwater."

Those who had hoped that the Mendell report would settle the location of the Los Angeles harbor once and for all were to be sadly disappointed. Its effect was just the opposite. Collis P. Huntington, who had ousted Stanford as president of the Southern Pacific Railroad in April 1890, was quick to realize that if the harbor were located at Santa Monica his company would once more enjoy the favorable position that it had held for so many years at San Pedro. Since the report had stated that a harbor could be built at Santa Monica, although at slightly greater cost, Huntington decided to gamble everything on Santa Monica.

It is uncertain exactly when Huntington decided to abandon San Pedro in favor of Santa Monica, but it was probably soon after the Mendell report was released. The first formal announcement was a telegram which William Hood, chief engineer of the Southern Pacific, sent Senator Frye in February 1892. Senator Frye's committee was considering an appropriation for San Pedro in accordance with the Mendell report, and this telegram warned that the Southern Pacific had found the floor of San Pedro Harbor to be so rocky that considerable difficulty was encountered in driving piles for the construction of a new wharf. For this reason, the Southern Pacific was abandoning San Pedro and constructing a new pier at Santa Monica. Hood's telegram was so convincing that the committee quickly threw out the San Pedro appropriation.

About two miles north of Santa Monica, the Southern Pacific selected the spot for its pier and named the location Port Los Angeles. The Los Angeles and Independence Railroad was extended to the pier by means of a tunnel and cut through the steep bluff, which faces the ocean at this location. According to the report of the Board of Harbor Commissioners, made in 1896, the pier at Port Los Angeles was:

> a very thoroughly constructed timber pier, the piles being creosoted and the superstructure carefully designed . . . The tracks of the Southern Pacific railway run to the extreme end of this pier, around which is a well-arranged system of mooring buoys, so that vessels lying at the pier can be breasted off, leaving them free to rise and fall with the swell. The pier is 4,300 feet long and terminates in five and one-half fathoms of water. It is the most carefully designed and thoroughly constructed ocean pier in the California coast.

After Hood's famous telegram, Congress held up further appropriations for the harbor until another board could settle the matter "once and for all." This new board consisted of five engineering officers of the army appointed by the Secretary of War. Colonel William P. Craighill was its chairman, and for this reason it is usually called the Craighill Board.

This board was appointed in July 1892, convened at San Francisco early in September, and then traveled south to Redondo Beach. Public hearings were held in Los Angeles on September 8 and 9. Several hundred people were present at these hearings, and they were about equally divided among Redondo, Santa Monica and San Pedro. C. M. Wells, president of the Chamber of Commerce, was chairman, but his opening remarks made it plain that the Chamber of Commerce was not taking sides, but was "simply aiding these engineers in collecting their information; and that is what this meeting is for."

Doctor J. P. Widney, founder of the town of Long Beach, was one of the principal speakers for San Pedro. He said that he had visited San Pedro Harbor several times with Stanford and that for fifteen years Stanford and the Southern Pacific had backed the development of a harbor at that place. Recently the Southern Pacific had changed its position, and Widney urged the board to find out who owned the land in back of the wharf at Port Los Angeles. He did not know for certain who owned this property, but some of his friends had been trying to buy it, and "the man said it was bid in for the Southern Pacific."

In October 1892, the Craighill Board filed a lengthy report with the Secretary of War. Redondo was quickly disposed of with the statement that it would not be advisable for the government to experiment with a floating breakwater, "especially as such a shelter is not needed for the protection of life or property, but merely for the occasional convenience of navigation."

San Pedro and Santa Monica were examined in detail, the board concluding:

> that the location selected by the Board of Engineers of 1890, at the present anchorage at the westerly side of San Pedro Bay under Point Fermin, is the "more eligible location for such harbor in depth, width, and capacity to accommodate the largest ocean-going vessels and the commercial and naval necessities of the country.

When the report of the Craighill Board was printed in the Los Angeles newspapers, it stopped all controversy for a short time. Most people believed that the findings of the board should be accepted in good faith, and the Chamber of Commerce ended its neutrality and strongly backed San Pedro.

But the Southern Pacific had no intention of giving up the fight, and work continued on the wharf at Port Los Angeles. When this wharf was finished in January 1894, much of the business which had previously gone to Redondo was now deflected to Port Los Angeles, which was closer to San Francisco. Business at the new wharf never came up to the great expectations of the Southern Pacific. In September 1894, the Southern Pacific was still running five trains each day to San Pedro, but only one to Port Los Angeles.

In June 1894, the Senate Commerce Committee began holding public hearings on the question of building a breakwater at San Pedro or Santa Monica. Advocates of San Pedro first stated their case; they were followed by C. P. Huntington, who asked for an appropriation of $4,000,000 for Santa Monica. William Hood, chief engineer of the Southern Pacific Railroad, spoke next; he was followed by E. L. Corthell, "a riparian engineer of national eminence," who stated that there was:

[269]

ample width of foreshore above high water under the bluff for several tracks. The owners of this property along the shore were not willing that any one road should have the entire ownership, and therefore they sold only a fifty-foot strip to the Southern Pacific Company. The right-of-way maps and the photographs of the vicinity show plenty of room for several more tracks the entire distance.

Corthell also claimed that currents at San Pedro were from east to west, and that this would wash large quantities of sand into the harbor, requiring constant dredging. Several supporters of San Pedro refuted this charge, but it still made a most unfavorable impression on the committee.

When the Senate first began considering the question of harbor appropriations for Los Angeles, it was generally believed that an appropriation would be secured for San Pedro without much difficulty. San Pedro had been recommended by an impartial army board; it was also backed by both Senators from California. But as the hearings progressed, the influence of the Southern Pacific lobby became apparent:

Four days ago there was a decided majority in the Commerce Committee in favor of following the wishes of the two Senators from California, but since the arrival of Mr. Huntington at the capital it is now a matter of great doubt where the majority will be found . . . C. P. Huntington was seen going the rounds of the hotels today, and although it was Sunday, he made no halt in buttonholing Senators.

After Huntington had finished his work, the Commerce Committee was so evenly divided that it was impossible to reach a decision. Finally, a motion was passed deferring action until the committee could "visit the two harbors and form an opinion of their respective merits." This was the so-called "Senatorial Commission" which never materialized, because no provision was made to pay the expenses of the trip to California.

In 1896 Congress was controlled by a bloc of economy-minded Republicans, and it seemed impossible to get a large appropriation for San Pedro. For this reason, it was decided temporarily to abandon plans for developing the outer harbor and concentrate upon getting an appropriation for deepening the inner harbor. For only $400,000 it was believed that the inner basin could be dredged sufficiently to provide fourteen feet of water at low tide. Huntington's representative in Los Angeles was asked to find out what attitude the Southern Pacific would take if the Free Harbor League decided to back such an appropriation. In a few days the League was informed that while "nobody was to be quoted as actually promising anything; it was all unofficial and confidential—but the League might go right ahead; the track was clear."

Three members of the Free Harbor League were sent to Washington, and they appeared before the River and Harbor Committee of the House on February 17, 1896. They were assured by the committee that favorable action would be taken on their request for dredging the inner harbor. Huntington was present at the hearing, but had no comment to make. Senator White later told newsmen that there was no opposition to the proposal.

Proceedings of the River and Harbor Committee were secret, but toward the end of March dispatches from Washington reported that Huntington had also appeared before the committee and asked $3,000,000 for Santa Monica. When the committee reported the River and Harbor Bill a few days later, it contained two harbor appropriations: $392,725 for San Pedro and $3,098,000 for Santa Monica.

This "double appropriation scheme" thoroughly divided the people of Los Angeles. The City Council passed a resolution favoring the double appropriation, and the Republican County Committee favored any appropriations for Los Angeles County, regardless of the area favored. Two mass meetings were held on the night of April 8; those favoring San Pedro met outdoors on the east side of the Court House, while the Santa Monica advocates met in Illinois Hall. The *Herald* reported that "Captain Steere of the Southern Pacific city offices is said to have engaged the hall and paid the charge therefore by check."

So much opposition developed to the double appropriation that the River and Harbor Committee withdrew both appropriations and substituted $50,000 for dredging the inner harbor at

San Pedro. This bill was passed by the House and sent on to the Senate, where it was referred to the Committee on Commerce. The Commerce Committee, by a vote of nine to six, restored the $3,000,000 Santa Monica appropriation.

Senator White of Los Angeles proposed another commission, with the money being appropriated in advance and given to the site recommended by the commission. This "reasonable" demand was rejected by the committee, and Senator White immediately announced that he would do everything possible to defeat the "Huntington steal," and would fight the entire bill if the "appropriation for Santa Monica harbor should be admitted in the face of reports of the army engineers."

Most California newspapers agreed with the Los Angeles *Times* that the Santa Monica scheme had been "conceived in sin and brought forth in iniquity." The San Francisco *Examiner* commented sarcastically that:

> The list of the nine members of the committee who voted for the Santa Monica steal has the suggestive sound of a burglar alarm. . . . There are two or three Senators in that lot whom it might be safe to meet on a dark night with a pocketful of money, but if a marksman wanted to bring down the greatest number of rascals with the smallest supply of rocks he could dispose of his missiles to better advantage in that quarter than anywhere else in the Capital outside of a joint meeting of the Committee on Pacific Railroads.

The River and Harbor Bill, with the double appropriation still intact, reached the floor of the Senate on May 8. Five days of hot debate followed, with Senators Frye and White taking the most active part. On Friday and Saturday, May 8 and 9, Senator White spoke at great length on the advantages of San Pedro as a deep-water harbor for Southern California.

Senator Frye replied on Monday with a long speech in which he defended Santa Monica. "There is plenty of room at Santa Monica for twelve tracks, for ten more tracks," he said. "Any other railroad can get it just as easily as the Southern Pacific Company did." He then attempted to fasten the blame on the Santa Fe Railroad. "Telegrams from the Atchison, Topeka and Santa Fe Railroad have been falling here upon Senators in the last ten days as the snowflakes fall in the winter storm."

The following morning, May 12, Senator White answered Frye's charges, and then proposed an amendment which would appropriate the money in advance, leaving the final choice to another board of engineers. This amendment, as finally approved by the Senate, provided:

> For a deep-water harbor of commerce and of refuge at Port Los Angeles in Santa Monica Bay, California, or at San Pedro, in said State, the location of said harbor to be determined by an officer of the navy, an officer of the Coast and Geodetic Survey, to be detailed by the Superintendent of said survey, and three experienced civil engineers, skilled in riparian work, to be appointed by the President.

The bill also provided for an appropriation of $2,900,000 of which $50,000 was made immediately available for expenses of the engineering board and other preliminary work. Later, the bill was approved by the House and sent to President Cleveland, who promptly vetoed the entire River and Harbor Bill on the grounds that the treasury did not have sufficient money to meet such tremendous expenditures. Congress promptly passed it over his veto.

The River and Harbor Bill had been passed in June, but it was not until October that President Cleveland got around to appointing the investigating board. Members of this board were Rear Admiral John G. Walker, Augustus F. Rodgers, William H. Burr, George S. Morrison, and Richard P. Morgan. All of these appointments were received with satisfaction in Southern California except that of Richard P. Morgan. Morgan's son was employed by the Southern Pacific, and it was known that at one time Morgan had "done the Southern Pacific an important service." Senator White made a formal protest to the president, and Cleveland wrote Morgan a letter inviting him to resign. Morgan would not take the hint.

For several days, beginning on December 21, 1896, the Walker Board held public hearings in the offices of the Los

Angeles Chamber of Commerce. Several weeks were also spent studying maps, charts and other technical information. Soundings were taken in both harbors, and borings were made all along the proposed breakwaters and at various places in the harbors.

The report of the Walker Board was filed March 1, 1897, and as everyone expected it recommended that the harbor be located at San Pedro. Four members of the board signed this report, but Richard Price Morgan wrote a minority report strongly advocating Santa Monica.

After 330 pages of technical information, the majority report concluded:

> While the physical advantages of the San Pedro location naturally leads to its selection, the advisibility of that choice is materially strengthened by the consideration of the extensive improvements of its interior harbor, already made. . . . The preponderance of physical advantages, therefore, which leads to the selection of the San Pedro location is in line with the requirements of the best public policy as to the matter intrusted to the decision of this Board.

Morgan's minority report cited nine reasons why Santa Monica was superior to San Pedro. In the first place, he claimed that San Pedro had an "arc of exposure" of 156 degrees compared to 104 degrees for Santa Monica; a chart was included to prove this point. In addition, San Pedro was "kelp grown," it would require a breakwater of 8,500 feet compared to only 6,500 for Port Los Angeles, and the Southern Pacific already had a wharf in operation at Santa Monica.

It was now up to the Secretary of War, Russell A. Alger, to advertise for bids and get the work started on the harbor. Alger had visited Los Angeles as a guest of the Southern Pacific before becoming Secretary of War, and at that time he had expressed a preference for a harbor at Santa Monica. He was also known to be a friend of Huntington, having had business dealings with him through lumbering activities in the northwest.

When Alger had been appointed Secretary of War, the people of Los Angeles expected trouble, and they were right. The Walker Board made its report in March 1897, but work was not started on the harbor until April 1899. Willard insists that "at least half of this time was deliberately wasted by Secretary Alger, in the desperate hope of throwing the issue back to Congress."

Congress was in extra session during the spring of 1897, struggling with the Dingley Tariff, and a meeting of the California delegation was called to consider what action should be taken. It was decided to have Senator White introduce a resolution asking the Secretary of War to inform the Senate "what action, if any, has been taken or is contemplated with reference to the making of contracts for the completion of . . . a deepwater harbor" at San Pedro.

Ten days later, the Senate received a letter from Secretary Alger stating that the bill called for a harbor of "commerce and refuge," which he interpreted to mean development of both the inner and outer harbors, but that there was not enough money available to do this. He also said that it would be necessary to dredge the inner harbor to a depth of thirty feet instead of twenty-one feet as estimated by the investigating board. Finally, there were a number of sunken rocks near the harbor entrance which had been overlooked by the Walker Board.

The hope of the Southern Pacific, as expressed by the New York *World,* was that Congress would "repeal the appropriation and reconsider the plan of spending untold millions in making a harbor where there is none." But Congress was in no mood to start another endless argument, and quickly passed Senator White's resolution calling upon the Secretary of War to advertise for bids without delay.

After the senate had passed this resolution, Alger referred the matter to Attorney-General McKenna for his opinion. The Attorney-General quickly replied that in his opinion there was no legal reason why the Secretary of War should not advertise for bids. Alger then made the excuse that there was no money available to pay for the advertising. The Los Angeles newspapers offered to carry the advertising free, but Alger replied that it would not be dignified for the War Department to accept charity, and that he was referring the whole problem to the Judge Advocate General.

Part of the $50,000 which had been appropriated to meet the expenses of the investigating board had not been spent, and the Judge Advocate General ruled that this could be used to pay for advertising. But before bids could be advertised, Attorney-General McKenna was elevated to the Supreme Court, and Alger proposed that the matter be submitted to the new Attorney-General, John W. Griggs.

President McKinley began to receive hundreds of letters which complained that Alger was stalling on the San Pedro breakwater, and he finally issued an order directing the Secretary of War to advertise for bids immediately. Alger was obliged to comply with this order, and on February 10, 1898 the sealed bids were opened in the office of the U.S. Corps of Engineers in San Francisco. War Department engineers had to pass on the bids, which was done two weeks later, but it was not until July that Alger found time to approve the bids and order a contract.

Work was not actually begun on the breakwater until the following spring, an event which the citizens of Los Angeles celebrated with a Harbor Jubilee on April 26 and 27, 1899. There were ceremonies and speeches in San Pedro followed by a barbecue, parade, and fireworks in Los Angeles. Climaxing the festivities, President McKinley pressed a gold telegraph key as a signal to dump the first barge-load of rock from Catalina Island. Los Angeles was at last to have a deep-water harbor—a dream of fifty years was about to be realized.

20

EL ALISAL:
THE HOUSE THAT LUMMIS BUILT
Dudley Gordon

*Charles F. Lummis—newspaper columnist, author,
museum founder, city librarian, and builder of one of Los Angeles'
most unique homes.*
Courtesy of Historical Society of Southern California.

To those who knew him, it was not surprising that Charles F.
Lummis would build a house unlike any ever built before or
since. Had he not already distinguished himself as author, editor, archaeologist, explorer, poet, athlete, librarian and scholar?
Weren't his achievements well-known as crusader, encyclope-

dist, linguist, critic, newspaper man, musician, *bon vivant* and glorious host? And didn't everyone know of his skill as historian, lecturer, photographer, translator, cook, Americanist, museum builder and, some say, actor? Was it not expected that he would become his own architect, contractor, builder, mason, electrician, plumber and cabinetmaker?

It is obvious that Lummis was unique, unlike any man who ever lived before. He was an original, unconventional he-man. His mind was as sharp as a steel trap. His muscles were as supple and tough as a tiger's, and he was forever flexing them when given the slightest encouragement. Although an active practitioner he was not content merely to live "the vigorous life" physically and mentally. He made a career of it—eighteen to twenty hours each day. Once he would have been described as a human dynamo, but that seems inadequate. Today it is more appropriate to say that throughout his long aggressive career he was an atomic pile on two sturdy legs.

The urge to build a home is deep-rooted in men. With Charlie Lummis it was a persistent passion. (The desire for an appropriate memorial to himself was probably in his mind.) With his own hands, and the help of an Indian boy, over a period of seventeen years at six to eight hours per day, Lummis built an eighteen-room dwelling-museum of boulders from the *Arroyo Seco*. He built a long-enduring home for his family, his posterity and the community for all time. Elsewhere it would be called a castle. He named it *El Alisal*, the place of the sycamores. It is one of Los Angeles' cultural assets and, when once visited, it will be forever cherished. It is now a state park and is maintained for public use by the Park Department of Los Angeles City.

In 1895 Lummis acquired three acres of boulder-strewn land on the west bank of the *Arroyo Seco* extending from Avenue 42 to Avenue 43. It was then "away out in the country" to the north of Los Angeles and possessed a good view of the growing city. It also possessed a gigantic sycamore with four enormous branches pointing out the directions of the compass. It was the sycamore which influenced Lummis' choice of the

[278]

site. The boulders determined the type of structure he would build. It is interesting to note that, years later, Greek George, one of the original drivers of Uncle Sam's only Camel Corps, identified the giant sycamore as the one under which he and his charges frequently rested on supply carrying treks between Los Angeles and the military outposts in the desert. The Camel Corps became a Civil War casualty when their patron, Lt. Edward F. Beale, was called back East for a new assignment. The patient, efficient camels were left in charge of inexperienced, unsympathetic men who preferred to use the mule with whose eccentricities they were familiar.

Having selected the site for his mammoth museum-home-memorial, Lummis rolled up his sleeves, spat on his hands and went to work in his characteristic whole-hearted fashion. Soon he had erected temporary quarters for his growing family. Then he turned his attention to the erection of the building that was to be his equivalent of a gymnasium for the next twenty years. From dawn until dusk thereafter he and his Indian boy helper hauled rocks and sand, mixed mortar, laid course after course of cobbles, and *El Alisal* began to take shape.

A constant flow of celebrities would call upon Lummis where they found him at his work. This kept up while they talked business. Often he would call down to them to climb the scaffolding and to "Bring up a bucket of cement as you come." One visitor wrote afterwards of being thrilled to see this Harvard-product man of letters attired in white duck overalls, with a red bandana on his head, go scampering up the scaffold in his bare feet in performance of the job at hand. Meanwhile he answered her questions, offered his observations and made pertinent suggestions. So impressed was this interviewer that she reported to her magazine as follows "He is as powerful muscularly as he is acute mentally, so that it can be readily seen that it is nothing but play for him to build a huge stone house."

After he had been wrestling with granite boulders up to three feet in diameter for ten years someone asked him when he expected to finish the building. In characteristic fashion he replied: "Why, never I hope. It is my gymnasium." Another

Lummis and his helpers hard at work on El Alisal.
Courtesy of Southwest Museum.

time he wrote "I would rather take pleasure in putting in 2,600 tons of masonry than in 2,000,000 strokes with a golf club—because it leaves a mark."

Using the gnarled old sycamore as a pivot about which life in *El Alisal* was to revolve, Lummis erected a U-shaped structure whose dimensions are ninety feet by sixty. The front, or long side, is a two-story affair faced with boulders. It overlooks Los Angeles whose culture he enriched as city editor of the *Times*, city librarian, editor of the *Land of Sunshine Magazine*, founder of the Southwest Museum, preserver of the San Fernando and San Juan Capistrano Missions and of our Spanish heritage in history, art, literature, song, cookery and street names. The northwest corner is adorned with a thirty-foot circular tower and a campanile or bell tower patterned after one of San Gabriel Mission. The circular tower enclosed Lummis' den where he wrote a number of books, all of which emphasized the theme of the slogan he originated—*"See America First."* It was from this den that he conducted his campaigns to make better Indians by treating them better, to preserve science from crackpots who would purge textbooks of any mention of evolution. It was here that he worked on what would have been his most outstanding achievement—his dictionary, concordance and encyclopedia on Spain in America from 1492 until 1850. He made detailed references on 30,000 index cards but was forced to quit working on it. The public and the scientific societies lacked Lummis' vision. They were not ready for such a noble project. As a result, we have had to spend multi-millions to buy the friendship of Latin America where, earlier, a few thousands would have provided us with knowledge of our neighbors to the south that would assure us their everlasting friendliness. As understanding between neighbors increases, the opportunity for misunderstanding diminishes.

The interior of the building demonstrates that Lummis practiced what he preached when he said "A man should put much of himself into the building of his home." From the floor of three feet of concrete to the joists of one foot in diameter there are evidences of his handiwork. Each joist was charred and rubbed until it displayed the grain under a satiny finish.

The ceilings are of two-inch redwood planks. The doors are four inches thick and dovetailed uniquely. Upon seeing one of these doors the observer realizes what Lummis meant when he declared "that any fool can write a book, and most of them are doing it—but it takes a man to make a dovetailed door." The windows are three inches thick and each is different from the others. One room has windows made from glass photograpic negatives of pictures made by Lummis in his extensive travels over the Southwest.

The fireplaces in each room are patterned after those found throughout New Mexico. They are located in a corner and the firebed is raised about eighteen inches above the floor. They are more efficient than our traditional ones and may be attended without bending over uncomfortably. Each fireplace is adorned with a fitting inscription. A typical one states: "A casual savage struck two stones together—now man is armed against the weather."

Windows are draped with fringed buckskin curtains. The walls are covered with ancient missal leaves of parchment, autographed letters and portraits from Theodore Roosevelt, Will Rogers, John Burroughs, Collis P. Huntington, Ernest Thompson Seton and John Muir with paintings by William Keith, Maynard Dixon, Gutzon Borglum and others, and with relics and mementoes from travels over North, Central and South America.

On the floors and over much of the furniture are an abundance of priceless Navajo blankets. Splendid specimens of Indian pottery, some of it prehistoric, are to be found wherever it could be tucked. The furniture itself is nondescript, because Lummis hadn't been able to fulfill his plan of making it. The bench and cabinet work which he did complete is worthy of the craftsman he was.

The ironwork—locks, hinges, keys, and guns, each has an interesting story. They came from old dwellings, missions, forts, temples in Mexico, Central Peru, Bolivia and our own Southwest. They are examples of the handicraft of Spain, the Pueblos, Aztecs, Incas, Mayans and Yankees. They, along with hundreds of items in his many collections, are memorabilia of his travels, explorations, excavations and contacts with primitive peoples. The lock on the front door (which is never opened) is as large as a child's head. The Toltec inscription on the door is the work of artist Maynard Dixon.

The walls of the museum, eighteen inches thick, are rose-tinted. The kitchen walls are shaped like those one would expect to find in a mosque. They are curved upward and terminate in a narrow skylight or vent. The whole of the ground floor may be cleaned in record time by the judicious use of a garden hose. Thus, the three major rooms, each eighteen feet wide and eighteen, twenty-three and twenty-seven feet long, were easily maintained.

Pictures, each an example of the artistry of fine western painting, and each a gift from the artist to Lummis, their intimate friend, are hanging from the walls. They are displayed in frames of copper facing—another example of Lummis' handicraft. All about the house one may enjoy the work of William Keith, Carl O. Borg, Ed. Borein, Alex. Harmer, Thomas Moran, George Townsend Cole, William Wendt and others.

The patio, fifty feet by seventy-five feet, with building and covered walks draped around three sides, faces north toward Sycamore Grove and Pasadena. Its vista includes the *Arroyo Seco* and the nearby Southwest Museum which adorns a steep acropolis on the left.

Once, after a hike along the river in the *arroyo*, Theodore Roosevelt remarked to Lummis that "Someday this will make the most beautiful park in America." Then, returning to *El Alisal*, they entered the kitchen where Lummis washed and Teddy dried the dishes. The Southwest Museum, which occupies the place in our culture which Lummis founded it to do, is an asset which any city would be proud to possess.

Dominating the patio, *Alcalde Mayor*, the old sycamore, stretches its massive limbs hither and yon, throwing a protective shade over the walk and nearby lily pool. Here lived the Horn Pout, fish who came to the surface when Lummis whistled. Here lived a mammoth African frog with voice almost as loud and lusty as Lummis'. Somewhere around was Methuselah, the turtle of unknown age. It was in the patio that the family ate many

[283]

of their meals. It was here where Lummis so often read or told Indian folktales to the children, his own or the neighbors'.

What celebrated guests have been entertained at *El Alisal* which was an American equivalent of a salon for three decades, from 1898 until 1928! Actors, musicians, educators, writers, statesmen, scientists, cowboys, artists, sculptors, singers, anyone who was someone and could wangle an invitation, was likely to be there, and to remember the event ever after.

The guest book contains inscriptions by Sarah Bernhardt, Madame Modjeska, Maude Allen, Mary Garden, John Muir, John Burroughs, Edwin Markham, Ina Coolbrith, Gutzon Borglum, Hamlin Garland, Ernest Thompson Seton, Mary Austin, David Starr Jordan, Frederick W. Hodge, Joaquin Miller. Also there are T.R., Eugene Manlove Rhodes, Douglas Fairbanks, The Duke of Alba, Charles Wakefield Cadman, Eleanor Hague, Harry H. Knibbs, Elizabeth Benton Frémont, Frank Gibson, Dr. J. A. Munk, the O'Melvenys, the Dockweilers, the Newmarks, Sumner P. Hunt, Joe Scott, John Comfort Fillmore, Will Rogers, Harry Carey, William Gibbs McAdoo, Arthur Farwell, L. E. Behymer and many, many more. In fact, until 1928 no other southern California home had been visited by so many contributors to American culture.

On such occasions as the Saturday night "Noises" or the meeting of the March Hares, laughter, song and hilarity would make the rafters ring. Lucky were those who were invited to be present. They were in for a good time which they would recall vividly decades later, for it was then that Lummis performed in his own inimitable fashion as a California host.

After the guests arrived they would assemble in the dining room where a trial would be held. Lummis, at the head of the table, dressed in a tight-fitting buckskin coat, covering a soft-bosomed, Spanish drawnwork shirt which revealed the vivid red Bayeta undershirt beneath, would call the court to order by rapping the table with an old-time Spanish pistol.

The culprits, or neophytes, who were charged with not knowing what a real, old California good time was, would be arraigned before the court by the *aguacil* or sheriff. The latter wore a large metal badge and carried a Spanish short sword suspended by a chain that ran about his shoulders like the branch of a boy's suspenders. Joe Scott, one of the city's leading criminal lawyers, would prosecute. They would be defended and after a time they would be formally acquitted and adopted into the family.

After the trial, dinner would be served by Lummis' Spanish gardener-troubadour. The menu for one of the dinners was:

Aguardiente de Albaricoque
Vino Blanco　　　*Hasta Acabar* (chicken)
Enchiladas a la Paisana (chicken)
Pollo al Alcalde　　*Califlor de Hoy*
Frijoes de Ayer　　*Papas al Infalable*
Macarones a la Andulusa
Queso a Don Carlos　　*Cafe a la Negrita*

Between courses the troubadour would circle the table singing Mexican and Spanish songs to his own accompaniment on the guitar. At each chorus Lummis would insist that everyone present join in.

A highlight at the "Noises" would occur when Lummis would put down his fork, pick up the Spanish pistol, and point it at someone around the table. Then that someone would be commanded to sing for his supper. Of course if he couldn't sing, he might dance, or tell a story or otherwise account for himself.

Following the dinner there would be music, singing, storytelling, and an entertaining exchange of anecdotes. At midnight the party would end and the guests would go home having enjoyed an evening of old-time hospitality freely extended and without price, except when funds were low, as they sometimes were; then a few of the "regulars" would see to it that Elena, the irreplaceable cook, had enough money to carry on.

The March Hares, intimates who were born in the same month as Lummis, year after year received the following invitation: "Dear Bunny, the hounds are after you. Postpone death, marriage, taxes and other disasters. Be here on March 1st. Cabbage at six. Madness begins later." And on that day artists, artisans, scientists, cronies from his old days as city editor of the Los Angeles *Times*, and others would assemble at his table for food, drink, song, sprightly talk and general good fellowship.

Fully aware of the fact that in this country private collections and inheritances are scattered or dissipated in a short time, Lummis sought to prevent that disaster by deeding to the Southwest Museum his complete historical, scientific and philological library and his artifacts from the Indians of Mexico, Guatemala, Ecuador and Peru and the native tribes of the Southwest. This he did in 1910 with the stipulation that its three museum rooms would be opened free to the public for stated hours each week, and that his family and descendants shall have tenure of the remaining rooms forever. This he felt would insure a beautiful and safe home to his posterity, forever free from rent, taxes or debts. It would insure to the public an important unique free museum of science, art and history; an example not only of durable architecture, but also of living ingenuity and devotion in the building of a home.

And so it remained until 1939 when, due to a shortage of funds, the Southwest Museum was no longer able to maintain *El Alisal*, having expended more than $27,000.00 on its upkeep over the years. There was the possibility that the property would be sold for a pittance when the League of Women Voters met to save the house and property as a memorial under the leadership of Mrs. J. L. Criswell and Marian Parks; others rallied to the cause. Among them were Althea Warren, the city librarian, Hobart Bosworth, Joe Scott, Marco Newmark, L. E. Behymer, Frederick W. Hodge, Grace Stoermer, Mrs. F. N. Noll, Mrs. W. C. Shults, Mrs. Leone G. Plum, Florence D. Schoneman, Orpha Klinker, Mary Workman, City Councilman Arthur Briggs and many others.

After an extended campaign and much unselfish work, the committees succeeded in inducing the State Park Commission to operate and maintain the Lummis property "for the benefit and recreation of the public." It is now maintained by the Los Angeles City Park Department and is available to the public on special appointment only.

El Alisal stands today a memorial to the peculiar genius of an unconventional man. His talents and achievements are largely unrecognized by *Angelenos* today though they are indebted to him more than they suspect. They would be surprised to learn that the King of Spain knighted him for his work of interpreting Spain's contribution to American culture. They will be surprised, too, when they visit *El Alisal* for most of them have been unaware that such a unique, interesting and highly significant building is being maintained by their taxes and for their enlightenment and enjoyment. This fine building is a jewel in the crown of *La Reina*. It is fireproof (except for the temporary room), weatherproof and an earthquake-proof jewel.

El Alisal was never finished as is indicated by the piles of boulders on the property. These were to be converted into still more rooms. The roof is not tiled for Lummis never reached the stage where he could make the tiles he intended to use. The iron grill work which he planned to hand forge was never begun, nor did he ever get to the task of building a ninety-foot Roman arched cloister on the front of the building. But wherever one looks he may see that Lummis followed his dictum that *a man should put himself into the building of a home.*

Literally as well as figuratively, this is what Lummis accomplished. Now the ashes of the genius that was Lummis are incased within the walls of the building upon which he labored so many years. They lie beyond a simple bronze plate near the main door. Upon this plate is inscribed the following:

> *He founded the Southwest Museum.*
> *He built this house.*
> *He saved four missions.*
> *He studied and recorded Spain in America.*
> *He tried to do his share.*

21

A NEGLECTED ASPECT OF THE OWENS RIVER AQUEDUCT STORY: THE INCEPTION OF THE LOS ANGELES MUNICIPAL ELECTRIC SYSTEM

Nelson Van Valen

The Owens River aqueduct has long been a favorite topic for investigation among scholars and journalists concerned with California south of the Tehachapi. Recently the aqueduct story even provided the basis for the Oscar-winning screenplay of the highly successful commercial film "Chinatown." Yet for all of the attention it has received, one significant aspect of the aqueduct story—the electric power aspect—has been consistently neglected. This essay seeks to remedy that neglect.

On Saturday morning, July 29, 1905, residents of the City of Los Angeles on picking up their copies of the Los Angeles *Times* read of a decidedly ambitious undertaking—a project to bring water to the city from the Owens River, 250 miles to the north. The project had its origins in a growing population's pressure on scarce water resources. A quarter of a century earlier, at the beginning of the boom of the eighties, Los Angeles had a population of 11,000. At the end of the decade, the city's population stood at 50,000, and at the turn of the century, at 100,000. At the date of the *Times* story, the population of Los Angeles was approaching 200,000. Especially during the last dozen years of this quarter-century of extraordinarily rapid population growth, the problem of supplying the city's increasingly numerous inhabitants with water became critical. In the eighties, there seemed no cause for concern, for the peak of the boom coincided with the beginning of a wet period during which the Los Angeles River, the city's principal source of water, rose to a record mean annual flow of 100 cubic feet per second. "We have water enough here in the river to supply the city for the next fifty years," declared the future Chief Engineer and General Manager of the city's water system, William Mulholland. But the mid-nineties witnessed the beginning of a dry period that continued for a decade. By 1900, the mean annual flow of the Los Angeles River had fallen to 57 second feet. In 1901 the river's flow was 53.5 feet, and in 1902, 45 feet. The Board of Water Commissioners insisted, "There is ample water"—but installed meters and raised rates in order to "stop waste." In 1903, the river's flow dropped another foot. In 1904 the river's flow reached a record low of 42.8 second feet. For ten days in the summer of that year, water was drawn out of Los Angeles reservoirs faster than it flowed into them—and newcomers continued to arrive. Mulholland summed up the situation. "Our population climbed to the top and the bottom appeared to drop out of the river." Out of this combination of circumstances emerged the Owens River project.

Although the preponderant majority of Los Angeles residents first learned of the project when they picked up their copies of the *Times* that summer morning in 1905, the idea was an old one; it had been put forward in the public press a quarter-century earlier. The idea first began to take the form of a specific project in the mid-nineties in the mind of Fred Eaton. In turn superintendent of the Los Angeles City Water Company, Los Angeles City Engineer, and in 1899–1900 mayor of Los Angeles, Eaton was thoroughly familiar with the city's water problem. He came early to believe that Los Angeles must someday supplement the flow of the Los Angeles River with water from an additional source, and in the mid-nineties concluded that source would be the Owens River.

> Mr. Eaton did not publicly discuss his ideas . . . [Mulholland explained in his first annual report as Chief Engineer of the Los

Angeles Aqueduct]. In the fall of 1904 and the early spring of 1905, Mr. Eaton on his own responsibility and at his own expense, began obtaining contracts and options on water-bearing property in Owens Valley. With these contracts and options in hand, he first presented the matter to representatives of the City of Los Angeles in the fall of 1904 and early in the year 1905.

Convinced, after months of investigation, both of the sufficiency of the Owens River water supply and of the feasibility of the aqueduct necessary to carry the water from the valley to the city, the Water Board came to an agreement with Eaton. Two days after the Owens River project became public knowledge, the Board requested the City Council to call a special election to authorize a preliminary $1,500,000 bond issue to purchase the necessary lands, water rights, and right of way in Owens Valley, and to make the necessary preliminary engineering investigation prior to the beginning of actual construction of the aqueduct.

Fifty miles from Los Angeles the proposed aqueduct dropped precipitously at two points a total distance of almost fifteen hundred feet. Thus the Owens River project was not only a water project; it was also a hydroelectric power project. Initially, however, there was little general awareness of the power implications of the project. That

> Little drops of water
> On little grains of sand
> Make a hell of a difference
> In the price of land

was immediately apparent to virtually everyone, and virtually everyone also recognized quickly that an ample supply of water was essential to the prosperity not only of Los Angeles real estate operators but of the city generally. But that a plentiful supply of cheap electricity might also have some bearing on the city's prosperity and that the proposed aqueduct might provide that supply—these facts were neither so immediately nor so generally apparent. City officials, perhaps fearful of arousing the opposition of the private electric utility companies, said almost nothing about the power potential of the aqueduct. Nor did the press have much to say about that potential. The *Times*,

[291]

for example, in breaking the story of the Owens River project made but one brief reference to electric power.

Within a week after the announcement of the Owens River project, however, the press began to recognize the project's potential for electric power development. "With electric power at nominal cost," declared a *Times* editorial, "the entire city—or at least all the principal streets—might be illuminated with brilliantly lighted lamps on ornamental candelabra." But the *Times* was clearly more interested in power than in light. "Look at the question of power for manufacturing," the editorial continued.

> Power to run factories could be supplied at about cost . . . and that cost would be so trifling as to be scarcely worth mentioning. Just think what such an inducement would mean in the way of transforming Los Angeles into one of the most important manufacturing cities in the country.

Yet despite the trifling cost at which aqueduct electricity would be sold, another *Times* editorial asserted, receipts from power and light sales would net the city $2,000,000 annually, a sum more than sufficient to discharge all expenses of aqueduct construction within a twenty-five year period. Other Los Angeles newspapers presented much the same argument.

In mid-August the City Council called the special election requested by the Water Board to authorize the $1,500,000 preliminary bond issue. Los Angeles voters approved the issue by a margin greater than that given any previous municipal issue. They did so, no doubt, primarily because they believed additional water was essential for the city's continued growth. "If we don't get the water," Mulholland once observed, "we won't need it." It seems highly probable, however, that the overwhelming nature of the vote was in part traceable to the assurances that electricity to be developed along the aqueduct would pay the cost of constructing the aqueduct and also assure the industrialization of Los Angeles. The city could, indeed, eat its cake and have it, too.

From the voting of these bonds, interest in the power side of the Owens River project increased markedly. Only two days after approval of the issue, Eaton called attention to what the *Times* called a "NEW SIDE TO OWENS PROJECT"—the power side. Eaton asserted that 65,000 horsepower could be developed within twenty miles of Los Angeles and an additional 25,000 horsepower one hundred miles from the city. Eaton's estimate of the city's annual revenue from the sale of aqueduct power was $1,000,000, a figure but half that put forward by the *Times* during the bond campaign but equivalent to four percent interest on $25,000,000, the estimated cost of building the aqueduct.

In part because they saw in cheap power a way of paying for expensive water, city officials were only slightly less enthusiastic than Eaton and the press. The Board of Water Commissioners, in its annual report for 1905, while clearly stating that the Owens River project was chiefly a water project, also called attention to the opportunities for power development. The Commissioners estimated the amount of electricity that might be generated along the aqueduct at 80,000 horsepower—an amount so large that even after meeting street lighting and other municipal needs, the city would have a large surplus available for sale. The Board concluded only slightly less optimistically than Eaton and the press, "The amount of revenue that might be derived from this source, together with the net income of the water department, would be sufficient to meet, if not the whole, at least a substantial part, of the indebtedness to be incurred by the city in completing this project."

In the summer of 1906, the Water Board—with the advice of other city officials and of the presidents of the Merchants and Manufacturers Association, the Municipal League, and the Voters' League—appointed a board of consulting engineers to review the city's aqueduct plans. Of eleven subjects for investigation assigned the engineers, only one pertained to power—the engineers were to estimate the amount of power that might be developed along the aqueduct—but of a half dozen major modifications of the city's plan recommended by the engineers, three dealt with power. The consultants estimated that 49,000 horsepower "would be available twenty-four hours per day, and seven days a week," but by raising the elevation of the aqueduct, adding storage reservoirs, and enlarging conduits the city could have available during hours of peak demand a total of

93,000 horsepower. The engineers concluded their report with the statement,

> The conditions for the economic development and mainte-nance of the power are very favorable, and its safety against interruption or diminution by drought and the permanent char-acter of the aqueduct, tend to make the power development fea-ture particularly attractive and valuable.

"The Board felt," according to one of the consultants, "as a power proposition alone, the aqueduct would be worth con-structing. . . ." He estimated the annual revenue to be derived from the sale of aqueduct power at $1,400,000, a sum sufficient to "pay all interest on the cost of the entire project."

As the engineering feasibility and financial attractiveness of aqueduct power development became thoroughly established, it became increasingly likely that aqueduct power would, indeed, be developed. But developed by what agency? By the private electric utility companies already in the field? Or by the city of Los Angeles itself? Although in a few years the issue of public versus private power would become one of the most important and most durable in Los Angeles politics, initially it aroused little interest. The *Times*, in a few years to become a principal champion of private power, declared that aqueduct power might be exploited by either private or public agencies. And the Board of Water Commissioners, soon to be charged with the development of what was to become the largest public power enterprise in the United States, in its annual report for 1905 ignored the issue completely.

What makes this lack of public discussion on the issue of public or private development especially striking is that the is-sue was present from the very inception of the aqueduct project, for private development was an important part of Eaton's plan. John Steven McGroarty, picturesque annalist of Los Angeles history, while likening Eaton to Moses and seeing him "perme-ated to the very soul" with "a great dream" "for the relief of a city that was well beloved by him," also notes Eaton's aware-ness of the opportunity for personal profit in the exploitation of aqueduct power. A less romantic chronicler of the city's growth,

Boyle Workman, similarly credits Eaton with "a blinding vision," but adds, "As an engineer, he knew it was feasible. He knew, also, that there lay an opportunity to build a personal fortune." Nor did Eaton himself make any effort to hide either his conception of the Owens River project as "a splendid opportunity to make money," an opportunity he had "had in view for a dozen years," or his reluctance to forego that opportunity. According to Mulholland, when he first conceived of the aqueduct project, Eaton thought of it as a project for private capital, but by the time he presented the project to the city, he was prepared to carry it out as a private project only if the city failed to act. The plan that Eaton finally presented to the city called for a marriage of private and public enterprise. Eaton was to secure and deliver to the city without cost all necessary land and water rights. In return he was to receive "the right to develop and own all the water power incident to construction."

But Eaton and the city were not the only parties interested in the Owens River. So, too, was the federal government. And Eaton's inability to promote the aqueduct as a combined public and private enterprise was in part the result of the opposition of federal officials. In the spring of 1902, President Theodore Roosevelt had signed the Newlands Act. The Reclamation Service created by that act soon began to investigate seven possible reclamation projects in California, among them one in Owens Valley. It was clear to city officials that if the Reclamation Service began actual construction work on the Owens Valley project Los Angeles would be denied Owens River water and the city's future growth would be very seriously curtailed. Hence the "aid" of the Reclamation Service was absolutely essential. Los Angeles officials sounded out Reclamation Service officials on Eaton's proposal of a combined public and private project. These officials, in Mulholland's words, "took the stand that they could not aid the City . . . unless the project was exclusively a municipal one." As the *Complete Report* explained a decade later, "Against a municipality seeking water for a large urban population, the government would not persist in its project, its policy being to promote the good of the greatest number." City officials promptly rejected Eaton's plan, insisting on "exclusive municipal ownership and control," and the Reclamation Service stopped all work in Owens Valley.

A few months after rejecting Eaton's plan for a combined public and private aqueduct project, the city received from another source a plan that called for a much larger ingredient of private enterprise. A local engineer, allegedly representing Eastern financiers, tentatively offered to build the aqueduct in exchange for power rights. Private capital could build and operate the aqueduct at far less cost than the city, the engineer urged, because private capital would be "out of the pale of political influences . . . which always arise when any municipality undertakes some project on a gigantic scale. Although nothing came of this proposal, it is significant both as an indicator of the growing awareness of the importance of the power side of the aqueduct project and as a foretaste of the impending conflict over the issue of public versus private exploitation.

Still another sign of increasing awareness on the issue of municipal or private development was the increasing frequency with which Los Angeles newspapers accused electric utility companies operating in Los Angeles of seeking to gain control of aqueduct power or, failing that, to block the entire Owens River project. No sooner did the *Times* discover the power potential of the aqueduct project than it also discovered that the potential perhaps fatally endangered the project's chances of adoption. The paper had heard what it termed "well-grounded rumors of a quiet combination of certain large interests against the Owens River scheme for business reasons." Although the *Times* named no names, it declared that if opposition to the aqueduct project did, indeed, develop, the opposition would "come in strongest force from the power and light interests." "A stream running 33,000 inches of water is enough to make any power producer jealous," the *Times* concluded. Mulholland was more specific, "The only opposition we are meeting is the Edison people. They fear Los Angeles will have too much power if we run this water down here from those mountains." Such allegations became so prevalent that the president of the Edison

Electric Corporation, John B. Miller, felt called upon to write to the Board of Water Commissioners to deny them. Miller wrote, "I desire to say to you as emphatically and as unequivocally as English can express it, that this company has not in any way opposed the city's plans for bringing water from Owens River."

Six months later the *Times* again charged that there was "underhand knocking" of the Owens River project by electric company officers. It was clear to the *Times* that whoever controlled the 100,000 horsepower of aqueduct electricity could "fix the price of power and light in Los Angeles," and this fact explained why the power companies were "knocking" the aqueduct. The *Times* charged specifically that the general manager of the Pacific Light and Power Company, Allan C. Balch, and an engineer retained by the Edison Company, F. C. Finkle, were "going about telling their friends and business acquaintances that the Owens River project is 'a scheme of graft,' an engineering absurdity, a financial chimera and an utterly impracticable proposition." Both men were said to have stressed engineering obstacles. Finkle, in addition, was said to have stated that he had made a survey of the flow of the Owens River for the Edison Company, the results of which were considerably less optimistic than those of the Reclamation Service survey on which the city was basing its plans. The *Times* feared that because Finkle was an engineer, his words would carry weight with businessmen innocent of engineering knowledge. The paper particularly feared Finkle's influence on bankers, "whose opinion might influence public action on a proposition to issue bonds."

Finkle categorically denied that the Edison Company had sought to have him "knock" the aqueduct project. He declared plausibly,

> The power companies now operating here would benefit vastly by the attainment of such a result, even should the city secure 100,000 horsepower in San Fernando Valley, because the 20,000 inches of additional water would so increase the population and industrial activity in Southern California as to consume all the output both of the power companies and the city at prices very profitable to the owners of power.

The data resulting from his investigation were the property of the Edison Company; Finkle had "never used them either for or against the city's Owens River project." Finkle also denied that he had made any allegations of graft—past, present, or prospective.

A few weeks later, the *Times* called attention to still another "knocker" of the aqueduct project—Samuel T. Clover, maverick Republican editor of the recently founded Los Angeles *Evening News.* The *News,* the *Times* charged, was the "subsidized organ" of the power corporations opposing the Owens River project, "the nominal editor . . . their employee." "Subsidized Sammy's" *Evening News* was doing openly what Balch and Finkle were doing undercover. According to the *Times,* the power companies were "knocking" the aqueduct project in order to impair the city's credit when it became time to sell aqueduct bonds. Alarmed at the prospect of municipal development of aqueduct power, the companies were determined to block the aqueduct project entirely or, at the very least, reduce its flow, and hence its power production, to a trickle.

The alleged power company opposition to the aqueduct project was not confined to the local scene. In June 1906, Mulholland and City Attorney W. B. Mathews, accompanied by a Chamber of Commerce delegation, went to Washington to work for passage of an act giving the city a right of way through certain public lands between Owens Valley and the San Fernando Valley. They found that a representative of the Edison Company had been on the grounds for two weeks and that Balch had "used the wires" to block the bill. By the time the spokesmen for the city arrived, this opposition, together with that of the congressman representing the settlers of Owens Valley, apparently had begun to have some influence on Interior Secretary Ethan A. Hitchcock. Mulholland found the Secretary "a very positive, domineering man," according to the *Times.* "But," the *Times* continued, "Mulholland was loaded with facts, and his emphatic way of stating facts had its effect." Furthermore, the city had on its side Frank P. Flint, Republican Senator from California and member of the Senate Committee on Public Lands, who had introduced the right of way measure, presumably at the behest of Los Angeles city officials. And the city also had on its side "two strong friends close to the President"—Chief Forester Gifford Pinchot and Geological Survey Director Charles D. Walcott. The whole matter was thrashed out in a conference with President Theodore Roosevelt. Roosevelt opened the conference by saying to the city's representatives, "You'll get your bill." He then proceeded to dictate a characteristic letter to Secretary Hitchcock, seated at his elbow, in which he said,

> I am also impressed by the fact that the chief opposition to this bill, aside from the opposition of the few settlers in Owens Valley (whose interest is genuine, but whose interest unfortunately must be disregarded in view of the infinitely greater interest to be served by putting the water in Los Angeles), comes from certain private power companies whose object evidently is for their own pecuniary interest to prevent the municipality from furnishing its own water. The people at the head of these companies are doubtless respectable citizens, and if there is no law they have a right to seek their own pecuniary advantage in securing control of this necessity of life for the City. Nevertheless, their opposition seems to me to afford one of the strongest arguments for passing the law, inasmuch as it ought not to be within the power of private individuals to control such a necessity of life as against the municipality.

The *Times* commented, "When the letter was completed and read, the Secretary found that he agreed with the President." The aqueduct right-of-way bill became law five days later.

But even after the passage of the aqueduct right-of-way act, the *Times* continued to fear power company opposition to the aqueduct. The "pin-head managers" of the power companies had said in public that they were friendly toward the aqueduct project, but in private they continued to fight it. Unable to defeat the aqueduct at the polls, power company agents were boasting that they would tie the project up in litigation, which even if unsuccessful, would so impair the city's credit that aqueduct bonds could not be sold. The *Times* made it quite clear, however, that the ultimate goal of the power companies was no longer permanently to block the aqueduct project. Persistent

[299]

efforts of the companies to kill the project had failed. Consequently "the power company schemers" had now "put about on another tack." The direction of this new course had been given in an "unauthorized and wholly baseless statement of the city's plans in their organ," . . . the *Evening News:* "It is not the purpose of the city to supply electricity, and a lease will be made to a corporation, the revenues to go to an expense fund. If a lease is not desirable, the right to use the power will be sold." As the *Times* pointed out, no one had been authorized to define the city's power plans, and no city official had presumed to do so. "The corporation organ" alone was responsible for the statement. The *Times* thought the statement highly significant. To the *Times,* it meant that the power companies, recognizing that they could not block the Owens River project, were trying "to hold up the project . . . until the city shall be forced to make an arrangement with them by which they can control the power."

As the issue of public versus private exploitation of aqueduct power slowly emerged, planning for the financing of the aqueduct continued. City officials wrestled with the problem of whether to install the proposed power plants concurrently with the construction of the aqueduct, or to delay power plant installation until the aqueduct was completed. The *Times* recalled "conservative" estimates that the power to be developed at the mouth of the aqueduct would yield an annual revenue sufficient to "provide for interest and sinking fund on the bond issues of $25,000,000 and leave about half a million a year to be used otherwise." Common sense, therefore, seemed to dictate that the power plants should be installed concurrently with the construction of the aqueduct, in order that they could go into operation and start yielding revenue when the first Owens River water rushed down San Francisquito Canyon. The *Times* estimated the cost of installing the power plants, transmission lines, and substations at $3,000,000. But Mulholland had earlier declared, "It will be time enough to take up the power end of it when we get the water down here," and he concluded his first annual report as chief engineer of the Los Angeles Aqueduct with this typical paragraph:

The proposed plan is to build the Aqueduct for the purpose of supplying water for municipal purposes, and after its completion, if the citizens of Los Angeles consider it desirable to install these power plants, they may subsequently be built as independent works. The installation of power has not been included in the Aqueduct estimates because the power situation is considered as wholly independent of the proposition of supplying water, and should stand on its own merits.

Surprisingly, in light of the expectation that aqueduct power would pay for aqueduct water, city officials adopted Mulholland's position. The City Council voted to submit a bond issue in the amount of $23,000,000 solely for the construction of the aqueduct; a power bond issue would be submitted independently at a later date.

At the beginning of the aqueduct bond campaign, the press appeared quite fearful of power company opposition to the bonds. In an editorial titled "The City's Enemies," the *Times* quoted at length from the Roosevelt letter, and charged that the chief opposition to the bonds was coming from the same power companies that the President had charged with opposing the right-of-way bill. The companies had offered to cease their opposition if the city would give them control of aqueduct power. The city had rejected their offer, however, and consequently the companies were seeking to defeat the bonds. The *Times* urged its readers not to forget that all of the opposition to the bonds was being inspired by power companies whose sole aim was, in the words of the President of the United States, "their own pecuniary interest." The liberal press, too, saw the hand of the private power companies raised against the aqueduct bond issue.

A fortnight before election day, however, the opposition of the power companies waned. "Their attempt to bluff and bully the city into giving them control of the power developed by the aqueduct had failed," the *Times* declared, "and they cannot make good their threat to defeat the Owens River bond issue." The companies had abandoned their fight against the Owens River project and their presidents had "publicly and unqualifiedly" endorsed it. The opposition that remained was insignificant; only the *Evening News* continued to oppose the bonds.

Support for the bonds was overwhelming. All of the city's major business and civic groups—coordinated by the Chamber of Commerce, the Merchants and Manufacturers Association, and the Municipal League—joined together to form an Owens River Campaign Committee. The city's major newspapers were also unanimously in support of the aqueduct bond issue. Supporters of the bonds, while primarily concerned with assuring the city an abundant supply of water, gave considerable attention to the power and light side of the project. Mayor A. C. Harper, for example, called attention to the power that would be developed along the aqueduct, and declared that in anticipation of the development of this power the city had already planned to establish its own municipal lighting system. City Attorney Leslie R. Hewitt pointed out that the aqueduct would provide Los Angeles with abundant power not just for lighting but for manufacturing as well. Equally important, receipts from the sale of aqueduct power would also assure the financial success of the entire aqueduct project. The *Times*, for example, again reassured its readers that the revenue to be derived from the sale of aqueduct power would be "more than enough to provide for interest sinking fund on the entire cost of the aqueduct and power plants."

Lured by a vision of a great city, a city with ample water and abundant electricity, an increasingly industrialized city, and convinced that this vision would become a reality at no cost to them, on election day Los Angeles voters went to the polls in greater numbers than at any previous special election and voted ten to one in favor of the aqueduct bonds, the bonds carrying in every precinct.

With completion of the aqueduct scheduled for the spring of 1912, city officials were obliged to turn to power development. A Bureau of Los Angeles Aqueduct Power was established: Ezra F. Scattergood, previously a consulting engineer for the Henry Huntington interests and for the aqueduct, was named Chief Electrical Engineer; and a second board of consulting engineers was appointed.

The southern end of the Soledad siphon,
eleven feet in diameter and over 8,000 feet long, an integral part of
the aqueduct construction project.
Courtesy of Los Angeles Department of Water and Power.

This second board of engineers was even more enthusiastic than the earlier board about the opportunities for power development along the aqueduct. A maximum delivery of 120,000 horsepower and 64,000 horsepower for a twenty-four hour period, an amount thirty percent larger than that estimated by the first board, could be developed at "an unusually low first cost." The completed system, furthermore, would be characterized by "the very highest degree of reliability in operation," and by unusually low costs of operation. In concluding their report, the consultants pointed out that in the preceding thirteen years, the demand for electricity in Los Angeles and vicinity had increased tenfold from 5,000 kilowatts in 1897 to 50,000 kilowatts at the time of their report. The city had "an assured and early market" for its aqueduct power. The *Times* commented, "If a private

[303]

corporation received such a report as this from its examining engineers its stock would immediately jump twenty-five points. . . ."

At the same time that they gave attention to the engineering side of the aqueduct power project, city officials also wrestled with the financial side. The Board of Public Works recommended to the City Council that it call a special election to authorize a power bond issue of $4,500,000. Although an issue in that amount would not be sufficient to complete an aqueduct power system—to do that an additional million dollars would be required—it would be sufficient to carry aqueduct power development to the point where it would be commercially serviceable." Mayor George Alexander sent a special message to the council urging prompt submission. The council fixed April 19, 1910, as the date of the special election.

Although for a quarter-century afterwards almost all Los Angeles power bond elections were bitterly contested, the city's first such election was "a formality." Support for the power bonds was almost as overwhelming as it had been for the aqueduct bonds. City officials were particularly active in urging adoption. Mayor Alexander issued a proclamation calling on the voters to approve the issue; Scattergood appeared before the City Club to urge that influential civic group to support the bonds; City Attorney Hewitt addressed the Federated Improvement Associations; and Mulholland and Mathews, the latter now Special Counsel for the Aqueduct Bureau, issued strong pro-bond statements. Perhaps even more influential was the virtually unanimous backing given the bonds by the city's business and civic organizations. The Chamber of Commerce, the Merchants and Manufacturers Association, the Federated Improvement Associations, and the Municipal League—all of these potent organizations, among others, urged the adoption of the power bonds. The city's newspapers unanimously endorsed the issue. The bonds carried by a margin of seven to one.

City officials in proposing municipal development of aqueduct power, business and civic groups and newspapers in endorsing the proposal, and voters in approving it were guided by several considerations. For one, almost from the first public announcement of the Owens River project five years earlier, and especially during the 1907 aqueduct bond election, voters had been assured that revenues to be received from the sale of aqueduct power would be sufficient both to meet the interest charges on the aqueduct bonds and to provide a sinking fund that would retire them in twenty years. In an expansive moment, Mayor Alexander had gone so far as to assert that power revenues together with those from the newly improved harbor would "wipe out the entire city indebtedness." Good judgment seemed to indicate, therefore, that installation of aqueduct power plants should begin promptly in order that the city could begin to realize large revenues from the sale of aqueduct power just as soon as Owens River waters began to flow through the aqueduct. Another compelling argument in favor of voting the 1907 aqueduct bonds had been the role of cheap power in the industrialization of Los Angeles; this argument, too, was now widely used in favor of the power bonds. And common sense reasons of economy also called for the earliest possible exploitation of the power potential of the aqueduct. If construction of power facilities were delayed until after the aqueduct was in actual operation, "hundreds of thousands" of dollars would have to be spent to detour water past construction work at the power sites; concurrent construction of the aqueduct and aqueduct power plants would obviate this waste. In sum, city officials and voters saw aqueduct power development as "a corollary of the aqueduct." "The voting of the power bonds was guaranteed when the aqueduct was undertaken," one newspaper observed. "It was an essential part of the project."

What needs to be explained, however, is not only why the power resources of the Los Angeles aqueduct were developed, but also why they were developed by the city of Los Angeles itself, rather than by the private electric utility companies already operating in the area. Benjamin Franklin is reputed to have asserted that the wisest measures of statesmanship are not the product of previous wisdom, but rather are forced by the occasion. In the decision of the city of Los Angeles to go into the business of generating electricity, however, both forces were at work. Clearly the construction of the aqueduct furnished the

[305]

occasion for that decision. It is equally clear, however, that the decision was also the product of previous wisdom.

During the first decade and a half of the present century, Los Angeles was the scene of the movement for municipal reform. A major impetus to reform was acute dissatisfaction with private utility companies. For a generation, city officials in their eagerness to obtain water, gas, electricity, telephone service, and street railways had granted extremely liberal franchises to entrepreneurs who would undertake to provide them. Poor service, high rates, and interference in the city's governance had ensued. Hence a primary aim of the reformers was to bring utilities under municipal control. Electric utilities were a prime target.

During the early years of the electric light and power industry, years of extraordinarily rapid growth, there was a general belief that it was inherently the least monopolistic of the public utilities. City councils looked to competition to prevent abuses in rates and services. Indeed so thoroughly was competition thought to be the natural and effective way to prevent abuses that virtually every city in the country granted several general franchises, some simultaneously, and some granted franchises to all applicants. It quickly became evident, however, that the electric utility industry was a natural monopoly, for competition produced a wasteful duplication of investment. Some other means must be found to control rates and services.

One proposed way to control the rates and services of electric utilities was government regulation. The earliest attempts were made on the municipal level. Some municipalities attempted regulation through ordinances or franchises; others established utility commissions. But regulation through ordinances proved to be "rigid, spasmodic and inept, if not corrupt," and regulation through franchises was similarly "inflexible, difficult to enforce and sometimes corrupt," while even large cities seldom could command the administrative and technical skills necessary to establish utility commissions worthy of the name. At best the jurisdiction of a municipality was too confined for effective regulation of a large utility system embracing several communities. Municipal regulation became widespread, but only rarely was it effective.

The evident general failure of municipal regulation gave rise to a widespread demand first for state and later for federal regulation. From the first, however, there were those who were skeptical of the ability of regulation by any level of government to control the electric utility industry.

During the years of the reform movement, three companies—the Los Angeles Gas and Electric Corporation, the Pacific Light and Power Company, and the Edison Electric Corporation—distributed electricity in Los Angeles. Yet the three companies did not directly compete, for they served different geographic areas of the city. The gas company—a product of earlier consolidations and a subsidiary of a San Francisco holding company, the Pacific Lighting Corporation, which also controlled the Pacific Gas and Electric Corporation and the Southern California and Southern Counties Gas companies, and the only one of the three companies that distributed most, 87 percent of its current for lighting purposes—operated principally in the lucrative central business district, where it also had a contract to furnish current for lighting the city streets. The Pacific Light and Power Company supplied most, 90 percent, of its current for power purposes, principally to Henry E. Huntington's electric railways, the Los Angeles Railway and the Pacific Electric, but it also furnished electricity for lighting in the southern and northeastern portions of the city. The Edison Company also supplied most, 75 percent, of its current for power purposes, but its lines reached 75 percent of the city's area and served almost half of the city's domestic consumers.

Although a provision of the city charter of 1889 authorized the City Council to regulate utility rates, not until 1904 did the council pass the necessary ordinance implementing the charter provision, and not until 1907 did the Council actually exercise its authority. At that time the council simply approved most of the existing rates. Mayor Arthur C. Harper, however, vetoed the domestic rate of eleven cents per kilowatt-hour. After a conference with the mayor and the councilmen, representatives of the electric companies agreed to accept a nine cent domestic rate, but the councilmen were obliged to enter into a secret "gentlemen's agreement" not to fix a lower rate for three years.

Despite the "gentlemen's agreement" of 1907, the following year the council entered upon its rate-fixing task much more earnestly. The electric companies, however, filed reports that City Auditor W. C. Mushet called incomplete and misleading, and refused the city auditor access to their books. Mushet nonetheless thought the nine cent domestic rate too high and urged a two cent reduction. He was convinced that the companies were exploiting the small light consumers for the benefit of the large power consumers. Mushet asserted, for example, that the Pacific Light and Power Corporation was selling power below cost to the street railway companies. Interested citizens presented similar charges. The Council, however, was unconvinced and perhaps also influenced by the "gentlemen's agreement" continued the nine cent rate.

By 1909 both the reformers and the companies were convinced of the failure of rate regulation by councilmanic ordinance. In its place both would substitute regulation by a permanent, non-political public utility commission. A utility commission bill largely reflecting the desires of the companies was approved by the council but vetoed by Mayor George Alexander. The council sustained the veto. The council then passed a second bill and overrode the mayor's veto of it. This ordinance was superceded, however, when at the December general election the voters approved an initiative creating the type of public utility commission desired by the reformers. The commission employed a group of nationally known utility experts that surveyed Los Angeles utilities and recommended upward adjustments of telephone and electric rates. The commission forwarded these recommendations to the council, but that body refused to adopt them. In July 1911, the members of the commission resigned. Municipal regulation of utilities suffered further blows when in a number of disputes between the city and the companies, the courts decided in favor of the companies. Thereafter the task of regulating public utilities was gradually assumed by the state. This failure of municipal regulation, either by councilmanic ordinance or by utility commission, to control the rates of the electric utility companies provided the reformers with considerable reason to adopt the alternative of municipal ownership.

But there was a second important, and closely related, influence making for municipal ownership of electric utilities in Los Angeles during the Progressive era. The city had received as part of its Spanish-Mexican heritage a tradition of municipal ownership and distribution of the water of the Los Angeles River. During the Spanish-Mexican period, the city held full title to the water of the river. The water was diverted from the river in publicly controlled ditches, called *zanjas*, from which all inhabitants might draw for irrigation or domestic purposes. Private enterprise was represented only by Indian women carrying on their heads jugs of water that they peddled from door to door for domestic use or by a water barrel mounted on a horse-drawn cart. After California was annexed to the United States, Los Angeles city officials felt obliged to provide an improved system for supplying water for domestic purposes. In 1868, apparently against the wishes of the majority of the city's voters, the city sold to a group of private capitalists a thirty-year contract to provide the city with water, from the Los Angeles River, for domestic purposes. The Los Angeles City Water Company—the name the capitalists gave to their organization—was to install an adequate distributing system, which the city was to have the right to purchase at the expiration of the contract. From the first the "thirty-year lease" was attacked on the ground that the company was making profits from the water owned by the people of Los Angeles. In the municipal election of 1896, the Republican platform charged that water could be supplied at one-tenth the rate charged by the company. In addition, the company's 200 miles of two-inch mains provided inadequate volume and pressure for fire protection or even for domestic service. Hence in 1898 the city authorities decided not to renew the contract. After a great deal of litigation, in 1902 the company reluctantly relinquished its properties, and the city returned to municipal distribution of its water resources. A charter amendment approved the following year precluded any future alienation of water resources from municipal control. The amendment required approval of two-thirds of the voters of any proposal to sell or lease any of the city's water or water rights. Municipal distribution brought improved service at substantially lower rates. The unhappy experience with private operation of the city's water system and the later success of municipal operation considerably strengthened the emerging sentiment for municipal ownership of utilities generally and of electric utilities in particular. This sentiment became especially evident when, with the inception of the Los Angeles Aqueduct project, water and power became so closely linked as to be almost interchangeable.

That the power resources of the Los Angeles Aqueduct would be exploited was a foregone conclusion. It was the considered opinion of two boards of consulting engineers that the opportunities for the economical generation of electricity along the line of the aqueduct were truly exceptional. Cheap electricity would find eager purchasers among manufacturers and householders alike—and attract additional manufacturers and home-seekers to Los Angeles—and power receipts would go a long way toward paying the high costs of constructing the aqueduct.

What is surprising is that the city of Los Angeles, instead of delegating the task to private capital, itself undertook to exploit aqueduct power. This action was the product of several forces. The Spanish-Mexican heritage of municipal ownership and operation of the Los Angeles water system combined during the American period with an unsuccessful experiment with private distribution of domestic water and a subsequent successful return to municipal distribution to produce an overwhelming general sentiment in favor of municipal operation of the city's water system. This sentiment embraced the water system's hydroelectric by-product. Municipal electricity was a corollary of municipal water.

Los Angeles was not, as were most American municipalities that resorted to municipal electric systems at the beginning of the present century, a small community neglected by private electric companies. Los Angeles was a sizeable and rapidly growing city served by three electric companies. Reformers were convinced, however, that the companies did not compete but rather cooperated to maintain high rates. Regulation, by city council and by public utility commission, had also failed to secure low rates. The aqueduct offered a third means of control. Perhaps municipal competition in the generation of electricity might secure lower rates.

Public reaction to the repeated charges that the already unpopular private power companies were seeking to block the aqueduct project or, failing in that, to get control of aqueduct power sites, and the determination of the conservation-minded Roosevelt Administration to prevent private expropriation of water power resources were additional forces leading to the inception of the Los Angeles municipal power enterprise.

22

THE DISCOVERY IN 1901 OF THE LA BREA FOSSIL BEDS

Mary Logan Orcutt

In order to preserve the record while it is still clear, this brief account of the discovery in 1901, by my late husband, William W. Orcutt, of the famous fossil beds on Rancho La Brea, is given, as I knew the story from his telling.

The Rancho La Brea, originally a part of an old Spanish grant, was acquired by Major Henry Hancock in the early 1870s. The presence of tar pits on the Rancho had been known from the earliest times, its name deriving from the Spanish word *brea*, meaning tar or asphalt.

The tar seepages were recorded by the diarist, Father Crespi, who accompanied Gaspar de Portolá on his expedition to Monterey in 1769. In the diary he states, that "on their way north they came upon tar springs, and used the *brea* as fuel for their camp-fire."

Early settlers in California, as well as the Indians, their predecessors, used the asphalt, exuding from the pits, for roofing their dwellings, caulking their boats, water-proofing their containers, and as fuel for their fires.

The occurrence of bones mixed with the asphalt had long been noted but they were generally assumed to be the skeletal remains of cattle, and other local animals, which had become trapped in the viscous mud in their search for water, and unable to extricate themselves, had perished. A favorite nickname of the tar pits was *La Huesomenta,* the bone-yard.

William W. Orcutt, by profession a petroleum geologist, was associated, shortly after his graduation in 1895 from Stanford University (where he majored in civil and hydraulic engineering, and geology), with the Union Oil Company of California, as head of their Geological Department.

Incidentally, this Geological Department is credited with being the first to be established commercially in the oil industry of that time. Mr. Orcutt was elected an honorary member of the American Association of Petroleum Geologists and, also, was a life member of the American Society of Civil Engineers.

In 1901, while exploring for oil sands and other oil indications on Rancho La Brea (as I have heard my late husband relate the circumstance), his attention was attracted to a curious mosaic of bones, embedded in the asphalt near the pool. Upon investigation, his knowledge of paleontology aided him in recognizing the bone pattern as being a part of the integument of the extinct ground sloth, an armored animal. On a second visit to the pits, with the proper tools, he was able to remove and to reassemble this mosaic.

Thereafter, from time to time, as his professional duties permitted, and with the consent and encouragement of Madame Hancock, then living on Rancho La Brea, Mr. Orcutt made many visits to the pits, laboriously removing, piece by piece, the fragile bones of the ancient fossils, which because of their brittleness and the tenacity of the asphalt in which they were embedded, could be removed only by unwearied patience, and meticulous skill. Often the cost of retrieving a single bone was a whole day's labor.

In the course of this excavation work, which Mr. Orcutt pursued alone, because he feared that the precious fossils might be broken by careless handling, he was rewarded, in 1906, by being able to remove from the asphalt the complete skull of a sabre-toothed tiger, the first entire fossil skull of this terror of the prehistoric animal kingdom, which, up to that time, had ever been found in the world.

With this rare find of a priceless fossil, Mr. Orcutt realized that information of this discovery of prehistoric animal remains should be given to some scientific institution qualified to carry on with the best of modern equipment the exploration and development of a project so important in interest to science and to the world in general.

Under these circumstances, it was natural that Mr. Orcutt should consult his alma mater, Stanford University, for advice in the matter. The Stanford officials informed him that, to their great regret, their Paleontological Department was not, as yet, equipped to develop adequately so important a project.

However, they advised that information of the discovery be given to Doctor John C. Merriam of the University of California, whose Paleontological Department was working along those lines and had facilities for exploration.

In accordance with this advice, shortly afterwards, Mr. Orcutt commissioned his friend and fellow-geologist, Mr. F. M. Anderson, who expected to visit Berkeley in the near future, to apprise Doctor Merriam of the discovery.

Immediately upon receiving this information from Mr. Anderson, Doctor Merriam wired Mr. Orcutt, and took the train for Los Angeles that evening.

Mr. Orcutt met Doctor Merriam at the train on his arrival, showed him the collection of fossils which he had exhumed, took him to the La Brea pits, and later arranged for a conference with the Hancock family, who graciously consented to grant Doctor Merriam the concession for exploration of the fossil pits which he requested, and soon thereafter work was begun in exploration at the La Brea fossil pits under the supervision of the University of California.

Later, concessions for digging at the pits were acquired by the Southern California Academy of Science, who issued a brochure on the discovery, and also by the Board of Supervisors of Los Angeles County, who operated in the interest of the County Museum.

The rest of the story of the La Brea Fossil Pits is history, and the product of the continued excavations may be viewed by

Fossil dig at Rancho La Brea, around 1910.
Courtesy of Los Angeles County Museum of Natural History.

visitors to the Los Angeles County Museum and to Hancock Park, where are assembled the greatest collection of prehistoric animal fossils in the world today. Rare fossil specimens taken from these pits have been acquired by leading museums in many countries. On arriving in Los Angeles in 1915, Theodore Roosevelt's first request was that he be taken to view these fossil pits and the fossil collection in the museum.

In our Los Angeles County Museum may be seen the articulated skeleton of the Imperial elephant, which in life is estimated to have been fifteen feet in height, and to have weighed from eight to ten tons. This is the only perfect fossil specimen of this huge beast on view in the world at this time.

Also, on exhibit at the museum are fossil specimens of the giant ground sloth, the sabre-toothed tiger, the giant "dire" wolf, camels, tapirs, and numerous fossil remains of the lesser carnivora, who roamed Rancho La Brea approximately forty thousand years ago, and by their presence in that prehistoric world give evidence of a climate, a flora and fauna much more tropical than exists in this locality today.

Several fossil specimens of animals new to science, exhumed from the La Brea pits by Mr. Orcutt, were given the name "Orcutti," in his honor, and in recognition of his discovery and introduction to the scientific world of what is now considered to be the greatest deposit of prehistoric animal fossils as yet known.

In conclusion, I desire to pay tribute to the late Madame Hancock, and to her son Mr. G. Allan Hancock, for their generous and wholehearted cooperation with the various agencies engaged in the exploration and development of this project, which is of inestimable value to the scientific world; also, as a citizen of Los Angeles, I wish to express my gratitude for the munificent gifts of this family to the public of Los Angeles City and County.

This philanthropy reached a high point in May 1915, when Mr. G. Allan Hancock, as a memorial to his parents, conveyed to the people of Los Angeles City and County, through their Board of Supervisors, title to the Hancock collection of fossils taken from the Rancho La Brea pits and the deed to twenty-five acres of land, in which the fossil beds are included. This tract of land, fronting on Wilshire Boulevard, in the heart of Los Angeles City, is known as Hancock Park, and is now being developed by the Los Angeles County Board of Supervisors as a museum illustrating in reproduction, as nearly as possible, the environment and form in which these fossil animals once roamed in this locality in the prehistoric world.

This park and these museums with their exhibits are the priceless heritage of the citizens not only of Los Angeles but of the world at large and they represent the philanthropy of their donors, and the devoted labor of countless workers in the field of science.

23

THE AVIATION MEET OF 1910

Marco R. Newmark

During the ten days between January 10 and 21, 1910, the eyes of the world were focused on Dominguez Field, the use of which Joseph and Edward Carson tendered, without compensation, as the locale for the first international air meet to be held in America.

The course was 1½ miles, 519.63 feet in length, and was in the form of an octagon. The meet was conducted under the auspices of the Merchants and Manufacturers Association. David A. Hamburger was Chairman of the arrangement committee; Perry W. Weidner was Treasurer and Lynden E. Behymer had charge of the sale of tickets. The other members of the committee were Fred L. Baker, Martin C. Neuner, Dick Ferris, William May Garland and Felix J. Zeehandelaar, Secretary of the Association.

A perusal of the newspapers of that not far-off time manifests the startling contrast between the records then established and the marvels of aviation today, when, in a few hours, man can travel from almost every part of the world to almost every other part; when airmen have soared through the stratosphere to an altitude of fifty-six thousand feet and have attained to a speed of six hundred miles an hour.

Both interesting and amusing, too, are the journalistic reports of the emotions of the spectators then as compared to our almost matter of fact acceptance of the infinitely more amazing accomplishments of aviation today.

*One of the more typical aircraft participating in the
Dominguez Field Aviation Meet.*
Courtesy of Spectrum, L.A. 200.

*One of the very unusual aircraft designs that were
at Dominguez Field during the air meet. Various lighter-than-
aircraft also were participants.*
Courtesy of Spectrum, L.A. 200.

THE AVIATION MEET OF 1910

Of interest, also, are a number of prophecies which were made by the authorities during the meet, concerning the future possibilities of aviation.

So much by way of preface. Let us now proceed to the task of resurrecting from the files of the contemporary newspapers an account of the meet, together with a few other items worthy of record, which appeared in the press before and subsequent to the meet.

On January 4, one article in the advance publicity recalled that Charles K. Hamilton had previously flown in two snow-storms and had gone up in a forty-mile wind, which we learn was the record for daring; and it is further related that the highest wind in which an airplane had hitherto flown was one of fifteen miles, and that this had been considered extremely dangerous.

Leaving these preliminaries, we will now enter upon a consideration of the historic Aviation Meet, which was attended by a total of 176,466 Angelenos and visitors from far and near; and of some of the more noteworthy of the events which distinguished the ten days of its duration, and also of some of the comments of reporters and editorial writers concerning the events and the reactions of the spectators who witnessed them.

That the government realized the importance of the meet to the development of aviation is demonstrated by the fact that it detailed Lieutenant Paul W. Beck, of the Signal Corps, to attend and make an exhaustive study of aeronautics and to make a report on the result of a night attack by a balloon force on a warship in San Pedro Harbor, the balloon, *Los Angeles*, having been put at the lieutenant's disposal by the Merchants and Manufacturers Association, which had recently purchased it.

There is no further reference to the attack, so that we do not know whether the plan was eventually actually carried out or not.

On the first day of the meet, Glenn H. Curtiss accomplished the first successful flight ever made in an airplane on the Pacific Coast. Using a biplane of his own invention and construction, he "negotiated" nearly a mile in the air, remaining

[321]

Marco R. Newmark

Mr. and Mrs. Glenn Curtiss at Dominguez Field as Mrs. Curtiss tries out the controls.
Courtesy of California Historical Society.

aloft nearly two minutes; and "he came to the ground only at his own volition," a performance which inspired this comment: "The hearts of five thousand persons were set to thumping as never before in their lives when Curtiss left the ground and soared like a bird through the air."

The writer continues, "An indescribable feeling comes over one when an aeroplane begins its flight. It is a feeling of awe and exaltation, of joy and fear. One's nerves grow tense; one's heart beats faster and one feels glad in the realization that he is living in the wonderful twentieth century."

Concerning the flight of a Wright machine, the enthusiastic journalist exultingly comments, "then, over the grass—before your startled gaze!—while your eyes are popping out!—why, man alive, look at that!—the airship picks up astonishing speed!—like an express train she is flying and hurrah!—she leaves the ground!—glides upward!—higher!—and higher, at one hundred miles an hour, off into the blue!—hip, hip—hooray!" (The punctuation is the journalist's.)

THE AVIATION MEET OF 1910

On the eleventh, two Curtiss biplanes, one carrying a passenger, one Farman biplane with Paul Paulhan, a member of the French Signal Corps, at the steering wheel and Masson hanging on for dear life behind him; two dirigibles, one piloted by Roy Knabenshue and the other by Lincoln Beachey; a Bleriot monoplane with Miscarol in the cockpit, and a captive balloon were all in the air at the same time. "Such a sight," said the scribe, "has never been witnessed before, anywhere" (and, it may be added, never will be again).

On the twelfth, Paulhan broke all records for height—4165 feet—in a biplane, a feat which inspired a prophecy that Los Angeles would ever be the biggest and brightest spot in aviation.

On the thirteenth, Paulhan took Mrs. Dick Ferris and Florence Stone, well-known stage stars of the day, on a flight, the first heavier than air flight by a woman on the Pacific Coast.

A performance of the fourteenth is of sufficiently amusing interest to justify a verbatim report: "Paulhan flew to San Pedro—over the site of the new fortification (Fort MacArthur), over the Palos Verdes Hills, out over the sea-swept cliffs of Point Fermin, out toward the breakwater and across the harbor.

"A sleepy deckhand on a tug looked, hastily rubbed his eyes, and looked again and shouted to the pilot. Then the shrill shriek of the whistle aroused the shipping and in a twinkling the harbor and the town awoke. Bells were rung and the crowd rushed out to see the aviator who had so strangely and silently swept across the sky.

"When the sound of the whirring reached some Chinese they looked above and with cries of terror threw themselves face downward on the ground. Another dip over a ranch house sent the domestic fowls scurrying for cover and nearly threw a patient cow into hysterics.

"After the flight, Edward Cleary, Manager of the Paulhan interests, threw his arms around the little man-bird and kissed him a dozen times on each cheek. It was a sight to make the eyes of the strongest man run with tears.

"The crowd went home happy in the knowledge that it had seen the greatest flight in modern times and had partaken in a world epoch."

On the fourteenth, also, appeared the following statement:

"If airships should ever be employed for warlike purposes and it is possible they may have to be used just once in order to teach the world the most terrible lesson of its history, they will render helpless and obsolete all the warships. Naval programs may as well be abandoned. A mercantile fleet carrying armed aeroplanes will be more than a match for any war fleet."

On the sixteenth, one of the dailies reported that S. H. Benoist claims to have invented an airship that will rise vertically, can poise in the air like a humming bird and return to the exact spot from which it started.

His invention did not materialize, but future developments were to demonstrate the validity of his idea in the gyroscope plane.

On the eighteenth, Paulhan again distinguished himself. He made a flight from the field over the San Gabriel Valley to the foothills which rise from the edge of Santa Anita, circled the race track and then to San Pedro—forty-five miles in one hour, two minutes and forty-two and four-fifth seconds, the longest cross-country flight the world had ever seen.

On the nineteenth, Paulhan, with Madame Paulhan as a passenger, made a flight which moved the reporter to this outburst: "To those who stood with upturned faces, wildly waving their hands and loudly cheering, while their eyes bulged with amazement, the sight of Paulhan and his wife skimming through the air three hundred feet above Redondo Beach and Hermosa and go down to the sea was a wonder of wonders. They were beholding for the first time the newest form of travel."

On the same date was published the following news item: "Interest in the army maneuvers was heightened when it became known that the Hague Peace Tribunal had just issued a bulletin asking all nations to sign an agreement which will make the throwing of bombs from aeroplanes 'unpermissible' in war."

*A pilot named Turpin, a passenger named Miss Ferris, and an
exciting trip into the sky in 1910.*
Courtesy of California Historical Society.

Any remarks concerning this idealistic gesture would seem
to be superfluous.

On the twentieth, a parade around the course nicely illustrated the transition from ancient to modern methods of land
transportation. There were men on horseback, in an oxcart, on
bicycles and motorcycles, in automobiles, in a carriage, and in
an aeroplane.

As a matter of interest, we record the following statement
made in a paper of January 25, 1910: "Charles K. Hamilton flew
in his Curtiss biplane across the border line of the United States
over the ancient Mexican city of Tia Juana, today, and then flew
back to the polo field at the Coronado Country Club without a
stop. He was gone from the field forty minutes and traveled
thirty-four miles.

"He then made a flight over the ocean, by moonlight, staying up three and a half minutes and alighted in the deep shad-
ows that had settled below the skyline.

"Two new records: 1. Flew farther over the water than
Louis Bleriot over the English Channel (in 1909). 2. It was the
first flight ever recorded where both start and finish were in
semi-darkness."

In this connection, it may be of historical interest to refer to an article in a Los Angeles paper of September 9, 1910, which we will quote verbatim: "Charles K. Hamilton offers to race an automobile at the Sacramento Fiesta of the Dawn of Gold at night." He said, "the conditions here for flying are perfect and I think I can give you something in the way of new records that will be worth telegraphing around the world.

"Night flights have never been attempted on account of the danger, except for a flight I made at Nashville, Tennessee, for the United States, for which I received a diamond-studded medal."

Returning now from digression to the air meet itself, we know, not only from the day to day reports of the many events which crowded its calendar, but from the subsequent editorials, that it was a complete success and we may conclude as well that the financial outcome was equally gratifying; for after paying all expenses and cash prizes plus $50,000 which had been guaranteed to Paulhan, William May Garland was able to announce that all subscribers to the fund with which the meet was financed would be repaid and in addition receive a bonus of fifteen per cent.

In appreciation of their brilliant organizing and conduct of the meet, the citizens of Los Angeles, under the chairmanship of Max Meyberg, on January 29, tendered to the members of the Committee a celebrative banquet at the Alexandria Hotel.

A concluding word on this air meet of thirty-six years ago may now be in order.

From the vantage point of our own era we may smile at the feats of aviation which in 1910 astonished the world; we may find amusing the intense enthusiasm and emotions they aroused in those who witnessed them; but as we smile, let us remember that not only was the meet the excellent and exciting show it was designed to be, but that it also accomplished the far more important objective of making a considerable contribution to the development of aviation; and do not let us forget that the achievements of our own age, not alone in aviation but in all fields, as marvelous as they may seem to us, are, too, but steps

A race between two dirigibles at the Dominguez Field air meet.
Courtesy of California Historical Society.

on the path to even much greater achievements in the future and will no doubt be contemplated by later generations with sentiments very closely akin to those which the triumphs of our predecessors in the past inspire in their successors of today.

24

THE SOUTHERN CALIFORNIA
REAL ESTATE BOOM
OF THE TWENTIES

W. W. Robinson

In 1849 sailors abandoned their ships in San Francisco Bay to rush to the California gold fields.

In 1922 and 1923 white-collar clerks in Southern California everywhere deserted good office jobs to become real estate salesmen. Only the dull-wits remained behind the counter and at the desk.

For a few years following 1920—with the war well forgotten—the influx of people to Southern California was a flood. Every state in the union contributed to the western migration that turned one end of California into vast "population areas" and caused the great real estate boom of 1921-1924, second in importance only to the famous boom of the Eighties.

Between 1920 and 1924 at least one hundred thousand people a year poured into Los Angeles alone. A real estate and building boom was inevitable and the joyous antics of the Eighties were duplicated in a milder way, with new features added. The building permits of Los Angeles told the story of what was happening. From $28,000,000 in 1919, their value rose to $60,000,000 in 1920, $121,000,000 in 1922—and in 1923 the grand total $200,000,000, exceeded only by the permits of New York and Chicago. The newcomers were home-seekers, hence the abnormal demand for real estate. Prices rose, quick profits developed and speculators were happy.

In two years fourteen hundred new tracts were opened in Los Angeles County and the real-estate-broker and civil-engineer elements numbered themselves in the thousands. Salesmanship became a fine art. College professors lectured on overcoming sales resistance. Preachers promoted. Each morning brokers' salesmen would gather in innumerable places for pep talks, mental shots-in-the-arm that would send them out tingling and leave them rag-weak by night. Rows of tiny flags waving before every piece of acreage gave Southern California a red, yellow and gala appearance.

Advertising was as fantastic as in the Eighties.

One dealer announced in the Los Angeles *Times* of June 17, 1923:

> $850 profit now. This is the best real estate investment offered today! We are *not* subdividers; we are manufacturers and are starting erection of a Two-Million-Dollar Worsted Plant. With our plant staked out we find some fine business frontage that we don't need. It's on Central Avenue and 108th Street.

In Carthay Center, lots were sold on the strength of their being fourteen minutes from Pershing Square, the heart of Los Angeles, *by subway*. That subway is still a lovely dream.

A mountaintop subdivision, "Rim of the World Park," with "cabin sites" at $150, was described as having "flower-dotted grass; mountain streams gliding between tall, cool pines; gentle balsam-spiced air; high, blue peaks nearby; a wisp of cloud in an azure sky." Quite true, but oh, how hard to get there!

Beach clubs, golf clubs, trout clubs, lake clubs, salt-water swimming clubs, artists clubs, all with fine club houses, extensive equipment and grounds, were organized daily. Full-page ads in the papers, with pictures of handsome structures, did the trick. If a bank clerk joined the Deauville Beach Club one day, the next morning on reading the *Examiner* he would regret that he had not joined the Gables Beach Club with its proposed taller building. Bridge-playing wives would urge husbands to go into the glittering Casa Del Mar at Santa Monica as an investment, the memberships being sure to rise next week. Real estate salesmen, as gullible as laymen, became charter members of the Belmont, the Fox Hills, the Sea Breeze or the Breakers. The telephone was used to announce to the unfortunate who took down the receiver that he had been elected to membership in the Bounding Boulder Hunt Club and would have an opportunity to get a mountain estate without cost except dues. Furniture stores expanded into emporiums, so great was the demand upon them for equipment.

Beverly Wood, five minutes north of the Beverly Hills Hotel, the "Switzerland of Los Angeles," was offered as a refreshingly cool retreat when "heat blankets Los Angeles," with homesites at $2,000 to $4,000.

In hundreds of tracts oil rights were sold with each lot. Dummy leases were recorded and fractional royalty interests went with every parcel of land.

Even the newspaper editorials were encouraging. The real estate editor of the Los Angeles *Times* on June 17, 1923, wrote:

> If any doubt lurks in the mind of any citizen, permanent or temporary, of Los Angeles, as to the solidity of foundation upon which the great structure of prosperity has been reared, a study of the figures upon the volume and value of manufactured products of 1922 should be sufficient to dispel that doubt. With the value of the output of Los Angeles industrial establishments hovering close to the billion-dollar mark in 1922, and with every prospect of exceeding that figure during the current year, the calamity howlers, who have seen Los Angeles prosperity and growth of the last two years only as a bright bubble subject to collapse at the first touch of adversity, have little ground to stand upon.

The motion picture colony at Hollywood was drawn upon to furnish color and entertainment at tract "openings," in addition to bands, barbecues and lot lotteries. Miss India Hughes, star of "The Common Law", presented a free "garden homesite" at Longacres on the afternoon of June 10, 1923, under the auspices of the promoters. Longacres was twenty-five minutes from Hollywood and the half-acre lots were $575. Jack Hoxie and his cowboys, always favorites among the realtors of the period, helped to "open" the townsite of Whitley, where streets

[331]

were paved not only with good intentions but with seven and a half inches of concrete asphalt.

Even so conservative and distinctive a homebuilding project as Palos Verdes Estates caught the fever. A subdivision of a huge old rancho, its hills and cliffs commanded a thrilling view of the sea. Improved with villas in the Mediterranean style, it has for years interested architects and "community builders." On Sunday afternoons even Palos Verdes gave free programs of music, Spanish dancing, stunt flying, athletic contests, aquaplaning and yacht racing. The Hollywood Legion Band of forty-five pieces and Gary's Hotel Hollywood Orchestra aided, while boy scouts and G.A.R. members took part in flag-raisings. There was a Kiddies' Tent at Palos Verdes, on these important afternoons, with playground teachers, physicians and free toys.

The most fun for observer or speculator during the period that began in 1921 was to take a free bus ride in Los Angeles and listen to the broker-spieler. It was not hard to take such a trip; in fact, it was very hard not to, for solicitors, with tickets in extended hands, flocked the streets. Agents scoured the southland for prospective passengers. A beautiful trip and a free lunch were the inducements. Here are bits, verbatim, from a travelogue delivered as late as July 1928, during a ride that started every morning on Wilshire Boulevard where the boom lasted until the fatal October of 1929. The wielder of the megaphone stands in the front of the bus by the driver. He has lungs. The megaphone speaks:

> Coming to Seventh and Alvarado Streets is beautiful Westlake Park. A few years ago this was a dumping ground for the City of Los Angeles. It is sometimes known as "Charlie Chaplin's Bath Tub," as all of his earlier comedies were made here . . .
>
> To the left is the site of the new Southern California Athletic and Country Club, which sold in 1916 for $12,500 and is now worth $700,000. . . .
>
> Just ahead on the right is Lafayette Park. It was given to the City by two old maids and is known as "Spooners Park." One of the original conditions imposed with this gift was that there would never be any lights or any smoking allowed. . . .
>
> The Talmadge Apartments are located on the next corner on the southeast side. This was given to Norma by her husband,

Prospective customers board a real estate promotion tour bus to be
taken to the Hollywoodland development.
Courtesy of Security Pacific National Bank
Photograph Collection/Los Angeles Public Library.

Joseph W. Schenck, president of the United Artists Moving Picture Corporation, as a birthday present. It cost approximately one
million dollars and was sold a few months ago for a reported
consideration of three million dollars. . . .

Across the street on the left is the beautiful Ambassador Hotel
and grounds. Just a few years ago this was the grazing place for
cattle. It was the dairy farm of Reuben Schmidt. Twenty years
ago Mr. Schmidt's father bought several thousand acres in this
district for about $125 an acre. . . .

The big white house across the street on the corner of Lucerne
Boulevard and Wilshire Boulevard was moved across the city
intact from Figueroa Street. The people never even moved from
the house and they held a party there during the moving. . . .

[333]

On the left you enter Fremont Place, one of the many residential parks of the city. . . . No. 56 is the former home of Mary Pickford before she married Douglas Fairbanks. Her rental there was $800 a month. . . . On the right the big house with the palms around it is a replica of the finest hotel in Hawaii. The palms are Hawaiian palms and were brought over here at an enormous cost. . . . Scores of millionaires, our most noted people, people of world-wide fame live on this street that was a barley field full of oil wells just three years ago. . . .

The large white school on the corner of Third Street and Rossmore Boulevard is the Marlborough School for Girls. Eight years ago this was so far out in the country that they refused to deliver milk there. . . .

This now brings us to the Wilshire Country Club. Memberships in this club cost $5000. Solicitors and salesmen became obnoxious, during the summer and fall of 1921, trying to sell memberships at $100 each. Today they are worth $5000 on account of the tremendous advance in the land that the club owns. . . .

In the distance on the hill you will see the large sign of Hollywoodland. Above this sign, on the top of the hill, Mack Sennett is building his beautiful home at a cost of over one million dollars. To the left you see the old Metro Studios. The last picture made here was Jackie Coogan's "Robinson Crusoe Junior". . . .

Crossing Hollywood Boulevard at Vine Street, the northeast corner recently sold for $6500 per front foot. . . . Continue to Franklin Avenue. The home on the northwest corner is that of Theodore Roberts. When they asked why he built his home at this point so high up, Mr. Roberts said he never wanted his view obstructed. Now look at these skyscrapers that have ruined Mr. Roberts' view. All of these limit height buildings have been completed in the last four years. Kathryn Williams, 1920 Vine Street, Larry Semon, 1938 Vine Street, Tully Marshall, 1950 Vine Street. These are just a few of the movie stars who reside in this vicinity. . . .

Coming back to the corner of Vine Street and Sunset Boulevard you will see the location of the old Paramount Studios. They have moved to the San Fernando Valley because of the profit which they can take on their location. They purchased two blocks for $250,000 and are now selling only one through the Frank Meline Company for $6,000,000. This property is being subdivided into high class business, income and residential property. Frontage on Vine Street is quoted at $3300 per foot. . . .

*Entrance to the Hollywoodland real estate development
in 1923. The famous "Hollywood" sign in Griffith Park was
originally an advertisement for the Hollywoodland tract.*
Courtesy of Security Pacific National Bank
Photograph Collection/Los Angeles Public Library.

This brings us to Cahuenga Pass. To the right is the Hollywood
Theater, where the life of Christ is portrayed each season. . . .
Now we'll turn north to our own tract. . . .

Because of its strategic position and because it merges on the
main highways, I don't hesitate to state that the streets will be
paved with pure gold for those persons so thrice fortunate as to
own land here. It is undoubtedly the best located of any ever
offered to any person in Los Angeles County. . . . The greatest,
safest, quickest opportunity for a sure fortune of all the ages. . . .

And now we're here. . . . My only wish is that you could
appreciate with the same certainty that I do the good fortune in
store for you. Follow my advice and buy one, or ten, of these lots,
regardless of the sacrifice it might mean. Ten thousand banks

[335]

may close, stocks may smash, bonds may shrink to little or nothing, but this tract and Los Angeles real estate stand like the Rock of Gibraltar for safety, certainty and profit. Don't be satisfied with six per cent on your money. Don't be satisfied with twelve per cent. Buy property like this and keep it, and as sure as the world moves it will pay you one hundred per cent to one thousand per cent and more per annum. Be among those who earn from one hundred per cent to ten thousand per cent. We offer you the opportunity. . . .

When the guests climbed out of that bus a free lunch was served. They then were led into a tent for a snappy lecture, to clinch the travelogue and the good food. Afterward they were taken out to the long rows of salesmen's "closing" offices, tiny frame huts looking like confessionals. Here, one to a hut, they were destined to sign on the dotted line.

The boom of 1921-1924 did not have an immediately sad aftermath. Real estate activity declined gradually but not disastrously. Building fell off, the death rate among brokers and surveyors was heavy and many a lawsuit was started against welching club-members. Bank deposits, bank clearings, retail trade and harbor commerce, however, increased for several years. Handsome buildings were left, as well as a network of highways for all the automobiles of the population area that is swallowing Southern California. The fever passed and the patient survived, until stricken with the paralysis of the Depression.

No longer did the gay little flags flutter over the open spaces of Southern California, announcing that orange groves, vineyards and fields of wild oats were being transformed into building lots and home sites, and carrying the cheerful messages of "Water? Yes"; "Sewers? Yes"; "Quick Turnover"; "It's a steal"; and "Sold," "Sold," "Sold."

25

THE BOOTLEGGER ERA IN SOUTHERN CALIFORNIA

Wendell E. Harmon

One of the most unique social reforms ever attempted in America followed the setting sun across the country on the sixteenth day of January 1920. At precisely one minute past midnight on the seventeenth the Eighteenth Amendment to the federal Constitution went into effect and the prohibition era began. While the last goodbyes to John Barleycorn were being spoken in New York, Californians still had three hours to perform their obsequies. But eventually midnight and one minute more came to the West Coast, a dry decade closed down upon the country. The thirty-sixth state, Nebraska, had ratified the Amendment just one year previously, and the Volstead Act had been passed by Congress over President Wilson's veto on October 28, 1919.

In Los Angeles an all-day service was held on the sixteenth in the Trinity Methodist Church to commemorate the passing of drink and the saloon. Those who had more reason to regret the passing than to commemorate it were unusually quiet. "The streets of the city were very quiet last night," reported the *Times* the next morning, "considering that it was the grand finale. Many parties, at which the flowing bowl was the big feature, were held in homes in all sections, but there was nothing like a public demonstration. At out-of-town cafes and clubs, however, things were different; there the expiring demon still had a kick, and some wild scenes marked his passing."

The imminence of prohibition caused a feverish scurrying about by many Californians to lay in supplies for the long dry spell ahead. All day on the sixteenth, floods of bottled and barreled goods, products of American stills, wineries, and breweries, poured into the border town of Calexico and on into Mexico where they could be stored or disposed of. Up to four p.m. on that day one hundred carloads of whiskey, beer, and wine had been received at that port of entry, and the border inspectors there had to devote all their time to checking the exports.

Once the lid snapped shut, enforcement of the Volstead Act was in the hands of a Prohibition Commissioner, working under the Treasury Department and with headquarters in Washington, D.C. Under him were a number of superintendents, each of whom was in charge of an area consisting of several states. Each state also had its own director under whom there were a number of lesser administrators.

Before six months of prohibition had elapsed, it was quite apparent that the federal government had bitten off a bigger bite than it could comfortably chew—at least with the resources at hand. Congress virtually washed its hands of the whole matter, and the Prohibition Bureau was left with a woefully inadequate budget. The Bureau averaged only 3,060 agents for the years 1920-1925, including clerks and stenographers, and was operating on an annual budget of around $10,000,000. With these resources, it was theoretically the duty of the government to prosecute 40,000 cases in the federal courts each year, to guard 18,000 miles of seacoast and border, to safeguard against diversion of 57,000,000 gallons of industrial alcohol, and to prevent the manufacture of intoxicating liquor in the kitchens or the basements of 20,000,000 homes.

The problems of enforcement in California during the prohibition era were similar to those which existed throughout the nation. The force of federal agents available for the job was small, and there was the perennial difficulty of obtaining the cooperation of local authorities. Added to this was the fact that federal courts could not possibly handle all prohibition cases, and the calendars of state and local courts were crowded beyond their capacities. Before the year 1920 ended, it was necessary for Paul F. Myers, assistant internal revenue commissioner, to come to San Francisco and Los Angeles to help enforce the law. Upon his arrival on the West Coast he said: "We are not going to play any favorites. As long as the prohibition law remains on the statute books it is going to be enforced, and there is going to be a better functioning on the part of all concerned." Early in 1922 Prohibition Commissioner R. A. Haynes announced from Washington a shake-up in the California enforcement organization and the dismissal of the state director for ineffectiveness.

The lax California enforcement situation forced President Coolidge in 1926 to issue an executive order empowering the employment of state, county, and municipal officers as federal prohibition agents. Proposed by Col. Ned Green, federal administrator for California, and applicable in all states, this order created a storm of protest in Congress where it was held to be a violation of states' rights. Green explained that the arrangement was necessary in California in order that local officers might cross their regular jurisdictional lines to enforce more adequately the law, since there were not always federal officers available.

Despite Green's explanation, protests against the President's order continued. Former Senator Albert J. Beveridge observed that "it is obvious that if local officers can be made national officers to execute one national law in a particular locality they can be made agents of a general and centralized government to enforce other laws in every locality." President Coolidge remained firm, and finally the Judiciary Committees of both the House and Senate agreed that the order was constitutional. But it was a hollow victory for the White House. No state officials were appointed as agents of the federal government and none were even recommended for appointment. President Coolidge's order was filed away as No. 4439 and the whole question was forgotten.

Most of the states, including California, were either unwilling or unable to spend large amounts of money on prohibition enforcement. It was not until 1923 that the Bureau of Census could make a separate listing of the totals each state paid out for

*An aerial view of the plaza area in 1924 before
demolition of many of the structures to make way first for Union
Station, then the freeway. This area was a focal point for
bootlegged whiskey and illicit sex during the prohibition era.*
Courtesy of Security Pacific National Bank
Photograph Collection/Los Angeles Public Library.

that purpose, and in that year the total of all forty-eight states was just $548,620. This amount was reported by only twenty-one states and California was among the remaining states which presumably expended nothing specifically for enforcement. It was not until 1929, when the states' total was $796,201, that California was listed as spending $1,767. In 1930 that figure jumped to $69,338 and in 1931 it rose further to $73,373.

Some aid in enforcement came from the local level. By January 1922, a total of fifty-six California cities and towns had "Little Volstead" ordinances, and twenty-six counties had similar laws. These statutes made it obligatory on the part of local officers to enforce the prohibition laws in their districts, and they also provided the municipality or county with the opportunity of acquiring a sizeable revenue in fines. In January 1921, the Los Angeles County Board of Supervisors as well as the Los Angeles City Council adopted such little Volstead Acts. The county statute prohibited the sale and distribution of liquor and the manufacture of home brew. Liquor could not be carried on the person without a legal permit, and permits could be granted only if the applicant had a legitimate use for intoxicating liquors. Penalty for violation of the ordinance was a fine not exceeding $300 or imprisonment not exceeding ninety days. The Los Angeles city ordinance was admittedly for the purpose of raising revenue for the city treasury from fines, and the chief of police announced that it would be enforced even to the close examination of soft drink stands.

California law enforcement officers had to face the same problems as did their colleagues in other states in stemming the tide of illicit liquor. Whether it was the use of illegal doctors' prescriptions, smuggling, or illicit distillation, no method of obtaining the prohibited drink escaped those who were intent on having it. Enforcement difficulties were magnified in California, however, because of a number of factors: the long coast line which virtually defied effective patrol, the presence of a long-established wine industry, close proximity to the Mexican border, a large percentage of foreign population, and a large number of pleasure-seeking tourists. It is impossible to say from what source Californians obtained most of their bootleg liquor

Wendell E. Harmon

during prohibition days, but a study of the cases which found their way into the courts or the newspapers leave one with the definite impression that the two principal pipelines came from the bootleg ships plying up and down the coast and from the backyard stills.

The saga of rum-running along the Pacific Coast rivaled in color and excitement the era of the daring pirate and his plundering escapades. The hazards for both the rum-runner and the pirate were great, but so were the rewards. Both considered themselves professionals and looked with high disdain upon amateurs who would attempt to compete with them. And just as the pirate of old had to be constantly on the alert against other buccaneers, the rum-runner had to be ever on guard against the hijacker.

The home base for the great majority of the coastal bootleg trade was Vancouver, British Columbia, where large export houses made no pretense of any other business than to send shiploads of liquor to the thirsting Americans down the coast. The liquor laws of British Columbia were not designed intentionally to allow business of this type to flourish, but loopholes in the statutes and law enforcement permitted it. In the province itself, liquor was dispensed through state liquor stores, but exporters could legally ship their merchandise to Mexico. Very few of the departing cargoes ever reached Mexico, however, and it was common knowledge that the holds were being emptied along the way. The situation could exist only because the exporters and their clique were firmly entrenched in provincial politics and defied any attempt to curtail their activities.

By 1926 smuggling from Canada had actually become one of the leading industries of the state. The Los Angeles *Times*, in a series of articles on the subject, reported that 150,000 cases of Scotch, valued at more than $10,000,000, were being sent into Southern California each year. Along the coast gin was retailing at $30 a case and brandy at $6 a gallon; Scotch, bourbon and cognac could be brought in from the sea for a price that ranged from $90 to $125 per case. Canadian whiskey brokers maintained agents in all major Pacific Coast towns, and orders could be taken, payments made, and deliveries promised in any of

[342]

them. Market quotations, probable average loss, and the expense per case of landing, fixing officials, and buying transportation were all matters of open discussion.

The importers were divided into several distinct classes. At the top was a small group of men who could afford enough equipment not only to transport the cargoes on the water but to see that they reached their destination on land safely. This meant that their equipment included an ocean-going boat, several shore boats for landing purposes, a fleet of trucks and fast rebuilt passenger cars, a good safe spot in which to store the liquor, and a good "mob" to protect their landings and transportation. The second class included those who bought "over the rail." They would make a deal with the first class and agree to accept delivery over the ship's rail. Most of them owned their own speed boats and once they had accepted delivery of their shipment, they were responsible for landing it without being detected by prohibition agents—which usually was not too difficult. At the bottom of the hierarchy were the hijackers who vied with the authorities to see who could first intercept shipments landing on the beaches. It was the losses to the hijackers and agents, plus the expense of bribing officials, paying property owners for good beach spots on which to unload, and the operation of the boats which brought the price of imported goods to a high level.

Four of the biggest bootlegging operators along the coast were Tony Cornero, Melvin Schouweiler, Tony Paragini, and Bill Nard, all wealthy enough that they were in the top class of rum-runners. King of the four was Cornero who, with his brother Frank, operated equipment valued at $105,000, exclusive of the lumber schooner which itself could carry 7,000 cases of liquor a trip.

These big-time exporters, and others like them, handled their goods mainly through the Vancouver firm known as Consolidated Exporters of Canada. Their ships would leave port with papers that called for a landing in Mexico or Central America, but usually only the ship's papers would reach the listed port. They would be cleared and returned by a bribed port official, leaving the vessel itself free to terminate its voyage at the most likely spot along the American coast. As a laden ship proceeded southward, prospective buyers would be notified by wireless and speed boats would meet the vessel thirty to sixty miles off shore. These boats would bring the cases in to a point just outside the breakers, where they would be transferred to still smaller craft and pushed on to the beach. There armed men would guard the approaches as the shipment was loaded into trucks. Favorite spots for operations of this type were Oxnard, Seal Beach, Del Mar, Oceanside, Laguna, Santa Barbara and Long Beach.

Even if the shipment reached the beach safely, there was no assurance that it would arrive at its intended destination, for it was at this point that the hijacker often came prominently into the picture. It was claimed that one truckload of liquor was hijacked on the way from San Pedro to Los Angeles, within fifteen minutes it was hijacked again from the first hijacker, and then recovered by the original owners half an hour later just as the truck reached Los Angeles. Activities of this type led to gang warfare in Southern California, and by 1926 the *Times* estimated that about twenty men had been shot in rum wars, about half of whom died. This situation continued until the 1930s when the New York *Times* correspondent wrote that California was wide open to the racketeer and gangster. "Alcohol is cheap and plentiful; hijacking is a favorite outdoor sport; gang murders are becoming episodical, and the police, fettered by political interference, espionage and other harassments, seem to be helpless."

The federal agents and local police were not entirely helpless to stem the flow of liquor, but their task was an immense one. During 1926 a corps of only fifty federal officers had the responsibility of watching over the conduct of 2,350,000 persons in the Southern California area of approximately 198,000 square miles. They were called upon to patrol 539 miles of coastline and 500 miles of Mexican border, and in addition they had to check monthly on the stocks of about 1,500 drug stores and keep track of about 3,000,000 gallons of wine stored in bonded warehouses.

The Los Angeles Police Department, which had three complete units devoted exclusively to the prevention and detection of imported whiskey, boasted one of the best law enforcement records in the Southland. This was largely due to a system instituted by Chief of Police James E. Davis known as "rousting." When the word spread that rousting was to begin, the police would go out on the streets of Los Angeles with pictures of the known offenders and arrest as many as possible. While evidence on those arrested would be admittedly inconclusive, they would be jailed until their attorneys could appear with writs for their release. This process would be repeated almost daily until sometimes a suspected offender might be arrested as many as six times in one week. Each time he would spend from a few hours to several days in jail, and before long many of them began to leave town.

A second major source of supply of contraband liquor for thirsty Californians was the illicit still. How many of these were in operation at one time or another during the prohibition era across the state is, of course, purely speculative; but any ambitious entrepreneur who wanted to set up one usually found a good market for his product. A commercial still representing an investment of $500 could produce from fifty to one hundred gallons of liquor daily at a cost of about fifty cents a gallon. The product could be sold for three or four dollars a gallon at or near the place of manufacture. At minimum profit a still operating at full capacity would pay for itself in four days. There was little to lose in having it seized, for another could be purchased and paid for within a short time.

The official records provide little help in determining just how widespread was illegal distilling in California, but they are interesting to note. In 1927 prohibition authorities seized 185 distilleries and 572 stills which were operating illegally. The total value of property seized during that year was $168,265. In subsequent years the numbers of stills taken in raids dropped materially until by 1932 it was down to 209; but in that year the total value of seized property was up to $3,743,474.

Statistics fail, however, to describe what was actually transpiring in this interesting and dramatic branch of the bootlegging industry. One of the first major raids in Southern California was made in January 1921, against the lair of suspected moonshiners in the San Fernando Valley. Agents found two large stills, thirty-six barrels of wine, several jugs of "jackass brandy," and about 3,000 gallons of mash. Before they could reach this loot, however, the officers were forced to make their way around 2,300 sacks of potatoes which had been banked in the front compartment of the basement where the still and supplies were located. The first big raid under the Wright Act (state enforcement statute adopted in 1922) in Southern California netted six offenders, $25,000 worth of illicit property, and a still which agents described as the most perfect ever confiscated to that time. The shack in which the paraphernalia was located was completely darkened from outside light, and the inside walls were tightly covered with red carpeting to render the establishment smoke and smell proof.

In July 1923, prohibition authorities uncovered what was believed to be the largest still discovered in the state to that time. It was located twenty feet below the surface in the Wilmington area and consisted of a labyrinth of secret passages, stills, mash vats, pipes, electric wiring and machinery. The cave, which also contained 400 gallons of whiskey along with all the equipment, was located by tracing a six-inch pipe from the top of a nearby windmill to the side of a barn in the rear of a residence. The pipe had been run high on the windmill to dispel distillery fumes which would give the location away.

Finding distilling equipment in a cave was nothing new to dry agents. The *Times,* in reporting the seizure of a still in a tent, was led to remark: "Stills have been found in houses, in garages, in subterranean passages, in the woods, among the eucalyptus trees, in canyons, stables, etc., but this is the first time one has been located in a tent." A short time later the *Times* could add a dairy farm to its list, for a still was found on such a farm near El Centro. The apparatus had been dismantled and hidden at various places around the premises under hay and dirt.

One of the most amusing raids on record took place in August 1924, when agents entered a house on West 78th Street,

*Los Angeles police investigate an illegal still during
the Prohibition Era.*
Courtesy of California Historical Society.

Los Angeles. The owner, a Mr. Bishop, told the inquiring officers that he "might have a drop or two around," whereupon
they promptly found a 100-gallon still in full operation. Mrs.
Bishop demanded immediately of her husband how "that thing
got into the house." Among the supplies on hand were 450
gallons of whiskey, 1,000 gallons of whiskey mash, and 2,100
pounds of sugar. When questioned about the sugar, Mrs.
Bishop told the officers that she had been expecting guests and
had simply laid in an extra supply.

In addition to rum-running and moonshining there were
other leaks in the prohibition dike. One of these was the unlaw-
ful diversion of sacramental wine. The National Prohibition Act
specifically exempted sacramental wine from its provisions with
the statement that "nothing in this title shall be held to apply to
the manufacture, sale, transportation, importation, possession,
or distribution of wine for sacramental purposes." This was one
of the legitimate purposes for which the wineries of California

[347]

and the other states could operate, but all such wine produced had to go into bonded government warehouses where it was closely supervised. Special permits were required to remove these goods, and permits could be obtained only by priests, rabbis, or ministers duly authorized by their ecclesiastical heads.

Prohibition was not a year old before this procedure was being exploited by those desperate for strong drink. In the fall of 1920 it was necessary for the Commissioner of Internal Revenue to issue an order restricting the issuance of wine for Jewish purposes to rabbis with actual congregations. Prior to this, it had been possible for a rabbi to obtain wine without proof that he had a legitimate congregation, and it was charged that some of them had secured the drink for their own use or to sell at speculative prices.

The Jewish community of Los Angeles resented the implications of the commissioner's directive, and issued a statement which pointed out that "the Jewish community at large is especially incensed that the Jewish good name should be prostituted to such purposes, and is therefore especially interested in the proper enforcement of the law." Rumors persisted, however, that bogus Jewish congregations were being organized for the sole purpose of securing wine withdrawals, and in March of 1921 an actual case of fraud came to light. The congregation of the Talmud Torah Synagogue of Los Angeles voted to dismiss Rabbi B. Gardner, and on departing the rabbi declared: "They kept calling for wine, wine, and more wine and, because I could not and would not supply it in the quantities which they require, they tried to break up the congregation. Then I resigned." The president of the synagogue explained that while the group had many fine people there were others who joined only for the purpose of getting wine, and when they could not get all they wanted, "they started a rumpus." Rabbi Gardner pointed out that when prohibition began the congregation had 180 members, but that it had subsequently increased by about one thousand members in fourteen months.

Whether it was going into legitimate or illegitimate channels, a large amount of wine was being released in California for sacramental purposes. In 1922 the total was 131,184 gallons, but in 1925 the figure dropped sharply to 45,757, the approximate level at which it remained until the end of prohibition. In withdrawals for this purpose, California ranked third in most years behind New York and Pennsylvania.

Another legitimate reason for the withdrawals of whiskey and wine from bonded storehouses was for filling physicians' prescriptions and for the use of hospitals and clinics. There was widespread violation throughout the country of this provision as well, and it was claimed that many doctors did little but write whiskey, brandy and wine prescriptions. There was no substantial evidence of flagrant prescription frauds in California, but ailing Californians apparently had no trouble in getting their favorite stimulants. During the prohibition era California doctors obtained an average of about 120,000 gallons of whiskey, 1,000 gallons of brandy, and 5,000 gallons of wine annually for their patients.

Whatever the source of supply, famished Southern Californians, like citizens in other parts of the country, did not have to go long with their thirst unquenched during the 1920s. In 1926 a New York *Times* correspondent wrote from Southern California that "at no time since prohibition went into effect has there been any difficulty here about securing whatever in the liquid line may be desired by anybody. While prices are approximately double what they were in pre-Volstead days, the supply is equal to all demands." Although the open saloon had disappeared, wines and liquors were served almost universally in the homes of the fashionable well-to-do element just as in the old days. The Southland was particularly hospitable to the large conventions which came to Los Angeles, and seldom did a visitor find it necessary to go thirsty. "The good settlers hold up their hands in horror," said the New York *Times*, "and the traffic goes on much as it does throughout the rest of the country."

26

UPTON SINCLAIR AND THE CALIFORNIA GUBERNATORIAL CAMPAIGN OF 1934

Donald L. Singer

When he died the obituaries were many and effusive in their lauding of his ideals. He was hailed as a man who had wrought many changes through his facile pen; as a gentle crusader who had fought strongly, but always fairly, for the many things in which he believed; and as a writer whose novels, though not considered great literature, mirrored the changing social scene for over half a century. Those journals which in 1934 excoriated him unmercifully and called him every name in the book—and then some—characterized him far differently in 1968 when they reported that Upton Beall Sinclair had died at the age of ninety in a nursing home at Bound Brook, New Jersey. Said one writer:

> Domestic reaction to his passing was courteous, as it tends to be when an aged ideologue slips away quietly to be judged. Even those newspapers whose current political postures make it obvious that, were it 1934 and not 1968, they would demand he be silenced, exhumed prepared obituaries which cited Sinclair's "many contributions."

First attaining fame in 1906 with the writing of *The Jungle* Sinclair spent the next three decades attacking every form of social injustice he saw. His prolific pen churned out works attacking such institutions as big business, the press, book publishers, higher education, and organized religion.

He moved to California in 1915 and while continuing his writing he found time to help organize the Southern California affiliate of the American Civil Liberties Union in 1923 and to dabble in politics. He ran as the Socialist candidate for the U.S. Senate in 1922 and as their gubernatorial candidate in 1926 and 1930. In 1933 he changed his party affiliation to Democratic and ran for governor on a platform known by the acronym of EPIC—End Poverty In California. To the surprise of many, he won the Democratic nomination and came very close to winning the general election. Deserted by most of the leadership of his own party and subjected to "one of the most scurrilous propaganda efforts in California history," Sinclair's zealous campaigning, aided by a tremendous volunteer organization, enabled him to garner 879,000 votes, about a quarter of a million short of victory.

This article examines those factors which made Sinclair's campaign so controversial, explains why this Socialist interloper was able to capture the Democratic nomination, and explores the methods and techniques used to defeat him.

Late in the summer of 1933 Sinclair received the following letter from a Gilbert Stevenson: "I have asked a half dozen people to meet you at my office Thursday, August 3 at 7 o'clock p.m. My office is in the California Hotel opposite the Miramar. . . ." Upon reading the letter Sinclair sent back a form letter indicating that he had no intention of becoming a candidate for political office at that time or at any time in the future. Stevenson was persistent, however, and continued writing letters to Sinclair.

These letters wore down Sinclair's resistance and he finally agreed to meet with Stevenson and his friends. Thus, on August 3, 1933, Upton Sinclair appeared before five members of the Sixtieth Assembly District delegation of the Los Angeles County Democratic Central Committee, in Stevenson's small office in the California Hotel in Santa Monica. Thus began the "most unusual and bizarre gubernatorial campaign in California's political history."

At the meeting Stevenson stated:

> It is evident that the next Governor of California will either be a Republican or Democrat. . . . The Republicans will probably put up a complete reactionary, and he will be elected. It is our

> hope that Upton Sinclair will register as a Democrat and stand as
> a candidate at the Democratic primaries, with a definite program
> which the people will understand. If he does this, he will get the
> votes of all forward looking elements in the Democratic party,
> especially the young people. . . . I am confident that Sinclair
> would sweep the primaries, and if so, would be elected.

It is interesting to note that Stevenson later became disillusioned with Sinclair and wrote some bizarre treatises on money reform and politics. These treatises had a definite anti-Semitic bias and fostered a belief in the notorious Protocols of the Elders of Zion.

Sinclair was duly impressed by Stevenson's address and told the group that he had a specific plan in mind as to how California might be saved and went on to detail his "two year plan for California." There was general discussion concerning the plan and, much to Sinclair's surprise, everyone in the room expressed complete approval of it.

He then told the assemblage:

> If I am your candidate for Governor, it will be for the purpose
> of putting my two year plan across. Let me make it plain that
> being Governor means nothing to me personally. I do not need
> fame . . . I do not need money . . . but I cannot enjoy the comforts
> of home . . . while I know that there are millions of others around
> me suffering for lack of the common necessities.

He proposed the slogan END POVERTY IN CALIFORNIA and suggested the bee as an emblem expressive of useful labor with the motto, "I produce, I defend." One of the members pointed out that the initials of the slogan spelled EPIC and these initials were heartily seized upon as a good name for the plan. More than a year before the date set for the general election, the California gubernatorial election of 1934 was under way.

Recognizing that he had no chance to win so long as he ran on the Socialist label, Sinclair went down to the Beverly Hills City Hall on September 7, 1933 and changed his registration to Democratic.

Though still committed to the principles of socialism, Sinclair claimed that:

> I am a Democrat by the same right that makes us Americans
> either Republicans or Democrats—I was born one. If by the

[353]

Donald L. Singer

*Upton Sinclair, at right, poses before one of his
EPIC touring buses.*
Courtesy of Historical Society of Southern California.

name Democrat you mean an advocate of the right of the people
to manage their own affairs, then I am still the Democrat I was
born.

He went on to explain that all of his Virginia-born ancestors had been Democrats and that the party had abandoned its
original principles and had been sold to "corruptionists" and
"the forces of Tammany Hall." Now that the party had been
"recaptured" by F.D.R., he could once again join.

Showing an awareness of political realities, Sinclair declared:

Fifty per cent of the people are going to vote a certain ticket
because their grandfathers voted that ticket. In order to get anywhere, it is necessary to have a party which has grandfathers.

He reminded the people of California that the first step in
making EPIC a reality was to register as a Democrat and to get
their friends and neighbors to do likewise.

After changing his registration Sinclair started his campaign in earnest. As befits an author, he wrote a book, *I, Governor of California and How I Ended Poverty: A True Story of the*

[354]

Future. In this narrative Sinclair wrote about his nomination, his victory, and his triumphant execution of the EPIC program. He also laid down the general principles of EPIC and spelled out these principles in great detail. Sinclair's plan included: a public body called the California Authority for Land (CAL) which would appropriate land that was idle, foreclosed, or to be sold for taxes, and turn it over to colonies of unemployed men for cultivation; a California Authority for Production (CAP) which would be authorized to acquire factories where the unemployed would make products to exchange with the CAL; a California Authority for Money (CAM) which would issue script to facilitate barter between the CAP and the CAL, and bonds to acquire factories and land. Sinclair also proposed to abolish the state's two and one-half per cent sales tax, and taxes on homes and ranches occupied by the owners and assessed at less than $3,000 and to impose heavy taxes on inheritances, incomes, public utilities, banks, and unimproved land. The EPIC plan also included a $50 a month pension for all widows with dependent children, invalids, and needy persons over sixty years of age who had lived in California at least three years.

Sinclair stated that EPIC could be started for "a very small sum of cash, perhaps five or ten million dollars," and that in less than a year the state would be able to wipe its slate clean of all obligations. He estimated that the proposed income tax would bring in between $35 million and $40 million per year.

Although Sinclair made some changes in the plan as the campaign progressed, no documentation was found to support Sinclair's claim that he had sent proofs of *I, Governor of California* to "fifty of the most qualified thinkers upon the subject and made several changes as a result of their suggestions." In talking to Sinclair about this point he said that he was hazy about some of the details of the EPIC campaign and could not remember the names of any of the "fifty thinkers."

While some financial journals merely shouted "Socialism" when confronted with the EPIC plan others took a long, hard look at it. Thus Sherwin Badger, editor of *Barron's*, presented a serious study of the EPIC campaign "with all the reasonableness it merits." He presented the plan in great detail, pointing out the naiveté of Sinclair's economic beliefs by stating:

> Mr. Sinclair appears to believe that a man who is reputed to be worth $1,000,000 has that amount of money on deposit in a bank, and that the bank in turn holds that exact amount in the form of currency. The fact of the matter is, of course, that only a small fraction of these deposits is in currency. Most of this wealth is represented either by securities or by tangible property. The minute that taxes upon the income produced by these securities or properties are increased, their value falls, and the more the value falls, the more difficult it is to sell at prices which will enable banks to pay off their depositors so that the depositors, in turn, can pay their taxes.

Critics of the plan also leveled charges at specific proposals. For example, the plan called for the elimination of the sales tax, which was the greatest single source of revenue in the state. This tax brought some $46,000,000 into the coffers in 1933. The plan did not attempt to show that revenue from new sources would compensate for this loss of revenue. In addition, "the proposal to exempt homes and farms assessed at less than $3,000 was not coupled with any estimate of the loss of revenue therefrom." The San Francisco *Chronicle*, an ardent anti-Sinclair paper, suggested that this recommendation showed that Sinclair was unaware that property was assessed on the basis of forty per cent of its value and that the proposed blanket exemption would bankrupt fifty-five of California's fifty-eight counties.

Taking cognizance of a particular criticism of the plan, Sinclair stated that he would not ask the people of California to buy the $300,000,000 bond issue to be floated by the CAM because he was certain that the federal government would take the bonds. No documentary evidence has been found to support this claim and it seems that it was either wishful thinking on Sinclair's part or, at best, the result of a vague promise made to Sinclair by Harry Hopkins.

As the campaign progressed, Sinclair finally modified his plan and in September 1934, issued *Immediate Epic: The Final Statement of the Plan*. In this work Sinclair either set aside for good or indefinitely postponed six important proposals of the original EPIC plan. Thus, for example, he hedged on the use of script, disassociated himself from the idea of pensions for the elderly, and again stated his desire to set aside the $300 million bond issue.

A few days after the publication of *Immediate Epic,* the Democratic party met in Sacramento for their state convention. The main purpose of the convention was to draw up a platform. Taking cognizance of the vigorous criticism of the plan and wanting to appeal to a broad section of the electorate, the party drew up a platform which looked very little like the plan in its original form.

Following the convention, speculation was rife that the modifications in the EPIC plan were made as a result of the advice Sinclair had received during his visit to President Roosevelt and from discussions he had had with New Deal Democrats in Washington and Sacramento. Sinclair was asked whether the changes in the plan, as put forth in *Immediate Epic* and the Democratic platform, were made as a result of conviction or in order to attract votes. Sinclair stated that the criticism of the plan had showed him that it needed changes in parts and that he had not thought through all the implications of his proposals. He candidly admitted that, as a result of talks he had held with certain Democratic leaders, whose names he refused to divulge, he had been persuaded that the umbrella of California Democracy was wide enough to cover varying points of view. He insisted, however, that the basic principles of EPIC were not compromised and that certain details were set aside with the idea that they would be picked up again when EPIC became a reality.

It was essential to the growth of the EPIC movement that it develop its own news organ; otherwise information concerning the campaign would never have been spread. The large newspapers of the state generally ignored Sinclair during the primary campaign and attacked him during the general election campaign. In fact, the only newspapers which opened their pages to news of Sinclair during the election were Manchester Boddy's *Illustrated Daily News* (Los Angeles) and the San Francisco *News.* Neither paper, however, editorially supported Sinclair.

Thus, toward the end of December 1933, the first issue of the campaign newspaper, *End Poverty*, made its appearance. The paper was dated December 1933—January 1934. Surprisingly enough, *End Poverty* was the private property of a former Hearst journalist who had a contract with Sinclair covering the distribution of expected profits. After five months of this unsatisfactory arrangement, however, the Sinclair organization took over the newspaper, along with its debts, and renamed it the *Epic News*.

To edit this news sheet the Sinclair forces chose a man who had been a reporter and political editor of the Los Angeles *Record*, a Scripps-Howard newspaper from 1918 to 1932. Reuben Borough was determined to make the *Epic News*, "the authoritative voice, not of Rube Borough, nor of Upton Sinclair, nor of Upton Sinclair's . . . End Poverty League, but, as near as I could, of the whole socially orientated people's movement in California."

Having read almost all the issues of the *Epic News*, the writer feels that Borough's lofty goal was not fully realized. While the newspaper did carry long articles on items that were not fully reported in other newspapers, most of the lineage was devoted to the activities of Sinclair and his running mates, news of the EPIC clubs and their work, charges against Sinclair's opponents, the mechanics of putting over a winning campaign, and exhortations to the faithful of the righteousness of the cause.

Borough, however, did achieve great success in his capacity as circulation manager of the paper. Starting with a state-wide circulation of 25,000, the newspaper reached more and more Californians until the five final editions each had a circulation of more than one million. The last edition prior to the general election reached the fantastic total of more than two million circulation.

Borough gives credit to Oliver Thornton, business manager of the *Epic News*, for conceiving the plan which helped the newspaper reach such a large circulation. While the first and last pages of the newspaper were the same throughout the state, the inside pages featured EPIC candidates for the assembly and state senate in a particular locale and were given over to local advertisers. In the remote and less thoroughly activated assembly districts these special editions ran between five and ten thousand copies, but in many areas of Southern California they exceeded one hundred thousand. Under this assembly district plan the *Epic News* achieved a free distribution (though it nominally sold for five cents) throughout the state. The newspapers were "carefully laid on the doorstep of the citizens by Epic Club members, many of whom had helped write the copy and make up the pages of the local section of the publication."

Sinclair was not the sole Democrat to want the party's nomination for governor in 1934. The administration in Washington, not wanting California to be "captured" by an interloper, urged J. F. T. ("Jefty") O'Connor, comptroller of the currency and former member of the prominent California law firm of McAdoo, Neblett, and O'Connor, to run for the governorship. At a California Young Democrats Convention held in the spring of 1934, O'Connor received the endorsement of the group by an overwhelming vote. On June 20, President Franklin D. Roosevelt offered to make a speech for O'Connor if he ran. Nevertheless, O'Connor decided not to enter the primaries, and later threw his support to George Creel.

George Creel had become famous during World War I when he headed the Committee on Public Information, that committee which was responsible for disseminating information relative to the war effort. While in Washington he met and became friends with William McAdoo, who was then secretary of the treasury. Following World War I, Creel again turned to his first love—journalism—and became a free-lance writer. He supported the New Deal in its earliest stage and in August 1933, was appointed N.R.A. administrator for California, the position from which he resigned in order to run for governor. During the ensuing campaign Creel presented himself as a regular or Roosevelt Democrat and charged Sinclair with being a Socialist in disguise.

During the primary campaign Creel furnished the voters with a sample of the deluge which was to come during the final election period when he charged that Sinclair had the support of the "Young People's Communist League of Los Angeles." In his rejoinder Sinclair pointed out that there was no such organization as the above-named one and that the supposed secretary of the legendary organization, one "Vladimir Kosloff," did not exist.

As a matter of fact, the Communist press vied with conservative journals in uncompromising condemnation of Sinclair and EPIC. The *Western Worker*, the official West Coast organ of the Communist party, suggested that Sinclair was more of an insidious threat to the proletariat than the Republican candidates since the latter were easily identifiable as "reactionaries" whereas Sinclair might easily deceive the workers into believing that he was a "liberal." In another article entitled "Fascist a la Mode," the *Western Worker* denounced Sinclair as a "social Fascist," while a Communist leaflet quoted Lenin's description of Sinclair: "an emotional Socialist without theoretical grounding."

Many years after the election, a writer for the *People's World*, the West Coast Communist newspaper, indicated that the Communist party had made a mistake in denouncing Sinclair since he was the only viable candidate whose ideas were not totally anathema to the party.

The third main Democratic candidate was Justus Wardell, the traditional Democratic leader of San Francisco. Wardell declared that Sinclair was a Communist and cited as his "proof" a recent book entitled *The Red Network*. This work, written by Elizabeth Dilling, also alleged that Mrs. Louis Brandeis and Mrs. Franklin D. Roosevelt belonged to the Communist party. Confusing Upton Sinclair with Sinclair Lewis, as so many people were prone to do, Wardell stated that Sinclair had proved himself an atheist by standing before a pulpit and saying, "If there is a God, let him prove it by striking me dead within the next minute."

Although numerous attempts, including phone calls to both by Democratic National Chairman James A. Farley, were made to get either Wardell or Creel to withdraw in favor of the other, both refused to do so, claiming that the other would hurt the state almost as much as would Sinclair.

The Republicans were rather quiet during this period because it was expected that, as a matter of course, the sole candidate for the Republicans would be the incumbent governor, James ("Sunny Jim") Rolph, Jr. His sudden death, however, on June 2, 1934, threw the G.O.P. primary open to all contenders, though it was now felt that the leading candidate was the former lieutenant-governor, now elevated to the governorship, Frank F. Merriam.

Governor Merriam had, like many Californians, emigrated to the Golden State from Iowa and had set up a real estate office in Long Beach. He was first elected to the state assembly in 1917, was elected speaker in 1923, and won the election for lieutenant-governor. Shortly after taking office he was plunged into the political maelstrom. A maritime strike broke out in San Francisco and, as a result of severe battles between strikers, police, and non-strikers, he called out the National Guard to quell the strike and police the San Francisco waterfront. Though this action undoubtedly cost Merriam some votes, one astute political observer reported that "Mr. Merriam has enormously strengthened his position . . . by his readiness to use troops in San Francisco and by his many speeches and statements denouncing radicalism."

Other candidates for the Republican nomination included former governor C. C. Young; John R. Quinn, former national commander of the American Legion and later Los Angeles County assessor; and Raymond L. Haight, a young progressive lawyer.

Haight, who was to play a vital role in the final election campaign, was also the sole nominee of the small Commonwealth party. Sinclair, who admired Haight, had met with him before the start of the campaign and urged him to join the EPIC ticket and run for attorney-general. Haight had turned down the offer, indicating that he had already conferred with the Reverend Robert P. Shuler who had agreed to support Haight's candidacy for governor. In addition to his ministerial duties, Shuler, a popular Los Angeles radio pastor, found time to be the leader of the Commonwealth party and a candidate for the United States Senate in 1932. Haight was a thirty-seven year old attorney who had long fought for clean government and had entered the race so as to give the voters a chance to vote for a "middle-of-the-road" candidate.

The feverish activity of the EPIC followers and exhortations of Sinclair had its effect as the following primary election results show:

DEMOCRAT

Upton Sinclair.................................... 436,220
George Creel..................................... 288,106
Justus Wardell 48,965
Milton K. Young 41,609

REPUBLICAN

Frank Merriam.................................... 346,329
C. C. Young 231,431
John Quinn....................................... 153,412
Raymond L. Haight 84,977

COMMONWEALTH

Raymond L. Haight 3,421

SOCIALIST

Milen C. Dempster 2,521

COMMUNIST

Sam Darcy 1,072

Foreshadowing the bitter general election which was to follow were the editorials carried in the state's two largest newspapers the day after the primary election. Said the Los Angeles *Times:*

> The Merriam-Sinclair contest is not a fight between men, it is a vital struggle between constructive and destructive forces. . . . Sinclair is a visionary, a consorter with radicals, a theorist. . . . No Democrat by the wildest stretch of the imagination . . . Sinclair is a political opportunist, whose sole chance of political success lies in his ability to fool a majority of the electorate.

The San Francisco *Chronicle* stated:

> The State faces an emergency which only resolutely united action can meet. The menace is real and is equally serious whether or not Upton Sinclair is elected Governor or would or would not have a Legislature committed to his fantastic program.

The New York *Times* cautiously commented that "Sinclair's victory is certain to raise up experimentation even more daring" while the Raleigh (North Carolina) *Times* stated that Sinclair's political philosophy is "dear to the heart of the most lusty Communist of the throat-cutting and shoot-em-at sunrise and loot-the-bank persuasion." One of the few newspapers which did not view Sinclair's nomination with distaste was the Bridgeport (Connecticut) *Post,* which said that "perhaps . . . Californians have decided that they would prefer a governor who has ideas to one who is merely a stuffed shirt or a figurehead."

Would the California electorate go along with Senator Hastings, a Delaware Democrat, who said:

> California Democrats have elected a disciple of Karl Marx in preference to a real Democrat. The people, however, can rectify this mistake by voting for Governor Merriam in November. . . .

or would they follow Sinclair, who told Californians that his victory in November would restore "useful, self-reliant citizenship to hundreds of thousands of human beings?" This was the question hanging over the minds of many persons as the general election campaign got under way.

Two days after he had been nominated Sinclair began a two-weeks trip to New York and Washington. The purpose of the trip was to call upon the federal officials whose aid he hoped to get for his EPIC projects, to explain the plan to them and to learn what the federal government was doing in these areas.

On September 3 he arrived in New York City and the next day he drove up to Hyde Park to see President Roosevelt and to seek his endorsement. The President was faced with a dilemma; if he endorsed Sinclair, he would alienate millions of conservatives; if he repudiated the California candidate, he would weaken his strength among many Democrats and among millions more who had followed him in 1932. As it turned out, the

[363]

President took neither course. Following the meeting of the two men, Marvin McIntyre of the White House secretarial staff explained to the reporters that Roosevelt had had a nice nonpolitical chat with Sinclair and that the President could not endorse Sinclair because "he does not interfere in local elections." McIntyre went on to say that if the President discussed politics with one candidate he would have to do so with all the candidates.

Later, however, Sinclair stated emphatically that the President talked a good deal about politics, and that the EPIC campaign was a prime topic of discussion. In a book written after the election Sinclair said that Roosevelt proclaimed himself to be in favor of EPIC and that he was going to come out for "production for use" in a national radio address to be given sometime toward the end of October. Sinclair then claimed to have replied to F.D.R., "If you will do that, Mr. President, it will elect me."

On October 22, 1934, Sinclair spoke to a San Francisco audience and reminded them that the President was going to make a speech in a few hours. The candidate said that if "President Roosevelt says what he told me he was going to say, I expect to be elected." That evening, President Roosevelt exhorted the American people to give to charitable organizations but said not a word about the gubernatorial election in California.

Sinclair asserted that Roosevelt's failure to live up to his promise was one of the three main reasons why he lost the election.

Did the President actually promise to come out for "production for use?" In the absence of any evidence to back up Sinclair's claim, perhaps Arthur Schlesinger, Jr.'s comment best summed up the situation:

> No doubt, like so many others in the excitement of the presidential evidence, Sinclair construed affability as assent. Or he may have transferred a Rooseveltian speculation from the future conditional to the future. . . .

When he got back to California the final campaign began in earnest. Looking back on the campaign almost four decades after it was waged it can be said that it was one of the "greatest smear campaigns ever waged in an American election." *Time* pointed out that "no one in American political history, with the possible exception of William Jennings Bryan, had so horrified and outraged the vested interests and was more open to abuse than was Upton Sinclair."

Not only did Sinclair have to battle the Republican party, as would be natural in any political campaign waged within a two-party system, but he also had to battle a large segment of the Democratic party, as well as the Communists and Socialists.

It might be thought that the Socialists, of all people, would throw their support to Sinclair. But this was not to be. The Socialist party in California declared Sinclair to be a "renegade" and warned the state not to trust Sinclair, while Norman Thomas, the perennial Socialist candidate for President, stated "Sinclair has promised the impossible," and told the country that the Sinclair prgram was "quite visionary." The Communists, too, both foreign and domestic, continued to do battle with the Democratic candidate for governor. The official Communist party paper in the U.S.S.R., *Izvestia*, had this to say of EPIC:

> Epic Upton has raised a cloud of "Epicdust" with his manifesto, which might cloud the view of some people at the very moment when the American Intelligence is so much in need of clear vision. Of course, this "Epic" cloud will dissolve itself. The "Epic" foundation will dry up. But the naivete of Sinclair should be punished. . . . We hope that he will be elected governor of California,

while Karl Radek, a leading Soviet official, was quoted as saying that the Democratic nominee was "stepping along the path of barren Fascism."

In California Communists regularly distributed anti-Sinclair literature at Sinclair rallies and the *Western Worker*, official party organ, continued to hit hard at the EPIC Plan, calling it, in derisive reference to the N.R.A. "blue eagle," "another addled egg from the blue buzzard's nest."

At first it appeared that the Democrats had patched up whatever differences had divided them during the primary campaign, for pictures taken at the Democratic State Convention held in Sacramento in September showed Creel, McAdoo, and Sinclair shaking hands and agreeing to battle the Republicans instead of each other. Two of the minor candidates, Dr. Z. T. Malaby and William McNichols, endorsed Sinclair at the convention.

Hoping to weld all factions of the party together, the convention drafted a platform that would hopefully appeal to many people. The Democrats "pledged themselves to protect the purity and sacredness of the American home, to protect ownership of property and property rights that were not in conflict with the general welfare," and, at the same time, they "pledged themselves to a policy of putting the unemployed at productive labor, enabling them to produce what they themselves are to consume."

This harmony, however, was shattered on the last day of the convention when Culbert Olson was easily elected state chairman of the Democratic party over Colonel William Neblett, Senator McAdoo's law partner. Neblett thereupon repudiated Sinclair and the platform, called Sinclair a Communist, and went over to the Merriam camp.

Other Democratic defections quickly followed. "Ham" Cotton, Creel's campaign manager and head of the W.P.A. in Los Angeles, stated that Sinclair had been nominated by "200,000 to 300,000 malcontents" and proceeded to organize the American Democracy of California in support of Merriam. The Wardell forces organized their own group (even at that point they did not want to associate with the Creel faction) called the Loyal Democrats of California. Naturally these "Loyal Democrats" were for Merriam. Judge Matt Sullivan became chairman of the Democratic Merriam-for-Governor Campaign Committee, a group which asked in a campaign pamphlet, "Is he in fact a dyed-in-the-red Communist? Sinclair will Russianize California and inflict on our people the curse of Communism?"

William Jennings Bryan, Jr., son of the "Great Commoner," organized the League of Loyal Democrats. Bryan, who had run a poor second to Sheridan Downey, Sinclair's running mate, in

the primary race for lieutenant-governor, declared that Sinclair
was:

> a Socialist interloper who offers not a single new or progressive
> idea and whose EPIC program is but a rehashing of the declara-
> tion of principles of the Anarchist-Communist party adopted at
> the convention at Pittsburg more than fifty years ago.

Even more damaging than the Democratic defections were
the pamphlets put out by the advertising team of Lord and
Thomas. This marked the first time, but certainly not the last,
that a political campaign took on the aspect of a commercial
sales campaign. " 'Out of his own mouth shall he be judged,'
said the opposition," and it was with this slogan in mind that
Lord and Thomas, helped out by the young enterprising advertising team of Clem Whitaker and Leone Baxter, culled material
from author Sinclair's numerous works which had been published over a period of twenty years.

Numerous "front" groups were organized and it was
through these "fronts" that millions of pamphlets were circulated and thousands of billboards put up throughout the state.
The physical assets of these organizations primarily consisted of
nothing more than a post office box, and, the only persons publicly identified as members were "chairmen" or an "executive
secretary." The most active of these "front groups" was the
United for California League. The League "quoted" from a
number of Sinclair's books in order to "prove" that the candidate was an atheist who advocated revolution, communism, free
love, and the scientific care of children. Quoting from *The Gos-
lings*, the League said that Sinclair had written that the P.T.A.
had been taken over by the Black Hand; in *Love's Pilgrimage*
Sinclair was alleged to have said, "the sanctity of marriage . . . I
have had such a belief . . . I have it no longer;" and in the novel
100% Sinclair was said to have called disabled war veterans
"good-for-nothing soldiers."

In *The Industrial Republic* Sinclair was supposed to have
come out in favor of "nationalized children," while a passage
from *Letters to Judd* was so garbled that it read "We are moving

[367]

toward a new American revolution. . . . We have got to get rid of the capitalistic system. It is close to breaking down."

At the same time that California Communists were calling Sinclair a "social Fascist," and "the Führer of Altadena," other anti-Sinclair groups were distributing literature picturing him as a wild-eyed Bolshevik. Thus the Veterans Non-Partisan League issued a pamphlet bearing the title *Is Upton Sinclair for Americanism or Communism? Here's the Answer*. The Women's Non-Partisan Committee for Merriam charged that Sinclair, by virtue of having contributed articles to the *New Masses* and having written such books as *Letters to Judd* and *The Profits of Religion*, was a "Communist writer," and the Save Our State League charged that Sinclair was supported by the Young People's Communist League of Los Angeles. It can be recalled that the last charge was first furnished during the primary campaign by George Creel. At that time Sinclair had shown that the organization was nonexistent.

In one of his campaign booklets Sinclair attempted to answer his opponents by stating that he was definitely opposed to communism and that he stood for peaceful change through democratic constitutional processes in contrast to the revolutionary means advocated by Communists. Unfortunately, the truth never caught up with the charges.

Billboards were another propaganda device used to condemn Sinclair. One read:

> Sinclair says: "Christianity has been the chief of the enemies of social progress. If the reader objects to my having fooled him, what will he say of the Christian church which has been fooling him for 1600 years."

The quotation was taken out of context from *The Profits of Religion*. In evaluating the causes of his defeat, Sinclair stated that he regarded this book, which he had written some sixteen years before, as the most important single factor.

Among the groups which used *The Profits of Religion* to substantiate their charges against Sinclair were the California League Against Sinclairism, which published a pamphlet entitled *Upton Sinclair Attacks All Churches*, and a group ironically named the League Against Religious Intolerance, which put out a small leaflet called *So the People May Know—That Upton Sinclair is Opposed to All Churches.*

Comments in the early 1970s by high Nixon administration officials regarding the alleged bias of the news media certainly could have been echoed by Sinclair, for the state's two largest newspapers, the Los Angeles *Times* and San Francisco *Chronicle,* used every propaganda device at their command to defeat him.

The *Times* took extracts from most of Sinclair's books and placed them in "boxes" on the front page of every issue during the last month of the campaign. These short quotations, set within black borders, attracted much attention and, according to Sinclair himself, were a major factor in his defeat. The newspaper "quoted" by leaving out words from the middle of a sentence, beginning a sentence after its real beginning, or ending a sentence before its real meaning.

A typical *Times* quotation was the following extract from *The Goose Step:*

> Fifteen years ago there was a strong movement for social justice in Oregon, led by reformers who fondly imagined that if you gave the people the powers of direct legislation they would have the intelligence to protect their own interests. We now see that the hope was delusive; the people have not the intelligence to help themselves. . . .

Sinclair pointed out that:

> the *Times* wanted the people to think I was expressing contempt for the people. . . . And so it garbled the last sentence. In *The Goose Step*, page 169, the word "themselves" is not followed by a period. It is followed by a comma, with the further words, "and the interlocking directorate is vigorously occupied to see that they do not get this intelligence.

Garbling a quotation from *Love's Pilgrimage,* the *Times* ran a cartoon portraying Sinclair as a bespectacled creature with long fingernails, enunciating the following words: "The sanctity of marriage . . . I have had such a belief . . . I have it no longer." One of Sinclair's fingernails was directed toward the picture of a happy family with a child climbing upon his father's back.

Interestingly, the impetus for the technique of quoting Sinclair out of context came not from the *Times'* management but

[369]

from an unidentified individual who showed up at the Times office one day loaded down with a stack of 3×5 cards containing quotations from Sinclair's many works. This "small man" showed his card file to the editor and editor-in-chief of the newspaper and the following morning the *Times* ran the first of its "boxes" on the front page. According to the managing editor, the use of these doctored quotations "turned the tide."

While the *Chronicle* did not use the Communist label with as much frequency as did the *Times*, Earl Behrens, the *Chronicle's* political editor, began every story with the words, "Upton Sinclair, erstwhile Socialist." In the September 28 edition Behrens reported that a nation-wide advertising campaign was taking place for a "slush" fund for the Sinclair forces. The editor noted that the advertisements had been placed in such publications as *The Nation* and *The New Republic* and included the names of such "prominent radicals" as Clarence Darrow, Oswald Garrison Villard, Theodore Dreiser and Margaret Sanger.

Not only was the metropolitan press against him, but the rural newspapers also opposed Sinclair. A survey of 129 daily and more than 400 weekly and semi-weekly newspapers showed that more than ninety per cent of these papers had tacitly or directly endorsed Merriam, five per cent were supporting Raymond Haight, and the rest had made no endorsement. No newspaper in California, with the exception of the *Epic News*, officially endorsed Sinclair.

For the first time Hollywood threw its mighty forces into political battle. Led by Louis B. Mayer, president of Metro-Goldwyn-Mayer and Republican State Committee vice-chairman, the film industry set out to smash Sinclair. The leaders' first move was to declare that they would be forced to move the entire motion picture industry out of California if Sinclair was elected. Thus, Joseph M. Schenck, head of Twentieth-Century Fox Studios, declared in Miami, "If Florida is on the alert it will benefit to the extent of $150,000,000 a year on the film industry if Sinclair is elected." However, Carl Laemmle, president of Universal Pictures, broke ranks and declared that Universal Studios would remain in California no matter who won the election. He stated "I never have cared a rap who was or was not governor."

The producers raised a campaign fund of half a million dollars, partly by assessing their high-salaried employees one day's wages. Though most actors and writers went along with this "request," some rebelled against the "Merriam tax." Jean Harlow and James Cagney led an actors' revolt against the assessment, while Gene Fowler organized a writer's committee for Sinclair.

The producers' main barrage against Sinclair consisted of a series of fabricated newsreels. Motion pictures were taken of a horde of "disreputable vagrants" in the act of crossing the "California border." The pictures were actually taken on the streets of Los Angeles with cameras from a major studio; the "vagrants" were actors on studio payrolls, dressed in false whiskers and dirty clothes, and wearing sinister expressions. These newsreels were spread across the screens of leading theaters in every city in the state.

Irving Thalberg, production chief at MGM, invented a character called the "Inquiring Reporter" who supposedly traveled around the state interviewing "typical" Californians, getting their reactions to the campaign. One of the melodramas was particularly interesting. In this film the "Inquiring Reporter" approaches a demure old lady sitting in her rocking chair. When asked for whom she was going to vote she replies that Merriam is her man; when asked why she is going to vote for Merriam she states, "Because I want to save my little home. It's all I have left in this world." In another "newsreel" a bearded man with a thick Russian accent declares for Sinclair. When asked by the interviewer why he is voting for Sinclair, he replied, "Well, his system worked vell in Russia, vy can't it vork here."

The effectiveness of Hollywood's crusade against Sinclair was summed up by the *Hollywood Reporter*: "This campaign against Sinclair has been and is DYNAMITE. It is the most effective piece of political humdingery that has ever been effected. . . ."

[371]

Donald L. Singer

Governor Merriam ran a shrewd campaign, declaring that his opponent was an "extreme Socialist" while stressing the positive features of the Republican state administration. In his public utterances Merriam stated that "there are no other issues before us except radicalism and Socialism." He called the EPIC proposals "flimsy and unreal . . . utterly misguided . . . completely impossible of realization . . . dangerously unsafe and destructive."

The incumbent pointed with pride to the special session of the California Legislature which had just concluded and through which he had forced measures dealing with old-age pensions, assistance for the unemployed, and relief for certain classes of debtors. He made a bid for the votes of the Townsend Plan advocates by declaring:

> I have recommended to the attention and scrutiny of the national government the . . . Townsend Plan and shall actually cooperate with the federal authorities in working out an equitable and sound plan designed to accomplish the purposes involved.

One newspaper reported that California's " 'good, grey governor' remained kindliness and tolerance itself" while his underlings carried on a vicious attack against Sinclair.

One Republican party official who attacked Sinclair for the candidate's alleged lack of patriotism was Earl Warren, district attorney of Alameda County and newly-elected Republican state chairman. He declared:

> In proportion as the size of the majorities can be made and the completeness of defeat of the Sinclair movement can be affected, to that extent can notice be given to the country that California is a safe place for constitutional rights and liberties. . . . We must fortify ourselves against a resolute purpose to overwhelm California with Communism.

The third man in the race, Raymond L. Haight, had little chance of winning, but his vote, if thrown to one of the two main candidates, could be the decisive factor in the election. It was with this thought in mind that a group of northern California businessmen went to Haight and urged him to withdraw from the campaign. In return for his withdrawal they offered him (1) any state office he wanted; (2) the United States senator-

*Stretching ingenuity to its limits, the Sinclair bandwagon
employed a fishing smack to advertise its candidate.*
Courtesy of Historical Society of Southern California.

ship in the event that a senator died while Merriam was governor; (3) a promise of support in the gubernatorial election in
1938; and (4) $100,000 cash. Haight refused to withdraw and
continued his campaign hitting hard at the theme that he was
the "middle-of-the-road" candidate.

During the last month of the campaign events moved fast,
and some of them proved inimical to Sinclair. He was heartened
by letters of encouragement from two famous men, one a
physicist and the other a poet. From his home in New Jersey,
Albert Einstein wrote, "You know indeed much better than I,
that nothing annoys people more than one trying to help them.
I heartily wish that in your case the matter may come out otherwise."

[373]

Donald L. Singer

Ezra Pound, from his home in Rapallo, Italy, scribbled on a large sheet the following message: "Congrats on nomination. Now beat the bank buzzards and get elected. 'Script' yr/best item. Vide exec."

The Sinclair forces were temporarily elated when letters arrived to prominent California Democrats urging Sinclair's election and bearing the famous green-ink signature of Jim Farley. The letter was promptly put on the front page of the *Epic News*. When Farley was questioned about this unexpected turn of events, he professed ignorance of the letter of endorsement. Emil Hurja, a wizard with figures and secretary of the Democratic National Committee, stated to the press that the letters were the result of a "clerical error" and never should have been sent in the first place. It was reported that F.D.R. himself called Farley in and reprimanded him for his carelessness in the matter.

Other prominent Democrats began to desert the Sinclair ship. Senator McAdoo, when asked if he were voting for Sinclair, evasively replied that he had to make speeches in Arizona and Utah in support of Democratic senatorial candidates and would not reach California until election day, while George Creel made public a letter to Sinclair in which he stated that Sinclair had violated a pledge to abandon his platform of "Immediate Epic" in favor of a compromise plan. Creel said that he was going to vote for Merriam and hoped that other Democrats would do likewise.

The same day that Creel's letter was made public, the *Saturday Evening Post* came out with its weekly issue and the lead article was entitled "Utopia Unlimited" and was written by one George Creel. In this article Creel blasted EPIC, claiming that the plan was economically unfeasible, and wrote that the platform adopted at the Democratic State Convention in September was different from that espoused by Sinclair.

In the final days of the campaign the Roosevelt Administration, believing that Sinclair would drag the entire Democratic ticket down to defeat, stepped in to try to persuade Sinclair to withdraw in favor of Haight. This scheme involved A. P. Giannini, president of the Bank of America and a prominent Roosevelt supporter; J. F. T. O'Connor, comptroller of the currency; and Raymond Haight. During the primary campaign Giannini had urged leading Democrats to unite behind a single candidate in order to defeat Sinclair. This effort having failed, "Giannini arranged to be kept informed on developments in the Haight and Sinclair camps."

In the last week of October, while he was in Washington on business, Giannini received a report from his San Francisco "contacts" that Sinclair was willing to withdraw in favor of Haight. Giannini then contacted O'Connor and informed him of this latest development. On October 27, O'Connor sent a confidential memorandum to Marvin McIntyre, a White House aide, urging administration support for a move to replace Sinclair. A copy of this memorandum was sent by O'Connor to Louis Howe, Roosevelt's close associate.

For the next two days Administration officials held a series of meetings on the matter. Known participants included McIntyre, Farley, and Henry Morganthau, secretary of the treasury. It was decided that O'Connor should fly to Los Angeles and, "if conditions seemed proper, suggest to Sinclair that he withdraw" from the race. That night, just before he left, O'Connor was told by Morganthau that the President wanted him to go to California. Thus, by indirectly endorsing O'Connor's mission, Roosevelt was violating his oft-expressed public policy of not intervening in state elections.

Actually the mission was doomed to failure before O'Connor saw Sinclair. Rumors of a possible withdrawal had led reporters to interview Sinclair before O'Connor arrived. The candidate told the press that he would never withdraw.

Upon his arrival O'Connor went directly to the home of Stanley Anderson, owner of the Beverly Hills Hotel and a close friend of Sinclair's. There the candidate and the comptroller had a two-hour conference. O'Connor suggested that if Sinclair felt his election were doubtful "some arrangements should be made." Sinclair ignored the suggestion. At no time did O'Connor ask Sinclair to withdraw from the race. The comptroller

explained later that he "saw the utter futility of such a suggestion," especially in light of Sinclair's statement to the press.

O'Connor's trip was not entirely in vain. He also talked to
Haight and Merriam. Haight was told that his chances of victory
had vanished with Sinclair's refusal to quit, while Merriam said
that he would make a statement to the press before election day
that his election would not be considered a repudiation of the
New Deal but was brought about with the assistance of many
Democrats. He also said that the Democrats "would not be forgotten" if he were elected.

Pleased with his success, O'Connor sent a lengthy report to
McIntyre, with copies to Farley and Morganthau. In his report
the comptroller stated that "I believe my most important work
on this trip is what we can expect if Merriam is elected Governor."

During the last days of the campaign O'Connor had lined
up additional Democratic support for Merriam and told friends
that he expected Merriam's winning margin to reach 300,000.

The President was evidently pleased with the way O'Connor had handled things in California, for when he returned to
Washington, F.D.R. told the comptroller, "Jefty, you must take
the party leadership in California," and offered him the chairmanship of the 12th District Federal Reserve Board, with offices
in San Francisco.

The last blow to Sinclair's candidacy fell on November 3,
just three days before election, when the poll taken by the *Literary Digest* was released. It showed Sinclair as the choice of only
25.72 per cent of the electorate while Governor Merriam was
picked by 62.31 per cent of those polled. While the poll turned
out to be extremely inaccurate (and was undoubtedly distorted
by the same factors which led it astray in 1936), it probably gave
whatever push was needed to defeat Sinclair. The candidate
later said that the poll "did us irreparable harm. It encouraged
our enemies . . . it shifted the betting odds. . . . Many people
were waiting to know which band wagon to climb onto—and
now they knew."

The voters, reflecting the high interest in the campaign,
turned out in record numbers on election day. The total vote

cast was 2,330,132; it exceeded by 916,044 the total in the previous gubernatorial campaign in 1930.

Sinclair received 875,537 votes, while Merriam garnered a total of 1,138,620 votes. The Commonwealth party candidate, Raymond Haight, got 320,519 votes. It was the first time since 1914 that the winning gubernatorial candidate received less than a majority vote in a general election.

Some political observers have concluded that Sinclair would have been elected it if had been a two-man race. The editor of *Epic News*, Reuben Borough, disputed this, stating that it is erroneous to assume that Raymond Haight took away votes from Sinclair. Borough pointed out that Haight's strength lay in the agricultural San Joaquin Valley and that the farmers disliked Sinclair because of his threatening to take over idle land. The editor felt that in a two-man race the farmers' votes would have gone to Merriam.

Although the EPIC movement did not accomplish what it had set out to do, it would be a mistake to write off the crusade as useless. The movement did produce a forceful Democratic party in California for the first time. Heretofore a minority party, the Democrats found themselves, at least in terms of registration, the majority party, a position which they have maintained ever since. Such progressive-minded men as Culbert Olson, Sheridan Downey, and Jerry Voorhis (all of whom ran on the EPIC platform in 1934), stepped into party leadership posts. These men, each of whom went on to hold high elective office, spoke for quite a different version of the Democratic party from that of McAdoo, Wardell, and Creel.

The EPIC crusade also contributed a leftward pressure on the New Deal. While the Liberty League was saying that Roosevelt had taken the nation down the Socialistic path, Sinclair's followers were claiming that the New Deal had not gone far enough. John T. Flynn noted the impact of EPIC on federal legislation when he said: "It was the sweep of the Townsendites, . . . and the EPIC planners that spurred F.D.R.'s interest and resulted in the passage of Social Security Act with old age pensions and unemployment insurance."

Equally as important, if not more so, was the fact that "Sinclair and the EPIC movement provided a means, which was in harmony with the American democratic tradition, through which the protests of thousands suffering from the great depression could be heard."

27

"HAM AND EGGS, EVERYBODY!"

Tom Zimmerman

━━━◦◦◦◦◦◦◦◦◦◦◦◦━━━

There is no better demonstration of how drastically unprepared the United States was to cope with the Great Depression's dislocations than the fate of the elderly. There was no federal pension plan, and by 1934 only twenty-eight states granted financial assistance. Old people had to fend for themselves, or get help from relatives or private agencies. This is why schemes like Huey Long's "Share The Wealth," Father Charles Coughlin's "National Union For Social Justice," and Dr. Francis Townsend's pension plan clubs received such an avid reception. As one disastrous year followed another, the elderly grew ever more desperate for relief. The Social Security Act of 1935 did little to assuage their fears. The monthly grant was small, and done on a matching basis with the states. Thus, while retired people in California got $35.00 per month, their counterparts in Mississippi got only $7.50. The situation was further complicated by the recession of 1937. What small hopes had been raised by a stronger economy in 1935 and 1936 were thoroughly wrecked. This disappointment set the stage for the last of the Depression era's pension panaceas: The California State Retirement Life Payments Act, more popularly known as "Ham and Eggs" or "$30 Every Thursday."

California has traditionally had weakly organized political parties. For this reason, grass roots movements, such as the Workingman's Party of California in the 1870s and the Progressives in the 1910s, have been central in bringing change to the state. Added to this was California's popularity as a retirement site. For these reasons, the state was the scene of feverish activity on the part of pension schemers. Technocracy, Upton Sinclair's End Poverty In California (EPIC), the Utopian Society, Mankind United, and Townsendism were greeted eagerly. But none of them had been successful. When Ham and Eggs came on the scene in late 1937, it found ready support among both veterans and rookies in the pension fight. A segment of the populace was as ready as ever to "support new movements and worship strange gods."

The basic form of the California Pension Plan originated with Robert Noble, a former divinity student and radio personality. He had his own weekly show and was a popular speaker at women's luncheons. He had his first brush with pension schemes during the EPIC campaign. Later, while in New Orleans touring on behalf of the Los Angeles Chamber of Commerce, he encountered Huey Long's Share The Wealth movement. When he returned to the West Coast, Noble proclaimed himself to be Long's California representative and lectured in support of the Kingfisher's plan. When Long was assassinated on September 8, 1935, Noble had to look elsewhere for involvement. He read Yale University Economics Professor Irving Fisher's theories on stamp scrip and developed a program he called $25 Every Monday Morning. He advocated distributing $25 in scrip every Monday to all people over fifty who were neither employed nor employer. It behooved the recipients to rapidly spend the scrip because 2¢ stamps had to be affixed to the pseudo money every Monday if they were to retain their value. The end result was a stimulated economy.

Noble needed an office for his slowly accelerating organization and secured space from the Cinema Advertising Agency, owned by Willis and Lawrence Allen. Willis, a former cheerleader at the University of Southern California, was no stranger to promotions. In 1934 he sold a hair-darkening tonic called "Greygone." Unfortunately, as it was more prone to making hair fall out than remove the grey from it, Willis was charged with using the mails to defraud. He was found guilty and fined $100. Lawrence was a lawyer and more restrained than his vociferous brother, but both became interested in Noble's plan and grew increasingly active in his organization.

On October 4, 1937, the Allens called a meeting of forty prominent members of the burgeoning movement at Clifton's Cafeteria in downtown Los Angeles. Willis held that it was time to get the plan moving. The membership was growing, but the scheme lacked direction. He recommended the election of a board of directors and the elimination of Noble, who was charged with wasting too much radio time attacking the corrupt regime of Los Angeles' Mayor Frank Shaw as well as lacking the skills necessary to build a statewide organization. The resolution was adopted, and Noble was advised that he would no longer be given radio air time or access to the money collected by the movement. In effect, the Allen dominated eleven man board had stolen $25 Every Monday Morning from its founder.

With their control of the organization secured, the Allens turned their attention to its enlargement. The most urgent need was a voice to replace Noble's on the radio. Their choice was Sherman Bainbridge, an experienced liberal speaker. It was he who gave the pension plan its nickname when he told an audience, "We must have our ham and eggs!" This offhanded phrase, used to indicate the difficulty of buying decent food under the existing pension system, stuck. Bainbridge's friend, Roy G. Owens, was also hired. He had formerly been vice president of a Cleveland manufacturing firm, but had lost his money when the business went bankrupt. He then turned his attention toward economic reform, becoming involved with the Utopian Society. Owens authored "The Righteous Government Act of 1936" which advocated the total control of the economy by a chief engineer-economist, who would distribute and regulate the value of all money in America. He planned to have this act implemented by Congress, but could never interest that body in it.

Even with the influx of new blood, $25 Every Monday Morning moved slowly until a story broke in San Diego about the suicide of sixty-four year old Archie Price. Price had retired to California with his life's savings. But the Depression slowly eroded his assets until by 1938, he was desperate. He entered

[381]

the office of a San Diego newspaper and told a reporter he would not face a life of misery and starvation, and planned to kill himself as a protest against his condition. On July 25, 1938, Price's body was found in Balboa Park. He had taken poison. A note was found on his body that said he had killed himself because he was "too young to receive an old-age pension, and too old to work." Price was buried in a pauper's grave by the city. The leaders of Ham and Eggs got wind of the story and prepared to take advantage of it. They arranged for a new funeral. Merkely's Mortuary handled the services at Glen Abbey Cemetery in Chula Vista. The Merkely Maids Brass Choir provided the music. Graveside speeches were delivered by Culbert Olson, Democratic candidate for governor, Sheridan Downey, Democratic candidate for United States Senator, and Sherman Bainbridge. A crowd estimated at five to six thousand, many with picnic lunches, attended. After scoring this publicity coup, Ham and Eggs was on its way.

When Bainbridge first arrived at the pension plan's Hollywood headquarters, he was aghast to find that there was no written act. Owens was put to work framing a constitutional amendment under the general outline of the warrant system established by Robert Noble. Once the act was written, Noble attempted to re-establish control of his organization by filing the name "$25 Every Monday Morning" with California Secretary of State Frank Jordan. The Allens countered this ploy by merely increasing the ante to $30 and changing the day to Thursday. Jordan titled the bill "Retirement Life Payments Act." The next step was to collect enough signatures on petitions to get the initiative constitutional amendment on the ballot since 187,000 signatures were required. The lists turned over to Secretary Jordan in August of 1938 contained 789,104 names, or 25% of the state's registered voters.

The amendment written by Owens retained the pension features of Noble's plan. Warrants of $30 were to be given to all people over fifty who were neither employed nor employers, to which 2¢ stamps had to be attached each week. The warrant with its fifty-two stamps could be exchanged at the end of the year for $1.00 in United States currency. The extra 4¢ would go to the state to cover the cost of the program (Section 7). The office of State Retirement Life Payments Administrator, who would carry out the "the spirit and the intent" of this act, was created to handle the new pension plan. The governor was directed to appoint either Owens, former Los Angeles City Councilman Will Kindig, or long-time Ham and Egger J. C. Elliott administrator within five days. His successor was to be chosen in the 1940 general election (Sections 3-6). The warrants were to be accepted for state, county, and city taxes and fees (Section 7). Any purchases made by state and local governments were to be paid 50% in warrants (Section 15), and all state, county and city workers were directed to accept up to 50% of their pay in warrants (Section 14). Dispersal of the warrants was to be accomplished through banks appointed by the administrator, which would act as Retirement Life Payment Agencies. If no bank could be secured, a Branch Retirement Life Payment Office was to be opened. These agencies were to receive 10¢ each week for every retired person assigned to them, and a 2% commission for all money collected for Warrant Redemption Stamps sold by them. These commissions were to be paid weekly, in either warrants or lawful money of the United States, whichever the agent preferred (Sections 20-25). The administrator was further empowered to appoint four assistant administrators, and as many other assistants, branch office managers, clerks, and deputies as he deemed necessary (Section 27). He was given the power to summon, and set the date for special elections whenever he proposed an amendment to the act (Section 37). To ensure the enactment of the totality of this act, any part of the California state constitution that conflicted with it was automatically repealed (Section 43). Also, if one aspect of the act was declared unconstitutional, only that section was stricken from the law, not the entire act (Section 45).

The Ham and Eggs movement did not involve itself unduly in the other aspects of the statewide elections in 1938. The only other of the twenty-five propositions they commented on was Number 1, a vicious anti-labor initiative. This limited effort was all the participation a segment within Ham and Eggs, led by Sherman Bainbridge, could urge out of the leadership. Bainbridge and his followers hoped to move $30 Every Thursday into the mainstream of California progressivism. The Allens were not interested, however, and the effort remained slight.

The Ham and Eggers had some effect on various representative office races. Under California's cross filing system, Earl Warren secured the nomination of both the Republicans and Democrats for attorney general. Seeking a friend in the office, the Allens instructed the faithful to write in the name of Carl Kegley, Willis Allen's lawyer. The race for governor was more confusing. State Senator Culbert Olson, an ardent New Dealer and long-time pension advocate, was the Democratic choice to oppose the incumbent, Republican Frank Merriam. Olson was evasive on the question of the California Life Payments Plan. He had to patch up his party, which was still badly split following Upton Sinclair's EPIC campaign in 1934. Convinced that his fence mending efforts would be ruined if he took a positive stand one way or the other on Ham and Eggs, Olson issued ambiguous statements on the movement. He continued this policy into the general election, neither supporting nor totally rejecting the pension plan. As a consequence, he received no official support from $30 Every Thursday. President Franklin D. Roosevelt chose the 1938 congressional elections for his disastrous attempt to prod the American people to support his friends and punish his enemies. California was the scene of one of his defeats. The White House supported incumbent William Gibbs McAdoo in the August 30 primaries. He was defeated by a veteran of the EPIC, Townsend, and Ham and Eggs movements, Sheridan Downey. He defeated Republican Philip Bancroft in the November general election, receiving broad liberal support, because, as *Nation* reported, despite "his enthusiasm for $30 Every Thursday, he is quite normal and would doubtless make a progressive Senator."

The big city dailies were primarily interested in the gubernatorial race, but donated sufficient space to the California Life Payment Plan (Proposition 25) to make their opposition clear. Even Manchester Boddy, who used the pages of his Los Angeles *Daily News* to trumpet the wonders of Technocracy, opposed Ham and Eggs. The labor and progressive press was predomi-

nantly concerned with defeating the anti-labor Proposition 1.
People's World, California's leading progressive newspaper, gave
all liberal causes a fair hearing. It offered no recommendation
on Ham and Eggs, but the arguments used in a debate sponsored by the paper were reprinted for the evaluation of its
readers.

As in all elections, numerous committees and citizen's
groups sprung up. Those opposed to Ham and Eggs received
millions of dollars in support from the traditional enemies of
progressivism in the state—such as the Chambers of Commerce, the railroads, the Associated Farmers, bankers, and the
California Manufacturers Association. The Southern California
Wholesalers Institute, the Southern California Retail Council,
and the Alliance of Retail Merchants recommended that their
members not accept the warrants because they would not hold
their value and were worthless outside the state. Other groups,
like the California Real Estate Association, the Affiliated Teachers Organization of California, the Southern California Restaurant Association, and the Hollywood Women's Club complained that the state's economy would be destroyed by the
inevitable failure of the warrants. The scrip's collapse in value
would lead to destruction of the school system, property values,
and usher in a killing inflation. Any program that required
matching funds from the federal government, whether it be
pensions or projects of the Works Progress Administration,
would be in jeopardy because there could be no matching of
warrants with United States currency. Although the warrants
would be worthless, their advent would spark a new migration
of destitute citizens from all over the country. Numerous articles were published by the state's daily newspapers examining
cases in which scrip schemes had failed. The point was repeatedly made that money's value rested on the degree of its acceptance by the people. Opponents claimed the warrants would be
rejected. The administrator was condemned as a dictator. Walter Davenport commented, "The man will be a dictator to a
degree that will cause Messrs. Hitler, Mussolini, and Stalin to
remove their helmets, genuflect, and write letters of admiring
congratulations." Fear that the state would be bankrupted be-

[385]

*Volunteers of America were one of the many groups
who tried to ease the tragic impact of the Great Depression by
setting up thrift shops in the 1930s.*
Courtesy of Spectrum, L.A. 200.

*Volunteers of America also operated employment agencies
for the unemployed.*
Courtesy of Spectrum, L.A. 200.

cause it was forced to accept the warrants for taxes was often expressed. Judge George Crothers opined that wealthy people would purchase the valueless scrip for 10¢ or 15¢ on the dollar and use them to pay their taxes. The liberals who opposed the plan generally did so for the same basic reasons as the conservatives and reactionaries. President Roosevelt referred to Ham and Eggs as a "shortcut to Utopia" that would surely fail. Upton Sinclair, Dr. Francis Townsend, Los Angeles Mayor Fletcher Bowron (who replaced Frank Shaw following a recall election), and Senator Burton Wheeler scored the administrator as dictatorial in nature and a harbinger of fascism. The amendment itself was generally condemned as the wrong way to assure fair pensions.

But such opposition was irrelevant to those caught up in the movement. Radio stations in Los Angeles, San Francisco, Sacramento, Fresno, Bakersfield, Stockton, Santa Barbara, and Hollywood presented daily half-hour shows sponsored by the Ham and Eggers. Three sound trucks constantly toured the state, and a Speaker's Bureau sent proselytizers to all parts of California to explain the plan. They constantly pointed out that there was nothing new in the use of warrants when money was scarce. The view of the Ham and Eggers as hairbrained dreamers was attacked. The most popular pamphlet of the movement, *Life Begins At 50 With $30 A Week For Life,* observed that progressive business executives, the finest legal minds, and others trained in sound business practice devised the act. "Theoretical and untried principles have been cast aside and only tested and proven ones used. Thus the Plan has assurance of success from the beginning." The notion that the $30 Every Thursday movement was solely for old people was rejected. It was pointed out that youth had nothing to look forward to except the W.P.A. With people over fifty deleted from the job market, and spending their $30 per week, the economic doldrums would vanish. The ideal of society under Ham and Eggs was expressed in a photo feature published in the movement's infrequently printed newspaper, *Ham And Eggs For Californians.* "In Our Neighborhood" featured a very young couple, Jim and Betty, who were finally able to get married and buy new things because Jim received a promotion when an older man voluntarily retired to get his pension. Stories of storekeepers who would accept warrants were published to oppose the general circulation newspaper accounts of wholesaler and retailer councils urging their members to reject the notes. But the chief pitch of the movement was that it would help people who desperately needed aid. Sherman Bainbridge wrote, "The measure provides the means by which the conveniences of life—food, clothing, and shelter—may be distributed to the people."

The Ham and Eggers suffered a setback when a major scandal attached itself to their movement shortly before the election. In 1937, Willis Allen needed money to buy radio air time. He accepted $130 from Captain Earle Kynette, head of the Los Angeles Police Department's "spy squad." Kynette had been directed by Mayor Shaw to restrain Robert Noble from further attacking his administration and aiding those who wished to shut him up seemed a good method. Kynette was later imprisoned as a result of his bombing the car of private detective Harry Raymond, who was investigating corruption in the Los Angeles mayor's office. For a time, the Allens supplied the captain's wife with money. When they stopped, Kynette sued them, claiming he had been promised one-third of the profits from the pension plan. The suit was settled in the Allens' favor, and Kynette remained in jail, with no part of the profits.

Smaller annoyances also marked the election. Harry Quinn of Denver sued the Ham and Eggs movement because he claimed to have originated the idea the Allens were so successfully promoting in California. The Ham And Eggs Restaurant on Wilshire Blvd. in Los Angeles brought suit against the $30 Every Thursday movement claiming that their business was being hurt because people thought they were connected with the pension plan. They demanded $50,000 in damages and an injunction against further use of the name "Ham and Eggs" by the pension movement. Like most nuisance suits, these evaporated soon after the election.

The polling went poorly for the Ham and Eggers. Their initiative was defeated by a vote of 1,143,670 yes to 1,398,999 no. Of the fifty-eight counties in California, only Kern, San

Diego, Merced, Madera, Mariposa, and Stanislaus Counties supported the measure. Earl Warren easily defeated Carl Kegley in the race for attorney general. Sheridan Downey defeated Bancroft, but by election time his ardor for the California Life Payment Plan was cooling. Culbert Olson was elected governor and turned his attention toward securing a more rewarding national pension system. The only victory the Ham and Eggers could derive from the election was the assistance they gave to defeating Proposition 1.

Yet the movement was by no means crushed by the defeat. The first post-election mass meeting, held November 13, 1938 at Los Angeles' Shrine Auditorium, was crammed as the leadership vowed to continue the battle. Willis Allen declared, "A special election is next in order. We are not giving up this fight. This is being demanded by the thousands of people seeking security."

While the die was cast to attempt to force a second election and the rank and file remained devoted and eager to work, there was trouble within the leadership. The Allens continued to hold sway over the board of directors, but some of its members felt the brothers' background had been the cause of defeat in November. Sherman Bainbridge was the most vocal in his condemnation of Allens' leadership. He scored them primarily on the profits they were reaping through their Cinema Advertising Agency, which handled all the advertising and secured all the radio air time for Ham and Eggs. While they were making thousands of dollars in agent's fees, they had paid their office help from $3.00 to $12.50 for a 48-hour week. The demand for their resignation was raised first by Bainbridge, and later by Board members Signa Erickson and Thomas Hammond for similar reasons.

But the Allens had total control of the new weekly newspaper, *National Ham And Eggs*, and the radio broadcasts, which were the only effective way of reaching the membership. Anyone who questioned their leadership was expelled from the organization and were attacked on the air, in print, and at meetings for selling out to the enemies of the pension movement. Besides controlling the means of propaganda, the Allens symbolized the California Life Payment Plan. Bainbridge's charges may have been published in city newspapers, but as far as effecting change within $30 Every Thursday, he did not have a chance. As a pension hopeful wrote him, "People don't want love. They want a pension." The members perceived that if anyone could get it for them, the Allens would. So Bainbridge, Erickson, and Hammond fell by the wayside and were ignored.

Dissatisfaction among the board members was not the only threat the Allens faced. A number of lawsuits were brought against them. The familiar charge that they used their Cinema Advertising Agency to make money off the old people they claimed to selflessly represent was resurrected by Helen Bartlett. She sued the movement on behalf of ten other former Ham and Eggs workers for back wages totaling $3439. She charged that she saw $40 checks paid on monthly installments for automobiles for Willis and Lawrence Allen, Sherman Bainbridge, and Treasurer Raymond Fritz. She testified that the secretaries were willing to work for $8 a week and less because they were led to believe the leaders received only $25 per week for expenses. The State Unemployment Department sued the directors of $30 Every Thursday for $4521, because, while the movement had paid out $327,329 in wages, they had paid the department nothing. Less serious problems also faced the Allens. Lawrence was being brought to trial by a woman he slapped at the Kynette trial in November. The former policeman was still restive and filed another lawsuit. This time Willis admitted that Kynette had loaned him the $130, but denied he offered him a percentage of the organization. The Junior Citizens, young people who supported Ham and Eggs, bolted the movement in protest to the dictatorial methods of the Allens and the profits they accrued through the Cinema Advertising Agency. $30 Every Thursday moved into the national spotlight when the Special House Committee on Un-American Activities, popularly known as the Dies Committee after its chairman, Martin Dies, came to Los Angeles in early November 1939. The committee claimed to have evidence that the Communist Party meant to seize control of the Ham and Eggs movement once it was voted in, and "ruthlessly wreck the state government as an opening wedge in its campaign to overthrow the government of the United States." Added to these difficulties was the continued opposition of President Roosevelt, Governor Olson, Dr. Townsend, and Upton Sinclair, as well as the much publicized change of heart by former supporters Gertrude Coogan, Carl Kegley, and Sheridan Downey. In answer to such charges, *National Ham And Eggs* warned its readers, "Remembering the barrage of baseless charges and futile lawsuits that featured the last campaign, Life Payments warns members to be on the alert, and ready themselves against any and all efforts to take their eyes off the ball. The opposition cloaked in all sorts of names and disguises will try anything to stop the enactment of our new bill."

The defeat suffered in November 1938 prompted the directors of Ham and Eggs to review their plan. The new bill, again authored by Roy Owens, was first presented in *National Ham and Eggs* on December 3, 1938. The trappings of Owens' second California State Retirement Life Payments Act were very similar to the previous one. The warrant scheme remained intact, and the administrator was not shorn of any of his powers. A few minor changes were made, however. Only two names appeared as possible candidates for administrator, Roy Owens and Will Kindig. Also, the appointee was assured his position until the election of 1944, and state and local government employees were no longer required to accept half their salaries in warrants. What significantly altered the second version of the Ham and Eggs amendment was the new 3% gross income tax (Section 15) and the Credit Clearings Bank (Sections 16-31). The new tax piled tax on tax as an item moved from manufacturer to wholesaler to retailer to consumer. In order to stimulate the use of warrants, the bill exempted all transactions consummated with them from the gross income tax. The Credit Clearings Bank of the People of California was to control all the money used by the state government and set up branch offices for the distribution of Retirement Compensation Warrants. Beyond these activities, the bank was also authorized to perform as a savings depository and a clearing house for checks, to make loans, and to carry deposits made by other banks. The new Credit Clearings Bank, therefore, was to have exclusive control of state monies and be the sole recipient of the agent's 2% commission on the sums collected for Warrant Redemption Stamps and Warrant Redemption charges.

Another important change in the California Life Payment Plan after its first defeat was the inception of a strong political organization. The first petition drive had been a stand-on-the-corner-and-collect-names affair. For the second attempt, the Allens hired George McClain to construct a political organization that would effectively cover the state. He basically followed the example set long before by Tammany Hall and more recently by the EPIC campaign. California was divided into north and south, with a man in charge of each section. Next, the state was separated into congressional districts with a district coordinator for each. The three or four assembly districts within them were each assigned an assistant district manager. The assembly districts were further broken down into ten sections, each with a section supervisor. He controlled fifteen precincts and appointed a precinct captain for each. The captain appointed four assistants. During the petition drive, each precinct captain dispersed voter lists to his workers. They were to collect signatures on the petition and discover if the voter was 1) a Ham and Eggs member, 2) going to vote for Ham and Eggs, 3) undecided, 4) opposed to Ham and Eggs, 5) going to vote against Ham and Eggs. The vast majority of the help was voluntary. It has been estimated that 20,000 circulators of petitions, 36,000 poll watchers, 12,000 telephone answerers, and 12,000 election day automobile drivers were involved.

Due to McClain's tight organization, the second petition campaign was even more successful than the first. On May 18, 1939, Willis Allen presented 1,103,222 names to Governor Olson in his Sacramento office. That evening Olson told a crowd of 15,000 Ham and Eggers gathered at the State Fair Grounds that he would name a date for the special election "that would be satisfactory" to them. He also stated that, while he was in sympathy with their objectives, he did not think the plan would work if enacted. Willis Allen favored voting on the measure as soon as possible, because special elections normally favor the supporters of the measure. The Ham and Eggers were at the height of their enthusiasm, and their enemies were disorganized and unprepared for another election. In order to dampen the spirit of the pension hopefuls and to save the state the $500-600,000 cost of a special election, Olson chose a previously established voting day five and one-half months away, November 7, 1939, to decide the fate of the California Life Payments initiative. Willis was less than thrilled with the date. He fully realized how difficult it would be to keep his followers at their present pitch for half a year. But *National Ham and Eggs* sounded a hopeful note, observing, "Let's go on to the glorious victory that will inaugurate a new era in our beloved state, and later in our beloved nation. It's a big job. But we accomplish big jobs."

The objections raised by Ham and Eggs detractors in 1939 were similar to those aired a year before. They charged that the administrator was granted dictatorial powers; that the warrants would not be accepted by merchants, wholesalers, and the general populace; that the plan would be a tragic failure with old people getting hurt worst of all, and that it was a case of expecting something for nothing. The differences between the two versions was by no means overlooked. The new gross income tax was condemned as an agent that would ruin commerce in California. Small businesses would go bankrupt, and large firms would simply leave the state. It was pointed out that in the case of sugar, a 3% tax would descend on the refiner, 3% on the wholesaler, and 3% on the retailer, making for a 9% rise in sugar to the consumer. Business people would have no choice but to close down or shift their base of operations. The Credit Clearings Bank was charged as being a method of increasing the power of the administrator and putting the finances of the state in the hands of a man who was untrained for the job.

To the Ham and Eggs faithful, the changes were easy to assimilate. They still wanted a pension above all else. Charges of dictatorial power on the part of the administrator did not bother them. The plan was an experiment, so wide leeway was needed in its implementation. Much was made of the continuing Depression, and the contingent unemployment of young people and pauperization of the elderly. *National Ham And Eggs*

[393]

asked, "Do you wish to help make war on poverty, misery, want and deprivation? We need YOUR help. We are going to create abundance for all the people. We will make jobs for youth, and security for senior citizens." A photo feature called "California Reborn" presented the bright future that awaited California as it followed John and Mary from the "tragic dictatorship of the money lords" to the "new world" of warrants. With their pension, the couple was able to travel and to go on shopping trips, thereby stimulating the entire economy.

The major adversaries were again the Chambers of Commerce, business groups, and a few concerned liberals against the Ham and Eggers led by the Allen brothers. The state's major newspapers were again in opposition to the plan. Only *People's World* and most labor groups supported the measure. The movement once again arranged meetings and radio broadcasts all over California, while pensioner hopefuls donated their time and money in hopes of getting their $30 Every Thursday. The previous measure drew more attention in the national press because 1938 had been an election year. But in California, the second act stirred the most concern because it seemed to have such a strong chance of passing. The progressive Commonwealth Club of California devoted an entire issue of its *Transactions* to a discussion of the plan, recommending a no vote. Pamphlet activity was greater than a year before, featuring titles like "Chaos In California!," "Hoaxing California," and "A Citizen Thinks About $30 Thursday, Ham And Eggs, And Himself." A billboard campaign was implemented, and radio time was reserved to speak against the amendment. The state had not been so passionately for or against anything since the EPIC campaign in 1934. This time there was no question of the feelings of the majority of citizens. Ham and Eggs was soundly defeated in a record 82.48% turn out by the registered voters. It did not carry a single county and lost in the popular vote, 993,204 yes to 1,933,557 no.

Ham and Eggs did not immediately collapse after this final rejection by California's voters. Meetings and radio programs continued, as did the newspaper. After the second defeat, Willis Allen declared, "The combination of millions of dollars and political treachery have proven too much to overcome . . . Olson, who was elected by the Ham and Eggers, has repudiated the people . . . and used the power of his office in the service of the banks and monopolies." The first task the Allens undertook was implementing an Olson recall movement. This was largely a move aimed at keeping the troops busy until a new petition campaign could be arranged. The northern California branch of the organization opposed this move, and the San Diego office split from the parent California Life Payments Plan. The rebel group called itself the Life Pension of the U.S.A. and supported Olson in his attempt to increase the payments arising out of the federal Social Security Act. The third petition drive opened in April 1940. Roy Owens' third version of the act was the same as the second, except the benefits were reduced to $20 in warrants per week. They could no longer be sued to pay taxes, and a three-man board replaced the single, all-powerful administrator. This initiative never garnered enough signatures to reach the ballot. In 1942 the Ham and Eggers finally got their chance to eke out some revenge against Culbert Olson. They supported Earl Warren, a long-time enemy of $30 Every Thursday, in his successful attempt to unseat the incumbent.

But the Ham and Eggers movement was finally dead. It had been overcome by the expanding European war. The dilapidated economy that drove ordinarily conservative people into the Allens' camp began to expand rapidly due to the orders pouring into American factories from the warring nations. After the United States entered the conflict, unemployment became almost non-existent. The small recession that followed the end of World War II was insufficient to frighten people into taking economic panaceas seriously. The growing Cold War with Communist Russia also contributed to an atmosphere that boded ill for groups who sought to tinker with the American political or economic system. In 1946 the Allens made their final attempt to revive interest in Ham and Eggs. A former Huey Long aide, Gerald L. K. Smith, was imported for the occasion and toured California trying to drum up support. But the effort was a failure. The "dirty thirties" and the economic desperation that accompanied them, were over.

[395]

The primary reason California's voters twice rejected the
Ham and Eggs amendment was that for all their reputation for
supporting odd causes they were not willing to enact a plan that
would revolutionize the state's economy. The decision was a
wise one. The California Life Payment Plan would certainly
have failed. In 1938 the means to pay for the warrants did not
exist. In 1939 the gross income tax would have paid for the
pensions, but to the detriment of the rest of society. Even if the
plan did not work, it had to be removed by another full constitutional amendment. If the warrant system had been found to
be in conflict with rights reserved by the federal constitution for
coining money and therefore declared unconstitutional, the administrator controlling California's economy through the Credit
Clearings Bank would remain. There was also good reason for
the voters not to trust the Ham and Eggs leadership. While the
Allens were not as blatantly corrupt as fellow pension schemer
Dr. J. E. Pope, or as politically ambitious as Huey Long, they
were promoters and were by no means above milking an issue
for all it was worth, or using their Cinema Advertising Agency
to make money while supposedly helping old people. Even as
cataclysmic an event as the Great Depression could not induce
the voters in California to experiment with the basic economic
arrangement of their society. Apparently most Californians' ap-
petite for bizarre utopias was cured by the sobering presence of
the polling booth.

The sad case of thousands of old people desperately grasping at a straw in the wind, seeking economic security in desperate times, was overlooked by most of the critics of the California Life Payment Plan. Eugene Lyons, reflecting on Ham and
Eggs' second rejection in *American Mercury,* wished that just
one state would adopt one of the strange money schemes that
were being so hotly debated so the rest of the nation could learn
a good lesson from the ruination of the experimentor. Upton
Sinclair, who had spent his entire adult life fighting for social
reform, derived a different impression from the Ham and Egg
movement. He understood how desperately the elderly wanted
increased pension benefits. Sinclair observed that it was easy to
laugh about the absurdity of the measure. But you could not

enjoy the laughter, "because you think about the frustrated dupes, of the pathetic old people who have labored all their lives to produce wealth and have seen their savings swept away in an economic cyclone and are now dependent and humiliated, many of them in desperate need. The old people demand relief and have a right to demand it."

28

SMOG COMES TO LOS ANGELES

Marvin Brienes

On a warm July day in 1943 a mysterious malady settled silently over downtown Los Angeles. Complaints of eye and throat irritation from citizens in the area began filtering into the city's Health Department, where officials responded routinely, dispatching several workers to locate the origins of the unknown irritant by walking in the direction from which the wind was blowing. Several days later the Los Angeles *Times* took casual note of the event, in a light-spirited article buried well back in the paper. "The atmosphere in the downtown area stunk—reeked yesterday," it began, explaining how some thought the "acrid ozone" had resulted from a heated conference in the mayor's office the previous day. Mayor Fletcher Bowron was struggling to end a streetcar workers' strike, but whatever "sulphurous fumes" had arisen in the discussions, health authorities agreed the atmospheric irritation "is strictly coincidental," except that the strike had pushed automobile traffic to its highest level in months, and an air blanket, the article continued, kept the exhaust fumes from rising "as they do under normal conditions." An accompanying photograph of a murky downtown revealed the severity of the attack, while its caption suggested that a new synthetic rubber factory was suspected of being the culprit. No one really knew what the cause was, and few of wartime Los Angeles' busy citizens would have thought it necessary to find out, had the problem promptly vanished.

But the distressing condition worsened daily. The automobile exhaust theory collapsed when the streetcar strike ended on July 23 with no change for the better, proving the circumstances were fortuitous as they were prophetic. Then, on July 26, the "gas attack" reached its height as a thick, smoky cloud, heavier by far than any experienced before, descended over the downtown area in the early morning hours and cut visibility to less than three blocks. Workers, the newspapers reported, "found the noxious fumes almost unbearable," and a municipal judge considered closing his court until conditions improved. At noon the siege ended. The dense haze lifted; after four hours of misery the brilliant summer sun shone again on Los Angeles. Concern, not humor as before, now prompted the front page headlines. Smog had come to stay.

It had been visiting, on and off, for at least three years by then. Few noticed how sick the air had been getting since the beginning of the decade, though by 1940 there had been clear signs in that direction. Weather Bureau readings the previous year documented the beginnings of a progressive decline in local visibility which was to continue until 1942. When smog investigators later examined old records, they found that neither wind speed, temperature, nor the amount of sunshine had changed significantly for decades. There was no reason to believe that natural haze of the Los Angeles basin could have been responsible.

A more ominous sign of trouble had appeared in June and July 1940 when people in the vicinity of the downtown Civic Center began experiencing eye and throat irritation. The frequency of such complaints mounted to a peak on July 9 when the discomfort struck "with such intensity in county buildings, particularly in the Hall of Records, that scores of Public workers and courtroom occupants continued their activities with the greatest difficulty." That same day the City Health Department's Industrial Hygiene Division was ordered to investigate. The subsequent study failed to reveal what had caused the incident, though officials deduced that the trouble at the Civic Center stemmed from "an abnormal concentration of smokes, gases and fumes from the many industrial plants—with the exception that the condition was worse in the vicinity of certain industrial plants which were known to emit irritating chemicals into the air." In the southwest area of the city, where eye irritation had been experienced also, oil refinery waste gases were blamed. But no one knew for sure. Another short attack hit on July 23, this time affecting the Los Angeles General Hospital where dozens reported discomfort.

After a brief respite, what was becoming known to local health officials as the "abnormal atmospheric condition," occurred again for short periods during the fall of 1940 and then in early summer of 1941. The worst attack during the latter year came December 10 and lasted four hours. When air samples were collected and analyzed, the results were inconclusive: aldehyde gas concentrations "probably" increased during the height of the attack, but sulfur dioxide, a key pollutant elsewhere, was within normal limits. Atmospheric conditions were blamed again.

On September 21, 1942, the mysterious affliction reappeared, this time in a Los Angeles preoccupied with the business of war. While irritation was again most severe downtown, the problem was clearly spreading elsewhere, as "the outlying districts were affected to a greater extent than at any previous time." The city's Industrial Hygiene Division, geared to protect workers from harmful environments inside industrial plants, and already struggling with that increasingly demanding duty, now extended its purview to include surrounding residential areas. Workers undertook, with what limited diagnostic tools they had, an inventory of the Los Angeles atmosphere. They discovered a brew of "ammonia, formaldehyde, acrolein, acetic acid, sulfuric acid, sulfur dioxide, hydrogen sulfide, mercaptans, hydrochloric acid, hydrofluoric acid, chlorine, nitric acid, phosgene, and certain organic dusts known to be irritants," for which scores of sources, ranging from fish canneries to oil refineries, could be blamed.

Here was the chemical testimony to Los Angeles' wartime industrial boom. By June 1942 the area had won over $3,000,-000,000 in war production contracts, and nearly tripled that in the following year. Los Angeles alone was garnering almost half

[401]

of all war contracts let out in California. One particularly significant impact was a trend of new and increasingly large-scale
industrial plants. In 1940 $4.4 million had been invested in 122
new plants. The following year, with investments up to $38.5
million, the number of new plants declined to 111. Spectacular
expansion occurred in those heavy industries most likely to present air pollution problems: rubber, nonferrous metals, all types
of machinery, and chemicals. At the same time the industrial
demand for electric power increased at breathtaking rates: for
its industrial customers alone, the Los Angeles Department of
Water and Power provided nearly 400,000,000 kilowatt hours of
energy in 1942, and well over a billion the following year. In
1941 the figure had stood at less than a third as much. Employment in manufacturing shot from 152,000 in 1940 to 446,000 in
October 1943, and the boosters of Southern California pointed
proudly to the new skyline of smoking industrial stacks.

By July 1943 the capacity of the Los Angeles atmosphere to
swallow the effluent of this activity had reached its natural limit.
With complaints now pouring into both the city and county
governments from Los Angeles, Burbank, Pasadena, and many
other areas in the county, the Los Angeles City Council ordered
an investigation of the "peculiar atmospheric condition," and
the County Board of Supervisors commissioned Health Officer
Dr. H. O. Swartout to cooperate with all interested parties in
ferreting out the cause of the "nuisance." Actually, the health
officials were already at work. Nine inspectors from the city
department were on watch in the streets, augmented by city
policemen who were requested to be on the lookout for unusual
sighting of smoke or evidence of fumes. The county assigned its
own Industrial Hygiene Division inspectors to join the search
and began air sampling on July 26. The city began its own sampling the next day. Health officials wisely concluded that the
problem had been in incubation for some years, and that no
magic, painless formula existed to end it. But this was subtle
thinking for the times. The public, and officials, had identified
one notorious contributor to the general pollution. In the downtown area where, so it appeared, the menace had come to life

[402]

first, stood the smoky, smelly butadiene plant on Aliso Street. It was here the fight against smog began.

The plant under scrutiny was a formidable, if unsightly, soldier in the war effort. With most of the world's supply of natural rubber in the hands of the Japanese, manufacturing a synthetic substitute received the highest priority from American war planners in the early months of 1942. Under the leadership of gruff William Jeffers, head of the Union Pacific Railroad, the Rubber Reserve Corporation supervised an enormous expansion in synthetic rubber production. With its petroleum industry well established and able to supply the raw material for synthetic rubber manufacturing, Los Angeles became the main west coast center for its production. Hastening to get the work begun, the Rubber Reserve ordered the conversion of the Aliso Street gas works facility of the Southern California Gas Company to the production of crude butadiene, a derivative of petroleum essential to the manufacture of rubber. The butadiene produced at the converted plant in the downtown area supplied the butadiene "feedstock" for several other plants, all of which were integrated to create the finished product. It was, wrote an observer, altogether unremarkable, "a sort of bailing [sic]— wire-constructed plant down in the industrial section" that "never amounted to anything."

Unfortunately, none of the baling wire found its way into pollution control devices. At a cost of $14 million, the converted plant went into production. Crude butadiene was formed there by combining steam with naptha and other materials under heat and pressure. The mixture then moved to a sealed chamber where it was cooled and cleansed of impurities by a water spray. The water would then be removed to another closed tank where most of the impurities absorbed from the butadiene were removed. To that point all fumes were well controlled, but following this cleaning process the water was pumped up to an open tank from which it then cascaded over open cooling towers on the building. It was here that the water, still "containing appreciable amounts of oil and other dissolved and suspended, odorous eye irritating chemicals," liberated its sewage. Pressures of time and expense, not primitive technology, accounted for the open cooling towers. Federal officials lamely explained that similar operations elsewhere in the country had never prompted complaints. But in Los Angeles the whiff of butadiene helped set off the first furor over smog.

Though the butadiene plant could not, by itself, account for the air pollution problems throughout the county, its emissions were severe enough to affect an extensive area from July to October 1943. Public officials endured a deluge of complaints blaming the butadiene residue for everything from lowered war morale on the part of defense workers to the corrosion of paint on automobiles. "There is no doubt," wrote Donald Carr, "that [the butadiene plant] did make a lot of smells for a short time." The *Pacific Coast Record* reported receiving daily outcries about the "terrific smoke nuisance." Hotel and restaurant owners noticed a "black carbon-like grease on furniture," linens, drapes, and carpets. By the end of August the county school superintendent reported employees were quitting their jobs because of the fumes. An air of desperation engulfed the tuberculosis ward at the County General Hospital, where 350 patients choked at the fumes. Futile attempts to seal off the hospital by shutting windows served only to make the wards more uncomfortably hot. At times not a corner of the facility could be kept free of the stench. Someone told Mayor Bowron that workers in plants in the area hardest hit were leaving their jobs," rather than work in gas-laden air," and that cars left standing in the streets near the butadiene plant had their finishes blistered by the fumes— which gave some hint, Bowron suggested, "of their serious effect on humans." Even the wheels of justice halted before the blue-gray pall, when Judge Roy V. Rhodes postponed a court session for the duration of a particularly bad attack. No other factory could compete with the Aliso Street plant for the attention of Angelenos.

Was there a menace to health, as well as to comfort? Bowron's allusion as to what the corrosive fumes might be doing to humans echoed a growing consensus among the afflicted. In the usual pattern of the attacks, fumes would spread out over residential communities along the foothills of the San Gabriel

Mountains. Trapped by the mountain barrier, the polluted air often blanketed the Pasadena area from noon until nightfall. It was not a phenomenon enjoyed by such people as had been lured to the area by its salubrious climate. A Pasadena couple pleaded for relief from chest congestion they blamed squarely on the fumes; from Altadena came a cry from a woman who had moved to California for her health, who now paced floors at night, the polluted air aggravating an old lung disorder. By October the Pasadena Chamber of Commerce heard that the fumes were "affecting health and the reputation of the community as a healthful city." Local public health officials joined in legitimizing such concerns. Dr. Swartout informed Bowron that "a definite health menace" existed in the vicinity of the butadiene plant; later he suggested eye irritation bore some responsibility for a recent increase in automobile accidents. Los Angeles City Health Officer Dr. George M. Uhl, at first noncommittal on the question, joined in the diagnosis by mid-September.

Away from the spotlight and ignored by the public, health authorities did what little they could do to alleviate the menace, as the Aliso Street plant riveted the attention of nearly everyone else. Because it was within city boundaries, relieved county officials sat decorously on the sidelines as Los Angeles City asked the Southern California Gas Company to do something about it. The company answered that it could do nothing: in operating the butadiene plant it was only an agent of the Rubber Reserve, and the Reserve had already decided the public ought to endure the smells for the sake of the war effort. Speaking for itself, the company indicated it would like to shut down the factory altogether. The city responded with a formal complaint filed with the Rubber Reserve, but the fumes and public demands for abatement continued. Tiring of the wait, Mayor Bowron wired a tersely worded threat to close down the plant by legal action. Obviously alarmed by the mounting pressures, Reserve Vice-President J. W. Livingston wired back an assurance of concern and hurried another agency executive, Stanley Crossland, to the west coast for a peace conference with the disgruntled city leaders.

[405]

Meeting in the mayor's office with Bowron, gas company, fire and health department officials, Crossland announced an apparent reversal of policy. The Rubber Reserve had already ordered construction of anti-pollution devices and would have them in place by December. A new cooling system would be installed, consisting of completely closed tanks and coils, with the scrubbing water isolated from the cooling water. Only clean water, after having absorbed heat from the scrubbing water, would be cascaded down the cooling towers. In the meanwhile a chemical palliative, then under development, would be added to the scrubbing water. There would be relief within sixty days, Crossland promised. As he left town people in Pasadena learned from the morning newspaper that "Gas Fumes Soon Will Be Eliminated." It was certainly no more than they expected.

From the middle of August to the first week in September, despite continued distress calls from the citizenry, local officials waited for relief in silence. But then the gas company put additional equipment into operation and increased butadiene output. Unfortunately, a low atmospheric inversion refused to co-operate with the war effort. Hugging close to ground level, a pall lingered over the downtown area, wafting along the San Gabriel foothills almost daily, enveloping one community after another. Finally, on September 8, the worst attack since July blighted downtown Los Angeles. When contacted by the Health Department, plant officials promised to install, within a week, a "new 'flotation' process" that would "considerably reduce the fumes." When no relief was achieved by the 14th, pressure from outside the city began mounting once more. Pasadena insisted on an immediate end to the fumes, whatever the Rubber Reserve timetable envisioned. On behalf of the supervisors, Dr. Swartout prodded city officials to take action. Patience had worn thin.

As nervous Rubber Reserve and gas company officials dunned Washington for War Production Board approval of the steel allocation earmarked for the anti-pollution equipment (production of which had not yet begun), the feisty mayor prepared to end the truce Crossland had arranged in August. "We all want to co-operate fully and completely with the war effort," he explained to the press, "but there is a limit to all things." Bowron phoned the gas company, threatened again to seek an injunction, and won some immediate concessions. The plant cut production down to twenty percent of capacity, and the company offered to gear future production levels to atmospheric conditions. A few days later, with complaints still pouring in, the plant was temporarily shut down completely. But Bowron, already decided on a war message to the City Council, recommended legal action "as promptly as possible."

The options open to the city were not happy ones. To do nothing but wait for December was perhaps the most difficult. By now public opinion had hardened into impatience; even the Grand Jury had passed a resolution demanding immediate action. Even as the councilmen met to debate their choices, the fumes were spreading over a five-mile radius, centering downtown, barely disturbed by a nearly motionless wind. The Aliso Street plant had been shut down on the previous morning, but few of the sufferers in this most severe attack since the trauma of July 26 stopped to take note. But if the butadiene fumes were a nuisance, the butadiene itself, as Reserve spokesmen pointed out, was needed to promote the war effort, and Bowron's drastic proposal raised its own dilemma. How was one to choose between having one's butadiene and not smelling it too? Patriotism and self-interest suggested Los Angeles ought to abide the fumes for a while longer. Some councilmen thought there had been enough delay and "pussyfooting," and pushed for an injunction. Caution prevailed, however, and the City Council set a hearing for the following day.

On September 22 the council listened to a wide spectrum of opinion. Foothill community representatives told their woeful, now familiar tale. Dr. Uhl reported that, far from being abated, the fumes were worse than ever. He took a hard line, recommending the plant be kept shut tight until the promised equipment was installed. Rubber Reserve, Defense Plant Corporation, and gas company spokesmen offered different views. They argued that there was a war on, and it was unreasonable to expect to fight in perfect comfort. Residents "can rest assured," noted one, "the boys on the battlefronts are suffering" also. The gas company's representative sought the middle ground, and proposed the plant's future operations be tied to atmospheric conditions. Not all the smells would vanish, he agreed, but some butadiene could be produced without causing major nuisance. In the end the council instructed Uhl to work with company officials "to keep existing nuisances to a practical minimum." The gas company's compromise would be given a chance.

It failed. Technicians at the plant added a highly touted chemical chimera to the scrubbing water. It helped very little, as the plant, closed since Bowron's threat, reopened production at a cautious twenty percent of capacity. Despite assurances from Charles L. Senn, director of the Health Department's Sanitation Section, who reported from the scene that "he could not detect escape of 'large quantities' of the objectionable gas," motorists driving through the downtown tunnels complained vigorously about fumes. Plant production edged toward forty percent within a week, when a bad smog attack forced another shutdown. The next day production resumed at the same level, but complaints to the mayor's office continued and within two days distress calls from General Hospital impelled Dr. Uhl to request another halt. Shut down until Friday night, October 8, the plant then started up again, worked through the weekend, only to close once more on Monday morning. Harassed gas company officials did not try to operate it again until the end of the month.

The ill-fated experiment revealed something of the problem's true complexity. It was no simple matter to balance the need for rubber against an equally essential need for breathable air. The compromise would have worked only if the butadiene plant's managers knew precisely the changing atmosphere's ability to disperse the gas fumes, precisely what contribution the butadiene plant was making toward the total air pollution problem, and precisely the tolerable limit for emissions. At the time there were no answers, only guesses, a circumstance assuring the attempt to find a tolerable fumes limit would not only fail, but increase frustration. The gas company needed to know,

Aerial view of downtown Los Angeles, taken from a U.S. Navy blimp, reveals limited visibility.
Courtesy of Security Pacific National Bank
Photograph Collection/Los Angeles Public Library.

before the public did, when production curtailments were indicated. There was no way to know. The difficulties were compounded by some puzzling differences over the incidence of discomfort. While the self-interest of some might be served by stone-faced denials that anything was wrong, in other cases disagreement was harder to account for. One day, for example, two members of the Los Angeles City Council visited the shutdown plant and left unable to agree on whether it was exuding odors or not. Beyond this, halting butadiene production did not necessarily mean the cooling towers, the main source of pollution, stopped operating, because scrubbing water might still remain to be cleansed and cooled.

Mayor Bowron's response rolled over such subtleties. In a scathing message to the city council he noted that the fumes were as bad as ever, and scored the members for having ignored his earlier call for legal action. The council voted narrowly to seek a remedy in the courts. The suit, remarked a city attorney assigned to the case, was "friendly in nature." But Councilman John Baumgartner echoed public sentiment more accurately: it was time, he said, "for the council to show it was working for the city and not the gas company."

The council's action brought a swift climax to the butadiene affair. Colonel Bradley Dewey, successor to Jeffers as head of the Rubber Reserve, flew in from Washington. Publicly disputing claims made recently by Bowron that butadiene was in surplus supply, he pronounced the lawsuit "contrary to the best interests of the war effort." But he had come to Los Angeles to help settle the uproar, rather than to debate its merits. The Los Angeles Chamber of Commerce arranged a dinner at the California Club to which a hundred prominent community leaders were invited. There Dewey made his case. A tall, stockily built gentleman with white hair and a soft, reassuring voice, Dewey drained all the tension from the air with some informal remarks. He had come to Los Angeles to reason, he told the assembly, not to dictate. The fumes were not harmful to health, even if "some interested party sold the mayor a bill of goods" to the contrary, but he admitted they were a real nuisance. At the close of his soothing talk the rubber "czar" promised that the long-awaited machinery would be in place by December, and that all trace of the fumes would be gone by the first of that month. "If it isn't," he vowed with theatrical sincerity, "you can call me a bum, and I will close down the plant myself."

Dewey's gesture of concern had an immediate effect. Some small show of bravado had attended the city's defiance of the Washington war planners, in the name of clean air. But all along there was uneasiness in the city council, a reluctance to demand this exemption from sacrifice. The suit had been forced upon it when Mayor Bowron washed his hands of the issue, and some of the councilmen now apologized for having voted for it. One after another, guests rose to ratify the new harmony, and the event took on the tone of a testimonial dinner. On the following day the councilmen voted unanimously to drop the suit, for which Dewey promptly thanked them "in the name of the war effort."

The butadiene controversy was over. For most of the remaining weeks of 1943 the Aliso Street plant stayed closed while the Oliver filters, flotation cells, and heat exchangers were installed as promised. No complaints were recorded when production resumed, just before Christmas. In February 1944 members of the county's newly created Smoke and Fumes Commission visited the site and reported it free of "any traces of these objectionable fumes." Through the rest of the war the facility continued in service, with more sophisticated control equipment eventually installed. It never became a perfect neighbor: occasionally in 1944 its fumes were detectable within a half-mile of the plant, and accidents were always possible. But the butadiene plant was no worse an offender in this respect than many other industrial establishments, and it ceased being a particular headache for authorities.

For a brief interlude Los Angeles enjoyed a sense of victory, stemming mainly from the widespread misconception which confused a general pollution condition with one notorious pollutor. The error was on the part of community leaders and much of the public, and was not shared by health department investigators, who earlier had distinguished between the butadiene problem and a "general smoke and fumes condi-

tion." As early as July observers had discovered that eye irritation was just as severe upwind from Aliso Street as downwind.
Soon investigators plotting the smog attacks learned that usually irritation began simultaneously at points ten miles apart,
convincing proof that no one source of emissions could be responsible. Minor attempts were made to educate the public.
When irritation persisted during one of the butadiene plant's
shutdowns, an official of the city and county defense councils
warned that "no single industry can be held responsible for the
smoke and fumes," and even Mayor Bowron named the plant
as only the worst of many offenders. At the time it gave wide
coverage to the butadiene controversy, the Los Angeles *Times*
suggested in its editorials that the fumes were too heavy "to
come from any one place."

The message was getting through very slowly, because the
fight to tame the butadiene plant had perfectly comprehensible
dimensions. It fit well into patterns already established. It had a
beginning, and an end. There was in it an attraction one could
never find in contemplation of massive pollution problems that
had been woven, over years, into the fabric of the metropolis. It
is small wonder that the insight of health authorities won so
little attention. In focusing on Aliso Street, Angelenos were de-
fining their newborn blight according to their taste for confronting it.

In the butadiene plant a solitary villain was isolated. In
itself this eliminated a number of potential complications: the
need for long, close investigation of thousands of possible offenders; the accumulation of basic scientific data in chemistry
and meteorology; planning for permanent, long-range control
programs. Abatement became a relatively simple matter of fixing something up or shutting it down, decisions dictated by
common sense. Experience with air pollution problems elsewhere, where known pollutors could be tied directly to the
known pollutants, appeared applicable to Los Angeles. Furthermore, the butadiene stench was no local responsibility. This,
too, helped make abatement seem simple, by placing the blame
on Washington—if not the world—and by reassuring local people that the problem was not their making. In 1943 it seemed

*The view wasn't much clearer at ground level as the Navy blimp
sailed past City Hall.*
Courtesy of Security Pacific National Bank
Photograph Collection/Los Angeles Public Library.

reasonable that an indignant telegram to the men in charge should be sufficient. And with the federal treasury underwriting the cost of control, no local business interests were threatened. The alacrity with which Los Angeles City challenged the Rubber Reserve reflected minds very much at ease. It was not often in the history of air pollution control that the right thing could be done for free.

One further attraction of the butadiene affair capped its apparent simplicity. Nothing new in anti-pollution devices was required to make the plant respectable, only the willingness to install them. Most people accepted this as a natural fact, when it was really pure coincidence. The idea that remedies might not be close at hand, or that technology had outstripped man's control, were hardly considered. In September 1943 the Pasadena Chamber of Commerce sent a thank you note to the gas company and others who had promised an early end to "this nuisance," in obvious expectation of closing its books on the matter. On August 16, making no distinction between the butadiene and general problems, the Los Angeles *Times* reported that "relief from concentrations of industrial gas in the downtown and other close-in areas within 60 days and entire elimination of the nuisance within four months was promised yesterday." Just after birth, smog was already accumulating its premature obituaries. They were read with interest in Pasadena, where some believed the prospects of "a 'second Pittsburgh' in this area" had been narrowly averted.

Only hindsight revealed the auguries hidden in the experiences of 1943. The first was an illustration of how much Angelenos cherished clean air. The health-restoring powers of the climate were axiomatic, and even the imperatives of the war effort were insufficient to cast them aside. In Pasadena, where many lived mainly for the climate, smog was immediately intolerable. The second was in the conflict of two desiderata, industrial production and air quality. As the butadiene affair progressed, the dilemma was poised but never really confronted, because it was possible to halt manufacture at the plant without disrupting the war effort. But the success of Dewey's visit is understandable only when one grasps how eager Los Angeles' leadership was to find a balance between the conflicting pressures. Dewey, after all, had brought nothing to Los Angeles with which to bargain except the occasion for a reconciliation, and perhaps his personality. The larger question was set aside, but it had arisen at least.

A third portent lurked in the attempt at regulating production so as to avoid serious pollution from butadiene. Its failure, and the subsequent closing of the plant, pointed out the logical development of a pollution control program that aimed at clean air without the scientific understanding necessary to reach that goal efficiently. In microcosm the butadiene plant situation mirrored the unique problem facing all Los Angeles. When the experiment of modulating the emissions collapsed from ignorance, the only resort was uncompromising abatement to the greatest extent possible. In the Aliso Street case, this meant shutting down the plant. What might it mean applied to all Los Angeles? A final augury lay in the gulf revealed between the public and the health officials. The butadiene incident had confirmed for the public simplistic assumptions about air pollution. At the same time the technicians were beginning to understand what a mysterious, even awesome, matter confronted them. A prevalent myth hints that, in these early years, officials shared fully in the naïveté of the public, but the opposite is more nearly true. In 1943 the public and control officials came to analyze their common problem in very different terms. It would have prevented much trouble in the future, had good lines of communication been open.

Even so, one could question how receptive people would have been to a sobering education. There was much to lose in waking from the butadiene dream. It is curious how tenaciously some held out, blaming the smog on butadiene long after the plant had been reformed. "You know," a citizen complained a year later, "such things are like piggeries. . . . Take them out in the country where they belong." Downtown jewelry workers insisted the old plant's fumes were interfering with their work. As late as mid-1945 many people mistakenly would "think butadiene" when smog caused eye or throat irritation. And when the plant finally ceased production after the end of the war,

[415]

many were surprised when the clean air of memory failed to return. When one has a problem, it soothes to think one knows the cause and can take after it with a vengeance. At the dawn of the smog era in 1943, that awful butadiene plant on Aliso Street was just such a comfort.

29

HELEN GAHAGAN DOUGLAS AND HER 1950 SENATE RACE WITH RICHARD M. NIXON

Ingrid Winther Scobie

Democrat Helen Gahagan Douglas lost the 1950 Senate race in California by a startling two-to-three margin—1,500,000 votes to 2,200,000. This election is still remembered because of the issues discussed, and even more because the successful candidate was thirty-seven-year-old Richard M. Nixon, at that time a Republican Congressman with two terms of experience. Douglas, age forty-nine, a beautiful, talented, and experienced opera singer and Broadway actress by profession, was in her third Congressional term.

The Senate contest is commonly and rightfully referred to as a classic example of a "Red smear" campaign. Unquestionably the issue of national security both at home and abroad, plus Douglas' alleged leftist leanings and the implication that she was a Communist, dominated campaign rhetoric. Nixon's vocal campaign workers used these issues to advantage and won the powerful backing of nearly all California newspapers.

But there were other factors, less frequently mentioned, that also influenced the election results. Nixon was more skillful as a debater and kept Douglas on the defensive throughout the campaign. In the words of one commentator who admired Douglas: "It was not red-baiting *per se* which defeated Mrs. Douglas so much as it was the [ineffective] strategy used to counter Nixon's unscrupulous demagoguery." Nixon had a highly skilled professional campaign manager who knew how to manipulate the California voter. Despite a Democratic edge of 3-2 in registration figures, Republicans had won most state-wide contests in California since 1942, in part because of the disorganized and divided state of the Democratic party. I also suggest that even if the Red issue had not been used in the campaign, Nixon might very well have still defeated Douglas. As a caustic anti-Nixon writer said: "There is a strong probability that Richard Nixon could have won the election . . . [even] if he had conducted a straightforward honorable campaign based on a discussion of the issues." He held economic, social and political views more in tune with California public opinion, or at least with political and financial centers of power, than did the idealistic Douglas. Finally, Douglas antagonized certain women's groups and thus lost votes on issues unrelated to Red-baiting.

At the beginning of 1950 the direction of the primary campaign remained in doubt. Although Nixon had emerged as the principal Republican candidate, two ideologically different Democrats had filed—Douglas and incumbent Sheridan Downey, a former "Ham and Eggs" New Dealer, recently turned conservative. In March Downey surprised his sizeable backing by announcing that due to ill health he was withdrawing from the campaign. Rather than throw support to Mrs. Douglas, whom he disliked intensely, he chose to back Manchester Boddy, longtime editor of the Los Angeles *Daily News*, and a man whose political outlook and personal temperament paralleled his own. Boddy jumped into the race immediately, and the primary gained momentum. Although Douglas seemed undaunted by this sudden change, she was forced to alter her approach to the campaign because her principal dispute with Downey had been his stand on the issues surrounding water use and development. For Nixon, Downey's withdrawal was probably considered a break as some Nixon people feared Downey unbeatable.

Although all three candidates—Nixon, Boddy, and Douglas—placed their names on both party tickets by means of cross-filing, the two Democrats concentrated efforts on capturing their own party's nomination. Douglas, better known, glamorous, and more articulate, campaigned primarily on her congressional record. Traveling to dozens of towns by helicopter, she made much of her strong support for Truman's Fair Deal legislation—to clear slums, extend social security, control rents, stimulate post-war jobs, and increase middle income housing. She stressed government control of both tidelands oil and the Central Valley Project which supplied half of California's water resources. She drew attention to her creative and instrumental role, as the fourth-ranking member of the House Foreign Relations Committee, in developing foreign policy, including aid to Korea, the Marshall Plan, and military aid to Europe as well as her co-sponsorship of the bill creating the Atomic Energy Commission. While acknowledging her opposition to the House Un-American Activities Committee, she continually repeated her sincere opinion that "the best way to keep communism out of our country is to keep democracy in it." Labor almost unanimously endorsed her, as did many of the Democratic county central committees. In contrast Boddy, although attractive and energetic and backed by Downey's campaign structure and many newspapers, appeared vague and abstract. He failed to elaborate clearly his principal theme—that the country must above all avoid another war and depression. He hedged on the issue of the Central Valley Project, but endorsed Truman's foreign policy.

Douglas and Boddy initially ran low-key campaigns. The latter's supporters, however, soon developed the Red-smear arguments that Nixon subsequently used so masterfully. In March, the vice-president of the California Democratic Women's League cried out that in light of Douglas' votes against HUAC appropriations and against Truman's 1947 bill for aid to Greece and Turkey, Douglas must be defeated. In these and other measures she pointed out that Douglas had sided with a small group of congressmen that included the "notorious radical" Vito Marcantonio, representative of the American Labor Party in New York State and darling of the American Communists, "on votes which seem[ed] more in the interest of Soviet

Helen Gahagan Douglas on the campaign circuit.
Courtesy of University of Oklahoma Library.

Russia than of the United States." On May 10, Boddy himself articulated the smear technique by declaring that "a small subversive clique of red hots had moved in on the Democratic central committees [by] . . . devious means." But more damning words came from Downey who joined in the fray in mid-May by repeating the unfair insinuations about Douglas' voting record and claiming her attendance record was poor, and by casting doubt on her overall ability to be a senator—arguments Nixon picked up in the fall. These vicious comments had no validity; indeed her attendance record was excellent and her reputation for hard and conscientious work was unexcelled. In the words of John W. McCormack, House majority leader: she was "one of the ablest, one of the most sincere and one of the most courageous legislators that I have ever had the honor to serve with in any legislative body."

Nixon, meanwhile, remained aloof from the Democratic clashes, in part because he wanted Douglas to win as he believed her an easier opponent for the fall election. It is also clear he hoped to win both nominations and thus avoid a fall contest. Conducting what he termed a "bipartisan campaign," he and loyal Pat crisscrossed California in a station wagon equipped with record player and loudspeaker. He touched on a variety of issues, campaigning hard for both Republican and Democratic votes. Claiming that Truman's Fair Deal was based on British socialism, he cried for a cutback in government spending and proposed specific alternatives to Truman's programs. He urged state rather than federal control of tidelands oil, pushed for rapid development of California's natural resources, and pressed for a stronger, more militarily aggressive foreign policy. He reminded his audiences of his persistent role in bringing Alger Hiss to trial and in drawing up the Mundt-Nixon Communist-control bill, both accomplished as a member of HUAC. But at the same time he called for caution against what he called "indiscriminate name-calling in the field of anti-Communist activities. Wild, unsubstantiated charges of disloyalty," he said, "could very well render a disservice to the security of our nation." It was tragic that in the autumn he did not heed his own advice.

The primary election results gave Douglas a commanding majority of Democratic votes, over 730,000 compared to Boddy's less than 400,000. But Nixon garnered more than 300,000 Democratic votes from the cross-filing system. The total popular vote thus revealed serious obstacles to the Douglas campaign. Nixon received slightly over one million votes in all, Douglas almost 900,000, and Boddy slightly over half a million. If Boddy's votes represented primarily conservative Democratic ballots, Nixon clearly held a significant advantage in the November Senate contest.

Although in June Nixon declared that his fall campaign would cover the gamut of domestic and foreign policy issues, by the end of the summer he clearly planned to concentrate on Douglas' stand on internal security and foreign policy, a decision reinforced, no doubt, by victories such as George Smathers' primary win over Claude Pepper in Florida. On September 18, Nixon opened his campaign and declared: "There will

[421]

be no name-calling, no smears, no misrepresentations in this campaign." This statement, to use a famous Nixon term, soon became "inoperative." But he continued, "to the extent that Mrs. Douglas does not reveal, or conceals, her record, I feel that I have an obligation to expose the record to the voters of California." He then proceeded to point to her congressional stands that to him demonstrated a lack of understanding of the international Communist conspiracy. Adding to the list of undesirable stands mentioned in Boddy's campaign, he cited her position against federal employee loyalty programs, subversive control bills, appropriations for HUAC, and contempt citations for witnesses refusing to answer certain questions before this committee. Not until later speeches did he use the damning insinuation that she revealed Communist sympathies because she voted with Marcantonio. But an early piece of Nixon campaign literature, dubbed the infamous "Pink Sheet" passed out by the hundred of thousands, emphasized the fraudulent assumption that because Douglas and Marcantonio happened to vote the same way on 354 issues, they were ideologically sympathetic to each other. This pamphlet concluded, after listing the parallel voting record: "Would California send Marcantonio to the United States Senate?"

Douglas' reaction to Nixon's barrage of slander was to fall back on the defensive and only occasionally to attack Nixon himself. In response to his accusations, she said: "He is throwing up a smoke screen of smears, innuendos and half-truths to try and confuse and mislead you." Nixon's answer to this was simply to say that he was not doing the smearing, but that her record was. She pointed out that Nixon too had voted with Marcantonio on numerous foreign policy issues, particularly foreign aid bills; but, she added, this did not make Nixon a Communist. It merely demonstrated that both Nixon and Marcantonio saw "eye to eye in voting against measures of vital importance to our program to stem the tide of Communist aggression around the world." Campaign statements passed out to supporters and featured in speeches attempted to clarify her position on civil liberties issues. For example, she had opposed the two federal security bills because there was no provision for the right of appeal; her votes against citations for contempt of Congress and against HUAC appropriations symbolized her fight to protect civil liberties of innocent individuals against the power of HUAC. Supporters pointed out that she had actually voted for numerous contempt citations but only those she recognized as justified. She opposed Communist registration acts because she felt that Congress instead should close loopholes in existing laws. In her speeches, Douglas did attack aggressively Nixon's negative record on social improvements and on foreign aid. But the emphasis remained on her own efforts to achieve peace and a strong America through international understanding, foreign aid, and internal social improvements—a positive approach that did credit to her ideals but one that failed to reach the voters as effectively as Nixon's innuendoes and slander.

Furthermore, the summer of 1950 proved to be a tense one, filled with suspicions and doubts on the international and domestic fronts. Lingering questions about the administration's China policy, aggravated by the hostilities that had broken out in Korea in June, the threat of increasing Russian and Communist involvement in that war, plus evidence that spies had been revealing our atomic secrets made people nervous, impatient, and very frightened. Americans needed concrete evidence of anti-Communist persuasion and action. People preferred to hear of Nixon's style of "vigilance against Communism" as in the Alger Hiss case or listen to Nixon's accusations that Truman's policies, soft on Communism, had led to the fall of the Chinese Nationalists and the onset of the Korean War. Many remained unmoved as they heard how Douglas had defended individual rights in security investigations, that the Communist takeover in China was inevitable, or that she had fought for aid to Europe—thus preventing Communist seizure of power— while Nixon had continuously voted to reduce such aid. As the New Republic pointed out after the election: "Mrs. Douglas fought back hard. But she was too often talking to those who were already for her and she could not reach enough of the other kind . . . Mrs. Douglas had a broom trying to sweep back the sea." Furthermore, the spurious association with Marcantonio, repeated continuously on radio and television and in newspapers "had a fearful impact. . . . Anti-Communist sentiment was at an hysterical peak. Nixon, a powerful and convincing speaker . . . made the most of this Moscow-created opportunity."

Despite the obvious advantage that Nixon reaped from the Communist issue, his commanding lead throughout the fall, as reflected in public opinion polls, suggests that other factors also contributed to a successful campaign. As noted earlier, Nixon had considerable skill in presenting issues in a way convincing to his audience. Douglas too could "turn on" an audience, but even some of Douglas' most loyal campaigners acknowledged Nixon's superiority in seizing on Douglas' weak points. In a forecast of these difficulties, the debating team captain at the University of California, Berkeley, wrote in April to Douglas:

> Early last week Rep. Richard Nixon spoke outdoors in front of our "Sather Gate." To the great surprise of most of us, who know him only by his voting record and his statements in the House Un-American Activities Committee, he gave a magnificent speech. He is one of the cleverest speakers I have ever heard. . . . The questions [from the audience] on the Mundt-Nixon bill, his views on the loyalty oath, and the problems of international communism were just what he was waiting for. Indeed, he was so skillful—and I might add, cagey—that those who came indifferent were sold, and even those who came to heckle went away with doubts . . .
>
> If he is only a fraction as effective [in his campaign] as he was here you have a formidable opponent on your hands.

In addition to his oratorical skills, which he would have used to advantage no matter what issues he had chosen to emphasize, Nixon had in Murray Chotiner a clever and devious campaign manager, "one of the fathers of the new synthetic Madison-Avenue-style politics in America." It might even be argued that Chotiner should receive principal credit for Nixon's victory, for it was he who devised Nixon's techniques in the campaign. This Beverly Hills lawyer made newspaper headlines with his admitted spy operations in 1972 directed against the McGovern campaign, successfully managed numerous California campaigns in the 1940s and 1950s. His formula for victory, a veritable bag of tricks, appearing first in written form for use in

1955 when he conducted seminars for all Republican state chairmen, gives real insight into the 1950 Senate race. One of his cardinal rules suggests a sound reason for Douglas' defeat: "Never attack the strength of the opposition." In Chotiner's words: "Mrs. Douglas, in desperation . . . started to debate Dick Nixon's issues . . . She was defeated the minute she tried to do it, because she could not sell the people of California that she would be a better fighter against communism than Dick Nixon."

In addition to his slick campaign organization, Nixon reaped benefits from the lack of effective Democratic party organization on the one hand, and substantial party defection on the other, conditions accentuated by the cross-filing system. As one liberal Democrat conceded, the Democratic party ran a "fantastically inept campaign" that hurt all statewide candidates. Douglas did receive support from many Boddy campaigners. In addition she rated all-out support from Washington. Luminaries trekked to California to praise Douglas, including Vice-President Alben W. Barkley, Attorney General J. Howard McGrath, Presidential Assistant W. Averill Harriman, Secretary of Labor Maurice Tobin, Secretary of Agriculture Charles P. Brannan, and Secretary of Interior Oscar Chapman. Others recorded five-minute spots for radio advertisement. But even this strategy, based primarily on the tactic of urging Democrats to vote a straight Democratic ticket, did not present a wholly united front. Most of these speakers, although strong for Douglas, made ambiguous statements about James Roosevelt's candidacy for governor or merely praised both Roosevelt and his formidable opponent Earl Warren—a stance that hardly strengthened the straight-ticket line.

This national support for Douglas also was undermined by "Democrats for Nixon" groups that organized in the primary and gained ground rapidly during the fall. A leader of the movement, George Creel of Wilsonian fame, announced the organization of his "Democrats for Nixon" group on September 29 with a vicious statement that repudiated Douglas and her "perverted point of view." At the end of October Creel came out with further accusations that even Nixon did not use— claims that she sympathized with Communists because she had

[425]

spoken before groups in 1945 and 1946 which were later classi-
fied as Communist-front organizations.

Capitalizing on this Democratic support, Chotiner sent a
pamphlet to California Democrats during the primary entitled
"As One Democrat to Another." This move infuriated both
Boddy and Douglas. One newsman commented: "It is surprising that [Nixon] . . . who poses as the soul of truth and honor
would permit such a deceitful device to be used to fool thousands of Democrats new to [Los Angeles] . . . county. As if that
were not enough, Chotiner put out another hate pamphlet
called "Is Helen Douglas a Democrat? The Record Says No!"
This completely distorted view of Douglas claimed that she
voted the Communist line in Congress and concluded: "How
will a real Democrat vote in this election? [For] . . . Richard
Nixon . . . a man who puts country above party."

Although Nixon reaped the harvest of votes in large part
by capitalizing on the public's anti-Communist sentiment, his
views on social, political, and economic matters also seemed to
coincide with California's general mood. This suggests that
Nixon held important advantages over Douglas on other issues
beyond that of anti-Communism. His position on questions of
corporate and individual taxation, government spending, labor
policies, and farm controls pleased the big ranchers, utilities,
and oil men. Nixon's firm conviction that California should control its tideland oil added to his popularity. Likewise his opposition to limiting water use in the Central Valley region to 160
acres per farm—a stand favored by Douglas—strengthened
Nixon's hand with the larger growers. This popularity with the
business community helped finance his campaign and doubtless
gave him an advertising edge over Douglas. The official record
does not prove this point since Nixon declared that organizations supporting him donated only $62,899, while Douglas re-
ported contributions of $156,172. But in the light of alleged irre-
sponsibility and dishonesty in subsequent Nixon campaigns,
one must discard this record as inaccurate. Nixon backers reputedly paid for seven months of billboard displays at a cost of
around $25,000 per month. It was even rumored that he had put
up billboards across the border in Mexico! Since a rule of

thumb suggests that billboards take up about ten to fifteen percent of a campaign budget, Nixon's total expenses may have run upwards of $1.75 million.

Finally, the fact that Douglas was a woman may also have hurt her. She denied this possibility vehemently, and from her own papers it is clear that numerous women's groups worked hard for her, both on grounds of her qualifications and her femininity. But it must be acknowledged that many people did not believe women were suited for high office. In addition, there are constant reminders throughout the newspaper coverage of the campaign that she by no means commanded support of all women's groups. One example concerned the Business and Professional Women's Clubs organized to work for female candidates running for political office. For months, a club in the Los Angeles area had planned a dinner in September at which both Nixon and Douglas were scheduled to debate the trend of Communism in the United States. Several days before the dinner, Douglas wrote to the sponsors that, due to the extension of the closing date of the current Congressional session, she would not be able to attend the dinner. Needless to say, it was a golden opportunity for Nixon to attack Douglas. The situation was worsened when Jimmy Roosevelt, who filled in for her at the last minute, proved unequal to Nixon's presentation. Given the overwhelming press support for Nixon, the event received exaggerated publicity. Nevertheless, it is clear that Douglas' refusal of the invitation damaged her reputation among professional women, particularly since some attributed the cancellation to her unwillingness to face Nixon. These reasons help explain Nixon's edge over Douglas, but in the final analysis his victory, which catapulted him into national prominence, resulted primarily from the dirty tricks skillfully devised by Chotiner to appeal to the lowest common denominator of human emotion.

The tragedy of this election was that a candidate of the high principles, courage, and talent possessed by Helen Gahagan Douglas lost. In so many ways she epitomized the ideal representative of a democratic people. She had entered politics because she felt compelled to help improve the lot of mankind. Visiting Vienna in 1937 she saw firsthand the terrifying atmos-

Helen Gahagan Douglas, Democratic candidate for the U.S. Senate, listens to the election returns.
Courtesy of Security Pacific National Bank
Photograph Collection/Los Angeles Public Library.

phere created by the Nazis. She left in haste, suddenly shocked out of the unreality of the theatrical world and thrust into a world threatened by war and fascism. She returned to California, first involving herself with the problems of migratory workers, and then moving on to the national scene. In 1940 she was elected Democratic National Committeewoman from California, and by 1944 she represented one of Los Angeles County's districts in the United States House of Representatives. In 1946 Truman appointed her an alternate delegate to the General Assembly of the United Nations.

Her votes in Congress reflected a remarkably consistent adherence to her belief in the democratic system and in the possibility for a better tomorrow. Never did political expediency govern her actions. Ironically it was this idealism that contributed to her defeat in the Senate race. She did not seek glory but rather worked diligently, often at tasks that went unnoticed, to influence legislation and national policy aimed at improving America and the free world. In 1949 she decided to run for the Senate, not out of desire for self-aggrandizement or with realistic hopes of winning, but because she strongly believed that Sheridan Downey's policies were detrimental to California.

Douglas' defeat ended her elected career, but by no means her productive life. After 1950 she appeared again on the New York stage and tirelessly devoted herself to causes she believed important. It is logical to wonder—did this vicious campaign scar her permanently. She answers this best herself in a recent interview. She recalls that on election eve, she sensed defeat was imminent. She knew her feelings the next morning would tell her if she really had entered the race to be of service or rather to seek higher office merely for the prestige. If she had participated to serve, her campaign had worth in itself, by raising the issues essential to keeping democracy alive. If rather she desired glory, her defeat could destroy her. She said: "When I woke up the next morning, Nixon didn't have control of my mind—because that's what it means to be permanently scarred . . . It means you *carry* that person who defeated you forever after. And I didn't carry Mr. Nixon. Thank God!"

[429]

30

REQUIEM FOR THE LOS ANGELES PHILHARMONIC AUDITORIUM

Henry A. Sutherland

When the Temple Baptist Church became the sole occupant of Philharmonic Auditorium on November 20, 1964, after fifty-eight years as a roommate of culture in manifestations ranging from symphony to professional wrestling, hardly anyone remained in Los Angeles who could savor the coincidence that it was remotely descended from a "Garden of Paradise," complete with Adam and Eve, the golden apples, and a serpent.

The garden and the Biblical progenitors of the race, or at least their plaster representations, were the creation of George (Roundhouse George) Lehman, a nineteenth-century visionary who was among the first to recognize Los Angeles as a great-city-to-be, and who pictured the northeast corner of Fifth and Olive Streets as its cultural center.

Lehman's dream, from which the story of the Philharmonic stems, dated from 1854, when Remundo Alexander, a sometime French sailor, built a home for his bride "out in the country" in what is now the 300 block of South Main Street. Alexander, in his voyaging, had been impressed with the cylindrical stone houses of North Africa, and decided to build one as a whimsical variation from the low adobes of Spanish-Mexican Southern California.

He built it two stories high, with eighteen-inch adobe walls and a conical shingled roof. *Californios* came from far and near to see the strange creation. Actually, it was octagonal in shape, but Los Angeles knew it then and forever as the "Round House." Whether Alexander was displeased with his handiwork, or whether he was overtaken by a sailor's restlessness ashore is not recorded, but two years later he sold the Round House and vanishes from our story.

The buyer was George Lehman, fresh from Germany and marveling at Southern California's genial climate, as would many a later arrival from the shores of the cold North Sea. "A second garden of paradise," he called the Southland, and determined to exemplify his conception with the Round House as a nucleus.

But whether for lack of a better model or simply with an eye to the main chance, Roundhouse George confused the "garden eastward in Eden" with the beer gardens of his native Rhineland. A beer garden the Round House became, and it was one of the first centers of public entertainment in a Los Angeles which, in 1860, numbered 4,385 inhabitants.

Extensive grounds surrounding the place fronted on both Main and Spring Streets. Roundhouse George developed them as a formal garden. He charged a small admission. There were "flying horses," evidently a primitive merry-go-round, for children, and as waiters hurried among the tables with trays of foaming steins, a little German band oompahed Wagner from a balcony until patrons might well have wondered whether Woden or Jehovah was in charge.

Except, of course, that George made the point abundantly clear in the plaster statuary ornamenting the grounds. Adam and Eve lurked in the shrubbery in testimony that this was truly an Eden. So, perhaps anachronistically, did Cain and Abel. The golden apples dangled temptingly, and the serpent coiled. A sign over the entrance identified the whole as the "Garden of Paradise."

When 1870 came, with its population of 5,738, Roundhouse George was still flourishing in his garden, despite competition as a community center from Los Angeles' first theater, the Merced, which opened at 418 North Main Street as the year ended.

In pursuit of his vision, however, Lehman sold out six years later, and one of the last notable events in the Garden of Paradise was an 1876 celebration of the centennial of American Independence. Some of California's newest Americans figured prominently. Ygnacio Sepulveda was chairman of the "literary exercises." Pío Pico won first prize for patriotic decoration of a business establishment.

Later, the Round House was used as a school. Still later, it was abandoned, its garden overgrown, and finally, in 1887, it was demolished.

The vision impelling George Lehman was one of a city extending far to the south of its dimensions of the time. He profoundly did not agree with the famous prophecy attributed to Hartley Taft that, "Never while wood burns or water runs will business come down as far as Fifth and Hill," where Taft made his home. Lehman foresaw the square between the Taft house and his own home on West Sixth Street—Block Fifteen of Lieutenant E. O. C. Ord's 1849 survey—as the center of the coming city.

In 1866 the City Council had set Block Fifteen aside to be a "Public Square or Plaza, for the use and benefit of the Citizens in common. . . . " It was a remnant of the four square leagues of land extending from the Old Plaza, with which Los Angeles was endowed at its founding by ancient Spanish law. Most of this patrimony had been auctioned off for trifling sums over the years at times when the city needed money.

The council moved again in 1870 with an ordinance permitting an "association of gentlemen," headed by J.M. Griffith, O.W. Childs, Andrew Glassell, J.S. Griffin, J.G. Downey and P. Beaudry, "to fence in and ornament with fruit or forest trees the aforesaid Block." "Los Angeles Park" was proposed as a name, but Central Park was commonly accepted for many years.

At one time or another the park was called by several other names—Public Square, La Plaza Abaja, City Park, Sixth Street Park and during one period, St. Vincent's Park, because of the proximity of St. Vincent's College on the present site of Bullock's downtown department store.

[433]

But on November 18, 1918, seven days after the signing of the World War I armistice, a rejoicing Los Angeles renamed it in honor of the commander of the American Expeditionary Force. It became Pershing Square.

The park beautification ordinance of 1870 found no more prompt and enthusiastic supporter than Roundhouse George Lehman. He planted the first trees in the square, near the corner of Sixth and Olive Streets and, as Mrs. Hartley Taft recalled many years later, toiled at watering them with "a big pail with a rope handle," which he carried "from his place across the street."

Lehman, however, was not without shrewd personal motives. He seldom was, despite a reputation for eccentricity. At about the same time he was beginning a "suburban" business community with a three-story building at Sixth and Spring Streets, and christening the area "Georgetown" in his own honor.

With the park safely established, he began buying property on its bordering streets and environs. According to the recollection of Boyle Workman (in *The City That Grew*), Lehman "bought property to the limit of his capacity, nor would he ever sell an inch of it."

One of his acquisitions was the site of the Philharmonic, a frontage of 165 feet on Fifth Street and 176 feet on Olive. George planned to build a theater or an auditorium there, the cultural center of his dream city, but it was not to be. Like that of many another pioneer, Lehman's vision outstripped his financial resources, and he fell victim to overextension. Workman recalls: "The time came when he could no longer meet interest on his mortgages, but even then he would not sell any of his holdings. In the end he lost all . . . and died penniless."

By this time, the early 1880s, Los Angeles was a town of 11,183 on the eve of a tremendous influx of population which still has not subsided. The flow was primed from a trickle by a passenger rate war which developed between the Southern Pacific and Santa Fe railroads in 1886. Fares from points west of the Missouri, which had averaged $100 one way and $150 for the round trip, melted under competitive price-cutting. At the climax, round trips were offered for as little as $15, and at one time, a single day, for $1, before climbing back to $50 for first class and $40 for second class one-way trips.

The rate war was paralleled by a wild boom in real estate. Passenger fare cutting, indeed, may have originated in the desire of the Santa Fe to dispose of its large landholdings, to settle the country quickly, stimulate business and industry, and create a broader base for its long-haul freight traffic.

But however it may have been, the boom swiftly got out of hand. Speculators flocked in. Visitors sold or gave away their return tickets. Developers and subdividers multiplied. Prices skyrocketed, and fortunes were made and lost overnight as real property changed hands at dizzy speed. Eastern financiers were attracted, and one of them, Phil D. Armour, was quoted as saying, "This is merely preliminary to a boom that will outclass the present activity as thunder to the crack of a hickory nut!"

By 1888 the madness had ebbed, but Los Angeles was on its way. The census of 1890 showed that the city of ten years earlier had quadrupled to a population of 50,395.

The decade had transformed George Lehman's dream of a great city from an eccentricity to an article of faith, and other hands were available to build the cultural center he envisioned overlooking Central Park. When it began, Los Angeles had a single theater. When it ended, there were three, plus a huge auditorium on Roundhouse George's site at the northeast corner of Fifth and Olive.

The growing city's need for new theaters was implicit in the decline of the old Merced. After its first years of glory, it had subsisted on a fare of minstrel shows and melodrama, including such standbys as *Uncle Tom's Cabin*, *East Lynne*, and *Ten Nights in a Bar Room*, but in 1876 it was leased by J. H. Wood and became Wood's Opera House.

"Opera House" appears to have been a name rather than a description of the entertainment, however. Wood made it strictly a variety theater, changing pace with boxing and wrestling shows and an occasional broad farce. One observer of the time called it "a typical Western song and dance resort . . .

[435]

where the actresses between acts mingled with the patrons. . . ." Wood went bankrupt in 1878.

For a time the theater served as an armory for a militia unit, the "Los Angeles Guards," but in 1883 it reopened as the Club Theater, another variety house. Heavyweight champion John L. Sullivan is remembered as a patron on at least one occasion, when he is pictured as amusing himself by tossing silver dollars at the dancing girls. Proper Angelenos of the day looked on the old theater as a scandalous place, and in 1887 the Los Angeles *Times* described a ball given there as a "prostitutes' carnival."

First of the new theaters was Childs' Opera House, almost immediately renamed the Grand Opera House, which was built in 1884 by O. W. Childs, pioneer tin and hardware merchant, on Main Street just south of First. Seating 1200, it was at that time the second largest theater on the Pacific Coast.

A second theater opened four years later, the Los Angeles, built by Mrs. Juana Neal on Spring Street between Second and Third, to vie with the Grand Opera House in the presentation of opera, musicals, and drama "direct from New York City."

In 1893, a third rival appeared when Dr. David Burbank opened the Burbank Theater opposite his home in the 500 block of South Main Street. Dr. Burbank is also remembered as the eponymous founder of the city of Burbank, developed on ranch properties he owned at the eastern end of the San Fernando Valley.

By 1965, both the Los Angeles Theater and the Grand Opera House were long gone, but the Burbank, which became a burlesque house in its later years, was still showing sexy motion pictures and live variety acts as the New Follies Theater at 548 South Main.

The relative opulence of two new theaters in the 1880s did not meet the city's need for a really large auditorium, however, and this necessity was supplied by Hazard's Pavilion, built in 1886–1887 for capacity audiences of 4,000 on the spot selected by Roundhouse George Lehman so long before.

Henry T. Hazard, who would be mayor of Los Angeles in 1889–1892, was the prime mover in the project. He was a son of

Captain A. M. Hazard, who arrived in Los Angeles across the plains in 1853, and who, coincidentally, was the first private owner of the auditorium site.

In 1866, at one of the last of the perennial municipal land auctions, Captain Hazard purchased the western half of the block extending from Hill to Olive on Sixth Street for $9.80, while his son-in-law, Hartley Taft, bought the eastern half for a like amount.

The combined cost would have been $20, but the city reduced it 40 cents because a fork of the old highway, El Camino Viejo, ran diagonally across the block from Fourth and Hill Streets to Fifth and Olive before crossing the present site of the Biltmore Hotel on its meandering way southwestward.

Twenty years later, when the pavilion was built, Henry Hazard's sister, Mrs. Mary Phelps, still lived at the northwest corner of Fifth and Hill, but the Olive Street end of the block had passed into other hands. Until then, the land had been used only as a horse and mule corral. Hazard and his associates reportedly paid $20,000 for it.

To build the pavilion, Hazard combined with Judge H. K. S. O'Melveny and C. H. Howland to form the Exposition Company, in which George H. Pike later acquired a substantial interest.

Construction began, and a clapboarded wooden building of 120 by 166 feet rose. The ceiling was 50 feet high. Double galleries ranged around three sides. Folding chairs formed the seating, so that the orchestra floor could be cleared for flower shows, citrus fairs, banquets, and balls. The cost was $60,000.

World War II servicemen would have recognized Hazard's Pavilion. Externally, except for its shuttered windows and cupola-topped square towers flanking the entrance, it resembled the huge, wooden, post theaters built at every military camp and base. But nineteenth century Los Angeles loved it. Carriages ringed the pavilion every night, while waiting teams stamped and switched at hitching posts.

Hazard's opened in April 1887, and the consensus was that it was not a moment too soon. The need for it had been demonstrated the previous January 20, when Adelina Patti was pre-

Hazard's Pavilion as it stood at the northeast corner of Fifth and Olive until May, 1905, when it was razed to make way for the Clune's Auditorium Theater, now Philharmonic Auditorium.
Courtesy of Huntington Library.

sented in Los Angeles for the first time. The Grand Opera House had been engaged. So had the old Turnverein Hall in the 200 block of South Spring Street, where musical events and drama were sometimes offered, although it was properly a ballroom.

For lack of a better place, the world-famed coloratura sang in Mott's Hall, the Seventh Militia Regiment Armory, on the second floor of Thomas D. Mott's building at 125–29 South Main Street. The hall lacked even a stage, and the lower floors housed a delicatessen, a fish and poultry market and grocery store. Because of the limited accommodations, promoters scaled the hall at $3.50 to $7.50, and a wag lampooned the admissions with the lines:

> Only to hear you, Patti,
> Only to hear you squeak.
> Only to pay seven dollars,
> And starve the rest of the week!

Nevertheless, a wall-bursting crowd jammed Mott's for the performance. The street in front was packed, too, and a man was stationed at an open window to wave a handkerchief when

[438]

the prima donna began to sing. Newspapers reported it as a triumph, and neither Patti nor her audience was distracted by the occasional crowing of roosters from the market below.

Three years later, however, it appeared that the economics of scarcity may have contributed to the excitement. Patti was billed in Hazard's Pavilion for February 7 and 8, 1890, to sing two evening shows and a matinee at $15 to $18 for the three. But despite prodigious trumpeting, advance sales were so unpromising that the concerts were cancelled.

Hazard's opened modestly with a civic flower festival, but a month later it presented the National Opera Company, with 300 singers, ballet dancers, and musicians, and "100 tons of baggage." During ensuing years many of the world's opera stars sang in the pavilion at one time or another.

But the great days of opera at Hazard's did not really begin until 1900, when Lynden Ellsworth Behymer took over, presenting the New York Metropolitan Opera in its first performance of Puccini's *La Boheme*. Nellie Melba, fabulous Australian soprano, sang the role of Mimi, with Fritzi Scheff making her American debut as Musette.

Behymer, affectionately known as "L. E." or "Bee," moved from Hazard's to its successor, the Philharmonic Auditorium, without missing a beat. He remained Los Angeles' principal impresario until his death in 1947.

The 1900 *La Boheme* is often misremembered as the American première at the Los Angeles Theater three years earlier. This event occurred on October 14, 1897, when the Del Conte Grand Opera Company of Milan sang the Puccini masterwork with Linda Montanari as Mimi, and Cleopatra Vicini as Musette. The performance was repeated October 16 and 19.

Behymer, who was born near Cincinnati, November 5, 1862, came to Los Angeles in 1886 as a bookseller's clerk, and became friendly with Harry C. Wyatt, manager of the Grand Opera House and later of the Los Angeles Theater. He became program editor of the Los Angeles Theater in the early 1890s, and from this worked into promotion, transferring to Hazard's through friendships with Martin Lehman and George P.

McLain, veteran Los Angeles showmen who were at that time managing the pavilion.

In 1901, he presented another great coloratura, France's Mme. Emma Calvé, in her memorable *Carmen,* and from the same stage such great voices as those of Mme. Ernestine Schumann-Heink and the tremendous tenor of Enrico Caruso. Between times, under the Behymer auspices, pavilion audiences heard the John Philip Sousa Band, the U.S. Marine Corps Band, and such orchestras as the Walter Damrosch and the Russian Symphony.

Thus Los Angeles had the Fifth and Olive Streets cultural center of which Roundhouse George Lehman dreamed, but to Gaslight Era Angelenos, "culture" meant the entire spectrum of human activity, including politics, prize fights, lectures, temperance rallies, revival meetings, banquets, balls, and even an occasional poultry show.

Hazard's was not looked upon primarily as a theater, despite appearances there of such actresses as Sarah Bernhardt and Helena Modjeska, and this attitude was expressed by the Los Angeles *Times Almanac* for 1897, when it said in describing the attractions of the city: "Three handsome theaters present most of the leading attractions from the East and Europe. There is also a large pavilion seating 4,000, where fairs, fruit shows, and occasional theatrical performances are given."

Politics debuted early in the pavilion under the sponsorship of the founder himself. Henry Hazard was a champion of a then prevalent move to divide California into two states, and in 1888, he joined with a committee including Dr. J. P. Widney, J. G. Downey, A. G. Moffit, J. G. Estudillo, Cameron E. Thom, Judge Robert M. Widney, Anson Brunson, Stephen C. Hubbell, and H. A. Barclay to call a convention.

Delegates from the Sixth Congressional District met in the pavilion to discuss the feasibility of forming a "State of Southern California" with its northern boundary at the Tehachapis. After lengthy debate, they appointed a committee on ways and means, but eventually the movement came to nothing.

Three years later, Hazard's welcomed its first President of the United States when President Benjamin Harrison addressed a capacity audience the night of April 22, 1891, and in 1896, William Jennings Bryan, "silver-tongued orator from the Platte," campaigned in the pavilion for "free unlimited coinage of silver" as Democratic nominee against William McKinley and the gold standard.

Curiously, Bryan appeared in Los Angeles under the sponsorship of Republicans rather than that of his fellow Democrats. In 1896 both parties split over the free-silver issue. "Gold Democrats" supported McKinley in the East, and "Silver Republican Clubs" sprang up throughout the hard-money West.

The party nose of California Democrats was badly out of joint when Bryan accepted the invitation of the Silver Republican Club of Los Angeles for a Fourth of July visit here, and McKinley loyalists jeered that the Silver Republicans were the "best Democrats in California."

Bryan and his wife were guests of honor at a gargantuan banquet in Hazard's Pavilion, and the candidate referred pointedly to the division of the parties when he said: "I used to think that all good was contained in the Democratic Party, and that all evil was concentrated in the Republican Party, but in the later years I have met so many bad Democrats and so many good Republicans that I have become more liberal in my ideas. . . ."

By 1904, the Republicans had resolved their differences, and were united when a rousing celebration of their party's fiftieth anniversary packed the pavilion.

Between political campaigns, Los Angeles attended rousing revivals at Hazard's, gave the "Demon Rum" his comeuppance at temperance rallies, and heard most of the outstanding lectures of the day, some educational, some patriotic, and some hilarious.

Notable among the revivalists were the venerable Dwight Lyman Moody and Ira David Sankey, conceded internationally to have been the outstanding evangelists and hymnologists of the nineteenth century. Sam Jones was another powerful exhorter heard at Hazard's on behalf of the "old time religion."

Lecturers ranged from humorist Mark Twain to Booker T. Washington, pioneer pleader for the Negro. In 1891, Henry M. Stanley, the African explorer, drew a capacity audience. Stanley's 1871 exploit in finding Dr. David Livingstone in "Darkest Africa" with a safari commissioned by James Gordon Bennett of the New York *Herald* had captured public imagination as no other adventure would until Lindbergh's New York-to-Paris flight. Then, as now, his casual greeting of the missionary when they met at Ujiji, near Lake Tanganyika, was a household word.

Other lecturers heard at Hazard's included Thomas Nast, *Harper's Weekly* cartoonist credited with breaking the power of "Boss" Tweed and Tammany in gas-lit New York; Lew Wallace, controversial Civil War general and author of *Ben Hur;* poet James Whitcomb Riley; Bill Nye, the humorist; and many another.

These were the days of theatrical stock companys, and two attempts were made to establish repertoire troupes at Hazard's. For a short time in 1893 the Park Theater offered stock drama at a 10-, 20-, and 30-cent scale plus 50-cent box seats, and in 1901, the Hazard's Pavilion Stock Company tried it again with such attractions as Ouida's *Under Two Flags.* But neither could cope with the competition of the Los Angeles and Burbank Theaters and the Grand Opera House.

Orchestral music had better luck. The Los Angeles Women's Symphony Orchestra, organized by Harley Hamilton in 1893, performed frequently at Hazard's in some of the earliest of its fifty-seven seasons, continuing until 1950, when it reorganized as the California Women's Symphony Orchestra. So did the Los Angeles Symphony Orchestra, which Hamilton formed in 1896 and led through twenty-three seasons. It was succeeded by the Los Angeles Philharmonic Orchestra in 1919.

From time to time, the pavilion lent itself to such odd purposes as a bicycling school and events sponsored by the Los Angeles Wheelmen, and, of course, to balls and banquets without number. On Memorial Days—Decoration Day, it was called then—and Fourths of July, it was a rallying point for the Grand Army of the Republic, and heard the still middle-aged veterans of the Civil War speak of storied battles and campaigns in almost the present tense.

Boxing or prizefighting as it was more often called, shared a common ground with opera in that it did not reach full stature at Hazard's until 1900, when Los Angeles was a hustling city of 102,479. Until then, the sport had been practiced in a demimonde status and on a relatively small scale, but when Thomas (Uncle Tom) McCarey became promoter at the pavilion, he brought it out of the upstairs-hall and railroad-yard arenas for presentation to big audiences.

McCarey was able to achieve the change largely through the prestige of a six-foot, two-and-a-half-inch, 220-pound young boilermaker, James J. Jeffries, who made Los Angeles his fighting headquarters after winning his first two bouts here, both by knockouts, in 1896. Three years later, on June 9, 1899, Jeffries knocked out Bob Fitzsimmons in eleven rounds at Coney Island, New York, and became heavyweight champion of the world. His subsequent appearances at Hazard's were sellouts.

A combining circumstance in the advent of big-time boxing was that California was one of the few states in the Union in which twenty-round bouts were legal. This state of affairs continued until 1915, when the Legislature banned boxing, except for four-round "exhibition" matches. The lawmakers relented and authorized ten-round professional boxing in 1924.

During the pavilion's remaining years, McCarey presented many of the most prominent boxers of the day, names such as Hank Griffin, Denver Ed Martin, and Philadelphia Jack O'Brien, and on one memorable evening he produced what must surely rank as one of the most dramatic incidents in the history of boxing.

To Los Angeles late in 1901 came John Arthur (Jack) Johnson, a young South Texan modeled as if by Praxiteles under a satin, khaki-colored skin. Johnson had fought himself out of opponents in his native Galveston. Now he began devastating West Coast heavyweights. Within a few weeks he was a familiar figure, clad like a Beau Brummell when he was flush and, good times or bad, in an air of regal arrogance.

Uncle Tom McCarey brought Johnson to Hazard's from Naud's Junction, in the Southern Pacific Railroad yards, where he made his local debut. On the night of May 16, 1902, he was matched with Jack Jeffries before a capacity crowd.

[443]

Jeffries was the younger brother of the champion and himself a promising heavyweight. Until the fight began, everything seemed to favor him. He was the more experienced of the two, and the great title-holder was one of his cornermen. But the shaven-pated Johnson, moving smoothly as a big brown cat, demolished young Jeffries in five savage rounds. Upon the count of ten he picked up his unconscious opponent, carried him to his corner and, with a guileful, gold-toothed grin, handed him to his shocked brother, the heavyweight champion of the world.

Thereafter, McCarey did his best to match Johnson and Jim Jeffries for the title. But he never was able to bring them together, and those who remembered Big Jim's expression that night of May 16 were sure they knew why.

It was easy in those days for a champion to "draw the color line," and a Negro heavyweight's prospects for a title bout usually varied in inverse ratio to his ability. This was still true more than two decades later when Harry Wills, perennially the outstanding contender, never was given a chance with champion Jack Dempsey. It remained so until the time of Joe Louis in the mid-1930's.

Jeffries had retired undefeated in 1905, "for lack of suitable opponents," even though Johnson was campaigning internationally at that time with sensational success. The two did not meet until July 4, 1910, when Jeffries was persuaded to come out of retirement as a "white hope" at Reno, Nevada. "Li'l Artha'," as the sportswriters were calling Johnson, had been champion for eighteen months then. He had finally won the title in Sydney, Australia, December 26, 1908, by knocking out Tommy Burns, successor to Marvin Hart, who had established a claim to the championship by elimination after Jeffries quit the ring.

By 1910, Jeffries was a husk of the boxer he had been eight years earlier. The laughing Johnson toyed with him, and apparently "carried" the old champion for several rounds before winning by a knockout in the fifteenth. Oldtimers still grow misty over the battle that might have been had Big Jim listened to Uncle Tom McCarey in 1902.

Curiously, prize fighting was one of the factors contributing to the finish of Hazard's in 1905, and building of the Philharmonic Auditorium began in the same year. Women flocked to the pavilion with their escorts for opera, drama, lectures, and religious services, but at other times the vicinity of Hazard's came to be considered "not quite nice."

In a 1952 letter to the Los Angeles *Times*, Mrs. Opal S. Corey, 1907-1908 secretary to the first pastor of the Temple Baptist Church, wrote: "When I visited here in August, 1900, three of us roomed at the northeast corner of Fifth and Olive Streets. Passing Hazard's Pavilion we looked straight ahead, as ladies did then, because of the sports hanging around the entrance."

For several years Central Park, across the street, had suffered from a somewhat sinister reputation. The shrubbery was heavy and concealing. Vagrants were believed to sleep in the bandstand. Holdups were common. E. A. Brininstool, an observer of the time, was quoted by W. W. Robinson as saying (in *The Story of Pershing Square*): "It was not safe to go through after dark, unless you packed a gun, as there were no lights in (the park). Bear in mind, that in those days (1895 or thereabouts) the park was a long ways from anywhere near the center of the business district and few people ever were seen there—day or night."

Addition to the neighborhood of the "fancy," or the "fight mob," as a later generation would say, did very little to improve the tone.

More importantly, however, the demise of Hazard's turned on the appearance on the scene of another man with a vision, Dr. Robert J. Burdette, who became pastor of the Temple Baptist Church immediately after its founding in 1903.

The church began with announcement in the newspapers "To the Baptists of Los Angeles" of an organizational meeting to be held July 17 in "the building formerly occupied by the First Congregational Church . . . at Sixth and Hill streets."

First Congregational, which occupied the corner from 1880 to 1903, had just moved to new quarters. The organizing Baptists rented the old church for $100 a month, but response to the

[445]

announcement exceeded all expectations and, from the first Sunday, attendance overtaxed the seating capacity of 1,200.

Dr. Burdette was a well-traveled man, and an admirer of New York's Old Trinity Church at the foot of Wall Street. At an early meeting, he told his church board that, "It is not by chance . . . that Old Trinity Church stands in the center of the commercial district of the United States," and urged: "Let us build a second Trinity Church here."

Temple Baptist Church was Dr. Burdette's first and only pastorate, in the formal sense of the word, and he was not a young man when he assumed it. Born in Greensborough, Pennsylvania, July 30, 1844, he grew up in Peoria, Illinois, and fought through the Civil War with the 47th Illinois Volunteer Infantry, notably in the Battle of Corinth, the Vicksburg Campaign, and the Red River Expedition. After the war, he became a newspaperman, first on the Peoria *Transcript* and later as editor of the Burlington, Iowa, *Hawkeye*.

From journalism, he turned to lecturing, and traveled much of the Midwest and East, on Sundays, according to the custom of the time, occupying pulpits of many denominations as an unordained minister. In 1899, several years after the death of his first wife, Dr. Burdette moved to Pasadena, where he met and married Mrs. Clara Bradley Baker, widow of Presley C. Baker, a Kentuckian and sometime colonel of Confederate cavalry. Colonel Baker died in 1893.

For more than a year before receiving a call from the new Temple Baptist Church, Dr. Burdette had served as acting pastor of the Presbyterian Church of Pasadena. In 1903, however, he was ordained as a Baptist minister, and Mrs. Burdette recalls (in *The Rainbow and the Pot of Gold*) that in delivering the charge to the new pastor, the Reverend A. J. Frost looked down on the five-foot, four-inch Burdette from a towering height, and said, "I thank God what there is of you is a Baptist!"

Although small in inches, Dr. Burdette was great in influence and in vision. A man of tremendous energy, he left a lasting mark on his denomination and on downtown Los Angeles.

Increasingly cramped in the old First Congregational Church, Dr. Burdette's flock cast a speculative eye at Hazard's

Pavilion, diagonally across the park. Early in 1904, they had rented the pavilion briefly for a Campbell Morgan revival, and during the summer they appointed a committee headed by C. R. Harris to investigate its possibilities as a home. Harris reported that Hazard's could be "made habitable for worship" for $1,000, and that it could be rented for $600 a month. On October 16, the church moved across the park, rechristening the pavilion for its own purposes, "Temple Auditorium."

Only a few weeks passed before the congregation resolved to act on Dr. Burdette's proposal to build a "second Trinity Church" in downtown Los Angeles. As a result, on January 21, 1905, a syndicate composed of Mrs. Robert J. Burdette, D. K. Edwards, Richard Green, and C. R. Harris concluded an agreement with the Exposition Company to buy Hazard's for $170,000.

This, of course, was a great sum, and the still greater cost of an edifice such as that envisioned by Dr. Burdette was hardly to be borne by the members of the church. It was from this situation that the fifty-nine-year partnership of the Temple Baptist Church and the cultural community of Los Angeles evolved. Mrs. Burdette recalls in her 1908 story of the founding of the church: "While . . . the expense of a downtown church was too great to be borne by any . . . membership that might . . . be gathered, it was possible for many of (the members) to make an investment in a business and auditorium block that should be dividend earning."

Thus, in February 1905, Temple Baptist incorporated the Auditorium Company, which still manages the affairs of the Philharmonic. It soon developed, however, that even this device would not serve to raise the amount of money needed. Mrs. Burdette recalls that attempts were made to interest wealthy Baptists in the East, but that these failed, and that "not one dollar of Eastern money ever went into the enterprise." She continues, "Having gathered all . . . possible stockholders in the Auditorium Company, it was evident that not one-third (of the stock) was to be held in the denomination, and that outside friends . . . must be . . . drawn in. . . . About this time, Theodore B. Comstock became interested, and not only invested his own money, but after careful consideration of the prospects, induced many friends to do the same."

Temple Baptist Church entered a long-term agreement to become renters "at about 25 per cent of what the space might otherwise produce." Directors of the Auditorium Company issued $300,000 worth of stock at par or higher, and floated a $300,000 bond issue, and in May 1905, Hazard's Pavilion went down under the wrecker's hammer. Mrs. Burdette added a kindly eulogy in her 1908 story when she wrote: "No matter how orthodox the tapeline, the measure of the life of this old building, dear to the hearts of the 'old timers', must stand 'feet' for demoralization and 'yards' for uplift. . . ."

Charles F. Whittlesley, admired for his work on Sullivan's Chicago Opera House, completed in 1903, was retained as architect, and construction went forward. When finished in the fall of 1906, the new Temple Auditorium was the largest reinforced concrete building in all of California, and the finest in a Los Angeles already approaching its 1910 population of 319,198.

Then, as now, it was composed of two units, a nine-story office building fronting 165 feet on Fifth Street and 65 feet on Olive, and the auditorium proper, adjoining on the north with a frontage of 111 feet on Olive Street.

The interior, with its intricately scrolled proscenium, familiar to generations of Angelenos, closely resembled that of Sullivan's Opera House, and it remains unchanged to this day. An elaborately worked Gothic exterior, rising to a mansard roof, ornamented both buildings until 1938, when a major "face-lifting" gave the Philharmonic its present clean, modern lines.

Opening night came November 7, 1906, with Behymer presenting the Lombardi Opera Company in *Aida,* coincidentally the same opera with which Hazard's had its musical opening nineteen years before. Next day the Los Angeles *Evening News* exulted: "Los Angeles, in the possession of this great new auditorium, now may truly be called the metropolis of the great Southwest."

*Central Park (later Pershing Square) and the newly built Temple
Auditorium, at the corner of Fifth and Olive Streets, around 1906.*
Courtesy of California Historical Society.

The opening was marred only by foreboding felt in some
quarters about the stability of the balcony. As far as Angelenos
knew, it was the first theater balcony ever built without supporting columns, and pessimists predicted that it would fall under the weight of an audience!

Four days later, on November 11, Dr. Burdette dedicated
the auditorium to the service of God. During the fifteen months
of building, Temple Baptist Church held services around the
corner in a Masonic Hall at 462 South Hill Street. From the first,
the curious association of religious worship and secular entertainment attracted comment and some protests, at least one ob-
jector quipping, "God gets into the auditorium only on Sundays—the devil runs it the rest of the week."

[449]

To this Dr. Burdette replied stoutly, "Let anyone who cries out against it . . . go buy some dive, tear it down, and on its unholy ruins build, for the good of man and the glory of God, a temple!"

Boxing never returned to Fifth and Olive Streets, but during one period of the auditorium's long life, professional wrestling did. It was ousted after a short time, however, when the manager complained, "Wrestling audiences get too excited. They tear up the seats."

Otherwise the auditorium, with its seating capacity of 2,600, fulfilled most of the purposes that Hazard's had served. It did not, of course, become the Philharmonic immediately. Fourteen years would pass before the Los Angeles Philharmonic Orchestra began its long tenancy in 1920, and gave its name to the theater. At first, Los Angeles tried to call its new music hall the "Theater Beautiful," but found the name unhandy, and for several years referred to it simply as the Auditorium, or the Temple Auditorium.

Most of the great names of opera who had sung at Hazard's returned to perform in the auditorium, and as the years passed were succeeded by new voices, Tito Schipa, Galli-Curci, John McCormack, and many others. In 1913, Behymer scored a triumph when he brought the Chicago Civic Opera to Fifth and Olive Streets for eight performances, headlined by that of Mary Garden, singing *Natoma* for the first time in the west. The impresario was compelled to post an $88,000 guarantee to insure the visit.

Curiously, except for the occasional tour de force such as an appearance by the great Russian ballerina, Anna Pavlova, ballet was never a major attraction until 1932, when the Ballet Russe de Monte Carlo played a resoundingly successful engagement.

Other uses were found for the auditorium. At one time, Los Angeles High School graduates received their diplomas on its stage. At others, it welcomed outstanding evangelists and spokesmen for many causes. Nor was the burgeoning motion picture industry tardy in taking advantage of the auditorium's large capacity.

In 1915, William (Billy) Clune, pioneer film exhibitor, rented the music hall as a motion picture house, and gave it a new name. It became "Clune's Auditorium" on February 8, 1915, for the world première of D. W. Griffith's history-making *Birth of a Nation.*

Los Angeles had followed the filming of the epic with fascination, and police swarmed around the auditorium on opening night, fearing that its glorification of the post-Civil War Ku Klux Klan would ignite race riots. No trouble materialized, however, and the film ran for two years, making Henry B. Walthall, Lillian Gish, Mae Marsh and Donald Crisp stars of the new drama form.

Other pictures followed, for shorter runs, and the movies held the stage until 1920, when the auditorium was rechristened again, this time with its present name. A year earlier, Los Angeles music acquired a fabulous "angel." The city was ready. Its population had soared to 576,073, and it ranked as tenth largest in the United States, for the first time surpassing San Francisco as the metropolis of California.

The new benefactor was William Andrews Clark, Jr., son of the Butte, Montana, and Arizona copper king. Clark had established a home, although not a legal residence, here in 1907, and during the remaining twenty-seven years of his life divided most of his time between Los Angeles and Paris. The younger Clark had played cello with the Saint-Saens Quintet organized here in 1910, and apparently developed a lasting interest in Southern California music.

On June 11, 1919, newspapers announced the organization of the Los Angeles Philharmonic Orchestra under the sponsorship of Clark, who guaranteed $100,000 for its support during the first season. Next year he doubled the amount, and eventually invested more than $3 million in the development of the orchestra. Clark's second wife, Mrs. Alice McManus Medin Clark, died seven months prior to the formation of the orchestra, and it was understood that he intended the Philharmonic as a memorial to her.

Organized around Harley Hamilton's old Los Angeles Symphony Orchestra as a nucleus, the Philharmonic played its

[451]

*Aerial view of Pershing Square, the newly constructed Biltmore
Hotel at left center, and the Philharmonic Auditorium at right
center, around 1925.*
Courtesy of California Historical Society.

first season in Trinity (now Embassy) Auditorium at Ninth
Street and Grand Avenue, under the baton of Walter Henry
Rothwell as first conductor, but in 1920 moved to Fifth and
Olive Streets, where it would be heard for the next forty-four
years.

Under Clark's sponsorship, during the 1920s it extended its
activities to include "Symphonies Under the Stars" in Hollywood Bowl during the summer months, and grew in reputation
until it was conceded to be one of the three or four ranking
symphony orchestras in the United States.

When 1933 came, and Clark brought the renowned German, Dr. Otto S. Klemperer, here as conductor, the Philharmonic was almost as much a Los Angeles trademark as
the towering new City Hall. By then the city was a giant of
1,238,048. Dr. Klemperer continued to lead the orchestra until
1940, when he resigned because of illness and was replaced by
Bruno Walter.

Clark had added to his stature as a philanthropist in 1926, when he deeded his home, library, and gardens at 2205 West Adams Boulevard, now the Clark Memorial Library, to the University of California at Los Angeles, subject to his own life interest. It was assumed that he would make a similar provision for the Philharmonic, but a crisis in the life of the orchestra came on June 14, 1934, when Clark died suddenly in his summer home at Salmon Lake, Montana. His will made no mention of the Philharmonic.

Into this breach in the late summer of 1934, stepped a group of business and professional men and women, forming the Southern California Symphony Association, a non-profit organization, for support of the Philharmonic's winter season and summer performances in the Hollywood Bowl.

A public subscription campaign was launched to assure the 1934-1935 season, and a similar drive has been mounted annually since then. In recent years, women have taken over the fund-raising mechanisms almost entirely, and support of the Philharmonic has become a social, as well as a musical enthusiasm.

Meanwhile, the Temple Baptist Church, oldest tenant at Fifth and Olive Streets, was experiencing reactions to the changing city which would end in its acquisition of full ownership of the auditorium it had called into being in 1906. C. H. Brainard, general manager of the Auditorium Company for the past thirty-one years, recalls how it came about.

It began in 1918, under the pastorate of Dr. J. Whitcomb Brougher, now retired and living in Oregon, he remembers. At that time Temple Baptist was still very much a minority stockholder in the Auditorium Company, and the congregation was growing a little restive under the old arrangement. The church was in the market for a new home, but true to Dr. Burdette's dream of a second "Old Trinity," would consider no site removed from the business and financial center of the city. Dr. Brougher led a drive to raise $500,000 to buy or build a new Temple Baptist Church in downtown Los Angeles.

As the fund increased, the Temple Baptist Governing Board invested it in sound, well-paying securities, pending the church's decision whether to buy or build. Stock in the Auditorium Company was included in these investments whenever it became available, and in this way Temple Baptist came to own so much of the stock that the congregation conceived the idea of acquiring all of it, and outright ownership of the Philharmonic Auditorium.

Years passed, and stock accrued steadily to the church, some of it by purchase and a considerable portion through gifts and bequests. The last of the original bonds were retired in the early 1930s, and Brainard recalls: "By the middle of the decade the First Baptist Church Governing Board held a controlling interest in the Auditorium Company. We bought the last of the stock in 1945."

Through the years, the interior of the Philharmonic underwent many renovations, one of the most extensive in 1931. In 1934, it was given a $50,000 refurbishing in time for a brilliant reopening with The Mikado.

Then came 1938 and complete restyling of the exterior under the direction of architect John Beelman at a cost of $200,000. There would be other interior renovations, notably in 1955, but by the end of the 1930s the Philharmonic had assumed the form in which it is familiar to present-day Angelenos.

The year 1938 was also notable for the appearance of a new major tenant in the Philharmonic, the Los Angeles Civic Light Opera Association, which would play there for the next twenty-seven years.

Since the rise of Hollywood, a tradition had developed in the legitimate theater that Los Angeles was a "motion picture town," and that audiences here would not support live musicals and drama. Edwin Lester, general director of the Civic Light Opera from its beginning, recalls that "it was not unusual for Broadway hit shows to make the trip across the country . . . to play San Francisco, and (to) bypass Los Angeles." This, although the city was then approaching its 1940 population of 1,504,277.

The theatrical world had become accustomed to calling Los Angeles "the worst show town in America," but the Civic Light Opera was to prove it one of the best. The Light Opera Association operates on a guarantor basis, and within a few seasons, as Lester notes, "being a guarantor became a sought-after obligation." But for the first season in 1938 there were just three guarantors, two in Los Angeles and one in San Francisco, all of them anonymous.

Light opera opened in the Philharmonic with a week's presentation of John Charles Thomas singing *Blossom Time*. It played to more than $41,000. The four-week initial season closed with *Roberta*, starring Bob Hope, then a brilliant young comedian. Lester recalls:

> The Civic Light Opera was on its way. San Francisco unshrugged its shoulders and took notice. We were invited to bring our company north. Our visit resulted in the formation of the San Francisco Light Opera Association to present our season there.
>
> As we gained in patronage, the increased resources made possible greater creativity, more lavish production. Distinguished casts have been a trademark.

But as the 1940s melted toward the 1950s, the success of the Civic Light Opera Association and the Los Angeles Philharmonic Orchestra could have been a source of public embarrassment as well as pride. With ownership of all of the stock in the Auditorium Company in hand, the Temple Baptist Church looked forward to a "divorce" of the spiritual and the secular, and devotion of the Philharmonic entirely to worship. But if this were done, the orchestra and the proud new Civic Light Opera would be homeless.

Temple Baptist and its Governing Board generously allowed the old association to continue from season to season. No one could have guessed that the 1906 marriage of culture and religion would endure for another nineteen years!

Flushed with optimism in the months following the close of World War II, Los Angeles seemed ready for expansion of its civic facilities. Publicly it was a time of freeway planning and projection of vast changes in the Civic Center. Privately, plans for vast new subdivisions, real estate developments, and a high-rise cityscape were forming. A group of distinguished citizens formed Greater Los Angeles Plans, Inc., a non-profit organization headed by Albert B. Ruddock as first president, for the purpose of building a new convention center and civic opera house.

In 1946, the group's real estate committee, headed by B. O. Miller, acquired two pieces of property as sites for the proposed buildings. One was a twenty-six-acre plot between Third and Fifth Streets, Figueroa Street, and Fremont Avenue, intended for an auditorium and convention hall, and the other a square on Sixth Street, opposite Lafayette Park, where the projected opera house would rise.

On April 3, 1951, the twin projects were submitted to municipal election voters as bond propositions totaling $31.5 million. They were rejected. Strong majorities favored each of the measures, but neither achieved the legally required two-thirds of the total vote.

Undiscouraged, proponents of the civic auditorium renewed the fight immediately. The Lafayette Park property was sold and attention concentrated on the downtown site. A plan for a huge, versatile edifice which would combine the functions of a civic auditorium, convention center, sports arena, and home for concerts and musical productions was developed.

It went to city voters on May 26, 1953, as a $27 million bond proposition, but the result was the same as in 1951. Despite enthusiastic support by the community and approval by a large majority of voters, the proposition failed to win a two-thirds vote. A little over a year later, a third attempt was made.

In 1954 the battle was spearheaded by a new organization, "Forward Los Angeles," led by Harry J. Volk, western head of the Prudential Insurance Company, as president. This time the plan called for three major buildings on the same downtown site as formerly. It envisioned a 15,000-seat auditorium also usable for sports events, an exhibition hall for trade and industrial shows, and a smaller auditorium for symphony, opera, and other musical entertainment.

Financing would require a $19.5 million bond issue, but it was emphasized that the bonds would be self-liquidating, so that the complex eventually would cost taxpayers nothing.

Again the community rallied to the support of the project, business, cultural, labor, and professional groups alike. Success seemed certain, but when ballots were counted the night of June 8, 1954, the result was another failure. The majority approving the civic auditorium complex fell just one per cent short of achieving the necessary two-thirds. It was a frustrating experience for a city of 1,970,358, mushrooming toward its 1960 population of 2,479,015 and its rank as the third largest city in the United States.

But the struggle was not abandoned. In February 1955, the County Board of Supervisors took an interest, and ordered a study of the legal framework which would govern the building of a large auditorium. The board was nettled that Los Angeles had no facilities to compare with the San Francisco Cow Palace, which had just been selected as the site of the 1956 Republican National Convention.

The following April, a bill which would authorize a county to lease any civic auditorium or convention hall it might build to a private, non-profit corporation began a successful passage through the State legislature. During the same month, the board appointed a Citizens' Advisory Committee to work out details of locating a music center and convention hall and financing it at no cost to the public.

As chairman, the supervisors selected Mrs. Dorothy Buffum Chandler, wife of Norman Chandler, president of the Times Mirror Company, controlling the Los Angeles *Times*. At this time, Mrs. Chandler was executive vice-president of the Southern California Symphony Association, and early in 1958 would become its president.

"We have no great theater, although we are one of the world's great theatrical centers," commented Chairman Roger W. Jessup. "I consider Mrs. Chandler the ideal person to guide this program to reality."

[457]

His remark was prescient, although this attempt, too, was doomed to failure. An executive group was formed, including Charles S. Jones, A. J. Gock, Gwynne Wilson, David Hearst, A. E. England, F. Marion Banks, Walter Brunmark, John A. McCone, and Edwin M. Pauley, with H. C. McClellan as vice-chairman and Robert Cannon as secretary. In September 1955, they recommended a professional survey to select a site, and the Board of Supervisors employed the Cambridge, Massachusetts, firm of Arthur D. Little, Inc., for the purpose.

The Little Report was submitted June 11, 1956, proposing a $50 million civic auditorium and music center to be built in an area bounded by Olympic Boulevard, Flower, Eighth, and Hill Streets. It would include a convention and exhibition hall accommodating 20,000, a music center seating 4,000, and two multi-story garages to park 5,500 automobiles.

Supervisors approved the plan on June 29, and next day the Civic Auditorium and Music Center Association of Los Angeles County, a non-profit corporation, was formed to tackle the job of financing and building the huge project. It appeared that at last the Southland was on its way toward achieving its long-sought cultural citadel.

But obstacles developed quickly. As architectural and financial plans progressed through the balance of 1956 and early 1957, problems and conflicts multiplied. County appraisals showed that acquisition of the proposed site would be much more costly than had been anticipated.

The days of the "1957 recession" came, with tight money, a shrinking market, and rising interest rates. The Board of Supervisors began to worry about increasing costs, and they were not alone. Members of the association became more and more concerned as estimates varied and conflicted, and it seemed impossible to arrive at firm figures.

At last, on July 29, 1957, the Citizens' Advisory Committee was compelled to recommend to the county board that construction of a civic auditorium and music center be postponed until a more favorable time. Supervisors agreed reluctantly, and thus a dozen years of effort to build a music hall by conventional means had come to nothing.

Almost two years passed before a new and thoroughly unconventional approach was proposed to an astonished county board. Its author was Mrs. Chandler, the chairman of the defunct 1955 committee. During the ensuing five years she would almost single-handedly create and arrange financing for a splendid solution to the old problem.

On behalf of the Southern California Symphony Association, Mrs. Chandler appeared before the Board of Supervisors on March 17, 1959, with an offer of $4 million, to be privately subscribed, toward a music center to be built on a seven-acre site owned by the county at the crest of the long slope on which the Civic Center stands.

Supervisor Frank G. Bonelli, then chairman of the Board, voiced the reaction of his colleagues when he commented, "In my fifteen years in public office this offer of donations of private funds to build public buildings is the most unusual I have ever heard."

It was estimated the project would cost "about $10 million," and it was utterly feasible. The seven acres, bounded by Grand Avenue, First, Hope and Temple Streets, had long been held by the county against future needs, but until that time no one ever had considered the summit of the Civic Center as an appropriate setting for a cultural acropolis.

The genesis of the proposal dated from four years earlier, March 17, 1955, when the Southern California Symphony Association held an "El Dorado Party" to raise money for its reserve fund, with the goal of providing a permanent home for the Los Angeles Philharmonic Orchestra. The party, attended by eight hundred men and women at the Ambassador Hotel, was so called because a Cadillac El Dorado sedan was given as a door prize. Within a few hours, a total of $400,000 was subscribed.

Until 1958, however, the purpose for which the reserve fund was intended lay dormant, and two events that year brought it to life. In January, Mrs. Chandler became president of the association, a post she would hold until 1962, when she became chairman of its board of directors. And in December, the reserve fund received two contributions of $100,000 each, one from Michael J. Connell Charities and the other from the James Irvine Foundation, in a letter signed by Myford Irvine.

With a base of $600,000 assured, Mrs. Chandler sounded a "call to arms" on January 12, 1959, when she told the annual meeting of the Symphony Association: "That home for all good music in Los Angeles need no longer be just a beautiful dream, but now has the portent of imminent reality. Through over a decade thousands have planned, suffered, worked. . . . Now is the time to unite and build it!"

Impressed by the offer of private funds, the Board of Supervisors directed L. S. Hollinger, Chief County Administrative Officer, and County Counsel Harold W. Kennedy to work with backers of the music center, and from then on events moved swiftly.

In July, the seventy-member Music Center Fund Committee was formed under Mrs. Chandler's chairmanship. Response from the community was immediate and beyond all expectations. In September, two Cornerstone Concerts played in the Hollywood Bowl swelled the fund by $115,500. The Los Angeles Civic Light Opera Association and the San Francisco Civic Opera Company, to be major tenants of the music center along with the Los Angeles Philharmonic Orchestra, joined the drive with a pledge of $250,000.

In 1960 Mrs. Chandler announced a $2 million increase in the amount pledged privately, from $4 million to $6 million, and in July of that year plans for the music center as originally conceived were presented to the Board of Supervisors by the architectural firm of Welton Becket & Associates.

They envisioned a single building, a stately pavilion, with gently curving walls of glass and dark granite surrounded by fluted white columns rising ninety-two feet to a sculptured, over-hanging roof, to front on a mall plaza overlying an underground parking garage for two thousand cars.

The music center plan did not reach its full extent until March 7, 1961, however. On that day Mrs. Chandler appeared again before the Board of Supervisors to say:

A giant plan has been conceived which will vastly increase the scope of the center. In this bold new concept, the entire area will be known as The Music Center, a Living Memorial to Peace. [It] envisions three buildings. The original structure, seating approximately 3,200, will be the Memorial Pavilion. Across the mall is planned a small 800-seat Forum, and adjacent to this at the north on Temple Street . . . an 1,800 seat performing arts Center Theater. . . .

It is proposed . . . that the Music Center Building Fund Committee extend its pledged obligation to completely finance, through private donation, the two additional buildings . . . This action increases the committee's pledge . . . from $6 million to $11 million.

This was a truly staggering sum, but it was by no means the final figure. Eventually, the music center would cost approximately $33,500,000. Eventually the Music Center Building Fund Committee would increase its pledge to $18.5 million, and on January 30, 1965, Mrs. Chandler would announce that this sum had been oversubscribed.

The amount raised during the five and one-half year campaign reached $19,023,723.42. Of this, $2.2 million, or almost twelve per cent, was realized through a direct-to-the-public "Buck Bag" drive begun soon after ceremonies which dedicated the music center site, September 27, 1964.

S. Mark Taper, financier and philanthropist who had previously subscribed the entire $1 million cost of the Mark Taper Forum, contributed an additional half million to match the first $500,000 raised in the Buck Bag Campaign.

Toward the balance of the total cost, a $13,730,000 issue of leasehold mortgage bonds previously had been floated by the Music Center Lease Company, a non-profit corporation formed under terms of an enabling act signed by Governor Edmund G. Brown in March 1960.

Ten weeks before the triumphant conclusion of the Music Center Fund Committee's campaign, the Temple Baptist Church picked up a final decree of divorce from public entertainment for Philharmonic Auditorium.

Construction of The Pavilion had been in progress under Peter Kiewit Sons' Company, contractors, since March 12, 1962.

Henry A. Sutherland

As 1964 wore on, the stately music hall neared completion, and its grand opening was set for December 6.

The Los Angeles Philharmonic Orchestra played its final season in the venerable auditorium to which it had given its name. The Los Angeles Civic Light Opera Association wound up its twenty-seventh year of tenancy. It fell to Leonid Kogan, the Russian violinist, to play the final concert at the Philharmonic on November 20, 1964, and his concluding number, Maurice Ravel's gypsy dance, "Tzigane," sounded a gay requiem for seventy-seven years of public entertainment at Fifth and Olive streets.

31

LOS ANGELES AND THE DODGER WAR,
1957-1962

Cary S. Henderson

Since its very beginning, professional baseball has been involved rather intimately with municipal politics. Indeed, at the turn of the century, a sizeable number of city council members in New York, Chicago, and elsewhere were partners in the ownership of local baseball teams. This gave them a direct stake in promoting their own team's welfare and in keeping out potential rivals. More recently this sort of linkage has all but disappeared, but political involvement in team decision-making has remained active. Since the 1950s most of the larger cities have vied with one another to attract major league franchises by persuading established teams to relocate or by creating new ones. The most peripatetic franchise has been the Athletics, once closely identified with Philadelphia, which moved in the 1950s to Kansas City, later to Oakland, and perhaps in the future to Denver. In each instance, they have had use of a modern stadium built and owned by the respective city.

Major league baseball is big business; at the same time it can also be a source of civic pride and a sort of personal identification for a city. Several examples come readily to mind: the Pirates *are* Pittsburgh, the Yankees are inseparable from New York, as are the Red Sox to Boston.

If one were observing the baseball scene during the mid-1950s, two other teams would have seemed to be permanently rooted in their respective boroughs, the New York Giants and the Brooklyn Dodgers. The latter were particulary noteworthy because they were highly successful, having maintained for over a decade one of the two or three best records in major league baseball. They were also accepted as an integral part of the Brooklyn scene, where they had played for half a century. The franchise was also a profitable one.

Restlessness, however, had begun to pervade the "Majors" by 1953, a restlessness sparked by teams which had experienced difficulties in league rankings and by falling box office receipts. For example, the marginal Boston Braves were transformed into the highly successful Milwaukee Braves, averaging 30,000 fans per game in a stadium built by a city-county partnership. Given generous rental terms, the club was made to feel welcome in its newly adopted city. Others followed: The Athletics, mentioned above, moved to Kansas City and the St. Louis Browns to Baltimore. These moves paved the way for many other relocations during the next few years.

However, the westernmost major league teams were still east of the Missouri-Mississippi River line, leaving larger cities of the west out of the big league picture, even though Los Angeles, San Francisco, Denver, and others appeared eager to obtain a franchise. "It is absurd," said Los Angeles mayor Norris Poulson, "to envision a population center of this size without major league baseball." Indeed, during the decade of the 1950s, Los Angeles had experienced tremendous growth and had become the nation's second largest city. The city's two Pacific Coast League teams, the Los Angeles Angels and the Hollywood Stars, seldom drew over 3,000 fans to home games, an obvious demonstration of an overwhelming lack of public interest in their fortunes. To right such widespread baseball apathy, Mayor Poulson eagerly sought to attract a winning Major league team to his city. He had declared himself to be a Dodger fan after watching them vanquish the New York Yankees in the 1955 World Series. The idea of the Dodgers moving to Los Angeles became one of his primary goals as mayor. But he was in for a fight. While elsewhere the marriage of civic pride and the sports business had been consummated smoothly, in Los Angeles it created a bitter emotional and legal struggle that left scars which are still discernable.

In New York City things were not doing well for two National League franchises, the Dodgers and the Giants. Brooklyn Dodger president Walter Francis O'Malley had for years been unhappy with the inadequacies of venerable old Ebbets Field, built in 1913. While winning league pennants in 1955 and 1956, the "Bums" had averaged only 16,000 fans per game. In an especially disappointing turnout, a mere 7,600 fans attended, with only two games left in the 1956 season. The Dodgers were leading the second-place Braves by but one game and the Braves were at Ebbets Field with two chances to wrest the pennant from the hometown Dodgers. Thoroughly disillusioned, *New York Times* sports editor Arthur Daley wondered after such dismal public turnouts whether Brooklyn deserved a major league team. Even though the Dodgers won the pennant, their attendance records were more indicative of a last-place team. The Dodgers could have been in the cellar for all Brooklynites apparently cared.

O'Malley had begun to wonder the same things as had Daley in his column. The Milwaukee Braves, who had lost the 1955 and 1956 pennants to the Dodgers, had bested the Dodger attendance in 1955 by 1,000,000 fans and in 1956 by 800,000.

The most obvious problem was the Dodger's Ebbets Field. There was no way that it could be satisfactorily improved; it had limited parking space and was near only one subway line. In the bargain, it was situated in a rapidly changing neighborhood. In his efforts to solve the stadium problem, O'Malley tried for several years to enlist New York officials in efforts to build a large modern facility in Brooklyn at a location where three subway lines converged. All the city had to do, said O'Malley, was to condemn the land and build the stadium. To this end, the Dodgers would contribute $5,000,000 and pay an annual rent in the same amount. In addition, he offered to pay the city 5% of gross receipts. This was substantially more than their new host cities had required of the Braves, Orioles, and Athletics, and O'Malley considered it to be a very generous offer on his part.

To underscore his determination, at the beginning of the 1956 season O'Malley announced that 1957 was the Dodger's last season in Ebbets Field. As a trial balloon, he scheduled seven games in Jersey City's Roosevelt Stadium. Attendance there proved to be better and gate receipts $100,000 more than if those games had been played in Brooklyn. But Roosevelt Stadium was also inadequate for O'Malley's purposes; the games played there merely pointed out that there were alternatives to a New York City site.

These goads to New York officialdom and O'Malley's implied warning produced little more than fruitless meetings. Mayor Robert Wagner in June 1957 called O'Malley's "demands" "ridiculous" and washed his hands of the matter, adding, "I have always in the past wanted to keep the Dodgers in Brooklyn . . . but now I'm not so sure."

Already, O'Malley had begun to look elsewhere. Mayor Poulson seized the initiative. It appears that he contacted O'Malley before or during the 1956 World Series, which Poulson attended. At the conclusion of the series O'Malley sent an engineer to look over a Los Angeles site suggested by Poulson in an area known as Chavez Ravine. The report has not been made available but it was obviously favorable because O'Malley firmly committed himself to Los Angeles and the Chavez site in early 1957 as a potential new home for his franchise.

Chavez Ravine had been acquired by the city through purchase with United States funds as a site for a public housing project during the tenure of Mayor Fletcher Bowron. Many acres had been legally condemned and most of the inhabitants were removed by court proceedings. A few, however, had chosen to stay, the money which had been offered for purchase of their property being held in escrow until they decided to accept it and move.

The land for the planned housing project was administered by the Los Angeles Housing Authority. Although building plans had been drawn up, construction had never materialized. A 1952 referendum had demonstrated the project's unpopularity, and the election of Poulson in 1953 put an end to all serious planning. Poulson, a Republican and a vigorous opponent of public housing, received the partisan endorsement of the powerful Los Angeles *Times*, which virtually ignored Mayor Bowron's 1953 mayoralty reelection campaign. An enthusiastic promoter and "back-slapping politician," Poulson envisioned better uses for the Chavez Ravine land.

In November 1956, Poulson appointed a "Blue Ribbon Commission" to look into the city's future parks and recreational needs. As the mayor had doubtless anticipated, they recommended that the city build a large, modern stadium in Chavez Ravine and that a $2,000,000 item be included in the 1957 budget for levelling the Housing Authority's 185 acres to get the project underway. Up to that time, the Dodgers had not been mentioned. Ironically, no one seemed to notice a major problem which would soon crop up: the land in question had been purchased by the United States government and was legally restricted to "public purposes only." This restrictive clause remained in the deed even though the city's Housing Authority had bought the land from the federal government in 1953 for a "bargain basement" price, in Poulson's words.

In the meantime, at the other end of the continent, O'Malley had decided in February 1957 to purchase the Los Angeles Angels franchise and ball park, Wrigley Field. Although he stoutly denied that the purchase signalled an intention to move to the City of the Angels, he did schedule a series of Dodger exhibition games at Wrigley in March 1958. In addition, it must be recalled that the Dodger president had announced that the 1957 season would be his last one at Ebbets Field, leaving the Dodgers without a designated ball park for the 1958 season. O'Malley and the other Dodger officials were obviously intent upon looking over the Los Angeles situation at firsthand. For his part, Mayor Poulson knew that the time for serious negotiations had arrived, and he had the fulsome support of the Los Angeles *Times* and the smaller-circulation daily, the *Herald Examiner*, as well. A few years earlier, the *Examiner* had suggested an attempt to bring the St. Louis Browns or the Washington Senators to Los Angeles. Poulson, however, wanted a winning team and he may well have suspected that O'Malley was on the verge of leaving New York. The purchase of the Angels franchise might have given Poulson a further clue as to O'Malley's intentions.

Formal efforts began in February 1957, when the youngest city council member, Rosalind Wyman, moved in a council meeting to invite the Dodgers to Los Angeles. She was asked by Poulson to gather together sportswriters and broadcasters to recommend "an orderly and feasible plan" for the realization of the move. The mayor also suggested that a select group of council members and Los Angeles County supervisors travel to the Dodger training camp at Vero Beach, Florida, to initiate open discussion of terms. A joint meeting of city and county officials convened and plans were made to "demonstrate to the officials of the Brooklyn Dodgers the sincerity of [Los Angeles'] interests."

In anticipation of unfolding events, there was a great amount of preparation on both sides. O'Malley formally invited the city-county delegation to confer with him at Vero Beach. Mrs. Wyman had already commenced deliberations with her informal committee on how to forge an attractive offer. O'Malley, while coming to look at the minor league team he had just purchased, also brought along an engineer to assess once again Chavez Ravine as a possible site for a proposed stadium. A graduate engineer himself, the Dodger owner gained a thorough firsthand knowledge of the terrain and its potential. After completing his study of Chavez, he made it clear that the Ravine was his only choice, primarily because of its close proximity to three freeways.

In the ensuing months of negotiating, city officials and sportswriters seemed to misunderstand who was wooing whom. O'Malley, by February 1957, had sold rickety old Ebbets Field to a real estate firm, had purchased a forty-four-seat jet airplane, and had acquired the Los Angeles Angels. He had, in fact, made a clear commitment to Los Angeles and he would either have to accept whatever the city offered or play in Jersey City. There is little doubt that O'Malley had firmly decided the California city had tremendous potential; he was therefore willing to talk seriously. On the other hand, the Los Angeles *Times* sportswriter Frank Finch thought O'Malley was making the city come to him. Actually, the opposite was the case: the Dodger president was at the city's mercy. Mrs. Wyman, nevertheless, was of the opinion that O'Malley was still wavering as late as September 1957. City council president John S. Gibson, Jr., thought O'Malley had made a positive commitment in April.

The Vero Beach talks made it clear that Los Angeles would offer the Dodgers 185 acres in Chavez Ravine and $2,000,000 for clearing it, but nothing more. O'Malley had hoped for a more generous offer, including a stadium built by the city and leased on terms similar to those offered by Milwaukee, Kansas City, and Baltimore. For such an edifice to be funded, however, a referendum would be required and Los Angeles city and county had a very thin record for approving anything involving large sums of money for construction. Over the next few months O'Malley continued his sporadic talks with Mayor Wagner and others in New York City, but anyone following the course of events there knew that a dead end had already been reached. Only Los Angeles was actively talking with O'Malley, and at Vero Beach that city's limited offer was made known. Indeed, Mayor Poulson had returned from that meeting confident that the Dodgers would open their 1958 season in Los Angeles.

One of the city's pawns in the negotiations was the $2,000,-000 which had been offered to help in grading hilly Chavez Ravine. This sum was included in the city's $104,000,000 budget referendum, which was approved by the voters in April 1957. In public statements the funds were said to be earmarked for building access roads for a proposed zoo and art gallery supposedly planned for Chavez Ravine. A map prepared for a council meeting on May 11, however, showed a large stadium adjoining the zoo. The art gallery was conspicuously missing from the new plans. No one had yet said who was going to build the stadium, but in June the city began condemnation proceedings to acquire the eighteen additional parcels of land needed to complete the 185 acres which had been offered to the Dodgers.

National League officials also met in May to approve the Dodgers' possible move to the west coast, but they expressed a preference for two teams to relocate there rather than only one. Poulson knew that the Giants were also ready to leave New York, so he established contacts between them and San Francisco Mayor George Christopher. In the talks that followed, the Bay City agreed to build a stadium and lease it to the Giants on very generous terms, something O'Malley could never expect from the City of the Angels.

News of the impending moves prompted Baseball Commissioner Ford Frick to order all parties concerned to refrain from discussing the matter in public lest it affect attendance in both the National and Pacific Coast Leagues. Enough was known about these venerable teams' plans, however, to stimulate the Judiciary Committee of the United States House of Representatives to begin a probe of a possible violation of the Antitrust laws. Chairman Emmanuel Cellar, whose district included Brooklyn, wondered aloud why, if baseball was a sport, teams were sold to the highest bidder. Nothing came of these long congressional hearings, but a great many problems and passions were aired in public.

Mayor Poulson, in July, appointed H. "Chad" McClellan, a prominent retired business leader, to be the city's official negotiator with the Dodgers. In August, after several talks with the Dodger owner, McClellan thought that O'Malley was holding out for 350 acres, which he must have known was out of the question. O'Malley was in no position to demand additional land, but perhaps he had not given up all hope. He was at least able to convince several people that all his options were still open.

Meanwhile, Los Angeles city officials had discovered that the restrictive clause in the Housing Authority's deed was liable to become a source of serious trouble. Poulson endeavored to get the Authority to find a way to "hold harmless" the "public purposes only" stipulation, but in reality it did not have the power to effect such a change. Only the courts had the power to adjudicate the matter.

As negotiations dragged on through June, Councilmen Harold Henry and Gordon Hahn urged greater speed, with Henry reminding the council that only a few years earlier the city lost a chance to land the Minneapolis franchise because Baltimore already had a stadium to offer them, and that had carried the day. But instead, seeds of dissension were soon to arise. In a later council meeting Everett Burkhalter announced his intention of changing the use of the $2,000,000 budget item by diverting it to needed improvements at places other than Chavez Ravine. He failed, but his attempt pointed out the problem involved in using public money for a private ball park. The mayor's budget thus remained intact, and on June 26, 1957, O'Malley announced that "the jig is up in Brooklyn" and added that "things are moving very intelligently in Los Angeles."

The Giants' announcement in August that they were moving to San Francisco made the stauncher pro-baseball council advocates still more impatient. Fears mounted that the city might "lose" the Dodgers after all. But such fears were not grounded in fact. O'Malley, noting that both college and professional football games in Los Angeles were the best attended in the nation, had already stated in February that, "If it becomes necessary for us to play any place other than Brooklyn, I think the final location is obvious. Then it would be a matter of picking the place with the greatest future." This factor, Los Angeles' great potential, meant more to O'Malley than the amount of acreage he was offered, a fact which should have been more evident to all concerned.

Council deliberations took on greater urgency in late September. Questions raised by Los Angeles *Times* sports editor Paul Zimmerman on September 12 appeared to summarize the doubts in many peoples' minds. "Time is running out" was a phrase often heard at both ends of the continent and Zimmerman wondered why the delay and hesitation: Was O'Malley promised concessions which were beyond the city's capacity to deliver? He may have expected 350 acres would be forthcoming but he should have known it was not possible under the circumstances. Perhaps, as Zimmerman implied, someone had given O'Malley that impression. Further, the editor asked, were the Dodger demands "outlandish"? Was it like the Minneapolis affair, too little, too late? One deadline which was approaching was the September 29 meeting of National League team owners,

[471]

at which all franchise changes had to be finally approved. The fact that an extension could be had for the asking was downplayed by Dodger advocates.

There was no doubt that O'Malley wanted either a city-built stadium or at least a 300-acre grant from the city. It was his estimate that the kind of stadium he had in mind would require that much land. In exchange for this amount of land, he would deed the city his Wrigley Field property, which consisted of nine acres and a small ball park. O'Malley's plans envisioned a beautiful modern stadium seating 55,000 people; ample parking lots situated so that fans could park on the level nearest to their seats; no posts or visual impediments would obstruct the view, in marked contrast to Ebbets Field which had obstructions everywhere, it seemed; and easy access to the nearby freeway system. All this would require 300 acres and possibly more, but the city had only 185 acres and was negotiating with the State of California for an additional 35 acres, still leaving the total some 80-95 acres short of O'Malley's requirements. This being the case, he would clearly have to accept the fact that the city might not be able to deliver the remaining acreage and that further insistence on the additional land would only increase the already evident opposition.

On September 16, the council, by a 11-3 vote, finally adopted a resolution setting out the terms on which it was willing to negotiate. This included "approximately 300 acres" in exchange for Wrigley Field, with the city retaining 50% of all oil and other mineral rights, if such were discovered under the Chavez Ravine surface. Actual city expenditures were to be limited to the $2,000,000 already budgeted for leveling, grading, and building access roads. The three dissenting votes were cast by John C. Holland, Earle Baker, and Pat McGee. Later, on a Holland-Baker motion, the council unanimously affirmed that the resolution did not commit the city to anything; it was only an authorization to negotiate, no more.

In return, the Dodgers would transfer to the city their Wrigley Field property and pay the city $500,000 to build a 40-acre recreational facility adjacent to the new Dodger property.

The Dodgers would pay the city an additional $60,000 a year to operate this facility for twenty years, after which time it would become Dodger property. Lastly, they would have to pay all additional costs involved in preparing the site and building Dodger Stadium. In order to forestall any rumors of a secret deal, the text of the proposal agreement was to be printed in all local newspapers.

The Los Angeles city council, however, had an established record for disharmony. One writer in 1961 labelled it "The Cave of the Winds," noting that its daily meetings were more like a debating society than a deliberative body. The mayor, it was noted, had no real power and the council was unlikely to agree on anything of significance. For dilatoriness, its reputation was well deserved, as subsequent events in the Dodger War demonstrated.

Proponents immediately hailed the September 16, resolution as a good deal for the city. As might be expected, Mayor Poulson was overjoyed. *Times* sports editor Paul Zimmerman, in an enthusiastic September 18 editorial, insisted that the taxpayers were getting a real break, in contrast to those of Milwaukee, Kansas City, Baltimore, and now San Francisco, where stadiums were built through public bonded indebtedness. By way of contrast, he pointed out that the Chavez Ravine acres would pay property taxes estimated at $300,000 a year. The Holland-McGee city council faction was not impressed by such comparisons.

Opponents did their best to delay the final agreement beyond the September 29 deadline. On the 17th, Holland moved for reconsideration of the terms, the motion losing by five votes to eight. He then asked City Attorney Roger Arnebergh whether the deal was legal and received the challengeable answer that it was merely the sale of city-owned property. It was no problem, said the attorney. Councilman Baker then asked whether the land could legally be sold without bids. "Not necessary," said Arnebergh, who further made it clear that the council could set any terms it wished as to how the land was to be used. On the 20th, another rumble was heard from Councilman

Rundberg, who explained in a public letter that, although he had voted for the September 16 resolution, his vote came only after Arnebergh's assurance that it was not legally binding.

It was evident that the opponents' stalling tactics would prevent an immediate vote on a final contract. As matters stood in late September, O'Malley would first have to accept the tentative offer and then the council would have to reconsider the matter again. In another ploy, Baker and McGee's resolution on the 29th to rescind Chad McClellan's authority to negotiate lost by four votes to eight, as did another motion by McGee to rescind the September 16 resolution, and by the same margin. Finally, Rundberg moved to create a group of civic leaders to discuss the benefits of a Dodger move; this motion was adopted. That same day Poulson extended an invitation to representatives of the Chamber of Commerce, the Downtown Businessmen's Association, the Board of Realtors, and others to assemble for that purpose.

Another rancorous council meeting followed on September 25. This time Holland made three dilatory motions, all of which were defeated. He moved that the council hire outside appraisers to evaluate the Chavez Ravine and Wrigley Field properties to determine whether the city was being cheated. When this was not acted upon, he insisted that the record be made absolutely clear that the September 16 resolution had no legal or even moral standing. He was not even able to get any action on his motion to make public a stenographic record of the proceedings, instead of the very general summaries which were customary. Mrs. Wyman argued that the hilly, unsightly, scarcely populated Chavez Ravine site would be suddenly transformed into a taxpaying paradise, which obviously swayed no opinions either. In one subsequent heated exchange, Councilman Corman accused Holland of obstruction, for which the accused demanded an immediate apology. Holland did, however, correctly predict that there would have to be a referendum on the contract. Another Holland motion was to delete the Dodger issue from the calendar for September 30. It was defeated but he did get an agreement to print enough copies of the proposed contract for distribution to the public. The only other motion to pass on the 25th was to make the September 30 regular meeting into a public session.

Mayor Poulson returned to Los Angeles on September 26 after a three-day absence, vowing to "put up the fight of my life" for the Dodger contract. Up until then the only concrete piece of action had been a unanimous vote by the county supervisors to provide $2,750,000 to build access roads to the proposed Dodger Stadium. It was, however, contingent upon "concrete evidence of its (Chavez Ravine's) contemplated or actual improvement by the city." The "evidence" awaited city council approval of a contract with the Dodgers, thus September 30 was set for a showdown. To be binding, a contract had to be approved unanimously on the first reading, which was supposed to occur at the September 25 meeting. For adoption on the second reading, only a two-thirds majority was required, meaning ten of the fifteen council members. But as the crucial September 30 meeting approached, the proponents counted only nine votes to the opposition's four. As Holland and McGee prepared crippling amendments and dilatory motions, Councilman Gordon Hahn, a staunch proponent, cut short his vacation to be back in time to cast the tenth vote in favor of the contract. "I was surprised to learn that the deal had not already been wrapped up," he told reporters upon arrival.

As expected, the September 30 session was heated and continued far into the night. Both sides marshalled their versions of evidence. The pro-Dodger faction displayed a large bundle of petitions on long, yellow legal pads, plus another fifty-foot long petition bearing even John C. Holland's signature. In addition, they could count on the enthusiastic endorsement of the Downtown Businessmen's Association, who forecast a glowing prospect to be realized from the economic stimulus the Dodgers would bring the city. Their case-in-point was the Milwaukee experience.

McClellan introduced the contract to the council as "the biggest bargain ever offered any major city to get a Major League team." A former Los Angeles Chamber of Commerce

[475]

president declared it "a terrific bargain." As the meeting ground on into the evening, unable to get beyond mere procedural matters, Poulson made a desperate move. He made a phone call to National League president Warren Giles with the announcement that "It's in the bag," prematurely counting the ten votes for the contract once the dilatory Holland-McGee motions had all been defeated. This was a "media event," staged before a select group of reporters who had been invited to the mayor's office for the occasion. He then called O'Malley with the same news, despite the fact that no vote had yet been taken.

Holland, McGee, and Baker predictably objected to this announcement and to the mayor's referring to their tactics in his call to Giles as "these shortsighted and petty efforts to block the continued progress of Los Angeles." Poulson's ploy may actually have worked to effect a ten-to-four vote to approve the contract that evening, which was his intention. O'Malley had already obtained an extension of time from National League officials until October 15 to complete his arrangements with the city council.

Council approval of the contract, however, was far from the last inning. In order to finally deliver the land to the Dodgers and to condemn the additional property, which the city was only loosely committed in the contract to use its "best efforts . . . to acquire at a reasonable price," a formal ordinance had to be adopted and another vote had to be taken. A further hazard was a public hearing on the ordinance, which was scheduled for October 7. Again ten votes would be required and Councilman Rundberg's vote was by no means certain. Mrs. Wyman later claimed credit for persuading him to vote in favor of the contract on September 30; the next year, however, Rundberg publicly recanted the deed.

The televised October 7 proceedings proved unpleasant for all concerned. After much confusion, the "public" was invited to comment. Despite the earlier enthusiastic endorsements, when council president John S. Gibson, Jr., called for the supporters of the ordinance to have their say, none responded. After an embarrassing silence he called for those opposed to speak and it appeared that the entire audience was of this mind. The reason for opposition ran the gamut from Mrs. Mary McFarland's opinion that the city deserved a better team than the Dodgers, to Mrs. Richard R. Suaso, who had previously been evicted from her home in Chavez Ravine to make way for the aborted housing project. If the land was so valuable, she asked, why weren't the property owners paid more for it?

A Dodger official, present for the meeting, answered whatever questions were posed by the council. Henry J. Walsh, president of the Brooklyn Baseball Club, fielded questions from council members with sufficient success to garner the required ten votes to approve City Ordinance No. 110,204. The formal date of promulgation was set for October 16, 1957. The ordinance essentially reiterated the wording of the contract previously adopted. This became the final authorization for enforcing the contract, but it was not destined to become effective until the fall of 1959!

The ordinance itself had some interesting features. To answer the criticisms that the land transfer was not in the public interest, the last "whereas" in the preamble clearly stated that, "whereas all of the foregoing is useful and convenient" in connection with the city's rights and powers, it was therefore declared to be in the public interest. That it would not go into effect for two years attests to the fact that a mere declaration on that point could not gloss over some very serious legal challenges.

Anticipating future problems, the city left itself several loopholes in the contract. As it was worded, the city was loosely obligated to convey to the Dodgers "185 acres, *more or less,* and will use its best efforts to acquire at a reasonable cost and convey additional land, to make a total of 300 acres, *more or less.*" Further, it stated that if the "public purpose" clause in the Housing Authority's deed could not be "eliminated or modified, this contract shall be of no further force or effect." This last disclaimer was inserted because court suits challenging the contract were expected and if the contract was declared invalid, the city would incur no obligations. The Dodgers, of course, knew this and signed the contract in full knowledge of the fact that they were liable for all costs if that should happen. As far as

[477]

land was concerned, the city had relieved itself of any obligation to deliver anything beyond the 185 acres, regardless of the contract's validity. The city did purchase an additional thirty-five acres from the state later in the year, making a total of 220 acres for Dodger use, pending legal sanction. Beyond that, a low maximum price of $7,000 per acre was established for any new acquisitions, perhaps to avoid having to purchase any more land. Although a moot point, it is known that little, if any, additional land was ever purchased.

No sooner had the ordinance been promulgated than two serious legal challenges erupted. A taxpayers' suit to restrain the mayor and council from consummating the deal had already been filed on September 23, 1957, by attorney Julius Rubin of Beverly Hills on behalf of two former Chavez Ravine property owners. By January 1958, Hollywood attorney Phil Silver, who was to be the most difficult obstacle for the Dodgers, filed a suit on behalf of taxpayer Louis Kirschbaum in the Superior Court in Pasadena. This suit cast considerable doubt upon the "public purpose" clause of the Housing Authority deed and the contemplated act of condemning further Chavez Ravine property for a private stadium.

The taxpayer suits delayed formal consummation of the "Dodger Deal" for another twenty-three months. But another and more immediate reason for concern was a referendum petition which began circulating as Dodger officials were in town to make the final arrangements for transferring the team to Los Angeles, finding housing accommodations and a place to play baseball until the new Dodger Stadium was completed. While the suits and the referendum were pending, no work could be done on the ball park, and O'Malley regretted that fact since delay would considerably increase construction costs. At the time he could not foresee just how long a delay was to be incurred.

A vote on Proposition B, the Dodger referendum, was set for June 3, 1958, the date for primary elections as well. The petition to force a vote collected 85,000 signatures, when only 57,000 were required. An armored car was hired to carry the documents to City Hall on November 14, 1957. On December 1, a majority of 77.36% of the signatures were declared valid and the referendum vote was ordered. In possible explanation for the larger number of signers, Councilman Ernest Debs, a Dodger proponent, suggested that "many petition circulators . . . have told the public, if you want the Dodgers to play ball in L.A., sign here." Poulson suggested that the signatures were obtained "through misrepresentation and confusion." The *Times* advanced the thesis that the largest number of petitioners were from outlying areas where people saw no immediate good for themselves and that "spite is the major prompter."

For whatever reasons, it was clear that the Dodgers and their supporters were in for a fight. What was never clear was where the money came from to sustain the "war of public relations" against the Dodgers. Most supporters were certain that Pacific Coast League San Diego Padres owner John Smith, who had recently built a new stadium on Mission Bay, was providing necessary funds.

"The Citizens Committee to Save Chavez Ravine for the People" was formed to campaign for "no" votes, while comedian Joe E. Brown (who was later the primary financial backer of the Minneapolis Lakers basketball team's move to Los Angeles) formed the "Committee on Yea for Baseball."

A running civil war over the Dodger issue constantly disrupted council meetings as Holland and McGee did their best to discredit the way the contract had been made. In late May 1958, for example, Holland unearthed a very cryptic "Dear Walter" letter in which Poulson appeared to be obscuring something deliberately shady. He also found a proposed joint statement by the city and county attorneys arguing for the contract's validity. On the top right of a photostat of the statement was the handwritten note "Vetoed in toto. W. F. O'M." This, Holland concluded, meant that "Mr. O'Malley was actually participating in the operation of our city and county governments as early as May 1957." Chavez Ravine might better be used, he suggested, for "a world scientific exposition" or something. He and Pat McGee claimed to be much offended by accusations that such charges and suggestions were "frivolous."

[479]

Another council meeting just prior to the referendum vote erupted into a shooting match. Holland was described as "red of face" as he, along with Rundberg and McGee, assailed the pro-Dodger council members. Rundberg demanded a grand jury investigation. "Blood pressures hit the ceiling," said the *Times* the following day.

All the while the council was barraged with letters from all varieties of protestors. One called the Dodger contract "taxation without representation." This letter was addressed to "Gentle-men and the Noisy Female Advocate of Baseball," referring to Mrs. Wyman. O'Malley, who had tried to stay out of the con-troversy, noticed the polls indicating a slippage in Dodger sup-port and jumped into the fray with a sharp denunciation of John Smith for his financial support of the campaign to keep the majors out of California. The city's two largest newspapers, however, were solidly behind the Dodgers, as the tone of their news coverage and editorials made clear.

The Los Angeles Dodgers, meanwhile, had begun the 1958 season in their new temporary home, the Los Angeles Coli-seum. Playing amid the furor of the referendum campaign, the players could not be certain where they might be playing next year. One thing, however, was certain: they were packing in record crowds. By June 6, 1958, in spite of their last place stand-ing and the strained political climate, their attendance was ahead of the Milwaukee Braves total for that date in 1957. The Dodgers' first *two-month* total attendance was more than had been seen at Ebbets Field during the *entire* pennant-winning 1956 season. A night honoring Roy Campanella, the Dodgers' great catcher who had been paralyzed in an accident before the season began, drew a paid attendance of 93,000, with an esti-mated 20,000 being turned away.

But Dodger Stadium, O'Malley's dream, was still far in the future. The Coliseum could accommodate more fans than any other baseball stadium was capable of seating. Thus receipts were not the main problem. Built for the 1932 Olympic Games, the Coliseum was oval in shape, while a baseball field requires a fan shape. Alterations to create a fan within an oval had cost the Dodgers $200,000. In addition the Dodgers and Giants had to pay $900,000 to liquidate the Pacific Coast League franchises from Los Angeles, Hollywood, and San Francisco. Nevertheless, despite paying a relatively high rental for the seventy-seven home games played in the Coliseum, net profits proved well worth the costs involved.

While the Dodgers floundered in the standings and prospered at the gate, the referendum campaign went into full swing. On May 25, Joe E. Brown, in an attempt to entice voters to approve the referendum, unveiled plans for the Dodgers' proposed ball park. It was to be, he said, "The baseball showplace of the world." Plans included a nursery, games, etc., for the children, express buses to bring passengers to the stadium, and a restaurant at the top where one could watch the game while dining. Endorsements for the "Vote Yes for Baseball" campaign included the "Doctors' Committee for Prop B" and "Disabled Veterans for Prop B." The latter was especially appropriate because it was Dodger policy to admit disabled veterans free.

In another of his unusual tactics, a little before the June 3 vote Mayor Poulson again called League President Warren Giles, urging him to issue a statement to the effect that the Dodgers would feel unwelcome if they lost the referendum and they might even leave Los Angeles. Holland doubted such a possibility, asking in a release to the press, "Does a hungry dog run away from a juicy bone?" He was certain the Dodgers would stay, especially since their gate receipts at the Coliseum were so attractive.

A few days before the referendum advocates staged a "Dodger Telethon," featuring such Hollywood personalities as Ronald Reagan, Debbie Reynolds, Carmen Cavallero, and Joe E. Brown, who urged its passage. The following day there was a televised "debate" where "the O'Malley" offered to answer all questions. One point he tried to emphasize was that, according to his estimates, the Dodgers would have to stay in Los Angeles for at least thirty years to recover the money lost in relocating. Wyman, McGee, Gibson, Holland, Poulson and others put on another televised debate on June 1.

[481]

On June 3, the voters trooped to the polls in record numbers. It was suspected that Prop B was the main reason for the huge turnout, although there were other important contestants on the ballot, politicians like Pat Brown, Goodwin Knight, Clare Engle, and others in a cross-filed primary election.

The Dodgers won the referendum, but only by a narrow 24,293 out of 666,577 votes cast. O'Malley, doubtless embarrassed by the slim margin, thanked the voters, thought the team would play better baseball, and hoped progress could be made soon on building Dodger Stadium.

O'Malley was aware, however, that it would take time to clear away the many remaining legal obstacles. As the litigation dragged on in the courts, matters became increasingly complicated for both the Dodgers and city officials. On April 28, 1958, with the baseball season barely underway and June 3 still in the future, Judge Kenneth C. Newell of the Pasadena Superior Court, issued a temporary restraining order barring any attempt to convey any city land to Dodger ownership. This meant that all the effort put into the referendum campaign would be in vain, at least for a while, regardless of the outcome of the vote. Newell's decree was based on the vulnerable "public purpose" clause in the Housing Authority deed, as argued by attorney Phil Silver in the complaint of Louis Kirschbaum against Los Angeles. A permanent injunction followed on May 2, which prohibited certification of the referendum's results before the vote had even taken place.

Another attempt to air the issues, instigated by Councilman Holland, began on May 15, in the midst of the referendum campaign, when a committee of the state legislature opened hearings on the Dodger "deal." John S. Gibson, Jr., managed organized testimony in favor of the contract and Pat McGee managed the opponents. On the second day of the hearings, John Anson Ford, chairman of the County Board of Supervisors, criticized what he called "the half-hidden fast moves that resulted in this strange deal." McGee added his opinion that San Francisco got a much better deal with the Giants. It was in the forum of these hearings that Councilman Rundberg publicly disavowed his vote in favor of the Dodger contract during the previous September.

Nothing came of the legislative committee's probe and no minds were changed by the hearing; it was merely another interlude in the long and bitter struggle. However, it produced an ominous prophecy from attorney Julius Rubin, namely that the Dodger case might go all the way to the United States Supreme Court.

Another and more involved trial began after the referendum on June 20, 1958, before Los Angeles Superior Court Judge Arnold Praeger. As described in the Los Angeles *Times*, the city and Dodger attorneys were arrayed on one side and the Phil Silver-Julius Rubin forces on the other, "lined up in battle formation." This maneuvering began in earnest as soon as the first witness, Mayor Poulson, was sworn in. He was able to respond to only one question in his two hours on the stand. Legal bantering kept him in silence the remainder of his time as witness. Once again the whole array of charges was examined. No, the city assessor testified, there was no deal to exempt the Dodgers from property taxes; no, the Housing Authority insisted, there had been no illegal pressure to alter the wording in the deed.

As the trial proceeded, Judge Praeger's questions to the defendants' attorneys became sharper and, not unexpectedly, on July 14 he issued a second temporary injunction, Judge Newell's being the first. In a thirty-two page opinion, he ruled that the city could not legally use public funds to buy or improve property for a private corporation. The contract was, he wrote, "ultra vires," beyond the city's lawful powers. As the city filed a formal appeal the next day, Praeger issued his permanent injunction on July 24. For some time to come the Dodger contract was in great legal jeopardy.

On January 14, 1959, six months after Judge Praeger's injunction, the Dodgers seemed to have won the victory. A jubilant Los Angeles *Times* in one and one-half inch headlines, announced that the California Supreme Court had unanimously ruled that City Ordinance No. 110,204 was a valid exercise of the city's power to use its best judgment as to what was in the public interest. Further, the court held that the city could legally "hold harmless" the "public purpose" clause in the City Housing Authority's deed.

This, however, was not the final chapter in the Dodgers' legal annals. Phil Silver, as Julius Rubin had predicted, filed an appeal to the United States Supreme Court in April, within the time limit set by the State Supreme Court, after which its decree would become effective. Silver's chief argument was that due process had been denied to Chavez Ravine property owners.

While all this uncertainty continued, the county supervisors withdrew their offer of $2,750,000 for building access roads, motivated by the prospect that the legal entanglements in the courts might go on for years. The supervisors indicated that if the final outcome was favorable, the money would be restored.

O'Malley's planned "baseball showplace" had to wait for yet another court to decide its fate. In the meantime, City Attorney Roger Arnebergh had approved plans for the grading of Chavez Ravine on the same day the California Supreme Court issued its opinion. He was persuaded to wait, however, when Silver reminded him of the risk involved should the United States Supreme Court reverse the state court's decision. Arnebergh did suggest that part of the $2,000,000 for the grading work might be advanced to the Dodgers as a loan, to be repayable if the court decided against them.

All efforts to thwart the Dodgers' ownership of Chavez Ravine seemed at an end when the United States Supreme Court dismissed the Silver-Rubin appeals on October 19, 1959. This left the California Supreme Court's decree as the relevant statement on the contract's validity. But there were still hurdles: for one, the land had to be possessed formally by the city and the remaining occupants removed.

There were many estimates of how much the land in Chavez Ravine was worth. Friends of the Dodgers tended to see it as a worthless piece of barren desolation. Sports columnist Frank Finch described it as "300 acres of steep hills, eroded gullies, weeds, stunted trees, and a few ramshackle dwellings, including an abandoned schoolhouse . . . densely populated by possums, skunks, jackrabbits, gophers, rusty tin cans, rotting tires, moribund mattresses, and broken beer bottles . . . an eyesore only a mile from the imposing Civic Center." O'Malley saw it as "an impossible wilderness," while a former president of the Chamber of Commerce judged it to be worthless and expressed gratitude that someone had finally found a use for it.

Opposition leader Holland, however, correctly pointed out that it was the only decent-sized parcel of land near downtown that was left to the city. Rundberg had obtained an outside consultant to appraise the tract earmarked for the Dodgers and was informed that its "commercial value" was as much as $18,000,000, assuming it was levelled.

In May, while the appeal to the United States Supreme Court was still pending, the eviction of the remaining Chavez Ravine tenants began when the city exercised its power of eminent domain. Technically this action had no relevance to Dodger Stadium but was merely the city taking possession of land to which it already had title, for the purpose of making improvements. This action precipitated the "Battle of Chavez Ravine."

The reasons underlying the subsequent conflict are still unclear, even after two decades. Mayor Poulson has suggested that, since the struggle took place in the early days of television news, television reporters were looking for something sensational to feature. In addition there was a marked difference between the Los Angeles newspapers and TV stations: the newspapers were enthusiastically for the Dodgers, and the Dodgers were anticipating that their games would be shown on pay TV, a prospect which was anathema to commercial TV stations.

On May 8 the few remaining residents of Chavez Ravine were evicted, some forcibly, and the TV cameras were very much in evidence to record the unfolding drama. The door to the home of two elderly ladies had to be battered down because they had locked it and refused entry to the police. They were not physically harmed, however.

It was different with the Arechiga clan. The elders of the family, ages seventy-two and sixty-eight, had several children, all adults at the time. They lived in two adjoining run-down houses in the Ravine. The senior Arechiga left only when a bulldozer began to level his house. Two of their daughters, Mrs. Aurora Vargas and Mrs. Glen Walters, had to be physically carried out of the house, Mrs. Vargas being photographed kicking and screaming. Mrs. Walters was pulled out of the house while resisting so violently that she was handcuffed and booked by the police. The clan mother threw stones at the evicters, while the grandchildren were "wailing hysterically." A rather dramatic photograph in the *Times* showed old Manuel Arechiga in the foreground watching the bulldozer destroy his home of thirty-six years. Adding to the melee were uncounted numbers of scurrying chickens, turkeys, and dogs. After the house was levelled, Mrs. Arechiga and some forty other persons went across the dirt street and stood in the now-vacant lot, watching the proceedings. The elders and their grandchildren decided to remain there, but the others eventually dispersed.

For ten days the elder Arechigas held out, living in a trailer furnished by a recreational vehicle dealer. They were provided with adequate supplies of food donated by sympathetic and concerned citizens. The *Times*, editorially, looked on these events as strange, pointing out that it was not a sudden, cruel eviction at all, notices having been posted almost two months before the evictions took place. Television, said the *Times* editor, had distorted the events because the Arechigas had known that since a 1957 court ruling they would eventually have to vacate. The sum of $10,500 had been offered for the Arechigas property in 1953, but they had chosen to refuse the money and remain in Chavez Ravine.

Mrs. Vargas was reported on May 16 as returning to the site of the old homeplace, shouting hysterically, "they're going to kill my children." She was sedated on a physician's orders and put to bed. Her sister, Mrs. Victoria Augustian, appeared soon after at a city council meeting with a copy of a legal complaint, one about to be filed by Phil Silver, asking $400,000 for houses and personal damages, pain and suffering, etc.

A particularly rancorous council session on May 11 attracted a large audience and extensive media coverage, including television cameras. Mrs. Augustian was there with her two children, as were Mrs. Vargas and Mrs. Walters, who had just returned from her preliminary hearing on the May 8 charge of resisting arrest. Placards in the audience urged "Justice for the Arechigas." Most witnesses cried out for more humaneness and one lady charged it was "communism" if their property was not restored. It was pointed out at the meeting that housing was available for all concerned, but that members of the Arechiga family had refused to accept it.

Also revealed at this meeting was the fact that the tenacious Silver had filed yet another suit, this one based on alleged "extrinsic fraud" in the land condemnation procedures because the intended use to be made of the land had not been made public. He further claimed that at the time the eviction notices were first posted in 1953, there were three bills in the Congress to stop public housing projects. Poulson knew about these bills, said Silver, a fact which Poulson admitted years later in his unpublished memoirs. He was a former congressman and in fact had suggested the bills in question, contending that the city should be free to use the land as it saw fit.

The Arechiga drama came to an abrupt halt on May 14 when it was revealed that Manual Arechiga owned eleven houses and was not a "poor" and "destitute" Mexican-American being deprived of his only possessions in the world. Both sides were taken aback and Poulson reportedly exploded in anger, flaying at the "ham actors on television . . . bleeding insincere tears up and down the picture tube." He denounced the "hypocrisy of the whole rigged demonstration." Councilman Edward Roybal nevertheless claimed that the revelation had changed nothing, a sentiment echoed by Holland and McGee. Public sympathy and support for the displaced Arechigas evaporated quickly, especially after the *Times* published pictures of all their houses, some obviously not slums. Council president Gibson publicly charged that the whole affair had been planned to embarrass the Dodgers.

By November 1959, O'Malley and the Dodgers had overcome all the legal hurdles, except for the required but relatively

Excavation for Dodger Stadium in Elysian Park.
Courtesy of Publicity Department, Los Angeles Dodgers, Inc.

uncontested zoning hearings. The ball park itself was changed from B-3 to B-2, but no serious problems arose from these proceedings.

Work was finally begun on the magnificent new Dodger baseball palace after the Dodgers' 1959 World Series victory over the Yankees. It was acclaimed the finest ball park in the world. Opening in 1962, it seated 56,000 people, each with an unobstructed view of the playing field. It was built at an eventual cost of $15,500,000, a sum considerably larger than the original $12,000,000 estimate.

In the years that followed 1958, the Los Angeles Dodgers won several National League pennants and regularly set baseball attendance records, averaging around 40,000 fans per game. For those who can't attend, games can be heard on KABC Radio, consistently the most popular radio fare particularly for the area's large Mexican-American population. As part of the terms

Dodger Stadium nears completion.
Courtesy of Publicity Department, Los Angeles Dodgers, Inc.

of the arrangement with the city, the Dodgers' property taxes reached $2,000,000 by 1972 and the forty-acre recreation field they built was still being used as a public park.

Once the stadium was under construction the Dodgers ceased being a political issue, although in the 1961 mayoralty race Mayor Poulson's close association with the Chavez Ravine issue may have cost him the election. Sam Yorty emerged the victor and Poulson retired from public life at age 65. He was given a golden lifetime pass to Dodgers games to show the team's gratitude for his efforts, but he has never used it for fear someone would call it a "payoff," although he often attends Dodger games.

The "Dodger War" could scarcely be called finished until 1972, when Mrs. Abrama Arechiga died at the age of seventy-five, defiant to the last. Poulson, on the other hand, always considered bringing the Dodgers to Los Angeles to be his greatest

[489]

political achievement. Another contented party was O'Malley, who, in retrospect, preferred his privately-owned stadium to renting one from a board of political appointees.

In a larger sense, O'Malley was an innovator, even a gambler, when he decided to pull up stakes and relocate across the continent to accept a contract whose terms he did not consider generous. He could easily have lost, as has been the fate of some franchises. Many cities and states have given significant tax breaks and other blandishments to induce business to relocate. Major league baseball and national football league teams have been especially favored, a proposition which has continued to be true: witness Anaheim attracting the Los Angeles Rams and Los Angeles trying to lure the Oakland Raiders to play in the Coliseum recently vacated by the Rams.

The Los Angeles Dodger story, however, is unique in the annals of sports history: the Dodger "deal" caused a bitter political, legal, and perhaps moral controversy; the city gave the Dodgers land instead of building a stadium and gave fewer acres than the contract seemed to promise; finally, the Dodgers built their own facility and are among the very few franchises who pay property taxes (although some teams pay more for rent than the Dodgers pay in taxes).

If one assumes the desirability of larger cities having "big league" baseball (as well as football, basketball, and ice hockey), the issue then becomes largely how they go about attracting teams. Since building a municipal baseball stadium was politically impossible, Los Angeles could offer only land and $2,000,000 for access roads. It must also be noted that the land in Chavez Ravine had never been considered valuable until O'Malley was attracted to it as a stadium site. The rough terrain seemed unattractive to everyone else who looked at it. Walt Disney, for example, refused to consider it as a site for his projected Disneyland. In a sense, then, it was O'Malley and the use he planned for the land that made the property valuable, whatever its potential could have been for others.

One might argue that the Los Angeles solution had some distinct advantages. For one thing, by building their own stadium the Dodgers committed themselves to their host city in a way no mere tenant is likely to do, as the much transported Athletics (Philadelphia, Kansas City, Oakland, and perhaps Denver) exemplify. From a city's viewpoint, if it builds a stadium, it must have some team or teams using it to make it profitable. One 1980 example is the Los Angeles Coliseum: The Dodgers no longer play there and neither do the Rams. The same might be true one day of the Oakland Coliseum. But Dodger Stadium and the Dodgers have roots, loyal fans, a fine ball park, and handsome profits. The "public purpose" served by municipal ball parks is to generate money through rents, concessions, and parking charges. The Dodgers have compensated by their annual local taxes. Los Angeles inadvertently found a workable solution, one that was reasonable and justifiable.

32

MYTH-MAKING IN THE LOS ANGELES AREA

W. W. Robinson

The Los Angeles area, beset always by waves of newcomers, has produced its full share of myths. Its people prefer to accept and to retell stories which seem good enough to be true, even if they are not.

Long before there was a Los Angeles and before California was looked upon by navigator Cabrillo, the whole region was shrouded in clouds of myth. As early as 1510, California—unseen as yet by white men—was reputed to be an island inhabited by black, passionate Amazons. The island phase of this myth had long persistence, but, needless to say, the Amazonian phase had a shorter life.

On the site of Los Angeles was the prehistoric Shoshonean village of Yang-na. The myth of its location at or near the southeast corner of present-day Commercial and Alameda Streets persists. Writers of the past, delving lightly into the archives of Los Angeles' Mexican period, came upon references to the Indian "rancheria of poblanos" at that spot in the old pueblo and concluded that there was the surviving Yang-na. Had they looked more deeply into the same records, they would have discovered that this rancheria was not Yang-na, but a segregated district, with approximately a ten-year life span (1836-1845), where were impounded the local Indians, most of them drifters from the secularized missions of Southern California.

Yang-na itself, with a probable location at or close to the land of the old Bella Union Hotel, had long since disappeared.

Chronologically, the widely held myth of the ceremonial founding of Los Angeles, in 1781, should be mentioned next. Permit me to hold this for special and climactic consideration.

The granting of ranchos in California began in 1784. As a heritage of the rancho period comes the myth—believed by many Angelenos as well as many other Californians—that the ranchos were grants directly from the King of Spain. Whenever a descendant of a rancho-owning family dies, his obituary is apt to state that his ancestor received "a grant from the King of Spain." This pleasant notion conceives of a benevolent Spanish monarch across the seas taking kindly thought of a "blue-blooded" Spanish soldier in a faraway California by rewarding him with a wide valley or a vast plain upon which to graze his cattle and raise his family. Actually, the necessity of royal approval for land grants outside of pueblo or presidio boundaries in New Spain had been done away with fifteen years before California was occupied by Spain. Supreme authority in New Spain during the Spanish period was vested in the viceroy, as representative of the king, with his seat of office in Mexico City. Under him were military chiefs, serving as governors in the outlying territories, including California. During the Mexican regime, the governors were answerable to the central government of Mexico. In California, during both periods, the concessions or grants of ranchos came from the governors or their representatives. The one exception was the grant of Sitio de la Brea (in Santa Clara County), which came from the viceroy himself.

The myth of the capture of Joseph Chapman, the first American to come to Los Angeles, is equally persistent. The most recent book on Los Angeles, socio-historical in treatment, preserves this story as factual. After all, it is so good it ought to be true! The myth is that Chapman, a member of Bouchard's coast-raiding party in 1818, was captured by being lassoed at Refugio Beach near Santa Barbara; that a pretty girl, of the Ortega family, pleaded with his captors and saved him from being dragged to death; and that, naturally, he married the girl. Actually, Chapman went ashore at Monterey, with two companions, while the city was under attack. He was arrested there and brought as a prisoner to Southern California. Probably in 1821, he became a citizen—a most useful one—of the Los Angeles area, and did marry an Ortega girl. The mythical aspects seem to have pioneer Angeleno Stephen C. Foster for their creator. His contribution to the Los Angeles *Express*, "First American in Los Angeles," was described by Bancroft as "an interesting sketch," but "purely fictitious so far as details are concerned." In spite of Bancroft's comment, and his detailed account of the whole adventure, few historians and few writers have been able to resist the happy tale.

In 1849, Los Angeles, eager to go into the real estate business, was surveyed for the first time. Out of the survey, made by Lieutenant E. O. C. Ord, came the myth—still going strong—that Ord was offered in payment either cash *or* lots in downtown Los Angeles, and that he chose cash. Quoting J. Gregg Layne, historian and delightful myth-maker: "Oh! that he [Ord] may never hear the wails of his heirs, to the third and fourth generation, for making this decision." Actually, Lieutenant Ord and the members of the city council were equally smart. Ord, with an eye to the future, wanted cash *and* land. The councilmen, also looking ahead to rising land values, insisted that Ord take cash only. He was paid $3000.

Another amusing myth, a favorite of Layne's, involves the Los Angeles delegates to the first constitutional convention, held in Monterey in 1849. These delegates were Manuel Domínguez, José Antonio Carrillo, Abel Stearns, Hugo Reid, and Stephen C. Foster. According to the legend, those traveling north on horseback spent the entire time during the journey arguing over whether the world was round or flat. Domínguez was reputed as holding to the flat-world theory and as asserting at every stop, "Gentlemen, I tell you she is flat!" Gregg loved to tell this yarn in the presence of members of the Domínguez family, espe-

One of Los Angeles' early myth-making depictions. A
fanciful artistic view printed as a lithography is the United States
Pacific Railroad Expeditions & Surveys (1852-1854).
This is Plate X, dated 1852.
Courtesy of Doyce B. Nunis, Jr.

cially if they were ladies. In fact, the story is nonsensical, for all
these gentlemen represented Los Angeles at its intellectual best.

The Joaquín Murieta myth hardly belongs to the Los Angeles area, yet the excitement over this imaginary bandit was
statewide. The publication, in the year 1854, of a small book
simply entitled *The Life and Adventures of Joaquín Murieta,*
launched California's best myth. The author was a Cherokee
Indian, John R. Ridge, who wrote under the name of "Yellow
Bird." Immediately, fiction became reality, and California's
"Robinhood" became the state's most popular and widely-seen
bandit. Murieta was said even to have visited the San Fernando
Valley. He was the answer to the Californians' yearning for
romance. When, a hundred years later, the University of Oklahoma Press brought out an edition, done from the rare original,
Joseph Henry Jackson was asked to write an introduction. This
he did, in detail and at length. Concluding, Jackson said that
author Ridge "died at forty with no inkling that the myth he had
manufactured practically out of whole cloth, would be a part of

his adopted state's tradition a hundred years later. . . . Since there wasn't a Murieta—at least not much of a Murieta—it was necessary to invent one."

The myth of the "Feliz curse" is stictly Angeleno and the creation of Los Angeles' most eminent myth-maker, Horace Bell. Los Feliz was a Spanish rancho within the present city limits, and it once belonged to members of the Feliz family. Bell accuses the highly respected Antonio Coronel of robbing the Feliz family of their rancho. A disinherited niece, he says, accordingly pronounced a fearful curse on the land of the rancho. The curse was effective, and when Rancho Los Feliz finally came into the hands of Colonel Griffith J. Griffith, he hastened to get rid of the curse-ridden acres by giving them—Griffith Park—to the City of Los Angeles. Over the years, whenever a flood or a fire hit Griffith Park, some young reporter on a local newspaper would come excitedly upon the myth and relate it as a new discovery. Actually, the "cursing" niece was well taken care of by the mother of Don Antonio Feliz, who, in the story, was robbed on his deathbed. Furthermore, the larger part of the rancho—including the Silver Lake area—is one of the older residential districts, well covered with homes, and quite immune to the floods and fires that are normal to the chaparral-clad mountain area that makes up much of Griffith Park. The myth now seems to be dying, for when a race riot took place a year ago in the park, not one newspaper thought to dredge out the "curse."

The San Gabriel Valley has been productive of myths about the naming of its ranches. Apparently none of the older historians, and none of the later place-name experts, came upon the obvious fact that the naming of the streams crossing the Valley preceded the naming of the ranchos. The priests of San Gabriel, sending out herds and herdsmen over the Valley's vast area, needed to name natural boundaries rather than beautiful expanses of oak-dotted or poppy-covered land. The San José Creek, named in early days for Saint Joseph, gave the latter rancho its name—Rancho San José, site of Pomona. A second small stream, the Santa Anita—a diminutive of Santa Ana—

Los Feliz Ranch house in Griffith Park, locale of the "Feliz curse."
Courtesy of Los Angeles County Museum of Natural History.

gave its name ultimately to Rancho Santa Anita. Finally, a third
tiny stream or *cañada*, the San Pascual, named for Saint Paschal,
bestowed its name on Rancho San Pascual, site of Pasadena and
Altadena. This stream is the original southeasterly boundary of
the rancho, and appears on *diseños* and in recorded documents.

Failure to recognize the logical way in which ranchos were
named has indeed resulted in the birth of a plethora of myths in
the San Gabriel Valley. Consult, for example, the mugbook history of Pomona Valley that was published in 1920, for a fanciful
account of the beginnings of Rancho San José. On the occasion
of the settlement there in 1837 by Ygnacio Palomares and Ri-
cardo Vejar, the author tells of the pleasure of San Gabriel's
priests at the coming of good Catholics. He goes on to say that
Padre Zalvidea "doubtless brought a small band of neophytes to
take part in the simple but formal service of dedication. . . .
Padre Zalvidea offered a mass of thanksgiving and pronounced
his benediction upon the families and their new possessions.
The day which they had chosen for the occasion was March 19,
the festival of San José, for which reason the new grant was
dedicated by Padre Zalvidea as the Rancho de San José." Unfor-

[498]

tunately for the story, the good Father Zalvidea—because of ill health—had been transferred to San Juan Capistrano in 1826. Furthermore, the story is in direct conflict with the facts disclosed by the rancho's *expediente* (land grant file) contained in the records of the United States District Court.

Especially in the San Pascual area of the San Gabriel Valley has myth-making seen a profuse flowering. Myths, purporting to tell the origin of "San Pascual," take many forms. In one, soldiers of the Portolá party—or even sailors far off at sea—saw the Altadena-Pasadena region blazing with poppies. Struck dumb at the sight, these pious men fell on their knees, and then arose to label the expanse "the altar cloth of Holy Easter," or San Pascual. In another form, the chief of the local Indians befriended Portolá—lost on his way back from the first trip north—smoked a peacepipe with him (contrary to Gabrielino custom), and was later baptized and called "Pascual el Capitan." In still a third appearance of the myth, the rancho was given on Easter Day, 1826, to Doña Eulalia Perez de Guillen, famous housekeeper of the mission—despite the fact that the canny priests of San Gabriel knew they had no authority to convey title to land. Take your choice, for all versions are completely mythical. If you are a realist, you will study the United States District Court records (now housed in the Bancroft Library, University of California, Berkeley) for a complete account of Rancho San Pascual and its ownership in the Mexican and early American periods.

The original myth-makers in the Pasadena area are many. They include such fine citizens and contributors to local history as Mrs. Jeanne C. Carr, whose story of Pasadena and Rancho San Pascual appears in the Lewis Publishing Company's *Illustrated History of Los Angeles County* (1889), and Dr. Hiram A. Reid, author of the hefty and valuable *History of Pasadena* (1895). Doña Eulalia herself, as confused about her age as about other details of her own story, occupies a high place among the early myth-makers. One of the handicaps all these worthies worked under was the unavailability then of the scholarship and on-the-ground research of Herbert Eugene Bolton.

[499]

The farthermost outpost of the San Gabriel Valley—Azusa—is utterly unable to free itself from the myth-makers. Bell Becker, special writer for *The New York Times Western Edition*, wishing to do something nice for this community with the puzzling name, made his contribution to his newspaper on November 9, 1962 under the title of "Whither Azusa?" After discussing the community and dismissing one derivation of the town that "has everything from A to Z in the U.S.A.," he stated that Azusa was originally a Mexican land grant known as "El Susa Rancho." The area, he continued, was sold to an Englishman, Henry Dalton, who renamed it Azusa Rancho de Dalton.

My letter to *The New York Times*, protesting the Beckerism, brought no response. In denying that there was a rancho named "El Susa," I asked, "Why is it that no newspaperman ever consults a place-name book?" I referred to Phil Townsend Hanna's *Dictionary of California Place Names*, which had been available since 1946, and to Erwin G. Gudde's *California Place Names*, which was published in 1949. They both showed Azusa as derived from Asuksa-gna or Asuka-gna, which was a Gabrielino (Shoshonean) name for the early-day Indian village located in the area. I could have gone into much more detail, with earlier and later references to the town's Indian origins. I fear, however, that the people of Azusa must continue to bear their cross, for the general public and all newspapermen prefer foolish and mythical origins to one that is factual and logical.

A personal adventure in myth-making might be mentioned. A few months ago, I turned on the television set to hear and watch Dr. Frank C. Baxter on his *Harvest* program. It was devoted to California place-names. One community after another was given fascinating treatment. Beverly Hills came up and Dr. Baxter asserted—to my dismay and with his usual relish—that the place was named for the hometown of founder Burton E. Green, given over the air as Beverly Farms, Massachusetts. In 1938, when I was writing a brochure on Beverly Hills, I made that mythical statement, owing to some difficulty I had in getting through to Mr. Green, head of the Rodeo Land

and Water Company, who was busy selling real estate. Accordingly, I relied on secondary sources. The myth was printed and given wide circulation. It was picked up and included in Hanna's and Gudde's place-name books—with full personal credit. There were later editions of these basic books and many other writers used the fictitious origin—including Irving Stone, when the magazine *Holiday* featured Beverly Hills in 1952.

Burton Green had long been disturbed over the misconception of the naming of his glamorous city. In a letter he wrote following the appearance of Stone's article, he said he had tried to correct the story but that it continued to crop up. "Actually," he went on, "the naming of Beverly Hills came about in this way: When I was trying to decide on a name for the city we were about to build, I happened to read a newspaper article which mentioned that President Taft was vacationing in Beverly Farms, Massachusetts. As I read the article, it struck me that Beverly was a pretty name. I suggested the name 'Beverly Hills' to my associates; they liked it; and the name was accepted."

Despite Mr. Green's earnest wishes, it appears that the Beverly Hills myth—vigorously launched by me—will attain immortality. It is repeated here to illustrate what happens when a myth once takes flight.

The apparent signatures of United States presidents on recorded United States patents, that confirm rancho or mission titles, have given rise to a pleasant California myth. It is reminiscent of the "King of Spain" myth. The presidents themselves, especially Abraham Lincoln, are credited with taking a very personal interest in salvaging titles for rancho or Church claimants. Actually, prior to 1833, land patents *were* signed by the president himself. In 1833, however, Congress authorized the president to appoint a secretary who would affix the president's name to patents. Under this authority, most of the patents confirming California ranchos or approved mission holdings were signed. In 1878 the president was authorized to designate an executive clerk to do the job. Until 1948 a specially designated clerk in the General Land Office (later the Bureau of

Land Management) affixed the name of the president to all land patents. Since 1948 the name of the president no longer appears on patents. They are signed by the appropriate clerk in his own name.

The myth of the great San Fernando Valley "conspiracy" should not be overlooked. According to its development by the Morrow Mayo-Carey McWilliams school of mythmakers, a syndicate (or perhaps two syndicates) of leading Angelenos conspired with the water board or the Department of Water and Power to initiate the construction of a 250-mile-long aqueduct. This would bring water to San Fernando Valley for the purpose of enriching the conspirators as holders of valley real estate. Usually, Harrison Gray Otis and Harry Chandler are named as the leading conspirators. They would be the obvious villains because of the anti-labor stand of their newspaper, the Los Angeles *Times*.

Actually, there were two syndicates. One was the San Fernando Mission Land Company, headed by L. C. Brand, which bought 16,000 acres of valley land in 1904—long before the Owens Valley aqueduct plan was worked out—with the hope of profiting from the building by Henry E. Huntington of an electric railway from Los Angeles to San Fernando. The other syndicate, the Los Angeles Suburban Homes Company, whose financial leader was Otto F. Brandt, bought 47,500 acres of valley land from the Van Nuys group, in 1909-1910, hoping to benefit by water from the aqueduct then being built, provided annexation of the San Fernando Valley to Los Angeles was possible. Counselor Henry O'Melveny advised that annexation was feasible. Both syndicates were speculative ventures by speculative-minded men. Both paid off—with the passage of years. The second syndicate is said to have made eight dollars for each dollar invested, a profit that would not seem overwhelmingly large in the light of later and recent valley transfers. My account of the "conspiracy" is based on a personal examination of the minutes of the board of directors of San Fernando Mission Land Company, and of the mountainous files of the Los Angeles Sub-

[502]

A fanciful view of the founding of Los Angeles in 1781.
Courtesy of California Historical Society.

urban Homes Company, discussions with some of the princi-
pals, and a close study of public records and of newspaper stories. Historians and writers continue to stub their toes in the San
Fernando Valley when dealing with questionable source material.

The myth that Los Angeles was founded with pomp and
ceremony seems indestructible. Apparently, most citizens of
America's third largest city want to believe that their city had a
splendid beginning. The available facts, however, point to the
simplest of starts—unattended by governor, officials, priests,
musicians, speechmakers, or ceremony.

When was the fancy story first launched? Not during the
Spanish or Mexican period, so far as records show. Not in 1852,
when Los Angeles presented its claim to pueblo land before the
United States Board of Land Commissioners. Attorney Joseph
Lancaster Brent, representing the city, offered the commissioners a copy of the regulations—the *Reglamento*—issued by Governor Felipe de Neve for the colonization of California, which
gave detailed instructions for setting up the pueblo of Los Angeles. He offered a transcript of the proceedings by which the
settlers were placed officially in possession in 1786 (five years
after the founding), as well as proof that the pueblo was raised
to the rank of a city in 1835, and that, in 1850, the city was
incorporated by American legislative action. Pomp and ceremony were completely absent from the account of the founding
given in the first Los Angeles city directory, issued in 1872. This
directory contained, incidentally, apparently the first attempt at
Los Angeles city or county historiography. The ambitious history of Los Angeles published in 1876, when many American
cities were observing similarly the centennial of the Declaration
of Independence, contained as simple an account of the town's
beginning as did the directory—with errors, to be sure, but free
of festive additions.

During the boom of the 1880s, when hordes of newcomers
poured into the Los Angeles area, considerable thought was
being given to matters historical. The newly started Historical

Society of Southern California was flourishing. Antonio Coronel, who had come to Los Angeles in 1834 (fifty-three years after the founding), and who was esteemed for his lively interest in early California customs, was being questioned by local historians eager to know about their city's beginnings. In 1889 he wrote a letter to Father J. Adam concerning the founding. I quote the essence:

> For the solemnities of the day a temporary shelter was erected. There a solemn mass was said by the minister of Gabriel, with the aid of the choristers and musicians of said mission. There was a salvo of carbines, and a procession, with a cross, candlesticks, and the standard with the image of Our Lady of Angels, which the women carried. This procession made a circuit of the plaza, the priest blessing the plaza and the building lots distributed.

Don Antonio, then 72, followed this account with a reference in his letter to the ceremony of giving possession, though the date and the name of the military officer were incorrectly stated.

If my findings are correct, Antonio Coronel is the "villain" who launched the "pomp and ceremony" myth. Where did he get it? He hadn't even been born when Los Angeles was founded. I suggest that his story—at complete variance with facts that are available—represents Los Angeles' collective memory of a different event: the fiesta of Our Lady of the Angels, celebrated, according to Bancroft, "with extraordinary ceremony" on the occasion of the formal dedication of the Plaza Church. Both Los Angeles and Mission San Gabriel joined in this affair, which took place on December 8, 1822, with José de la Guerra y Noriega chosen by the *ayuntamiento* as *"padrino."*

The Coronel version passed almost intact, but with improved phraseology and the addition of the governor's presence and his speech "full of good advice," into historian J. M. Guinn's *Historical and Biographical Record of Los Angeles and Vicinity,* which appeared in 1901. Later in the same year Charles Dwight Willard incorporated the Guinn account in his *History of Los Angeles.* Willard, a true newspaperman, added that the ceremony "was probably the most extensive and the most impressive that was ever held over the founding of an American city."

Thus arose, in my opinion, a myth out of what was as simple a founding as any village, any town, any city ever had anywhere. So far as is known, eleven families and four soldiers—unaccompanied by governor, priests, choristers, or musicians—unpacked their mules and built their first rude shelters—with the heads of families being assigned house and farm lots. The Willard story today dominates all later stories of Los Angeles' founding. (Consult, for proof, the latest books on the Los Angeles area by those two genial commentators on the local scene, Remi Nadeau and Bill Murphy.) Newspaperman Ed Ainsworth, who loves both ceremonies and anti-ceremonialists, says—alas—that it doesn't make any difference how the city was founded! Los Angeles newspapers, called upon each year—just before September 4—to say something nice about the founding, almost always assign the job to fledgling reporters. These young myth-makers come up with interesting features of their own, and if anyone were foolish enough to collect their descriptions—I have been that foolish—an amusing potpourri would be the result. In the year 1962, unfortunately, the Los Angeles newspapers forgot all about the significance of September 4. Not till September 5, the day after the anniversary of the founding, did they comment on the few sorry celebrants who had gathered in Olvera Street to toast the nearly forgotten birth of their city.

The Catholic Church has sometimes been accused of fostering the ceremonial myth. Actually, from Father Palou, who wrote perhaps the first account of the founding (published in 1787), to Father Maynard Geiger, California's current Franciscan historian, the Church has voted for the simple story. To found a pueblo was not a religious affair; it was a civil matter. It should be remembered, too, that the early Franciscan missionaries did not look with favor upon either pueblos or privately owned ranchos. Their letters continually reveal their opposition and note that the Indians who worked for pueblo authorities or for rancheros set poor examples for mission neophytes.

The collection of material about the founding and the founders, made in 1931 by the Historical Society of Southern California, remains today the best source. It was published in one volume in commemoration of the city's one hundred and fiftieth anniversary. This assemblage helps to demonstrate that all facts about Los Angeles' early days are important and that the non-ceremonial simplicity of the founding of America's third city is in itself dramatic.

All of us who try to tell the local story are to a degree mythmakers. It is impossible for any historian, whether of high or low degree, to get all the facts; it is impossible to maintain complete impartiality; and it is natural to yearn for romance. My hope is that I have not launched any new myths in this summary.

EPILOGUE:
THE CONTRIBUTORS

The authors who have written the essays included in this anthology come from varied backgrounds. Yet, they all share one thing in common—a love of history. What follows are brief biographical sketches of the contributors and an indication of the issue from the *Annual* or *Quarterly* publication in which their essay was originally published. Those essays which appeared with footnotes are indicated by an asterisk (*) at the end of each identification citation.

* * *

ROBERT W. BLEW, a secondary school teacher in the Los Angeles City School District, earned his B.A. and M.A. degrees at the University of California, Los Angeles. He completed his Ph.D. in History at the University of Southern California in 1973. His doctoral dissertation was on "*Californios* and American Institutions: A Study of Reactions to Social and Political Institutions." He has authored a number of articles for various publications and is a member of the Los Angeles Corral of Westerners. [*Quarterly*, LIV (Spring 1972): 11-30.*]

MARVIN BRIENES received his Ph.D. in History in 1975 from the University of California, Davis. He earlier completed his B.A. at City College, New York and M.A. at Brooklyn College. He is currently in the Interpretive Planning Section of the California Department of Parks and Recreation and is a partner in the historical and archaeological consulting firm of Brienes, West & Schulz, Davis, California. [*Quarterly*, LVIII (Winter 1976): 515-532.*]

Contributors

PAUL M. DE FALLA was active on the Los Angeles scene in numerous historical activities ranging from various committees to historic preservation. He was the founder of the Los Angeles City Historical Society in 1977 and died shortly thereafter. His original essay was simply entitled "Lantern in the Western Sky" and appeared in two consecutive issues. The first part of that study has been edited for inclusion in this anthology. [*Quarterly*, XLII (March 1960): 57-88; (June 1960): 161-185.]

GLENN S. DUMKE received his B.A. and M.A. degrees from Occidental College and earned his Ph.D. in History from the University of California, Los Angeles, in 1941. For a number of years he served on the faculty of Occidental College before moving into administration as Dean of the Faculty of that institution. He was President of San Francisco State College (now University), 1957-1961. When the office of chancellor was established for the California State College and University System, he was appointed vice-chancellor in 1961 and became chancellor in 1962. He retired from that post in 1982. He presently resides in the San Fernando Valley. [*Quarterly*, XXIV (March 1952): 14-25.*]

JAMES A. FISHER, a graduate of Sacramento State University, received his Ph.D. in History from New York State University, Stony Brook, in 1971. He presently resides in Sacramento. For a period of time he taught Afro-American history at the University of California, Davis, campus. [*Quarterly*, LI (Winter 1969) 313-324.*]

STEPHEN C. FOSTER was born in Maine in 1820 and was educated in local schools in East Machias. He entered Yale College in 1836, graduating four years later. Four years of teaching in Virginia and Alabama schools followed before he went to New Orleans to study medicine at the Louisiana Medical College. He completed his training in Missouri with a local doctor in 1844. He trekked overland to Santa Fe, New Mexico in 1845 and tried to push on to California via Chihuahua and Sonora, a journey disrupted by the Mexican War. Returning to Santa Fe, he subsequently joined the Mormon Battalion as an interpreter. The battalion arrived in San Diego on January 20, 1847. Los Angeles was entered on March 16, 1847 (the subject of Foster's recollection published in the anthology). Fluent in Spanish, Foster quickly found his niche in Los Angeles. Appointed alcalde in 1848, he held numerous appointive and elective offices during his long life in the city. He married a daughter of Antonio María Lugo and was survived by two sons when he died on January 28, 1898. He was a founding member of the Historical Society of Southern California. [*Annual,* I, Pt. 3 (1887): 46-52.]

DUDLEY C. GORDON was long active in affairs historical in Los Angeles and in the Historical Society of Southern California. He retired from Los Angeles City College in 1963 after thirty-three years as an instructor in English to devote himself completely to matters historical, including the publication of numerous articles and a number of books, the more important being his biography of *Charles F. Lummis: Crusader in Corduroy* (1972). He died in 1982 at the age of eighty-three. [*Quarterly,* XXXV (March 1953): 19-28.]

JAMES MILLER GUINN, born in Ohio in 1834, was trained as a teacher at Antioch and Oberlin colleges. He was a veteran of the Civil War, distinguishing himself as a Union soldier in a number of important battles. Invalided from active duty, he sought the healing climate of California and there resumed his school teaching career, interrupted for a brief period by prospecting. He became a permanent resident of Southern California in 1869. He was one of the organizers of the Historical Society of Southern California, filled every Society office and edited the Society's *Annual Publication* the last decade of his life. He was an undisputed "authority on the history of early Los Angeles" and contributed numerous articles to the *Annual.* In addition he penned five massive historical tomes relating to his adopted state and regional home. He died in Los Angeles, a month shy of his seventy-fifth birthday, September 24, 1918. [*Annual,* 3, Pt. 3 (1895): 40-50; 5, Pt. 1 (1900): 70-77; 7, Pt. 1 (1906): 5-12.]

WENDELL E. HARMON. No information available. [*Quarterly,* XXXVII (December 1955): 335-346.*]

CARY S. HENDERSON earned his B.A. and M.A. degrees from the University of Florida and his Ph.D. from Duke University. He is presently associate professor of history at James Madison University in Harrisonburg, Virginia. [*Quarterly,* LXII (Spring 1980): 261-289.*]

ABRAHAM HOFFMAN, a doctoral graduate of the University of California, Los Angeles, teaches in the Los Angeles Unified School District. He has authored two books, the most recent being *Vision or Villainy: Origins of the Owens Valley-Los Angeles Water Controversy* (1981), a book which won universal critical acclaim. He has also contributed articles to a number of scholarly publications, including the Society's *Quarterly.*

FRANKLIN HOYT was an outstanding historical specialist on the subject of Southern California railroads and railways. He contributed eight articles on these subjects to the *Quarterly* between 1950 and 1954. He taught for many years in Burbank secondary schools. [*Quarterly,* XXXV (September 1953): 195-212.*]

HARRY KELSEY, president of the Historical Society of Southern California in this centennial year, is the chief curator of history in the Los Angeles County Museum of Natural History. He graduated from Regis College and received his Ph.D. in History from the University of Denver. Prior to coming to Los Angeles, Dr. Kelsey served with the Colorado Historical Society and headed the Michigan Historical Commission for five years. He has been with the Los Angeles County Museum since 1971.

Author of several books and some fifty articles in historical journals, he is currently completing a biography of Juan Rodriguez Cabrillo.

MAYMIE R. KRYTHE received her B.A. from Wittenberg University and M.A. from the University of Southern California, with further graduate work at the universities of Jena and Berlin. She taught for many years at Long Beach Polytechnic High School. She contributed numerous articles to the *Quarterly* between 1951 and 1956. Her contributions included a four-part article on "First Hotels of Los Angeles," another on the Pico House, a biographical study of "Madame Modjeska in California," among others. She also authored a biography on Phineas Banning. She died in 1969 at the age of eighty-four. The essay published in this anthology was Part I of her four-part article on "Daily Life in Early Los Angeles." [*Quarterly*, XXXVI (March 1954): 28-39.]

MARCO R. NEWMARK was a frequent contributor to the *Quarterly* between 1942 and 1956, following in the footsteps of his illustrious father, Harris Newmark, whose *Sixty Years in Southern California, 1853-1913* is a classic. Mr. Newmark's numerous articles range across a broad spectrum of subjects, but biography is a major component. He was president of the Historical Society of Southern California from 1940 to 1942. Born in 1862 in Los Angeles, he died in 1959. [*Quarterly*, XXVIII (September 1946): 103-108.]

DOYCE B. NUNIS, JR., editor of the *Southern California Quarterly*, the publication of the Historical Society of Southern California since 1962, received his B.A. degree from the University of California, Los Angeles, and two masters and a Ph.D. in History from the University of Southern California where he holds the rank of professor. He has authored and edited thirty-three books, numerous articles and book reviews since 1960. His scholarship has been recognized by two Awards of Merit from the American Association for State and Local History, election as a Fellow of the California Historical Society, and an Award of Merit from the Society for his editorship of the *Quarterly.*

MARY LOGAN ORCUTT presented her essay originally at the annual luncheon for the First Families of Los Angeles at the Statler-Hilton Hotel in 1953. She was the wife of Professor William W. Orcutt, the man who discovered the scientifically important La Brea fossil beds in 1901. [*Quarterly*, XXXVI (December 1954): 338-341.]

LAWRENCE CLARK POWELL served as the University Librarian at the University of California, Los Angeles, 1944-1961, when he became the Director of the Clark Library and founding dean of the UCLA School of Library Science. He retired in 1966 and became associated with the University of Arizona for the ensuing decade. A prolific author of books, essays and reviews, his bibliography numbers in the hundreds of titles. His book, *California Classics*, is a classic in itself. He lives in active-writing retirement in Tucson. [*Quarterly*, XL (December 1958): 325-336.]

JOHN W. ROBINSON, a teacher by profession, has taught for some years in the Newport-Mesa Unified School District. For over twenty years he has backpacked the San Gabriel Mountains. History is his second vocation. He has authored such books as *Trails of the Angeles, The Mount Wilson Story, Mines of the San Gabriels, Mines of the San Bernardinos, Los Angeles in the Civil War Days,* and *The San Gabriels: Southern California Mountain Country.* He has contributed much to enrich the local and regional history of Los Angeles and Southern California. [*Quarterly*, LVII (Spring 1975): 1-17.*]

W. W. ROBINSON was the dean of the historians of Los Angeles at his death, age eighty-one, in 1972. Two years before he died, Jimmie Hicks honored his life and work in a book entitled *W. W. Robinson: A Biography and a Bibliography*, published by the Zamorano Club in 1970. His impressive contributions to Los Angeles and California history are many. He was a gifted historian and a talented writer. [*Quarterly*, XLV (March 1963): 83-94.*]

INGRID WINTHER SCOBIE received her Ph.D. in History from the University of Minnesota, specializing in twentieth-century political history of the American West. She is currently a member of the Department of History, Texas Women's University, Denton. Widowed several years ago, she recently married John Williams. [*Quarterly*, LVIII (Spring 1976): 113-126.*]

DONALD L. SINGER, since 1982 president of Crafton Hills College, Yucaipa, California, earned his four academic degrees from the University of Southern California: B.A., M.S. in Education, M.A. in History, and a Ph.D. in Higher Education in 1970. He has written a number of articles and co-authored a textbook on United States history. [*Quarterly*, LVI (Winter 1974): 375-406.*]

SARAH BIXBY SMITH (Mrs. Paul Jordan Smith) wrote a California classic in her wonderful autobiography, *Adobe Days*, published in 1925, with a revised edition in 1926, and a third revision published in 1931. Her maiden name was Sarah Hathaway Bixby. She authored a number of books of prose and verse and died in 1935, age sixty-four. [*Annual*, XI, Pt. 3 (1920): 63-76.]

HENRY A. SUTHERLAND, a native of Illinois, became a newspaperman after his graduation from the University of Chicago in 1929. He moved to Los Angeles in 1935. In 1962 he joined the staff of the Los Angeles *Times*, serving in various editorial capacities until his death, March 6, 1970. [*Quarterly*, XLVII (September 1965): 303-331.]

THOMAS WORKMAN TEMPLE II, a native son of Los Angeles, was an excellent local historian, with a particular gift for translating Spanish documents pertaining to the city of Los Angeles and its environs. A major contribution was the Society's *Annual* for 1931, celebrating the 150th anniversary of the founding of the pueblo in 1781. He was also an excellent genealogist, specializing in Southern California Hispanic families. He graduated from Santa Clara University and earned a law degree from Harvard. He died in 1972 at the age of fifty-seven and was buried in the cemetery of Mission San Gabriel, an institution with which much of his historical work was connected. [*Annual*, XV, Pt. 1 (1931): 148-149.]

THEODORE C. TREUTLEIN, a Fellow of the California Historical Society, is a recognized authority on the history of the American Southwest. He is also well versed in the history of Spanish and Mexican eras in California. Author of numerous books and articles, he is emeritus professor of history in California State University, San Francisco. [*Quarterly*, LV (Spring 1973): 1-7.*]

NELSON VAN VALEN was raised in northern New Jersey and Southern California. He did his undergraduate work at Swarthmore and, after military service in signal intelligence during World War II, his graduate work at Claremont. After a half-dozen years in Asia, Europe and Africa with the University of California and the University of Maryland overseas programs, he joined the History Department at Beloit College, where he is presently chairman. [*Quarterly*, LIX (Spring 1977): 85-109.*]

VIOLA LOCKHART WARREN served as associate editor of the Society's *Quarterly* from 1958 to 1962. She was widely known for her published contributions on various aspects of California's medical history. Three of her articles on that subject appeared in the *Quarterly* in 1952, 1959, 1959-1960 (in two parts). She also served as a director of the Society for several terms. Wife of the founding dean of the School of Medicine at the University of California, Los Angeles, Stafford L. Warren, she died in 1968. [*Quarterly*, XLIV (March 1962): 31-41.]

FRANCIS J. WEBER has served as archivist for the Archdiocese of Los Angeles since 1962. Ordained to the priesthood in 1958, he has served a variety of priestly posts ranging from a professorship at Queen of Angels Seminary, chaplain to St. Catherine's Military Academy (Anaheim), to pastor of Mission San Buenaventura. He is currently director of Mission San Fernando and the new Archival Center built at the mission in 1981. He is a prolific author; his publications, focusing primarily on the history of the Catholic Church in California, are numerous. For his work as archivist he has received an Award of Merit from the California Historical Society, with a like award to the Archival Center in 1983. [*Quarterly*, LVIII (Summer 1976): 137-142.*]

IRIS WILSON ENGSTRAND, Mrs. Paul Engstrand, received her collegiate education at the University of Southern California, capping her studies with a Ph.D. in History. She is currently professor of history in San Diego University. A widely published author, her books include a biography of William Wolfskill, a history of San Diego, and her critically acclaimed *Spanish Scientists in the New World: The Eighteenth Century Expeditions.* She is a frequent contributor to scholarly journals and is active in many historical organizations on the local, state, regional and national levels. (Her essay was published under her maiden name, Iris Ann Wilson.) [*Quarterly*, XXXIV (September 1957): 242-250.*]

TOM ZIMMERMAN, a native of Los Angeles, received his B.A. and M.A. degrees in American history from Loyola-Marymount University. He is a candidate for the Ph.D. in History at the University of California, Los Angeles. His dissertation will focus on the use of media, particularly photography, in the promotion of Los Angeles from the 1860s to the Great Depression. [*Quarterly*, LXII (Spring 1980): 79-98.*]

INDEX

Compiled by Anna Marie and Everett Gordon Hager

INDEX

INDEX

INDEX

[543]

This centennial volume was designed by Ward Ritchie with print coordination by Museum Reproductions. Set in Palatino type by Donnelley/ROCAPPI, Inc., printed by McNaughton & Gunn, Inc. in a limited edition of 500 copies.